Beena George

Exploring Information Systems Outsourcing: The Role of
Social Capital

Beena George

Exploring Information Systems Outsourcing: The Role of Social Capital

Managing Inter-organizational Relationships for Successful Outcomes

VDM Verlag Dr. Müller

Imprint

Bibliographic information by the German National Library: The German National Library lists this publication at the German National Bibliography; detailed bibliographic information is available on the Internet at http://dnb.d-nb.de.

Any brand names and product names mentioned in this book are subject to trademark, brand or patent protection and are trademarks or registered trademarks of their respective holders. The use of brand names, product names, common names, trade names, product descriptions etc. even without a particular marking in this works is in no way to be construed to mean that such names may be regarded as unrestricted in respect of trademark and brand protection legislation and could thus be used by anyone.

Cover image: www.purestockx.com

Publisher:
VDM Verlag Dr. Müller Aktiengesellschaft & Co. KG , Dudweiler Landstr. 125 a, 66123 Saarbrücken, Germany,
Phone +49 681 9100-698, Fax +49 681 9100-988,
Email: info@vdm-verlag.de

Zugl.: Houston, University of Houston, Diss., 2006

Produced in USA and UK by:
Lightning Source Inc., La Vergne, Tennessee, USA
Lightning Source UK Ltd., Milton Keynes, UK
BookSurge LLC, 5341 Dorchester Road, Suite 16, North Charleston, SC 29418, USA

ISBN: 978-3-639-01860-8

The completion of this work has been the culmination of a long journey, a journey I was able to complete only because of divine grace and support from family, teachers, and friends.

**This dissertation is dedicated to my husband, Kurian,
and our children – Sanjay, Sunita, and Sheila.**

TABLE OF CONTENTS

LIST OF TABLES

LIST OF FIGURES

Chapter 1

INTRODUCTION

1.1 Introduction

The notion of outsourcing – making arrangements with an external entity for the provision of goods or services to supplement or replace internal efforts – has been around for centuries. Kakabadse and Kakabadse (2002) track one of the earliest occurrences of outsourcing to the ancient Roman Empire, where tax collection was outsourced. Closer to home, in the early years of American history, the production of wagon covers was outsourced to Scotland, where they used raw material imported from India. In the 1830s the English textile industry became so competitive that the Indian textile manufacturers lost the contract to supply the fabric (Kelly, 2002). Outsourcing remained popular in the manufacturing sector, with part of the assembling in many industries (e.g., garment, cigar, and toy industries) sub-contracted to other organizations in locations relatively close to the manufacturer where the work could be done more efficiently. However, there was a radical change in the manufacturing sector in the early seventies when production was outsourced to suppliers in Asia (Vaze, 2005). It was not long before the idea of outsourcing was applied to the procurement of IS services; IS outsourcing as is practiced today in the information systems domain was developed by EDS[1] in the early sixties. However, information systems (IS) outsourcing garnered the spotlight in practice and research only after the landmark Kodak outsourcing deal[2] in 1989 (Dibbern et al, 2004).

In the past fifteen years since the Kodak deal, IS outsourcing[3] has seen an explosion in quantity and scope. The number and value of outsourcing deals has increased, with client organizations willing to outsource a wide range of IS services. A Gartner study conducted in 2004 placed global IS outsourcing[4] at $176.8 billion in 2003, and forecasted that this will grow to $235.6 billion in 2007, and to $253.1 billion in 2008 (Reported in Souza, 2004). The IT Services Contract Tracker, a service of analyst firm Datamonitor and outsourcing consultants Everest Group gives a slightly different number, but also reports that IS outsourcing is on the rise. According to that study, the combined value of global outsourcing deals increased by 37 per cent to $163 billion in 2004 (Reported by McCue, 2005). Another study by TPI reports similar findings; it also points out that 67% of all global outsourcing deals were IS outsourcing deals. Thus it appears that IS outsourcing is a practice that is here to stay.

From its beginnings as a cost-cutting tool, outsourcing has evolved into an integral component of a firm's overall business strategy (Linder 2004). Outsourcing is also motivated by other factors such as improved quality of services, faster time-to-market, and reduced headcount. In a survey conducted by Hewitt Associates (Business Wire, 2002) of more than 500 Chief Financial Officers and senior executives in the United States (the outsourcing leader), ninety percent indicated that they believed using outside resources to perform non-core functions of their business increases shareholder value. Since the typical client organization's core competency is not in the creation of IS (Rockart et al, 1996) outsourcing some IS responsibilities to vendor organizations would enable them to conserve critical resources to focus on strategic

---

[1] Electronic Data Systems
[2] Eastman Kodak outsourced its information systems function in 1989 to IBM, DEC and Business Land.
[3] Information systems (IS) outsourcing is "the delegation to a third party the continuous management responsibility for the provision of an IS service under a contract that includes a service level agreement" (Fitzgerald, 1997). A more detailed discussion of IS outsourcing is presented in Chapter 2.
[4] The term global outsourcing is used to refer to all outsourcing deals across the world, and includes both outsourcing to vendors in the same country and outsourcing to vendors in other countries. The former is referred to as domestic outsourcing and the latter as offshore outsourcing.

1

priorities. Thus, while conventional drivers of outsourcing such as cost-cutting still exist, organizations are increasingly turning to outsourcing for strategic reasons. Yet, even as client organizations turn to outsourcing with expectations of strategic benefits and operational efficiencies, there are reports that many of these deals fail to deliver expected benefits. One of the cited reasons for this failure is the breakdown in relationship between the outsourcing client and vendor organizations. It is the intention of this study to examine this client-vendor relationship to gain a better understanding of the impact of the relationship on the outcome of the outsourcing project.

1.2 IS Outsourcing Categories:

IS outsourcing includes a range of services; Gartner Dataquest divides IS outsourcing into four categories: data center outsourcing[5], desktop outsourcing[6], network outsourcing[7], and applications outsourcing[8]. These activities differ in the nature of skills required and in the costs and impacts to the organizations (Kern, Willcocks, and vanHeck, 2002). Because of this disparity in capabilities required among categories, this research focuses only on one of these categories: applications outsourcing. Further, the nature of the interactions and the relationship between client and vendor is determined by the particular service or product that is outsourced (Kakabadse and Kakabadse, 2000). Applications outsourcing encompasses application development, management, and enhancement. In 2002, application outsourcing comprised 21% of the worldwide IS outsourcing total of $161.9 billion. While IS outsourcing is expected to grow at a compounded annual growth rate of 7.3% until 2007, applications outsourcing is growing at a compounded annual growth rate of 7.8%. It is the second fastest growing category behind network outsourcing, which is growing at a rate of 9.3% (Gartner Dataquest Forecast, 2004).

While outsourcing to vendors within the United States is growing at a rate of 10-15% annually, outsourcing from U.S. clients to offshore vendors (offshore outsourcing) is growing at a rate higher than 25%, according to a study by the Meta Group (www.ebstrategy.com). Forecasts from Meta Group indicate that offshore outsourcing will grow from seven billion dollars in 2003 to ten billion dollars in 2005. The escalating demand for IS resources, a focus on cost controls, and a recognition of global "centers of excellence" primarily drive this move towards offshore outsourcing (Krishna et al, 2004). In a comparative study of offshore and onshore IT outsourcing, a study in the McKinsey quarterly reported a savings of 50 to 70% through offshore outsourcing. It is estimated (0.6 probability) that by 2005, at least thirty percent of Global 2000 companies will have a sourcing strategy that includes offshore solutions (Terdiman, 2001). In the applications outsourcing area, offshore resources are reasonably mature and clients are comfortable going to offshore vendors. Meta Group (2004) predicts that by 2009, an average organization will be sending 60% of its IT applications work offshore. The international aspect of these transactions significantly impacts the complexity of these arrangements (Halvey and Melby, 1996), and as a result the failure rates are higher than when

---

[5] Data center outsourcing is a contract/relationship involving the day-to-day management responsibility for operating server/host environments, including distributed servers and storage (Gartner, 2004)
[6] Desktop outsourcing is a contract/relationship involving the day-to-day management responsibility for operating desktop/client environments (Gartner, 2004)
[7] Network outsourcing is a contract/relationship involving the purchase of ongoing network or telecommunications management services for managing, enhancing, maintaining and supporting premises or core network infrastructure or enterprise telecommunications assets (including fixed and wireless) (Gartner, 2004)
[8] Applications outsourcing is a contract/relationship involving the purchase of ongoing applications services for managing, enhancing and maintaining custom or packaged applications software in the server/host or desktop environments (Gartner, 2004)

2

outsourcing to domestic vendors (Foote, 2004). Given the growth of offshore outsourcing and the increased risks associated with it, this research will examine the client-vendor relationship in the offshore applications outsourcing context.

1.3 Problems in Outsourcing:
The Culprit: Relationship "Disconnect"

Clients take up IS outsourcing as a means of obtaining services and/or products more effectively and/or efficiently. Vendor organizations also come into the outsourcing relationship with their own expectations. While providing the necessary services and value to the customer, they hope to benefit from the relationship financially as well in the form of additional business opportunities in the form of additional projects with the same client or referrals to other clients (Corbett, 2001). However, the reality is that many such well-intentioned relationships end in failure. The most common meaning of "failure" in the outsourcing context is that the contract for the outsourcing project is cancelled prior to completion. A secondary definition includes projects that do not meet expectations: projects that are not delivered on-time, those that prove unsuitable for intended purposes or are unprofitable for the life of the IS.

A report by Gartner (2003) states that half of all outsourcing projects will be considered failures; Gartner paints an even more alarming picture of IS outsourcing. "A staggering 80% of IT deals do not achieve desired results" (Gartner, 2003). A Forrester Research report published in February 2004 paints a better picture with only more than 40 percent of outsourcing relationships failing to deliver expected value. These outsourcing failures cost US companies between \$30 billion and \$40 billion a year in lost time and expense. Exact statistics on outsourcing failures are hard to find because they are rarely reported; naturally, organizations may be reluctant to publicize those failures. Whatever the actual percentage may be, it is true that any failed outsourcing project is costly to both the client and the vendor. In addition, when considering the dependence of the client organization on the outcome of the outsourcing deal, the problem gains additional significance.

Clients and vendors initially create a contract which established the product and processes required for the completion of the outsourced project. However, both parties have potentially divergent expectations about the product and the processes. Problems develop due to a "disconnect" (Hirschheim Porra, and Todd, 2001) between the client and the vendor, resulting in unmet expectations and poor performance. The ensuing dissatisfaction could lead to lack of commitment and unwillingness to exert effort to maintain the relationship (Commeiras and Fournier, 2001). The stability of the relationship is thus compromised (Huston and Robins, 1982) resulting in non-completion of the project as originally planned.

Vendors would like to develop and maintain a long-term relationship with the customer. In interviews conducted at vendor organizations for this research project, many vendor representatives stated that "repeat business" was the ultimate indicator of success for the vendor organization. Repeat business occurs when the client expresses a preference for a particular vendor for continued exchange and interaction. This preference is created during the ongoing exchange relationship between the client and the vendor. Another frequently mentioned and related indicator was "referrals from existing clients to obtain new business." In the competitive outsourcing market, some organizations thrive and some attain "preferred partner" status while others are not able to establish themselves. In fact, the "annual client retention rate" is recognized as a measure of success from the vendor perspective (Corbett, 2001), and many

3

vendors tout these numbers in their marketing material and on their web sites as a reflection of their capabilities.

While the vendor organizations' viability depend on managing and completing outsourcing projects well, the clients have significant efficiency and effectiveness issues at stake in these relationships. As the end-users of the product of the outsourcing arrangement, they have the most to gain from a good relationship. Thus, the expected outcomes from an outsourcing project are 1, completing the project while meeting the expectations of both organizations and 2, a continuing relationship between the client and vendor organizations that can leverage the learning that has occurred in previous projects.

Organizations are becoming increasingly aware of the importance of relationship management. In the IT Index 2001 survey, client organizations identified relationship management as one of the three most factors determining success in outsourcing, along with identifying the vendor with the right capabilities and crafting the right contract. According to Barthelemy (2003), contract management and relationship management are the mutually exclusive hard and soft sides of outsourcing management. Contract management is the creation and enforcement of contracts for the supply of a product or service. The contract cannot stipulate issues such as cooperation, coordination, and trust between clients and vendors (Currie, 1998); this is the domain of relationship management. The results of a survey conducted by the KPMG consulting group revealed that dissatisfaction with the relationship has resulted in more than seventy percent of customers not planning to renew their contract (TPI, 1999). However, few client organizations have taken formal steps to address this crucial issue; only a quarter of client organizations using the ten largest outsourcing vendors provide training for their personnel on how to manage relationships with vendors (Violino and Caldwell, 1998). Vendor organizations pay a bit more attention to this issue; vendor organizations train their personnel in relationship management and people management (Jones, 2000).

Though relationship management is a relatively under-explored area in IS outsourcing research, its importance in the overall success of the outsourced project has been noted. In couple of the earliest works in this area, Klepper (1994 and 1995) identified various elements of relationships such as dependence, trust, cooperation, functional conflict, and communication that are important in the outsourcing context. McFarlan and Nolan (1995) recommended that organizations focus on the relationship rather than on the contract to achieve success in outsourcing. Grover et al (1996) noted that as the outsourcing marketplace becomes increasingly competitive, the nature of the client-vendor relationship and its management are of fundamental importance. Recognizing the risky nature of outsourcing (Aubert et al, 1999), researchers have stressed the need for relationship-building mechanisms that can deliver on the promises of outsourcing for both client and vendor. Rockart et al (1996) stress that to obtain the full benefits from IT outsourcing, the IT manager in the client organization must be able to recognize the nature of the relationship and manage it accordingly. Studies have also looked at the effect of specific relationship elements on the success of the outsourcing relationship (Kern and Blois, 2002; Lee and Kim, 1999; Sabherwal, 1999). In his research, Goles (2002) found that the client-vendor relationship mediates the link between the capabilities of both organizations and outsourcing success. Thus, academic research and reports from practitioners indicate that solutions to many problems associated with outsourcing can be found by understanding the relationship between client and vendor.

It is not surprising that researchers in the area of outsourcing have identified the importance of relationship elements in outsourcing success. While mainstream economics emphasizes only the contribution of financial capital and human skills to economic activity, a high degree of social cooperation is required to accomplish such work (Wright, 2000). Granovetter (1985) argued that most economic behavior is embedded in social relationships. He contends that neoclassical economists who assume that markets operate based on the rational self-interest of individuals are mistaken. Economic behavior can be better explained through embedded relations, both within and among organizations. Social relations guide economic behavior, and are not just a consequence of economic actions. Following this reasoning, this study also approaches the study of IS outsourcing from a social perspective, focusing on the dyadic relationship between client and vendor.

1.4 Research Questions

The costs of a failed applications outsourcing project, while significant, are not contained within itself, but are exacerbated by the costs of lost opportunities for both client and vendor. Recognizing the significant role that the relationship plays in determining the outcome of applications outsourcing, this research examines the relationship between client and vendor in the operationalization stage and the execution and completion of the applications outsourcing project. Using case studies based in the interpretive paradigm, these relationships are studied from the client and vendor perspectives. Thus, the <u>primary research question</u> is

> *How does the client-vendor relationship affect the execution and completion of the applications outsourcing project?*

Acknowledging the growth of offshore outsourcing, especially in the area of applications outsourcing, this research also examines the effect of cultural differences between clients and vendors on the offshore applications outsourcing project. Thus, the <u>secondary research question</u> is

> *How does the difference in national cultures between the clients and vendors in the offshore applications outsourcing situation affect the development of the client-vendor relationship and hence the outcomes of the applications outsourcing project?*

1.5 The Following Chapters

This book has eight chapters. A summary of the following seven chapters is presented below.

Chapter 2: In this chapter, previous research on outsourcing literature is reviewed. This review identifies various issues associated with the phenomenon of IS outsourcing and highlights the paucity of research in the area of outsourcing relationship management.

Chapter 3: Inter-organizational relationships have been the focus of much research in the disciplines of management and marketing. These studies have formed the basis for the few studies that have addressed relationship issues in outsourcing research in general and IS outsourcing research, in particular. A review of the different characteristics of relationships (for example: communication, commitment, trust) that have been identified in previous research on inter-organizational relationships is presented in this chapter. The description in this chapter sets the stage for the integrative framework presented in the chapter 4.

Chapter 4: The theoretical framework used in this research is discussed in this chapter. This research applies the concept of social capital[9], a term that originated in Sociology, in

---

[9] Social capital can be defined as the access and resources available to members in a relationship.

5

separate works of various researchers. Nahapiet and Ghoshal (1998), through a systematic review of previous work on social capital, identified and categorized the elements that comprise social capital. They then examined how social capital contributed to the exchange and combination of knowledge necessary for the development of new intellectual capital within an organization. Nahapiet and Ghoshal (page 261; 1998) suggested that their work could be extended to examine the relationship that develops through ongoing inter-organizational exchanges. This research extends the concepts developed in Nahapiet and Ghoshal's work to examine the client-vendor relationship in the area of applications outsourcing.

Chapter 5: The proposed methods for data collection and analysis, as well as the reasons behind these choices are discussed in this chapter. The interview-based case study method is the primary tool for data collection. Intentional analysis, which is appropriate for analysis of data of this type, was used to examine the data, guided by the concepts provided by the theoretical framework.

Chapter 6: Based on the analysis of the interview data using the social capital framework, descriptions of relationships in the context of an outsourcing arrangement were constructed. Ten such case descriptions are presented in this chapter.

Chapter 7: This chapter presents a cross-case analysis to answer the questions that were posed in this research. Additional insights regarding the outsourcing process are also discussed.

Chapter 8: In this chapter, insights gained from the examination of outsourcing relationships using the "social capital" theoretical framework are presented. Further, the merits of this framework are assessed and the implications of this research for both practice and research are discussed.

Chapter 2

REVIEW OF OUTSOURCING RESEARCH
2.1 Introduction

The primary purpose of this chapter is to review this research on information systems outsourcing. As a necessary prelude to the research presented in this dissertation, existing research is reviewed to identify what aspects of the outsourcing phenomenon have received attention and which have lagged behind.

The following sections of this chapter are organized as follows. The first task in the next section is to define IS outsourcing as it applies to this research. Applications outsourcing and offshore outsourcing are discussed next. In the third section of this chapter, existing research in IS outsourcing is reviewed. This review is organized into topics that match the issues and challenges a client organization will face as it moves through the outsourcing lifecycle. This use of the client organization perspective is not a matter of personal choice, but a reflection of the research that has been done in IS outsourcing, where the spotlight until recently[1] has been on the client perspective. Lee (2000) divides the outsourcing research that has been done so far into two stages. The first stage presented the client view predominantly, while the current (second) stage of research considers both client and provider views. The chapter concludes with a chart that links the major research issues to the different stages in the outsourcing life cycle.

2.2 Outsourcing Defined:

Information systems researchers have proposed many definitions of outsourcing. Mitchell and Fitzgerald (1997) emphasize the continuing nature of the outsourcing process and define information technology outsourcing as "the delegation to a third party the continuous management responsibility for the provision of an IT service under a contract that includes a service level agreement." Focusing on the contractual nature of the outsourcing arrangement, Kern (1997; p.37) defines outsourcing as" a decision taken by an organization to contract-out or sell the organization's IT assets, people, and/or activities to a third party vendor, who in exchange provides and manages assets and services for monetary returns over an agreed time period." These IT services could include "all or part of the technical resources, the human resources and the management responsibilities associated with providing IT services" (Clark et al, 1995). The outcome of such arrangements is "a service or product that has a distinct business function and fits into the customer's overall business operations" (outsourcing-law.com).

Outsourcing is seen as an occasion for rebuilding the organization and the outcome of outsourcing is a leaner and more competent organization; this is the message conveyed by the definition at the web site of the Outsourcing Institute, which reads: "Outsourcing is nothing less than a basic redefinition of the organization. Outsourcing suggests an organization focused on a few, well-chosen core competencies supported by long-term outside relationships for many of its other activities and resources." Loh and Venkataraman (1992) also see outsourcing as a new means for governing, but focus only on the IT infrastructure: "We argue that IT outsourcing represents a fundamental point of departure in how organizations govern their IT infrastructure, and hence could be viewed as an administrative innovation."

---

[1] In one of the rare studies that focused on vendors, Levina and Ross (2003) examined the reasons behind vendor efficiency. They conclude that the efficiency of the vendor stems from the fact that the vendor is able to develop a set of competencies based on client needs and market conditions and control the delivery processes across multiple clients.

Building on these definitions, information systems outsourcing is defined in this study as

> "an arrangement between two organizations, the client and the vendor, in which the vendor provides the client with specific IS products and services, based on a formal agreement between the two organizations."

2.2.1 Applications Outsourcing

"Applications outsourcing is a contract relationship involving the purchase of ongoing applications services for managing, enhancing and maintaining custom or packaged applications software in the server/host or desktop environments. It includes services specifically delivered in support of the life cycle of applications such as consulting/advisory services, applications development, integration, deployment and support services" (Gartner, 2004) Rus and Lindvall (2002) emphasize the knowledge-intensive nature of this work; they identified two types of knowledge that are necessary for this activity – business domain knowledge and technical knowledge. Thus, as Constantine and Lockwood (1993) have noted, this activity requires a synthesis of knowledge from different sources. When applications development or enhancement is outsourced, the exchanges occur across organizational boundaries, thus making it even more difficult to coordinate and manage. In addition, the combination of many complex factors such as changing technologies and dynamic environments make applications outsourcing complex (Kern, Willcocks and vanHeck, 2002). As the outsourced activity becomes more complex, the harder it becomes to manage and to achieve a satisfactory outcome. In such a situation, relationship management becomes even more important and has considerable impact on the product of outsourcing as well as on the satisfaction of both parties (Klepper, 1994; Lee and Kim, 1999; Marcolin and Mclellan, 1998).

2.2.2 Offshore Outsourcing

"Offshore outsourcing" is the delegation of responsibility for management and delivery of IT services to a vendor who is located in a different geographical area (from the client) (Sabherwal, 1999a). High labor costs and the shortage of qualified engineers in the US coupled with the availability of well-qualified but less expensive resources in other countries make offshore outsourcing attractive to developed economies. Even the recent furor over offshore outsourcing has not cut the interest in offshore outsourcing. An IDC research report produced in October 2004 states that the worldwide market for offshore IT services will grow from nearly $7 billion 2003 to $17 billion in 2008. Most offshore spending by U.S. companies will be on applications, particularly custom application development, application management, and systems integration.

India is recognized as the "offshore leader" in information systems outsourcing (Gartner, 2004); other major players are Canada, China, Ireland, Mexico, and Philippines India has a considerable impact on the US offshore market; of the $9.5 billion software exports from India in 2003, the United States accounted for 60%. Apte et al (1997) found that access to trained professionals was considered one of the advantages while difficulties in verbal and data communications were found the greatest disadvantage in global outsourcing. The absence of a language gap combined with the availability of a vast pool of software professionals trained in diverse technologies makes India particularly attractive for offshore outsourcing to US companies (Rajkumar and Dawley, 1998).

Offshore outsourcing is not without its challenges; in a Gartner survey of 219 clients conducted last year, more than half failed to realize the expected value from offshore outsourcing (cited in "Shifting Work Offshore? Outsourcer Beware". BusinessWeek Online; Jan 12, 2004). The geographical separation and cultural differences have posed a challenge for offshore vendors in the management of outsourcing arrangements. Information and communication technologies help overcome some of the problems posed by distance; additionally, vendor organizations supplement these tools with face-to-face meetings on a regular basis. To alleviate the problems caused by cultural differences, vendor organizations invest in cultural training; Krishna, Sahay, and Walsham (2004) exhort client organizations to do the same to create an environment of mutual understanding that will support all the activities required to complete the delivery of the outsourced service.

2.3 Review of Outsourcing Research Literature

Organizations engaged in the outsourcing process face various issues at the different stages from inception to termination and researchers have studied different aspects of outsourcing over the past years (Lee et al, 2003). In making the decision to outsource, the organization must first consider the determinants of outsourcing as well as the benefits and risks; these are the issues addressed in the first three sub-sections. Indiscriminate outsourcing has the highest chance of failure; particular care needs to be taken in determining what activities need to be outsourced and in selecting the vendors. These are the issues addressed in sub-sections 4 and 5. The legal and organizational structuring of the outsourcing arrangement are the subjects of the next two sub-sections. The last three sub-sections deal with the operationalization and outcomes of the outsourcing arrangement.

To identify articles to be included in the review, leading IS journals (MIS Quarterly, Information Systems Research, Journal of Management Information Systems, European Journal of Information Systems, and Information Systems Journal) and the Proceedings of the International Conference on IS were scanned, starting with issues from 1989, the year of the Kodak outsourcing agreement. Using the reference lists from articles obtained from these sources, articles from other journals were also selectively obtained, in a snowballing process. Not all the articles obtained are included in the review below; instead, a representative sample of articles to show the key areas of research has been presented.

2.3.1 Why do client organizations outsource?

Cheon et al. (1995) present a theoretical framework for understanding determinants of a organization's outsourcing strategy; the decision to outsource IS functions stems from the interaction of two factors: the organization's dynamic environmental conditions and the extent to which the organization needs to fill gaps in its IS resources and capabilities. Thus outsourcing is driven by factors external to the organization, as well as organizational needs and IS capabilities. Similarly, Clark, et al. (1995) identifies four categories of outsourcing determinants: technology forces, technology management forces, industry forces and organizational forces.

A review of the IS outsourcing research shows that various researchers have identified specific factors in these different categories. For example, Reponen (1993) and Slaughter and Ang (1996) list organizational staffing issues as one of the determinants of outsourcing – lack of availability of technical staff within the client organization and/or the opportunity to obtain technical experience from vendor organizations. Thus, companies with smaller IS budgets are more likely to outsource than companies with larger budgets since they may not have the requisite resources within; also, organizations with decentralized IS functions are more likely to outsource than organizations with centralized functions (Sobol and Apte, 1995).

Beyond pure cost reduction, the opportunity to focus on core competencies while improving IS performance motivate organizations to consider outsourcing (McFarlan and Nolan, 1995). DiRomualdo and Gurbaxani (1998) suggest that the underlying conviction behind these determinants is that IS can be used to achieve better results in organizational endeavors and creates value for the organization. In summary, the research review shows that the determinants of outsourcing have shifted from pure cost-reduction to more strategic reasons. Further, examining the years of publication of these articles, it appears the reasons behind outsourcing is an issue that was of great interest in the initial periods of outsourcing research, but is no longer a central theme of outsourcing research.

As a sidebar, researchers have also commented on the role of technology in supporting IS outsourcing. Clemons et al (1993) put forward an interesting hypothesis that IT aids the "move" towards outsourcing by reducing transaction costs without increasing transaction risks. Transaction costs arise from various information-intensive activities such as searching, monitoring, and coordinating and IT can be employed to reduce these costs. The use of IT does not produce any additional risks, and thus would cause firms to outsource more. Hirschheim et al (2004) also discuss this enabling role of IT in outsourcing; the communication and distributed work that is necessary for outsourcing is made possible by the advances in technology.

2.3.2 What are the benefits from outsourcing?

Benefits are intimately connected with the determinants of IS outsourcing identified in the previous section. Thus, benefits of outsourcing include cost reduction, rapid development time, access to leading-edge technologies, and easing of IS management tasks (Clark, et al., 1995); yet, most organizations identify cost reduction as the primary benefit (Ang and Slaughter, 1998, Currie and Willcocks, 1998, Lacity and Hirschheim, 1995, Smith, et al., 1998, Sobol and Apte, 1995). In a study which considered differences between organizations in Finland, Japan, and the United States with regard to outsourcing practices, Apte, et al. (1997) find that companies in all three countries considered the potential for cost reduction and the opportunity to focus on the strategic use of IS as important advantages of domestic outsourcing.

Though Loh and Venkataraman (1992a) do not find a relationship between business performance and outsourcing, a later work by Loh and Venkataraman (1995) find some evidence linking outsourcing and favorable organization performance. Fowler and Jeffs (1998) see outsourcing as a means for introducing change into the organization. Similar to the results found in industry surveys, these studies also indicate that while cost reduction may remain a priority, there is more recognition of the strategic benefits that are available from outsourcing. Thus, cumulatively three primary classes of benefits have been identified: strategic, economic, and technical (Grover et al, 1996; Lee and Kim, 1999; Saunders et al, 1997).

2.3.3 What are the risks of outsourcing?

In one of the earliest studies of outsourcing, Lacity and Hirschheim (1993) strike a cautionary note about outsourcing; they exposed several myths about outsourcing prevalent in the media at that time which suggested that outsourcing could provide benefits that organizations could not otherwise achieve. Clark, et al. (1995) identified some negative consequences of outsourcing, including increased costs and risk, loss of flexibility and increased information systems management complexity. Earl (1996) determined different sources of risk in outsourcing including uncertainty and loss of innovative capacity. Aubert et al (1998 and 1999) identifies the risk factors such as lack of experience, uncertainty, and task complexity which can lead to undesirable consequences like unexpected transition and management costs, lock-in, cost escalation and service degradation. Natovich (2003) contends that the client may actually be adding additional vendor related risks such as adversarial relationships to traditional project risks (for e.g.: cost overruns, schedule slippages).

The research reviewed in the following sections address challenges in different phases of the outsourcing lifecycle that prevents organizations from realizing the benefits discussed above and/or worse, end up facing undesirable consequences from poorly managed risks.

2.3.4 How should client organizations select vendors?

Research has identified criteria that clients can apply during the vendor selection process. In selecting vendors, the clients should naturally consider technical competence (Klepper, 1995); other desirable characteristics include reputation, trustworthiness (Nam, et al., 1996), vendor stability, and quality (McFarlan and Nolan, 1995). Organizations may consider using multiple outsourcing vendors to obtain benefits from vendor specialization and to maintain contractual and technological flexibility (Gallivan and Oh, 1999). Huber (1993) recommends using external consultants to help in choosing the right partner and in negotiating agreements, particularly when the client does not have much experience with outsourcing.

2.3.5 What activities should be outsourced?

Frameworks that help client organizations determine the activities to outsource based on the organization's dependence on the function and its importance to the organization have been proposed (for e.g. McFarlan and Nolan, 1995; Lacity et al, 1995 and 1996). McFarlan and Nolan propose a 2X2 framework that places the IT functions of the organization into four categories that should be "insourced[2]" or "outsourced". The two dimensions used in the evaluation of the IT functions are the function's importance to the organization and the dependence of the organization on the IT function. Lacity et al's framework also has four categories: critical commodity, critical differentiator, useful commodity, and useful differentiator. The evaluation is based on two dimensions: contribution of the function to business operations and contribution of the function to business positioning. Critical differentiators are IT functions that are critical to business operations and distinguish the organization from its competitors; insourcing is the preferred option here. The useful commodity is diagonally opposite; since these are not critical to the business and do not serve as a means of differentiation, these can be outsourced. Critical commodities should be "best sourced", that is, insourced or outsourced depending on their content and value to the organization; these are critical to the organization, but do not differentiate the organization from its competitors. The last set, the useful differentiators, provide only marginal benefits even though these are differentiators, and should be eliminated.

Aubert et al (2004) examine the outsourcing decisions of 335 organizations; their results show that the asset specificity, uncertainty, and technical skills required for the IT function determine which activities are outsourced. When there is considerable uncertainty about the requirements and deliverables for an IS function, client organizations would be unwilling to outsource that activity. If the activity requires a high degree of technical skills, it is more likely

---

[2] IS functions are provided by the in-house IS staff

11

to be outsourced. Asset specificity would reduce the level of outsourcing; since these may lead to costly lock-in situations. These findings suggest that clients should outsource IS services selectively, ensuring that the requirements for the service is clearly defined. Further, as discussed in the section above, the client should ascertain that the vendor has the technical capabilities and has a solid reputation for excellent service and trustworthiness.

2.3.6   What are the different outsourcing models?

Currie and Willcocks (1998) identify four distinct approaches to sourcing; three of these involve getting an external vendor to provide IS services: total outsourcing to a single vendor, joint venture or strategic alliance, and using multiple suppliers. The fourth approach is to use resources available in-house, that is, insourcing. When entering into agreements with vendors, five types of contract-based relationships may be defined: tightly defined service contract, short and flexible service contract, partnership based on formal contract, flexible partnership based on trust and strategic alliance (Fitzgerald and Willcocks, 1994).

Kishore et al (2003) identify four types of outsourcing relationships, which they term support, alignment, alliance, and reliance. In a support relationship, the role of the vendors is limited with the client keeping most activities in-house. In the alignment relationship, the client obtains the vendor's expertise as needed on a project basis. In the reliance relationship, the client depends extensively on the vendor for IT services. In the alliance relationship, the client and the vendor work together in close partnerships. To sum up, in the ten years of research (from Fitzgerald and Willcocks, 1994 to Kishore et al 2003), the different client-vendor relationships possible in outsourcing have been viewed as a continuum ranging from discrete transactions governed by tight contracts to alliances where both client and vendor work together collaboratively towards a win-win situation (Clark, et al., 1995, Klepper, 1995, Marcolin and McLellan, 1998). Clients and vendors may determine a model for their project based on their particular technical requirements and organizational and environmental constraints.

2.3.7   What should be included in contracts? What is the role of the contract in the management of the outsourcing arrangement?

The contract defines the outsourcing arrangement and structures the interactions of the client of the vendor in the outsourcing arrangement; it includes mechanisms to determine if these provisions are met. According to Macaulay (1963), a contract has two distinct elements: "rational planning of the transaction with careful provision for as many future contingencies as can be foreseen, and the existence or use of actual or potential legal sanctions to induce performance of the exchange or to compensate for non-performance" (pp. 266). MacNeil (1978, pp. 895) described contracts by the following norms: "permitting and encouraging participation and exchange, promoting reciprocity, reinforcing role patterns appropriate to the particular kinds of contracts, providing limited freedom for exercise of choice, effectuating planning." While Macaulay's definition focuses on the sanctioning and restraining capabilities of contracts, MacNeil's description directs attention to the capability of the contract to promote relational cooperation between organizations.

Most contracts include three key components: product definition, intellectual property protection and payment terms (Whang, 1992). DiRomualdo and Gurbaxani (1998) interviewed senior executives of companies that have outsourced some or all of their IT and recommended that the outsourcing contract be designed to anticipate and manage change. The specific type of contract created for an outsourcing arrangement depends on the nature of the product or service that is outsourced. Fitzgerald and Willcocks (1994), based on an in-depth analysis of contracts and partnerships in large and medium-sized organizations in the UK, identifies six different types of outsourcing contracts: time and materials, fixed fee, fixed fee plus variable element, cost plus management fee, fee plus incentive, and shared risk and reward. A contract could combine any of these six types. Fixed term, fixed price contracts are usually preferred over open-ended, or time and materials contracts in outsourcing (Currie, 1996).

The contract may be an occasion for opportunistic behavior by the vendor, since the vendor has more knowledge of the technology (Lacity and Hirschheim, 1995) while the client may be beguiled into thinking of the relationship as a partnership (Lacity and Hirschheim, 1993; Lacity and Willcocks, 1998). Kern, Willcocks and van Heck (2002) offer an interesting explanation for the possible opportunistic behavior on the part of the vendor. The vendor may suffer from "winner's curse" where the vendor has bid for the contract at such a low rate that the vendor cannot provide the services the client requires within the pricing structure.

Contracts are seen as the solution and the problem in different studies. Inattention to contracts can result in financial loss and lock-in and Huber (1993) recommends that organizations create a clear and complete contract. However, Brynjolfsson (1994) reports that most organizations have been writing less detailed contracts with vendors, since it is impossible to identify all conditions to be included in the contract as requirements and technology are changing and evolving. Further, contracts cannot provide a solution to all problems in the relationship and undue dependence on the contract will only create additional problems in the relationship; governance mechanisms based on mutual awareness and understanding are preferred (Clark et al, 1995). Sabherwal (1999a) reiterates that a balance between structure and relationship elements such as trust improves performance in IS outsourcing and enhances the likelihood of outsourcing success.

2.3.8   What is outsourcing success? How can it be assessed and/or achieved?

Success is a difficult variable to operationalize and "satisfaction" is commonly used as a stand-in to evaluate success in an outsourcing relationship (Lee and Kim, 1999). It is often used as a catchall term to capture the organizational representatives' assessment of the output of the outsourcing project and the interactions between client and vendor organizations in the process of completing the project. As Goles (2001) points out, organizations enter into outsourcing arrangements to achieve strategic, technical, and economic benefits and it would be reasonable to assess the success of these arrangements by whether these expectations were met. In a survey to determine the determinants of outsourcing success, Goles (2001) evaluates success using assessments of strategic, technical, and economic benefits, evaluation of equity, and evaluation of satisfaction. Equity captures the notion whether benefits attained are proportional to the resources invested by either party. Satisfaction is used as an overall measure of success in this study.

Grover, et al. (1996) find that outsourcing success is affected by the level of service quality and the quality of the client-vendor partnership. It also varies depending on the asset specificity and the complexity of the function outsourced (Grover, et al., 1996). Assessments of success vary depending on who is doing the assessment; Hirschheim and Lacity (1998) note that different outsourcing stakeholders have different expectations and perceptions of IS performance and success. Based on a survey of small to mid-sized US banks, Heckman and King (1994) suggest that differing levels of satisfaction will result in different behaviors exhibited by the organizations: collaborative, switching, and contending behaviors.

To achieve success in outsourcing, relationship management and business planning should complement contractual arrangements (Marcolin and McLellan, 1998). Koh and Ang (2004) identify behaviors that the client and vendor organizations should exhibit to ensure outsourcing success. Clients should provide clear definition of expectations, make payments promptly, and have qualified staff dedicated to the project. The vendor organizations' obligations include effective management of resources, dedicated project staffing, knowledge sharing, and effective knowledge transfer. Quinn and Hilmer (1994) recommend that organizations should develop core capabilities and promote continuous innovation in the outsourcing project by leveraging the resources of both organizations. To establish the solidarity that is required for both organizations to work together, Kim and Chung (2003) stress that relationship management is essential.

2.3.9 What is involved in the management of the outsourcing project?

Not many studies have been done in this area; however, the limited research (Goles, 2001; Grover et al, 1996; Kern, 1997; Kern and Willcocks, 2000; Lee and Kim, 1999) supports the viewpoint of practitioners that management of the operationalization stage is a significant determinant the success of the outsourcing arrangement (Casale, IT Index, 2001). The operational stage of the outsourcing arrangement is characterized by information and resource exchanges as well as social exchanges to effect the creation and exchange of the product or service. Additionally, financial exchanges have to be completed to meet the contractual requirements (Kern and Willcocks, 2001). The parameters for the exchanges have been set in previous interactions and documented in the contract. The contract and the management capabilities of the client and the vendor influence the outcome of this stage (Lee and Kim, 1999). Management capabilities include capabilities associated with project management, IT management and relationship management.

Researchers recommend that clients retain adequate in-house capabilities (Saunders et al, 1997), establish feedback systems to ensure sharing of knowledge and innovation (Quinn, 1999), and develop formal monitoring mechanisms for effective management of the outsourcing arrangement (McFarlan and Nolan, 1997). Managing a single vendor to meet expectations is a challenge, but management challenges are compounded when working with multiple vendors. Cross (1995) points out that change management, conflict resolution, and knowledge transfer need to be carefully monitored in this situation. Experience is the best teacher; over time all parties gain an increased understanding of the others' expectations, making negotiations and operations easier to manage (Willcocks and Choi, 1995).

2.3.10 What are the factors that affect the relationship between client and vendor?

In one of the earlier studies on client-vendor relationships in IS outsourcing, Klepper (1994) finds a positive relationship between client-vendor relationship and outsourcing success. Saunders et al. (1997) further note that partnership arrangements are more successful than contract-based relationships. From a historical perspective, there has been a move from outsourcing arrangements defined by transaction based contracts to relationships based arrangements, which require closer interactions and sharing of risks and benefits by clients and vendors (Kakabadse and Kakabadse, 2000). The major conclusion from earlier research that examined the success of the outsourcing arrangement was that the client-vendor relationship "critically needs managing"; outsourcing success depends not only on achieving the service levels and meeting contract terms, but also on the relationship between the two parties (Kern, 1997; Willcocks and Kern, 1998).

Some researchers have presented a different perspective. While the studies above stress the importance of the relationship, Fowler (1998), Hancox and Hackney (1999), Lacity and Hirschheim (1993), and Willcocks et al (1995) doubt that a partnership, a relationship of mutual cooperation, can exist between the outsourcing client and vendor organizations since a common goal is not shared. While it is true that the desire for profit-maximization would lead the client and vendor organizations to have different goals, they do have a common goal in the outsourcing arrangement: the successful completion of the outsourced product or service, and it is around this agreement that a relationship is built.

Having established the importance of relationships, researchers turned to examining different elements of relationships such as trust, commitment, and flexibility to determine their impact on the outcome of the outsourcing arrangement. In the outsourcing context, Grover, et al. (1996), Lee and Kim (1999); and Sabherwal, (1999b) have found significant relationships between trust and outsourcing success. Lander et al (2004) examine trust-building mechanisms in outsourcing and find that while clients and vendors concur trust is important, creating trust in an outsourcing relationship is difficult because the perceptions of clients and vendors about trust-building mechanisms differ. Another important consideration in the relationship is flexibility. Clark et al (1995) and Lacity et al (1995) consider the key to a successful client-vendor relationship to be flexibility – the client should be able to change service requirements if necessary and the vendor should be able to change the means by which the service requirements are met. Kern and Blois (2002) commented on the importance of establishing norms such as flexibility, solidarity, and information exchange at the onset to avoid failure. Other researchers have focused on different relational aspects: cooperation (Grover et al, 1996; Kern, 1997), cultural compatibility (Lee and Kim, 1999), coordination (Sabherwal, 2003), expectations of continuity (Kim and Chung, 2003), and dependence (Klepper, 1995; Lee and Kim, 1999). Goles (2001) included a number of these relationship elements in his research; significant relationships were found between the presence of these relationship elements and success of the outsourcing arrangement.

Researchers have also looked for frameworks that would encapsulate the various relationship elements in the outsourcing arrangement. The contribution of Kern and Willcocks to this area of research is notable; they present different frameworks to explain the IS outsourcing relationship. In a 1998 paper, using concepts from contract theory and relational exchange theory, Willcocks and Kern described interactions between the client and the vendor at two levels, the contractual level and the cooperative level. At the contractual level, more tangible exchanges between the client and vendor were included such as product or service exchanges, financial exchanges, asset and staff exchanges and information exchanges. 'Social adaptations' is the last factor in this category; this factor of the contractual level refers to those formal mechanisms that have been implemented to create a cooperative atmosphere. At the cooperative level, the framework included social and personal bonds, communication, investments in time and knowledge and development of mutual goals and objectives. The framework was used to examine the interactions in an outsourcing arrangement between the UK Inland Revenue and its outsourcing vendor EDS. Willcocks and Kern report that this "exploratory framework" had "considerable applicability in terms of coverage of issues" (page 43), but needed additional work.

Kern and Willcocks (2001) refine their previous framework (Willcocks and Kern, 1998) to identify the various interactions and exchanges in an outsourcing relationship. The two foci for analysis in this framework are the contractual nature of the outsourcing relationship and the embededdness of that relationship in the social bonds between the organizations at personal, group, and organizational levels. The interactions that were included in the previous framework were part of this framework as well; however, in this framework, instead of separating these exchanges into two contractual and embededdness categories, these were grouped together, indicating that the economic exchanges were embedded in social relationships (Kern and Willcocks, 2001). Kern and Willcocks feel that the framework does not capture the dynamic nature of the outsourcing relationship; they comment that "the static view" (page 345; Kern and Willcocks, 2001) may limit the usefulness of the framework in explaining the development of the relationship in the outsourcing arrangement. However, this was the first framework that combined social, economic, and contractual characteristics of the operationalization stage of the outsourcing relationship. Though the framework appears to include client and vendor perspectives, Kern and Willcocks discuss the framework from the client's point of view.

In a later article (2002), Kern and Willcocks used the interaction model proposed by the Industrial Managing and Purchasing group (IMP) to describe the IS outsourcing relationship. The IMP model was the outcome of Phase I (1976-1982) of the IMP group and encompasses both short-term transactions and long-term relationships in dyadic buyer-supplier arrangements. Four main classes of variables are included in the model; these variables affect and are affected by the interaction: the elements of the interaction process; the parties involved; the environment; the atmosphere characterized by cooperation, closeness, and power. However, Kern and Willcocks concluded that while the interaction approach's focus on exchange issues provide some insights into IS outsourcing relationships, it is not sufficient by itself to provide a complete picture of the IS outsourcing relationship.

Another significant work in this area is that of Goles (2001). Goles' objective was to investigate the relationship elements that influence the success of the outsourcing arrangement. Using data collected via a survey from 175 respondents in client organizations and 191 respondents in vendor organizations, the model was tested. The study showed once again that the customer-vendor relationship is critical to the success of an outsourcing arrangement. The relationship leverages the capabilities of the organizations in a good relationship, enhancing the likelihood of success. In a poor relationship, the organizations will have to expend effort on the relationship and will not be able to concentrate on the outsourcing project. This study also highlights the difference between client and vendor perspectives; vendors are more sensitive to the relationship dynamics and believe that the relationship factors are important. Examining the various factors, both clients and vendors did not consider cultural compatibility and coordination to be important. Communication, cooperation, and flexibility are significant for the vendor, but not for the client. The client considers interdependence important, but the vendor does not.

2.4 Charting Research Issues to the Outsourcing Lifecycle

The review in the sections above has focused on the different topics addressed by researchers. Based on conversations with outsourcing consultants and a review of outsourcing articles in business journals and publications of consultancy and research groups (for example,

Gartner, TPI), other questions relevant to outsourcing clients and vendors were also identified. The stages of the outsourcing life cycle identified by Lacity and Willcocks (2000) are used as the basis for the classification of questions. While there are other players in the outsourcing arrangement such as consultants and sub-contractors, these questions are raised from the perspective of the key players: the client and the vendor.

Table 2-1: Outsourcing Process: Questions

Outsourcing stage	Questions raised from client perspective	Questions raised from domestic vendor perspective	Additional questions raised from offshore perspective
Partner Selection	How is contact with vendors established? What are the differences in establishing contact with local versus offshore vendors? What are the determinants in vendor selection? Who are the players/stakeholders involved? What are their roles and expectations? How are these assessments made?	How is contact with clients established? What are the factors that influence the choice of client and market? Who are the players/stakeholders involved? What are their roles and expectations? How are these assessments made? What are the different business models possible? Is there a preference for one particular model?	How can the move to offshore markets be accomplished? I.e. what is the mode of entry?
Evaluation and Negotiation of Contract	What are the factors considered? Who are the players/stakeholders involved? What are their roles and expectations? Is there a (perceived) power and knowledge imbalance? Why? How does it affect the	What are the factors considered? Who are the players/stakeholders involved? What are their roles and expectations? Is there a (perceived) power and knowledge imbalance? Why? How does it affect the	

17

	process?	process?	
Product: Finalized Contract	What is included in the contract? What is not? Why?	What is included in the contract? What is not? Why?	
Operationalization/ Management	How is the "relationship" operationalized, developed and maintained? How does this affect the outcome of the outsourcing arrangement?

What is the influence of the contract in this process?

What are the factors necessary for a successful relationship? | How is the "relationship" operationalized, developed and maintained? How does this affect the outcome of the outsourcing arrangement?

What is the influence of the contract in this process?

What are the factors necessary for a successful relationship? | What is the influence of the geographic and cultural distance on this process? |
| Evaluation: Ongoing | What are the monitoring procedures? | What are the monitoring procedures? | What is the influence of the geographic and cultural distance on this process? |
| Evaluation: Final | What are the benefits achieved?

What are the problems/risks? How is success defined? | What are the benefits achieved?

What are the problems/risks? How is success defined? | |

While the review of research shows that many of the questions on the client side have been addressed, much more needs to be understood about vendor behavior. Initial steps in this direction have been taken by researchers such as Levina and Ross (2003) and Goles (2001). Offshore outsourcing research has focused on the differences in cultures and the geographical separation and recommended ways to overcome this cultural and geographical distance (for e.g., Krishna and Sahay, 2004). Others have looked at country-specific characteristics and how the specific strengths and weaknesses of each country affects its potential as an outsourcing location (for e.g., Nair and Prasad, 2004 on a state in India; Zatolyuk and Allgood on Ukraine, 2004).

As discussed above, there is a growing interest in the area of relationship management, much still remains to be done. A better understanding of the client-vendor relationship is necessary as the relationship is a crucial factor in determining the success of the outsourcing arrangement, which also remains an elusive concept. The need for research to be directed to this area is documented in recent review articles on information systems outsourcing (for e.g., Hui and Beath, 2001 and Lee et al, 1999). Hui and Beath (2001) separate the outsourcing process into various stages: decision making, negotiation and project activities; they also classify research issues as related to the contract, the capabilities of client and vendor, market forces and institutional forces, and prior commitments. Based on their review, Hui and Beath identify issues in outsourcing on which more research is needed; studying issues associated with the operationalization of the contract and the impact of relationship elements on the outcome of the outsourcing arrangement is seen as a priority. Lee et al (1999) present a historical overview of IS outsourcing research and state that researchers have advanced to the stage where they can and need to start to direct their attention to relationship issues.

A more comprehensive review of outsourcing research is undertaken by Dibbern et al (2004). With the goal of providing a framework for synthesizing, and integrating existing outsourcing research in its first decade, they review and categorize a number of the research articles that appeared in leading IS journals as well as conference proceedings from 1992 to 2000. As the review in the preceding sub-sections also showed, Dibbern et al reveals that there is a great deal of diversity in terms of research objectives, as well as the theories and methods used in the research. Based on this comprehensive review, they identify gaps in the IS outsourcing research, which present future opportunities for research. Four significant areas were identified as needing further study: understanding the dependent variable, "outsourcing success", and understanding of the vendor perspective, understanding the client-vendor relationship; and, understanding changes in outsourcing over time. The goal of this study is to contribute to research in these identified areas, primarily the client vendor relationships in IS outsourcing, by examining both client and vendor perspectives on outsourcing.

2.5 Theoretical Underpinnings of Outsourcing Research

The primary referent discipline for IS outsourcing researchers has been strategic management research. Strategic management has ""traditionally focused on business concepts that affect organization performance" (Hoskisson et al, 1999; pp.418). Since organizations exist within a competitive environment, they have to make choices to survive. It is these choices that the field of strategic management must address; these choices include: "the selection of goals; the choice of products and services to offer; the design and configuration of policies determining how the organization positions itself to compete in product markets; the choice of an appropriate level of scope and diversity; the design of organization structure, systems and policies used to define and coordinate work" (Rumelt, Schendel and Teece, 1999). This range of issues defines two basic questions: How do organizations behave? Why do they behave differently?

Early works in the field of strategic management include Chandler's (1962) *Strategy and Structure* and Ansoff's (1965) *Corporate Strategy*. These early works focused on internal strengths and weaknesses and looked at the fit between strategy and structure. The next major contributions to strategic management research came from industrial economics; two theories that have predominantly been applied to IS outsourcing research developed from this stream: transaction costs economics theory and agency theory. Swinging back to an internal focus, more recent studies focus on the resource-based view of the organization. While this stream has its roots in Edith Penrose's work in the late fifties, it became a dominant framework in the strategic management area only in the nineties.

Whether focusing internally as with resource-based view of the organization, or focusing externally with contractuarian theories (Hodgson, 1998), the focus of these works has primarily been on economic efficiency. However, with an increasing recognition of the social embededdness of all economic action (Granovetter, 1985), strategic management researchers have been looking for other explanations for organization performance. At the same time, researchers in the marketing discipline, recognizing the need to shift from a product characteristics focus to a customer retention focus, have been honing in on "all activities aimed at establishing, developing, and maintaining successful relational exchanges" (Morgan and Hunt, 1994).

Reviewing the theoretical lenses applied in IS outsourcing research, a similar shift can be observed. While the traditional strategic management theories from the competence-based and contractuarian themes were applied in earlier research, recent work, especially on relationships, has started to incorporate such relational perspectives. A good example is Kern and Willcock's application of the IMP interaction model, which considers not only the economic aspects, but also the behavioral aspects of the interactions that describe the outsourcing relationship.

2.6 Conclusions

Looking at the research foci, most of the research has been undertaken from the client's perspective, providing a lopsided picture of outsourcing. In addition, while the initial decision making as well as the evaluation of outcomes have received considerable attention, the operationalization stage, where the client and the vendor work together has received very little. The relationship that regulates the interaction between the client and the vendor during this stage has been studied by a few researchers (for example, Goles, 2001; Kern and Willcocks, 2001), and the importance of the relationship in determining the performance and outcome of the outsourcing arrangement has been established.

While previous research has established the criticality of the relationship and identified factors that come into play in the relationship (such as trust, commitment, flexibility, coordination, cooperation, cultural compatibility, and dependence), much more needs to be understood about the establishment and development of these relationship factors and how they affect the work processes and exchanges in outsourcing arrangements. Such an examination will provide insights into how the relationship between the client and vendor organizations, the performance of both organizations, and the outcome interact and shape one another over time.

Chapter 3
ATTRIBUTES AND PROCESSES IN
INTER-ORGANIZATIONAL RELATIONSHIPS

3.1 Introduction

In the first chapter, the focus of this research was specified as inter-organizational relationships in an outsourcing context, specifically in domestic and offshore applications outsourcing arrangements. Review of research on IS outsourcing relationships in the second chapter has shown that research on outsourcing relationships is still in its infancy. However, there is a vast amount of research on inter-organizational relationships and buyer-seller relationships in other business disciplines (e.g., Marketing and Management). IS outsourcing researchers typically draw upon this work to explain the IS outsourcing relationship. For example, Kern and Willcocks (2002) apply a model developed in research on buyer-supplier relationships in the manufacturing sector.

The review in the previous chapter identified characteristics of relationships (for e.g., trust, commitment, and communication) that have an impact on the success of the outsourcing arrangement. These characteristics are discussed in more detail in this chapter. These characteristics can be separated into attributes (e.g., trust, commitment, and flexibility) that are necessary for the well-being and successful outcome of the relationship and processes (e.g., cooperation and communication) by which these attributes are developed and sustained in inter-organizational relationships (Lambe et al, 2000).

Articles for inclusion in the review presented in this chapter were obtained in three different ways. Articles were retrieved based on a search conducted using the names of these attributes and processes in electronic databases Academic Search Premier, Business Source Premier, and JSTOR. Articles referenced by researchers studying IS outsourcing relationships were also collected. A snowballing process was applied as well, with referenced research in retrieved articles leading to new articles.

The next section of the chapter contains a brief discussion of what constitutes inter-organizational relationships. Following that, the attributes, processes, and outcomes of inter-organizational relationships are discussed. The last section summarizes the findings from this review of inter-organizational research.

3.2 Relationships

The basis for all inter-organizational relationships is exchange; as Van de Ven and Koenig (1975) state, "a relationship occurs when two organizations make a transaction of resources of any kind." This statement does not capture a complete picture of relationships. While transactions are necessary for a relationship, not all transactions lead to relationships. Emphasizing the continuity of interactions required for relationships, Oliver (1991) defined relationships as "the relatively enduring transactions, flows, and linkages that occur among or between an organization and one or more organizations in its environment." Similarly, Holmlund and Tornroos (1997) define relationships as "an interdependent process of continuous interaction and exchange between at least two actors in a business context." The interdependency arises from the realization that one's success depends on the partner's success also (Dant and Schul, 1992). Thus, the defining properties of relationships are continuity and mutuality. This continuity also implies that a relationship can change over time due to changing factors in the environment as well as within the relationship.

An organization becomes involved in a relationship with another organization to attain its goals or solve problems it cannot solve alone. This is true in applications outsourcing, either because the organization does not have the resources or is not willing to acquire or expend the resources necessary to accomplish the particular task itself. This resource dependence motivates the organizations to identify an external provider and establish an agreement for the provision of these services with this provider, thus satisfying the three conditions necessary for two organizations to enter into a relationship: resource dependence, awareness of external sources for resources, and agreement between the organizations (Van de Ven and Koenig, 1975). Once the organizations enter a relationship, this relationship needs to be managed to achieve successful outcomes as determined and expected by the organizations involved.

Goles (2001) pulls together these concepts and defines the outsourcing relationship as "an ongoing linkage between an outsourcing vendor and customer that has a long-tern orientation and a mutual recognition and understanding that the benefits attained by each firm are at least in part dependent on the other firm" (page 30). A similar definition is proposed here; a "client-vendor relationship" in the outsourcing context can be defined as 'a linkage between a client and vendor that is characterized by ongoing exchanges governed by mutual agreement'.

3.2.1 Unit of Analysis

In research on dyadic inter-organizational relationships, the unit of analysis naturally is the relationship between the two organizations (e.g., Mohr and Spekman, 1994; Sobrero-Roberts, 2001). Data are collected from organizational representatives, usually at the management level, to obtain insights about the inter-organizational relationship (Arino and De La Torre, 2003; Narayandas & Rangan, 2004).

3.2.2 Levels of Analysis

The "reality of organizations is shaped by the constant interplay" of various levels at which interaction may take place (Adler and Kwon, 2002; page 35), primarily the inter-organizational and interpersonal level in inter-organizational relationships. When two organizations are in an exchange situation, individuals who are in the roles of boundary spanners in both organizations tend to interact with each other more often than do their other colleagues within the organizations. These individuals accept and process the information from the partner organization and represent the interests of their own organization in inter-organizational exchanges. The boundary spanners are required to balance the competing expectations of their organization and the partner organization and their actions have a significant part in defining the relationship between the two organizations (Perrone, Zaheer and McEvilly, 2003). Over time, the interpersonal relationship attributes exhibited by the boundary-spanners get institutionalized in a process akin to structuration (Giddens, 1984), evolving into stable arrangements between the two organizations. Although the individual boundary spanners may leave the organizations, new occupants of these roles internalize these orientations in performing their duties. Thus, an examination of the inter-organizational relationship requires an examination and sense-making of these inter-personal exchanges.

3.3 Attributes of Inter-organizational Relationships

The attributes and processes identified from the review of IS outsourcing research appear in the first column of Table 1, and references to a few articles from IS outsourcing research where these attributes or processes have been examined appear in the second column of the table. In the following discussion, some of these attributes have been grouped together because of conceptual overlap. For example, the concepts represented by consensus (Kim and Chung, 2002), solidarity (Poppo and Zenger (2002), information sharing (Willcocks and Kern, 1999), shared knowledge (Duncan, 1998; Lee and Kim, 2003), shared vision (Kern, 1997), integration of common structures and processes (Goles, 2001), and mutual understanding (Kishore et al, 2003) appear to be captured in the three meanings of "shared understanding" as defined by Thompson and Fine (1999). Therefore, the discussion of these concepts is summarized under the title "shared understanding." Similarly, since dependence of one party on another is a major source of power for the latter, the attribute of power (Klepper, 1995) is not discussed separately from dependence. Not all the articles in the second column have been mentioned in the following sub-sections; the list of references is intended to identify attributes studied in IS outsourcing research and indicate the prominence of some attributes in outsourcing research.

Table 3-1: Attributes of Inter-organizational Relationships

Attribute	References
Trust	Goles, 2001; Grover et al, 1996; Kern, 1997; Klepper, 1995; Lander et al, 2004; Lee and Kim, 1999; Marcolin and McLellan, 1998; Welty and Beccera-Fernandez, 2001; Willcocks and Choi, 1995
Commitment	Goles, 2001; Kern, 1997; Kishore et al, 2003; Klepper, 1995; Lee and Kim, 1999; McFarlan and Nolan, 1995
Flexibility	Duncan, 1998; Goles, 2001; Grover et al, 1996; Lacity et al, 1995; Poppo and Zenger, 2002; Willcocks and Kern, 1999
Consensus	Poppo and Zenger; 2002
Solidarity	Kim and Chung, 2003
Information sharing	Willcocks and Kern, 1999
Shared knowledge	Duncan, 1998
Shared vision	Kern, 1997
Mutual understanding	Kishore et al, 2003
Integration	Goles (2001)
Cultural compatibility	Hancox and Hackney, 2000; Kern, 1997; Lee and Kim, 1999; Willcocks and Kern, 1999
Dependence	Goles, 2001; Lee and Kim, 1999; Sun et al, 2002; Willcocks and Kern, 1999
Power	Klepper, 1995

The attributes discussed in this section are trust, commitment, flexibility, shared understanding, cultural compatibility, and dependence. Trust is considered central to a relationship, with the presence of trust promoting other attributes. For example, Geyskens et al (1996) show that trust begets commitment in supplier-customer relationships. Trust also and lubricating processes like cooperation while controlling the potential negative effects of others (e.g., conflict) (Selnes, 1998). Relationship attributes other than trust are classified as relational norms in inter-organizational research, following Macneil (1980). Norms are mutually agreed upon standards for behavior in a relationship (Heide and John, 1992) and set the stage for harmonious interactions.

3.3.1 Trust

Trust is crucial wherever risk, uncertainty, or interdependence exist (McKnight et al. 2000). Risk, uncertainty, and dependence are characteristic of the relationship between a vendor and client in the outsourcing situation. Trust in interpersonal and inter-organizational contexts has been the topic of innumerable studies (Anderson and Weitz, 1989; Anderson, 1990; Clark, 1995; Das and Teng, 1998; Doney, Cannon and Mullen, 1998; Dwyer, Schurr, and Oh, 1987; Fontenot and Wilson, 1997; Garbarino and Johnson, 1999; McKnight and Chervany, 1998; Mohr and Spekman, 1994; Morgan and Hunt, 1994; Rousseau et al, 1998; Ring and van de Ven, 1994; Willcocks and Kern, 1998). Trust is defined as the expectation that the partner can be relied on to fulfill their obligations (Anderson and Weitz, 1989), behave in a predictable manner, and act fairly even when the possibility of opportunism is present (Zaheer et al, 1998). Thus, trust has three core components: reliability, predictability, and fairness.

Trust is necessary for the successful development of inter-organizational relationships (Anderson et al. 1989; Arnett et al. 1994; Fontenot et al. 1997; Matthyssens 1994; McKnight et al. 2000; Mohr et al. 1994; Ring and VandeVen 1994). Similarly, in the outsourcing context, researchers (Grover et al. 1996; Lee et al. 1999; Sabherwal 1999; Willcocks et al. 1999) have found significant relationships between trust and outsourcing success.

An important reason that trust is important is because it reduces the likelihood of opportunism. Opportunism is the pursuit of self-interest with guile (John 1984; Joshi et al. 1999). Either party or both in an exchange relationship can exhibit such behavior. In previous outsourcing research, it was noted that the problem of opportunism by the vendor was evident in the structuring of outsourcing contracts (Duncan 1998; Lacity et al. 1995), since the client organization lacked the knowledge the vendor possessed. Lee (2000) comments that while opportunistic behavior may produce some benefits in the short-term for the organization that initiates such behavior, the expectation that the relationship will have a long-term orientation will curb such actions. Further, during a long-term relationship, the other party in the relationship has time to retaliate, and any gains from short-term oriented opportunistic actions will be negated (Joshi et al. 1999a).

3.3.2 Commitment

Commitment is "a desire to develop a stable relationship, a willingness to make short-term sacrifices to maintain the relationship, and a confidence in the stability of the relationship" (Anderson and Weitz, 1992). Client and vendor commitment has been found to be positively related to outsourcing success (Kern, 1997; Lee and Kim, 1999).

In the relationship literature, two forms of commitment have been identified: calculative and affective. Calculative commitment is driven by an objective assessment of a continued relationship with the other organization and the likelihood of significant value creation. Often, investment by one party in assets specific to the exchange is seen as evidence of commitment and leads to greater cooperation (Heide and Miner, 1992) and increased expectations for continuity (Geyskens et al, 1996; Heide and John, 1992). Affective commitment stems from the organization's attachment to the relationship (Wetzels et al, 1998). This form of commitment goes beyond contractual agreements and incorporates an emotional obligation to work together for the success of the relationship.

3.3.3 Flexibility

Flexibility is a type of relational norm, a shared value regarding appropriate behavior within the relationship (Joshi and Stump, 1999). Examining buyer-supplier relationships in manufacturing, Joshi and Stump (1999) define flexibility as the shared expectations that organizations will be willing to modify the original terms of the contract to take into account unanticipated contingencies. Thus, flexibility reflects the mutual trust that parties will not take advantage of each other when unexpected changes in the environment provide opportunities (Heide, 1994). Flexibility in dealing with each other demonstrates that the organizations value the relationship and are willing to make considerable efforts to sustain the relationship (Das and Teng, 1998). Macneil (1980) working in the area of contract law, has also recognized that such action is necessary for trust building.

In IS outsourcing, Clark et al (1995) and Lacity et al (1995) consider the key to a successful client-vendor relationship to be flexibility. The client should be able to change service requirements if necessary, and the vendor should be able to change the means by which the service requirements are met.

3.3.4 Shared Understanding

Thompson and Fine (1999) identify three possible meanings for shared understanding. The first possibility refers to the "notion of distributed knowledge"; information is distributed among specialized teams. A second possibility relates to the "notion of collective knowledge," including similar representations of task requirements and procedures. The third meaning pertains to the "notion of consensus." Consensus is the extent of agreement between parties. While shared understanding in all three forms has an effect on inter-organizational relationships, consensus is found to help in the coordination of actions between two parties (Thompson and Fine, 1999).

Collective knowledge leads to an intensive exchange of information and can promote innovation (Obstfeld, 2002). Husted and Michailova (2002) contend that a shared understanding of the subject matter helps overcome problems in the transfer of knowledge between organizations and individuals in these organizations. Fortgang et al (2003) found that organizations who failed to develop a consensus on the expected outcome and the means to achieve that outcome failed to realize the potential from the inter-organizational arrangement.

As in other inter-organizational relationships, shared understanding is important in inter-organizational relationships as well. There should be mechanisms to share information (Willcocks and Kern, 1999) between the organizations – a means to distribute knowledge, a shared means of interpretation to develop a common understanding of the information that is shared (Duncan, 1998) – the existence of collective knowledge, and a shared vision and agreement regarding the outcomes of the project (Kern, 1997) - consensus. Heeks et al (?) and Krishna et al (2002) find that the development of shared understanding is even more important in offshore outsourcing.

3.3.5 Cultural Compatibility

Organizational culture is "a socially constructed, cognitive reality that is rooted in deeply held perceptions, values, beliefs, or expectations that are shared by, and are unique to," members of one organization (Adler, 2001). It is the "pattern of shared beliefs and values that help individuals understand organizational functioning and provide norms for behavior in the organizations" (Deshpande and Webster, 1989). While culture aids in regulating activities within the organization, it may act as a hindrance when employees from different organizations have to work together.

Outsourcing practitioners have commented that a degree of compatibility between the client and vendor organizations, particularly in terms of culture and project discipline is required for success in outsourcing. Willcocks and Kern (1998) found that the absence of cultural compatibility created problems in achieving outsourcing objectives, in a study completed at an organization in the United Kingdom. However, other research has found no relationship between cultural compatibility and partnership quality (Lee and Kim, 1999) or outsourcing success (in results of survey reported in Goles, 2001). However, in interviews reported with outsourcing managers in the same study, Goles found a contrary finding. The managers he spoke to stressed the importance of cultural compatibility. Goles explained the inconsistency in these findings to be a result of the differing perspectives of the managers and the survey respondents who primarily dealt with operational issues.

3.3.6 Dependence

The existence of inter-dependence in an inter-organizational relationship implies that the organizations need each other's skills and/or assets to achieve their goals. Henderson (1990) has noted the importance of managing dependence between organizations in creating successful relationships. Increasing reciprocal dependence between partners promotes cooperation and commitment and results in favorable evaluations of exchange partners (Gundlach and Cadotte, 1994; Sivadas and Dwyer, 2000). However, when an organization perceives an asymmetry in dependence, the organization that is more dependent is less satisfied with the relationship (Dwyer, et al., 1987, Klepper, 1995, Macneil, 1980). This asymmetry in dependence may be because one organization contributes more in the relationship or has made specific investments in the relationship, giving rise to switching costs. In such situations, the imbalance vests one organization with more power to control or influence the other organization (Pfeffer, 1981). The asymmetry in dependence may be viewed by the weaker party as a possible cause for reduced commitment and opportunistic behavior on the part of the stronger party. It is possible that the more powerful partner could be looking for chances to exploit the relationship; however, if there is a desire to sustain the relationship, the powerful partner will try to ensure that any appearance of exploitation does not exist (McAlister, Bazerman and Fazer, 1986). .

In an outsourcing context, Lee and Kim (1999) found a negative relationship between mutual dependence and the clients' perception of partnership quality; i.e. perceptions of higher mutual dependence are related to perceptions of poor relationship quality. They offer a possible explanation that clients may perceive increased dependence on the vendor as leading to loss of control and increased switching costs, causing the client to view the relationship in a negative light.

3.4 Processes in Inter-organizational Relationships

The processes identified from the review of IS outsourcing research appear in the first column of Table 2, and references to a few articles from IS outsourcing research where these attributes or processes have been examined appear in the second column of the table.

Table 3-3: Processes in Inter-organizational Relationships

Process	References
Communication	Goles, 2001; Grover et al, 1996; Kern 1997; Krishna et al, 2004; Lee and Kim, 1999; Sun et al, 2002; Willcocks and Kern, 1999
Coordination	Clemons et al, 1992; Lee and Kim, 1999; Sabherwal, 1999; vanFenema, 1997
Cooperation	Goles, 2001; Grover, 1996; Kern, 1997; Klepper, 1995; Loh and Venkataraman, 1992; Willcocks and Kern, 1999
Conflict management and resolution	Aubert et al, 1998; Goles, 2001; Klepper, 1995; Lee and Kim, 1999; Marcolin and Mclellan, 1998; Natovich, 2003
Performance management and monitoring	Kishore et al, 2003; Quinn and Hilmer, 1994

In this section, the processes of communication, coordination and cooperation, conflict resolution and management, and performance monitoring are discussed. These activities are necessary to develop and sustain the attributes discussed above. An iterative relationship exists between these processes and the attributes discussed in the previous section. For example, cooperation leads to trust, which leads to increased willingness to cooperate, which generates more trust in turn, and so on (Selnes, 1998). These processes and contribute to the well-being of the inter-organizational relationship and facilitate the meeting of the goals of both organizations.

3.4.1 Communication

Communication between organizations is necessary to develop and sustain inter-organizational relationships (Anderson and Weitz, 1989; Anderson and Narus, 1990; Das and Teng, 1998; Fontenot and Wilson, 1997; Joshi and Stump, 1999; Mohr and Spekman, 1994; Paun, 1997). The definitions of communication emphasize that it is a bi-directional process, allowing for exchange of meaningful and timely information between parties (Anderson and Narus, 1990; Klepper, 1995). In the outsourcing context, "communication is more than the day-to-day exchange of project related information between client and vendor; it is also concerned with open revelation of needs and resources related to the future of the relationship" (Klepper, 1995). Communication increases trust (Kern, 1997; Selnes, 1998) and cooperation and commitment (Oikkonen et al, 2000). As can be expected, communication has been found a significant determinant of outsourcing success (Goles, 2001; Grover et al, 1996; Lee, 1999).

3.4.2   Co-ordination & Co-operation

Coordination and cooperation are associated notions; cooperation brings about the coordination necessary for joint activities to be productive, though cooperation is not necessary for coordination. Cooperation characterizes the 'atmosphere' in which the interactions take place, while coordination refers to the management of activities to achieve a common goal. Cooperation refers to "the willingness of a partner organization to pursue mutually compatible interests" (Das and Teng, 1998). In doing so, both parties may have to sacrifice some autonomy (Fontenot and Wilson, 1997). Not surprisingly, Grover et al's (1996) and Kern's (1997) research has found that cooperation is necessary for the success of an IS outsourcing relationship.

Coordination is a characteristic of successful relationships, where organizations synchronize their activities to accomplish a common set of tasks (Arnett et al., 1994; Fontenot et al., 1997; Matthyssens, 1994; Mohr et al., 1994) Sobrero and Schrader (1998) identify two forms of coordination: contractual coordination and procedural coordination.   Contractual coordination refers to "the mutual exchange of rights between the parties involved in a relationship"; the mechanisms to achieve contractual coordination are derived from the legal agreements between the two organizations. Procedural coordination describes "the extent to which the parties coordinate their processes by exchanging information," helping them adjust their activities to each other. The nature of the task determines the form of coordination to be employed. When there is more "sticky, that is, context-specific" information, organizations may invest more in procedural coordination mechanisms (Sobrero and Schrader, 1998).

3.4.3   Conflict Management & Resolution

Conflicts are inevitable in relational exchanges (Dwyer, et al., 1987; Mohr and Spekman, 1994; Morgan and Hunt, 1994); indeed absence of *all* conflict may signal the end of a relationship, since it is but natural that when two firms work together there may be differences of opinion on execution of the project (Dwyer, et al., 1987). Conflict is the divergence of goals, roles, and procedures between the parties in the relationship. Conflicts can be resolved when disagreements are replaced by "agreement and consensus" (Robey, et al., 1989). When disputes are resolved amicably, they actually contribute to the well being of the relationship, by provoking effective communication, monitoring, and balance in the power distribution (Anderson and Narus, 1990; Dwyer, et al., 1987; Fontenot and Wilson, 1997; Morgan and Hunt, 1994). Trust building activities, such as cooperation and communication, will result in increased functionality of conflict (Chenet et al. 1999; Morgan et al. 1994). Similarly, in outsourcing relationships, the manner in which conflicts are handled and resolved has implications for the relationship (Klepper, 1995).

3.4.4   Performance Measurement & Monitoring

In inter-organizational relationships, monitoring the partner's performance provides the organization an opportunity to assess the partner's compliance with the agreement and detecting deviations from expected behavior. Based on work by Heide (1994), Aulakh et al. (1996) identify three types of monitoring mechanisms: output control, process control, and social control. Output and process controls determine the extent to which compliance with the original agreement takes place in the outcome and the means used to achieve the outcome (Heide, 1994). Aulakh et al. describe social control as a proactive means of monitoring, whereby the partner organization is encouraged to perform the required activities through "mechanisms of social pressure". In socially controlled relationships, monitoring takes place through interpersonal interactions, which encourage "shared beliefs and mutual identification" (Aulakh et al; p.1014)

In the outsourcing context, the complexity of the tasks and the extended duration of the contract require that both parties institute tools for monitoring and evaluation (Beccerra and Gupta, 1999; Dwyer, et al., 1987; Heide, 1994; Paun, 1997). Due to the ongoing nature of the project, continuous monitoring is necessary in these relationships (Quinn and Hilmer, 1994). Both organizations have to come to an agreement on these performance measures and monitoring processes to develop a successful relationship and ensure a satisfactory outcome. Kishore et al (2003) recommend that the monitoring mechanisms and competencies[1] be matched to the type of relationship[2]. In the support and reliance type of relationships, output controls (as discussed above) will be most effective since the IS services picked for outsourcing in these types of relationships is typically well-defined and the expected costs and benefits can be quantified to a great extent. In the alignment type of relationship, applicable when the specifications and outcomes are more ambiguous and dynamic (for e.g., in the outsourcing of application systems development or implementation of new software), process controls are more effective. In the alliance type of relationship, social controls are preferred; this means that organizations need to pay special attention to the development of trust and interpersonal relationships.

3.5 Outcomes of Inter-organizational Relationships: Satisfaction

In an exchange relationship between two organizations, satisfaction can result based on the evaluation of the outcome and the processes used to achieve that outcome. Satisfaction is a catchall concept, reflecting the assessments of all aspects of the relationship: the output, the process, and the realization of expected benefits (Geyskens, Steenkamp, and Kumar, 1999; Groenroos, 1994). There are two aspects to satisfaction: economic and non-economic. Economic satisfaction is related to the quality of the product and captures the success of a relationship in terms of goal attainment; it is a response to the benefits and rewards from the relationship with the partner. Ring and Van de Ven (1994) find that in assessing these benefits, organizations look beyond the notion of equivalence of benefits and costs to obtaining equitable returns. The concept of equity is related to fair dealing and aims to capture whether each organization has received expected benefits proportional to their investments. Non-economic satisfaction refers to the response to the interactions with the partner, and assesses if these were "fulfilling, gratifying, and easy" (Geyskens, Steenkamp, and Kumar, 1999; p. 224). The focus is similar to that in Groenroos' (1994) conceptualization of functional quality, which aims to capture the quality of the process and the interactions through which the product was delivered.

Satisfaction with the project usually brings about other benefits that the client and vendor organizations view as positive business outcomes. Client organizations that are satisfied with an outsourcing relationship are likely to see the relationship as effective and are likely to want to sustain it (Klepper 1995). Selnes (1998) finds that when buyers are satisfied, they are likely to want to not only continue the relationship, but enhance the scope of the relationship. Thus, the clients' satisfaction results in benefits for the vendor: repeat business (measured from the vendor

---

[1]The competencies mentioned by Kishore et al (2003) are based on technical and contract management capabilities. E.g., ability to call and evaluate bids, maintaining technically competent staff within the organization to provide technical expertise to vendors.
[2] In a support relationship, the role of the vendors is limited with the client keeping most activities in-house. In the alignment relationship, the client obtains the vendor's expertise as needed on a project basis. In the reliance relationship, the client depends extensively on the vendor for IT services. In the alliance relationship, the client and the vendor work together in close partnerships.

perspective as the retention rate), preferred status, enhanced reputation, and referrals. When the vendor feels that the benefits received were in line with their investments and the client was fair in its dealings, the vendor will also want to have a long-term relationship with the vendor. In such long-term relationships, both client and vendor can leverage the learning that occurred in the first project.

While the amount of repeat business or retention rate provides a quantitative measure of the success of the relationship, the nature of the relationship is indicated by the status afforded to the vendor by the client. Morgan and Hunt (1994) note that the goal of relationship management is to earn the position of preferred partner by developing trust in exchanges over time. Thus, a second measure of success for a vendor organization in an inter-organizational relationship is the ability to attain preferred partnership status. Preferred partnership status guarantees that the vendor will have a agreed-upon share of the total outsourcing requirements for the organization; preferred partners are also included in the earlier stages of the outsourcing decision-making process when the client organization is making a decision on whether and what to outsource (Crutcher et al, 2001).

Repeat business and preferred status with existing partners enhance the reputation of an organization. It is important for vendor organizations to maintain their reputation by fair business dealings and competent service (Anderson et al. 1992; Matthyssens 1994). This reputation serves the vendors not only in subsequent interactions with the same client, but is also a source of referrals, which is a form of "reputational endorsement" (Nahapiet and Ghoshal, 1998).

3.6 Conclusions

In the preceding sections, the characteristics of relationships that have a positive impact on the outcome of IS outsourcing have been briefly examined through a review of management, marketing, and IS outsourcing research. This review provides support for the importance of these attributes and processes in IS outsourcing arrangements. Researchers of inter-organizational relationships have also proposed research frameworks that combine various relationship attributes and processes to provide a better understanding of these relationships. IS researchers have drawn up on these frameworks, often in an eclectic fashion, combining concepts from various sources such as the IMP interaction model and Macneils' relational exchange theory. Willcocks and Kern's work provide good examples of such approaches. The application of these models and/or the underlying analyses of these models to IS outsourcing have given us insights into the IS outsourcing relationship. Yet, it remains to be explained how these attributes and processes interact among themselves and with other contextual factors to enable the exchanges in IS outsourcing and produce the desired outcome. The detailed examination of the different attributes has provided a valuable base for the future examination of the relationship. This research builds on such work and aims to address this issue through an examination of outsourcing relationships using the theoretical framework presented in the next chapter.

Chapter 4
THEORETICAL FRAMEWORK

4.1 Introduction

Following Walsham's (1995) recommendation that a researcher embarking on interpretive case studies "create an initial theoretical framework which takes account of previous knowledge" (Walsham, 1995, p.76), a theoretical framework is developed and presented in this chapter. A theoretical framework lays out the key constructs related to the phenomena being studied and the presumed relationships between them (Huberman and Miles, 1998). It functions as a sensitizing device helping the researcher identify emergent themes in the data and as a structuring device helping the researcher make sense of the results of the study (Walsham, 1995). Thus, the framework serves as a guide for the exploration and presentation of possible explanations for the phenomenon under study, the client-vendor relationship in the applications outsourcing context.

From the review of research in the previous two chapters, it is evident that relationship management in outsourcing is an area can benefit from further investigation. It is also clear that there has been considerable work done on examining the factors that contribute to the success of inter-organizational arrangements. Studies have analyzed the dyadic relationship between organizations and established the positive influence of relationship attributes such as trust and commitment on the performance of the inter-organizational alliance (for e.g., Cannon and Perreault, 1999; Mohr and Spekman, 1994).

Research in information technology outsourcing has echoed these findings. To cite an example from outsourcing research, Kern (1997) found that clients consider the vendor's commitment – another relationship element – as necessary for the success of the outsourcing arrangement. The strongest support for the role of the relationship comes from Goles (2001); the results of his survey showed that without a "good" relationship, the outcome of the outsourcing arrangement can be disastrous. However, while these and similar studies establish the importance of the relationship and the various relationship attributes and processes in determining the outcome of the inter-organizational arrangement, they do not explain exactly how these influence the outcome. The goal of this research is to address this issue and thus explain the relationship between various relationship elements and the outcome of the outsourcing arrangement.

Nahapiet and Ghoshal (1998) present an insightful analysis of how different relationship elements fit together and comprise social capital. Social capital is defined as "the access and resources available in an exchange relationship." Social capital contributes to the development of conditions conducive to the exchange and combination of knowledge resources. Though they focus on the creation of knowledge within the organization in their work, they suggest that the basic analysis can be extended to examine the relationship that develops in inter-organizational arrangements and the effect of the relationship on the outcome of the arrangement. As a framework that integrates different themes emerging from the review of relationship management research in the previous chapters, an extension of Nahapiet and Ghoshal's framework to the inter-organizational setting is believed to be appropriate for the examination of the client-vendor relationship in IS outsourcing

This chapter begins with a review of the concept of social capital, and is followed by a review of Nahapiet's and Ghoshal's model. Building on this review and supplemented by a discussion on the processes required to execute and deliver the product of applications outsourcing, the theoretical framework that guides this research is constructed in the following section of the chapter. This framework is subsequently used in the analysis of the empirical data in Chapters 6 and 7.

4.2 Social Capital

Social capital has a long intellectual history in the social sciences. The first usage of the term "social capital" in the contemporary sense is that of Lyda J. Hanifan in the thirties. The term was reinvented by Jane Jacobs in the late 1960s, and subsequently elaborated upon by Glenn Loury in the late 1970s (Lin, 2004). Current conceptualizations of the term have their roots in the work of Coleman and Bourdieu, as discussed below.

The concept has been applied in various contexts: For example, Ainsworth (2002) examined the role of social capital in migration patterns and Cechhini and Raina (2002) found that social capital had a facilitating role in the implementation and acceptance of networking technology in an Indian rural community. In organizational research, Kostova and Roth (2003) studied how social capital facilitated coordination between sub-units in a multinational organization, while Kanter (1994) explained how social capital at the individual level facilitated business partnerships.

Information systems researchers have also been intrigued by the concept of social capital. In April 2002, Communications of the ACM devoted an issue to the topic, with the primary theme being the contribution of the Internet and online communities to the development of social capital. Trust is a central component of social capital; Erickson et al (2002) discuss how trust can be developed in online interactions by permitting participants to identify other participants and their activities. Smith also describes a tool for developing trust; this tool can be used in the context of bulletins boards and in Usenet by tracking threads and authors. Other articles in this issue focus on the role of various participants in promoting trust and collaboration. Hiltz and Turoff comment on the role of the teacher in encouraging participation and collaboration in asynchronous learning networks, while Bruckman visualizes a new Internet-enabled learning environment where peers and elders (besides teachers) also facilitate student learning. In a paper similar in flavor to these CACM articles, Oxendine et al (2003) compare two cities' attempts at developing electronic networks and find that the city with more trust and cooperation between its citizens are able to build and sustain a network better than the other. Most of these articles focus on trust; trust is indeed an essential component of social capital, but it is only one of the elements of social capital. None of these articles captures the depth of the concept of social capital, though they all touch upon the essence of social capital as the "glue that holds networks together" (Preece, 2002; page 38).

4.2.1 What is Social Capital?

In European social thought, Pierre Bourdieu first used the term "social capital" in 1972 (Turner, 1990). Social capital was defined by Bourdieu as "the sum of the resources, actual or virtual, that accrue to an individual or a group by virtue of possessing a durable network of more or less institutionalized relationships of mutual acquaintance and recognition" (Bourdieu and Wacquant, 1992). Bourdieu sees social processes as being shaped by the economic infrastructure. However, agents are not puppets in these social interactions; they possess their own internalized cognitive structures that they use to deal with the world and thus alter their levels of capital.

Coleman (1986) considered social capital to be defined by its function; social capital was defined as the sum of the processes within and between groups that allow individuals to accrue benefits. Putnam's (1993) definition follows the functionalist slant of Coleman's; he explains social capital as the features of social organizations that facilitate coordination and cooperation for mutual benefit. Thus, social capital is the set of expectations for action within a collectivity that affect the goals and goal-seeking behavior of its members. While Bourdieu defines social capital as a fungible property of individuals, Coleman's and particularly Putnam's usage of the term suggests that social capital is a collective property of the group (e.g., civic spirit) that bestows benefits on the group.

In general, the concept of social capital reflects the fact that members in a social structure are able to secure benefits by virtue of their membership in such structures. There are two predominant conceptualizations of this term in current research. One conceptualization emphasizes structural considerations and focuses on the value accrued to the individual from being a part of the structure. In this stream of research, the social structure itself is seen as providing value by providing access to information and other resources (e.g. Baker, 1990). Another stream of research emphasizes the relational aspect of social capital (Fukuyam, 1995; Putnam, 1993). Here, social capital is derived from the nature of the relationship, not the structure itself. The relationship is defined by trust and trustworthiness (Tsai and Ghoshal, 1998), obligations and expectations (Coleman, 1990), norms and sanctions (Coleman, 1990), and identification (Hakanson and Snehota, 1995). Relationships characterized by these elements would lead to cooperative behaviors and result in productive outcomes in the form of material benefits for both parties (Nahapiet and Ghoshal, 1998; Zaheer at al, 1998). As can be readily seen, these conceptualizations are not mutually exclusive; as Adler and Kwon (2002) point out there is an advantage in combining these perspectives. Social capital accrues from the pattern of the linkages and the quality of the linkages; this view is favored by some researchers (e.g., Loury (1992), Pennar (1997), and Woolcock (1998)).

Social capital exists at multiple levels; for instance, Fukuyama (1995) noted that social capital can be observed at the family level as well as at the national level. Organizational researchers (Kostova and Roth, 2003; Peng and Luo, 2000) have addressed this issue by proposing a multiple level approach, a "micro-macro model for social capital formation" (page 16; Kostova and Roth, 2003). This formulation recognizes the fact that relationships and hence social capital are formed at the individual level between members of the organizations participating in the inter-organizational relationship. These individuals act as "boundary spanners" (Zaheer et al, 1998) and it is their continuing interaction that enables the "maintenance and reproduction of this social asset" in the inter-organizational relationship (Lin, 1999; page 32). Information and perceptions about the partner organization are communicated throughout the organization by these boundary spanners, transforming the private social capital that they have accumulated into a "public good" (Kostova and Roth, 2003). Thus even in the absence of direct contacts with members of the other organization, individuals in one organization will form shared perceptions about the other organization based on the interaction of these boundary spanners, thus creating social capital at the organizational level.

In summary, social capital encompasses many aspects of the social context, such as the "social ties, trusting relations, and value systems" that enable productive behavior (Tsai and

Ghoshal, 1998). It comprises both the network and the assets that may be mobilized through that network (Bourdieu, 1986; Nahapiet and Ghoshal, 1998). Social capital can take many forms: structural, relational, and cognitive, but every instance of social capital facilitates activities of units within the structure (Coleman, 1988; Nahapiet and Ghoshal, 1998). Portes and Sensebrenner (1993) identify another essential characteristic of social capital, stating that "value introjection" is possible because social capital prompts individuals to behave in "ways other than naked greed." Thus, social capital can be understood as "the features of a relationship that bind together the participants in the relationship, enabling them to exchange resources and making it possible to work together in a productive manner."

4.2.2 How is Social Capital Created and Enhanced?

Social capital is created when units within a social system interact with one another (Bourdieu, 1986). In fact, social capital cannot develop when there is no interaction or exchange between the units and will be depleted by the lack of interaction. The exchange and the attendant reciprocity between the units of the social system underlie the creation as well as use of social capital (Bubolz, et al., 1998). It also follows that inter-dependence between the units promotes social capital, since it is this mutuality that will ensure that the units continue to interact and exchange resources. However, dependence is a double-edged sword; it has been noted that when one party feels more dependent on the other, it can lead to the erosion of social capital and of the relationship (Fukuyama, 2000).

Communication between members is an integral part of this interaction and is necessary to develop social capital. Another factor that contributes to the development of social capital, particularly in work settings, is the clarity in the definition of the task for which the group has been formed (Kogut and Zander, 1996). Such clarity delineates the boundaries of the group (Boland and Tenkasi, 1995), within which group members can develop unique codes and means for communication, enhancing the development of social capital. Further, social capital improves with age; Coleman (1990) stressed the significance of the duration of a relationship in the development of social capital.

Adler and Kwon (2002) sound a cautionary note about the risks associated with social capital. Developing and maintaining social capital in the relationship involves considerable time and effort, which may take away from the work at hand. While positive benefits may accrue from social capital in the initial stages, in the later stages of a relationship embedded practices can obstruct change, preventing appropriate responses to the environment. Strong ties can inhibit opportune action, by causing "organizational inertia" (Portes and Sensenbrenner, 1993) or inducing dependence. This potential for confining and counter-productive outcomes from social capital underlines the necessity for an organization to constantly monitor its interactions with its partners and the environment.

4.2.3 How Does Social Capital Produce Value?

Social capital acts as a lubricant in relationships, enabling effective governance. It can minimize the transaction costs associated with negotiation and enforcement, imperfect information and layers of unnecessary bureaucracy in relationships. Relationships rich in social capital provide effective governance through commonly agreed monitoring schemes and mutual understanding and trust between parties. High levels of commitment and low levels of opportunism characterize these relationships (Joshi and Stump, 1999). Further, the cooperative behavior that stems from social capital is conducive to the efficient exchange of resources, reducing production costs for the organization.

Social capital affects activities within organizations and its relations with other organizations, across sectors and with society. Social capital promotes greater coordination among individuals and between departments within a organization. As Nahapiet and Ghoshal (1998) show, the organization setting is conducive to the development of social capital and this gives the organization an advantage in the completion of work processes. Similarly as organizations establish stronger relationships with one another and social capital in the inter-organizational relationship increases, they will work together in the future on other business projects beyond the scope of the original project (Kostova and Roth, 2003). However, social capital cannot replace financial resources and technical and business expertise; it only serves as a necessary complement to these resources, ensuring the effective use of these resources.

4.2.4 Organizational Advantage from Social Capital: Nahapiet and Ghoshal (1998)

Nahpaiet and Ghoshal (1998) build on Ghoshal and Moran (1996)'s critique of market-based theories, particularly, transaction cost theory, where they present the notion of "organizational advantage". Advocating an organizational economy perspective, rather than one based on a market economy, they argue that organizations are not mere substitutes for structuring efficient transactions when markets fail, but possess unique advantages for managing certain economic activities. Applications of transaction cost theory overlook this aspect, and thus are "bad for practice". Transaction cost theory is criticized as a "static theory" applicable only to situations where markets and economies foster the uncontrolled growth of opportunism. Organizations actually have an advantage over markets in that they are able to "leverage the human ability to take initiative, to cooperate, and to learn." When organizations are unable to create an internal environment that is conducive to the generation of trust and commitment, they will fail to achieve those benefits that accrue from cooperation and team work. Nahapiet and Ghoshal (1998), in turn, explain how organizations can enjoy "organizational advantage," by employing "social capital" to generate an environment that is conducive to the creation of "intellectual capital."

4.2.4.1 Social Capital and Its Dimensions:

In Nahapiet and Ghoshal's treatise, social capital is defined as the access and resources available in an exchange relationship; social capital thus has the potential to influence processes of knowledge creation in exchange relationships. Based on a comprehensive review of the previous work on social capital, Nahapiet and Ghoshal (1998) identify three dimensions of social capital: the structural, the relational, and the cognitive. To distinguish between the structural and the relational dimensions, Nahapiet and Ghoshal (1998) rely on Granovetter's (1985) discussion of structural and relational embeddedness. The structural dimension refers to the pattern of connections – "who you know and reach and how you reach them." The relational dimension refers to the assets that are rooted in these relationships, such as trust and commitment. While previous researchers have recognized the importance of mutual understanding and sharing of knowledge among parties (Cohen and Levinthal, 1990; Kogut and Zander, 1992), Nahapiet and Ghoshal were the first to specify a separate third dimension of social capital, the cognitive dimension, to include these elements. The cognitive dimension facilitates a common understanding by relying on shared representations and interpretations. Table 1 provides definitions of the three dimensions in Nahapiet and Ghoshal's framework, which elaborated on these concepts in the intra-organizational setting.

Table 4-1: Definitions of social capital dimensions and elements from Nahapiet and Ghoshal (1998)

Element of framework	Definition
Structural Dimension:	
Network ties	Links that provide access to resources
Network Configuration	Properties of ties between groups that affect the flexibility and ease of information exchange
Appropriable organization	"Organization" created for one purpose may provide a source of valuable resources for other purposes
Cognitive Dimension	
Shared codes & language	Codes organize sensory data into perceptual categories and provide a frame of reference for observing and interpreting the environment. Shared codes provide a common conceptual apparatus for evaluating the likely benefits of exchange and combination. Shared language facilitates communication
Shared narratives	Tools that facilitate the exchange of meanings and tacit experience – e.g. stories
Relational Dimension:	
Trust	Multi-dimensional; indicates a willingness to be vulnerable to another party, arising from (1), belief in the good intent and concern of exchange partners, (2), belief in their competence and capability, (3), belief in their reliability, and (4) belief in their perceived openness
Norms	Shared beliefs of what constitute appropriate behavior; reflects a degree of consensus in the social system. Examples: cooperation, flexibility
Obligations & Expectations	Commitment or duty to undertake some activity in the future
Identification	A group sees themselves as one with another group of people

Nahapiet and Ghoshal comment that while the separation of social capital into dimensions and their elements is necessary for analytical purposes, inter-relationships may exist among dimensions and within a dimension. For instance, trust, one of the elements of the relational dimension in Nahapiet and Ghoshal's analysis, is necessary for the development of shared norms, which is yet another element of the same dimension. Research has shown that trust is necessary for the development of norms such as commitment (Ganesan and Hess, 1997) and cooperation (Rindfleisch, 2000). It is also possible that a relationship exists between the dimensions of social capital; it is reasonable that without access (an element of the structural dimension), it is not possible to develop the elements of the relational dimension or enhance the elements of the cognitive dimension.

4.2.4.2 Intellectual Capital

While "social capital" has been the subject of research for the past few decades, "intellectual capital" has become a popular term in the literature of business and management more recently (Roslender, 2000). Intellectual capital is considered a major source of competitive advantage to an organization (Bouty, 2000). Intellectual capital has been broadly defined as the sum of an organization's knowledge resources (Bell, 1997; Knight, 1999). It encompasses the models, strategies, unique approaches and methodologies organizations use to perform their business activities (Bell, 1997). Nahapiet and Ghoshal (1998) equated it to "the knowledge and knowing capacity" of organizations. Intellectual capital takes three different forms: human or internal capital, structural or organizational, and external capital. Human capital is the capabilities of the individuals in the organization that are required for the organization to conduct its business and provide solutions to customers. Structural capital is the sum of the capabilities of the organization to meets its market needs. It is "the hardware, software, databases, patents, trademarks, and everything else of organizational capability that supports employees' productivity" (Bontis, 2001; p.45). External capital defines an organization's vital relationships with external stakeholders including customers, competitors, and the community (Kampmeier, 1998; Knight, 1999; Roslender, 2000; Saint-Onge, 1996; Stewart, 1994).

In summary, intellectual capital can be understood as the knowledge resources of the organization that contributes to meeting customer needs and competing in the market. Thus, technology that embodies business processes and its management are part of intellectual capital (Bontis, 2001). As discussed in Chapter 2, many organizations today turn to outsourcing as a means of acquiring this intellectual capital. The results of an information technology outsourcing arrangement may be new technology, new means of using existing technology, provision of technology-related services or a combination of the three. As Das (1994) expresses succinctly, "new technology may be new wine in an old bottle, old wine in a new bottle, or new wine in a new bottle." As a manifestation of the knowledge resources held by the client and vendor organizations together, the result of every outsourcing arrangement is the creation of new intellectual capital, in at least one of the three forms.

4.2.4.3 Social Capital Facilitates the Creation of Intellectual Capital

The primary argument in Nahapiet and Ghoshal (1998) is that social capital facilitates the creation of new intellectual capital in organizations, by providing an environment conducive to the combination and exchange of resources. Combination and exchange have been identified as the two processes that generate new intellectual capital at the group level. New intellectual capital is the result of combining the knowledge resources of different individuals; this is dependent on the exchange of such resources between the parties. Exchange enables the reallocation of resources, stimulating potentially new and productivity-enhancing combinations of resources. Such combinations can also lead to the creation of additional resources by stimulating the learning and innovation potential of the individuals involved (Moran and Ghoshal, 1999). Thus, following Schumpeter (1934) Nahapiet and Ghoshal note that the resultant new intellectual capital may be created through radical change, producing something that is entirely new, an innovation, or new intellectual capital may be created through incremental change, a combination of existing knowledge, or an enhancement to an existing routine.

The argument is presented in the form of several hypotheses that relate the social, relational, and cognitive dimensions of social capital to conditions that facilitate the processes necessary for combination and exchange. Figure 1 provides a graphical representation of Nahapiet and Ghoshal's arguments. A basic requirement is that the opportunity to combine and exchange resources exists; this is determined by accessibility of resources and is the first condition necessary for combination and exchange. Even if the opportunity exists, individuals may desist from exchanging and combining resources; however, if the individuals feel that something worthwhile may come out of the process, they may feel encouraged to participate in the processes of intellectual capital creation. This anticipation of value is the second condition necessary for combination and exchange. Additionally, the individuals involved in the exchange will be motivated to exchange and combine if they believe that they can appropriate some of the value from the exchange. Thus, a third condition is that, individuals must be motivated to contribute to the process of intellectual capital creation.

However, even if these three conditions exist, lack of ability to assimilate and apply new knowledge may act as a barrier to combination and exchange of resources (Szulanski, 1996). Nahapiet and Ghoshal term the capability to overcome this barrier "combination capability"; this is the fourth condition necessary for the combination and exchange of intellectual capital. Various researchers have studied this phenomenon, recognizing its importance in achieving organizational advantage and acknowledging the "inertness of knowledge" (Kogut and Zander, 1992). For instance, Cohen and Levinthal (1990) applied the label "absorptive capacity" to the critical "ability of an organization to recognize the value of new external information, assimilate it, and apply it".

Nahapiet and Ghoshal emphasize the bi-directional structuring relationship between social capital and the work-process and its outcome: intellectual capital. They include a feedback loop from the creation of intellectual capital to social capital. Social capital enables exchange and the exchange supports and develops social capital in a "dialectical process" (Nahapiet and Ghoshal, p.259), leading to the co-evolution of social capital and intellectual capital. This is consistent with the work of Bourdieu (1986, 1992) which emphasizes the interaction of man and the social world, of the producer and the product, in an effort to overcome the agency-structure dichotomy in the social sciences. This consistency is to be expected since Nahapiet's and Ghoshal's conceptualization of social capital is based primarily on the work of Bourdieu.

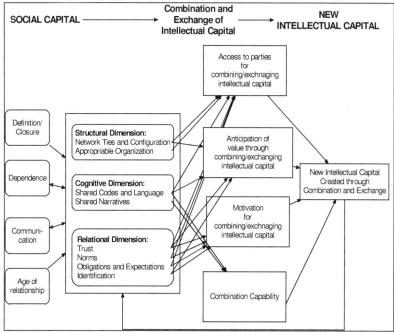

**Figure 4-1: Social Capital in the Creation of Intellectual Capital
(Nahapiet and Ghoshal, 1998)**

Nahapiet and Ghoshal identify four factors that affect the development of social capital.

1, Age of the relationship: Social capital is built over time; it takes time to produce the stability and continuity necessary for the development of social capital. So, it is more likely that social capital will develop in long-term relationships than in short-term transactions. Additionally, social capital will be valued more in long-term relationships while factors such as price will be valued more in short-term transactions.

2, Communication: Social capital is developed through frequent interactions. Communication between the parties promotes the development of the cognitive and relational dimensions of the social capital. In many inter-organizational settings, communication patterns and mechanisms are defined by the structures put in place for the inter-organizational project.

3, Dependence: Another factor that affects the development of social capital is the relative dependence of the people on each other. Social capital is unlikely to develop where there is no reason for either party to be dependent on the other. However, perceptions of asymmetric dependence can negatively affect the development of social capital, especially the relational dimension.

4, Closure: Definition of task boundaries and teams provides an environment in which trust and norms of cooperation and coordination as well as sharing of codes and language can be developed. Thus definition or closure aids in the creation of social capital.

4.2.4.4 About Criticisms of Nahapiet and Ghoshal's Conceptualization:

Nahapiet and Ghoshal present a model where the social capital promotes the creation of intellectual capital. Locke (1999), in criticism, argues that social capital cannot be the cause for intellectual capital, and that the relationship should be reversed. Nahapiet and Ghoshal (1998) do not suggest that intellectual capital is created only by social capital. Knowledge can certainly be created and used by single social units. However, where an exchange situation exists, the development of social capital increases the production of intellectual capital, by providing the conditions necessary for the exchange. Bouty (2000) in her research on exchanges between researchers also noted that social capital operates as a regulatory and critical factor in the knowledge exchange process. Additionally, Nahapiet and Ghoshal acknowledge that the creation of intellectual capital can lead to the enhancement of social capital in the relationship; the feedback loop from intellectual capital to social capital in the model is indicative of that relationship (See figure 1).

4.2.4.5 Research Based on Nahapiet And Ghoshal's Work:

Judging by the number of articles in academic journals as well as trade journals that use the term "social capital," the concept seems to have a certain appeal to researchers. Nahapiet's and Ghoshal's elucidation of the concept of social capital and the identification of its dimensions have attracted considerable attention. In this section, a few examples of research that apply this conceptualization of social capital are briefly described[1].

Llewellyn and Armistead's (1999) work focuses on the different dimensions of social capital identified by Nahapiet and Ghoshal; they examine the extent to which business processes associated with service delivery in a large telecommunications company exhibit the structural, relational, and cognitive features of social capital. The findings suggest that social capital elements are present in successful processes, enabling the resolution of conflicts and making the service delivery more efficient. Kumar and Worm (2003) show that social capital enables smoother and productive exchanges in negotiations between Chinese and North American business managers, helping bridge the cultural divide.

Gold, Malhotra and Segars (2001) find that technical, structural, and cultural infrastructures that maximize social capital are a necessary for effective knowledge management. Tsai and Ghoshal (1999) test the propositions relating social capital and value creation within organizations. Their study examines the interrelationships among selected elements from the three dimensions of social capital at the business unit level, the influence of different dimensions of social capital on resource combination and exchange and, the contribution of resource exchange and combination towards intellectual capital, in the form of innovations.

4.3 Applications Outsourcing: Execution of Projects

Applications outsourcing comprises applications development, enhancement, and customization. As previously noted, applications outsourcing requires the combination of at least two different types of knowledge from sources in both organizations: business domain

---

[1] For a more detailed review, see Appendix 6.

knowledge and technical knowledge. Armstrong and Sambamurthy (1999) note that in the development of applications, sharing of perspectives, pooling and assimilation of knowledge and development of shared understanding is essential.

Applications outsourcing produces value only when the individuals working on the project bring together their skills and knowledge (Tiwana, Bharadwaj, and Sambamurthy, 2003). Information systems development has been recognized as a socio-technical process where objectives of multiple stakeholders must be reconciled to effect the integration of knowledge required to create the final product (Iivari, Hirschheim, and Klein, 1998; Nelson and Cooprider, 1996). This is especially true in the case of applications outsourcing, where individuals from different organizations work together. Similar to the problems faced within organizations when the various stakeholders in the information systems development process cannot be induced to share resources, problems can also occur in applications outsourcing when the differing objectives of individuals involved in the project create hurdles to sharing, ultimately leading to a result that fails to produce the desired value.

When individuals from either organization need access to resources held by members of the other organization, structures must be in place to provide this access. In most organizations, channels are put in place to ensure that requests and responses are directed to the right individuals. If such access is not present, it can cause uncertainty and ensuing problems in the applications outsourcing project (Sabherwal, 2003). To avoid conflicting interpretations of requirements and evaluations of the project, it is necessary to include the contributions of all stakeholders in the applications outsourcing project (Constantine and Lockwood, 1993).

An additional challenge to the sharing that is required for the completion of the applications outsourcing project is the "stickiness" of knowledge (Szulanski, 1996; Tiwana, Bharadwaj, and Sambamurthy, 2003; von Hippel, 1994); stickiness refers to the difficulty in knowledge transfer. In all applications development and maintenance, this is a challenge because the knowledge that is to be shared may be collective and complicated; additionally, the source may not be motivated to share and/or the recipient may not be able to absorb the knowledge. In the applications outsourcing context, this may even be more of a challenge because this information needs to be shared across organizational boundaries.

Thus, it can be seen that an environment conducive to the sharing of resources between members of both organizations is a necessary condition for the completion of the applications outsourcing project. Such sharing will promote the integration of technical and business knowledge of various participants from both organizations and produce a mutual understanding and agreement on how the results of the outsourced project can support the client organization's business needs (Tiwana, Bharadwaj, and Sambamurthy, 2003).

4.4 Theoretical Framework

In various discussions of social capital, it has been accepted that social capital is created and sustained through exchange, and enables such exchange to take place. Likewise, the exchange and combination of resources is the crux of applications outsourcing as well. Extending the social capital analysis from Nahapiet and Ghoshal to the applications outsourcing context, it can be argued that social capital inherent in the client-vendor relationship could support the work processes of the representatives of the client and vendor organizations and impact the final outcome of the outsourcing arrangement. In turn, social capital in the relationship would be affected by the performance and outcome of the work processes, regulating further interactions in the relationship.

4.4.1 Inter-organizational Relationships in Applications Outsourcing: a Social Capital Analysis

In the applications outsourcing situation, two organizations come together with the stated purpose of creating something new out of the combination of their knowledge pool. It is true that one organization, the vendor, comes in with a profit motive, while the other comes in with a business need. However, the goal of the outsourcing arrangement is the creation or provision of something that did not exist before in that particular form. Once these two organizations establish contact, they move through the process of establishing a relationship. While the contract stipulates the organizational structure and interactions necessary to fulfill the objectives of the outsourcing arrangement, a strong relationship characterized by elements such as trust, norms of commitment and cooperation, and shared understanding is necessary to support the activities required to complete the processes required for the outsourcing arrangement. These characteristics of the outsourcing relationship are central to the success of the applications outsourcing arrangement. And, as the discussion in the second section of this chapter shows, these are the elements that constitute social capital. Hence, it is believed that it is appropriate to build upon this model to examine the applications outsourcing phenomenon. The following table (Table 2) relates aspects of the outsourcing relationship to the various elements of social capital as described by Nahapiet and Ghoshal (1998).

Table 4-2: Social Capital Elements in the Applications Outsourcing Context

Facet of social capital	Definition	Evidenced in outsourcing relationship as
Structural Dimension:		
Network ties	The links that provide access to members of both organizations	Established through formal channels such as contracts and service level agreements and through informal channels such as personal bonds
Network Configuration	The structure for interaction between the two organizations	Defined by contract or through the development of informal/personal ties
Appropriable organization	The roles and routines defined for one task may be applied to a similar task	Transfer of engagement routines to other projects
Cognitive Dimension:		
Shared codes & language	Shared codes ensure a common understanding of the concepts and context associated with the task. Shared language provides a means for sharing information about activities.	Shared understanding of the goals of the outsourcing arrangement as well as the activities and associated metrics of the outsourcing arrangement

Shared narratives	Shared narratives cut across different contexts, facilitating the exchange of practice and tacit experience	Sharing of experiences
Relational Dimension:		
Trust	Multi-dimensional; indicates a willingness to be vulnerable to another party, arising from (1), belief in the good intent and concern of exchange partners, (2), belief in their competence and capability, (3), belief in their reliability, and (4), belief in their perceived openness	Trust between organizations
Norms: shared values of what constitutes appropriate behavior	A degree of consensus in the social system	Norms such as commitment, cooperation, and flexibility
Obligations & Expectations	Expectations for the future	Expectations for business opportunities and growth
Identification	A group sees themselves as one with another group of people	Similarity in cultures develops

Figure 4-2: Theoretical Framework

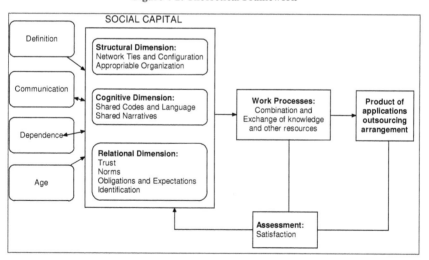

The structural dimension of social capital comes into play in the applications outsourcing context primarily by determining the access between units for exchanging knowledge. The elements in the structural dimension are network ties and configuration, and appropriable organization. The contract initially defines the levels at which interaction between parties will

43

take place, the frequency of interaction, and the format of interaction, and thus defines the access and the patterns of access of the relationship. However, as the project progresses, ties may also develop informally. Interpersonal contacts perform vital roles in problem solving, in exchanging social values and information, and in demonstrating commitment and credibility (Hakansson, 1982). Personal contacts also serve to reduce the impact of geographical separation (Ford, 1998), which would be particularly important in offshore outsourcing.

The term "appropriable organization" refers to the notion that an organizational structure created for one purpose may provide a source of usable connections and information for other, different purposes. In the business context, "appropriable organization" refers to the notion that roles and associated functions defined for one project can be transferred easily from project to project, and helps in mobilizing the resources necessary for the completion of the project. Within the context of an outsourcing arrangement, the procedures developed for carrying out one outsourcing arrangement may be transferable to another arrangement. Thus, appropriability of routines and structures creates the efficiencies of scale that enables outsourcing vendors to provide requisite services to their clients and be profitable.

Creation of an intellectual product by the joint work of two or more units requires a considerable amount of sharing. According to Nahapiet and Ghoshal (1998), this sharing can occur through shared language and codes, and the sharing of narratives. A common language promotes interaction and exchange of information. Shared codes enable the construction of common conceptual models and provide a frame of reference for observing and interpreting the environment. For example, in the development of embedded software, hardware and software engineers use terms and models that are specific to their context. The sharing of narratives, tales of experiences and situated practices, enables "the combination of imaginative and literal observations and cognitions" (Nahapiet and Ghoshal, 1998; p. 254), thus allowing the transfer of context-specific knowledge between organizations. For example, when outsourcing the development of an application to a provider with no domain experience, the client will provide descriptions of the manual processes that are used in the business to the vendor. In applications outsourcing, it has been noted that sharing of ideas and experiences and tacit knowledge are crucial to the success of the development and implementation of applications. The cognitive aspects of social capital are thus crucial in the development of the new technology, by providing the means for the interaction between the client and vendor organizations.

The relational dimension of social capital includes trust, norms, obligations and expectations, and identification. Trust has been the subject of much research, as previously discussed and this model affirms the centrality of trust in relationships. Norms are "shared values" (Joshi and Stump, 1999), an agreement on what is appropriate in the relationship. Trust is necessary to create norms, and behavior that does not violate norms builds trust. Creation of norms requires effort on the part of both parties in the relationship. Obligations are expectations developed within the relationship, regarding the future. A long term-orientation towards the relationship is required to build up these elements of the relational dimension of social capital. Identification is the process by which both parties in the relationship accept similar values and standards. They are able to coexist with each other's beliefs about what values, goals, and behaviors are important and appropriate. In a reciprocal relationship, this compatibility enhances trust, commitment, and a concern for collective processes and outcomes, which aids in the transfer of knowledge and creation of intellectual capital (Sarkar et al, 2001).

Nahapiet and Ghoshal (1998) include a feedback loop from the newly created intellectual capital to social capital, to indicate that the creation of intellectual capital by the joint effort of the parties involved affects the continued development of social capital in the intra-organizational relationship. This representation of the feedback without inclusion of any controls could be considered sufficient, given the focus of their model on the creation of organizational advantage through creation of new intellectual capital. In the applications outsourcing situation, where the two organizations involved do not share a common profit motive (Lacity and Hirschheim, 1999) and are motivated rather by the goal of "self-maximization" (Henderson, 1990), the inclusion of assessment of progress towards the outsourcing objectives of both organizations is particularly important.

Assessment of the progress on the applications outsourcing project would encompass the economic and non-economic aspects of satisfaction (Geyskens, Steenkamp, and Kumar, 1999). The economic aspect of satisfaction is a judgment on the outcome of the outsourcing arrangement; and is captured by the notion of equity; that is, both parties will receive benefits commensurate with their investments, though not necessarily equal. Concurrently, both organizations would assess the interactions and the process through which the IS service or product is delivered, leading to the non-economic evaluation of satisfaction. If the assessments are satisfactory, it may result in continuity and enhancement of the scope of the applications outsourcing arrangement. The result of unsatisfactory assessments may be the dissolution of the outsourcing arrangement, reduction in scope of the outsourcing arrangement, or a determination not to extend additional business opportunities to the other organization.

Social capital is built through exchanges; thus the age of the relationship affects the development of social capital. As the client and vendor organizations interact, they learn about each other and can determine whether there is a good match between the organizations. Each organization will make the determination to continue in the relationship only if they are satisfied with it. Thus, relationships that have lasted for a long time are more likely to be rich in social capital, as the client and vendor organizations have developed mutual trust and understanding and a means to work together in harmony.

Mutual dependence is one of the factors that lead to effective inter-organizational relationships. When organizations are inter-dependent, since one's success depends on another, there is a motivation to ensure that the outcomes are positive for all involved, rather than just for one party (Nahapiet and Ghoshal, 1998). When organizations have alternative means of acquiring the technology or the intellectual capital and are capable of doing so, they may feel less obliged to the partner (Nahapiet and Ghoshal, 1998). Mutual dependence produces high levels of social capital, especially, its relational aspects. This relationship between the relational aspects of social capital and dependence is bi-directional; increase in trust and norms of commitment and coordination will encourage the organizations to be more receptive to the other's ideas and accept more dependence (Gundlach and Cadotte, 1994).

Ongoing exchange is necessary for the development and maintenance of social capital (Bourdieu, 1986; Nahapiet and Ghoshal, 1998). Interaction and communication increases the levels of the cognitive and relational dimensions of social capital, particularly. As the organizational members interact through formal and informal channels, they get a number of opportunities to share their ideas. With the revelation of needs and resources related to the outsourcing relationship (Klepper, 1995), communication increases trust and cooperation between the organizations. Communication, in various forms, is an integral part of organizational procedures (Nahapiet and Ghoshal, 1998). This communication is necessary for maintaining the linkages between the different parties in the outsourcing arrangement. The relationship between social capital and communication is also bi-directional. As aspects of social capital like trust and identification increase, the organizations will be motivated to communicate and share more. When an organization perceives the other as espousing similar goals and values and exhibiting trust-worthy behavior, the organization is more likely to share information with the other.

The definition of the task and processes to accomplish the task through legal documents like the contract provides formal boundaries for the relationship between the two organizations. The closure that is implied by this definition assists in the development of trust, coordination, and sharing of information between the members of the organizations involved in the outsourcing arrangement. The contract serves also as the starting point, establishing the relationship between the two organizations.

In the initial discussions on outsourcing (Chapters 1 and 2), it was noted that the relationship was only one factor in determining the outcome of an outsourcing arrangement. The model presented above appears to focus on relationship to the exclusion of everything else. However, it does recognize the importance of the contract in the initial structuring of the relationship, as well as in providing the definition or closure necessary for social capital to develop in the context of a particular applications outsourcing arrangement.

The technical and management capabilities of the vendor and the client are also significant in outcome of the applications outsourcing arrangement. It has been assumed here that the client and the vendor have satisfied themselves about the other parties' capabilities. Again, while those capabilities are not explicitly included in the model, it can be seen that those capabilities do enter the model by their influence on the cognitive dimensions and the relational dimensions of norms and identification.

In addition, the environment in which the interactions between the organizations take place could affect the development of social capital and intellectual capital. Environmental changes, such as the availability of new alternatives, could affect the level of dependence between the organizations.

In summary, the framework described above contains the significant elements discussed in previous outsourcing research. It provides a view of the process of outsourcing and identifies key factors in the building and management of an outsourcing relationship. The framework can be used to examine the outsourcing process from the perspective of the client or the vendor organization.

Recapitulating the discussion above, applications outsourcing requires establishment and development of a relationship between client and vendor. Empirical research indicate that many IS outsourcing arrangements fail because of a disconnect between the parties. Social capital is the access and the resources that are available in an exchange relationship, and contributes to the conditions necessary for the combination and exchange of knowledge that is necessary to obtain a successful outcome in an applications outsourcing project. Thus, the research question "how does the client-vendor relationship contribute to the execution and completion of the outsourced project?" can be rephrased in terms of social capital as "How is social capital developed in the relationship between an outsourcing client and vendor, and how does this capital contribute to the performance and outcome of the outsourcing arrangement?"

4.4.2   Culture and the development of social capital

Leveraging global resources for software development is rapidly becoming the norm.   IS organizations in more than 50 nations currently develop software for the global outsourcing market (Carmel and Agarwal, 2001).   In this context, it is reasonable to examine the additional challenges faced in offshore outsourcing.   Certainly, part of the challenge rises from the geographical distance separating the two organizations, requiring additional attention to coordination of tasks.   In addition, the difference in national cultures[2] may affect the development of the relationship, and thus, social capital.

Culture can be seen as the sum of the basic implicit assumptions, the resulting norms and values, and the explicit artifacts shared by a group (Trompenaars and Hampden-Turner (1997). Individuals with different national backgrounds hold different but stable assumptions, beliefs, and expectations about many aspects of life, including accepted behavior in organizational settings (Hofstede, 1982).   However, effective interaction between people presupposes a common understanding among the interactants about how to communicate and behave (Trompenaars and Hampden-Turner, 1997).   When this understanding is not present, it may lead to problems in the exchange of information and resources.

Trompenaars and Hampden-Turner (1997) identify several dimensions important to business practices on which national cultures may vary.   Cultures may vary on the relational orientation, which focuses on the emphasis placed on rules versus relationships.   A universalist culture would focus more on rules, and thus pays more attention to contracts.   A particularist, on the other hand, views relationships as more important, and believes there are several perspectives on reality respective to each participant.   People from different cultures may differ on the level of identification with the group, with communitarian cultures being more accepting of authority and joint responsibility, in contrast to individualistic cultures.   Differences can color the actual interaction as well, with some cultures preferring a more neutral orientation, while some reveal their thoughts and feelings freely.   Management of time and specificity are other dimensions on which cultures vary.   When these differences are significant, it can create problems in relationships.

Harris and Dibbern (1999) examined the effect of national culture on the development of trust and cooperation in business relationships between business executives from companies in France, Holland, and the United Kingdom.   Their results indicated that the individuals from the different cultures sought different types of relationships and used different criteria to decide on cooperation.   For instance, the French individuals depended more on the structures within the contract to maintain the relationship, while the Dutch sought the development of mutual understanding to foster a long-term relationship.   The British looked for more short-term relationships than the Dutch and the French.   These differences have implications for the development of social capital in the relationship.   When organizations do not see the benefit of long-term relationships, it is difficult to develop social capital in the relationship, particularly the elements of the relational dimension such as trust and cooperation (Nahapiet and Ghoshal, 1998; Ring and Van de ven, 1992).   The preference for one dimension over the other (French preference for structural dimension and Dutch preference for the cognitive dimension) raises intriguing questions.   Is one as successful as the other in achieving the outcome of the

---

[2] People within cultures vary; however, an average or most predictable behavior can be identified for a national culture (Trompenaars, 1998)

relationship? Is it necessary to develop all three dimensions of social capital to sustain a long-term relationship?

Thus, it can be seen that cultural differences can have an impact on relationships and the elements of social capital, even when individuals are from countries that are proximal. In offshore outsourcing, individuals from different national cultures have to interact with each other to integrate their knowledge and produce the desired outcome. Therefore, similar to the restating of the first research question, the second research question can be restated in terms of social capital as "Do cultural differences create difficulties in the development of social capital between organizations?"

4.4.3 Social Capital in the Outsourcing Lifecycle:

Returning to the set of questions presented in the table at the end of Chapter 2 which identified issues from an outsourcing lifecycle perspective, additional questions that can be raised based on the social capital framework are added for each stage. Further, elements of social capital addressed in the original questions (2nd, 3rd, 4th columns) are identified and added as a separate column in Table 4-3 (fifth column). The first four columns are the same as in the original table, while the sixth column contains the additional questions based on the social capital framework.

While it is true that the outcome of the outsourcing arrangement can be realized only as organizations move thorough the operationalization stage, the relationship and elements of social capital are developed throughout the outsourcing life cycle. Interactions at every stage of the lifecycle have an impact on the relationship and the outcome of the outsourcing arranging. Therefore, Table 4-3 includes all stages of the outsourcing life cycle.

Table 4-3: Further Research Questions using concepts from the theoretical framework

Stage in the outsourcing process	Questions raised from client perspective	Questions raised from domestic vendor perspective	Questions raised from offshore vendor perspective	Element of the social capital framework	Further research questions raised by the social capital framework in the outsourcing context
Partner Selection	How is contact with vendors established?	How is contact with clients established?	How is contact with clients established?	Ties	How are the ties established – formal vs. informal means? What are the benefits of these ties? What is the nature of those ties – for example, friendship? What are the functions accomplished using those ties?
Selection of partners	What are the differences in establishing contact with local versus offshore vendors? What are the determinants in	What are the factors that influence the choice of client and market? Who are the players/stakeh olders	What are the factors that influence the choice of client and market? Who are the players/stakeh olders	Assessment: economic and non-economic satisfaction	

48

	vendor selection? Who are the players/stakeholders involved? What are their roles and expectations? How are these assessments made? What is the role of external parties?	involved? What are their roles and expectations? How are these assessments made?	involved? What are their roles and expectations? How are these assessments made?		
			How can the move to offshore markets be accomplished? i.e. what is the mode of entry?		
				Trust	How is initial trust established?
				Obligations and expectations	How do obligations and expectations from previous relationships with vendors come into play here? What is the influence of referrals?
	What are the different business models possible? Is there a preference for one particular model?	What are the different business models possible? Is there a preference for one particular model?		Appropriable organization	Is the "appropriability" a consideration in initial sourcing decision for vendor?
Evaluation and Negotiation of Contract	What are the factors considered? Who are the players/stakeholders involved? What are their roles and expectations?	What are the factors considered? Who are the players/stakeholders involved? What are their roles and expectations?	What are the factors considered? Who are the players/stakeholders involved? What are their roles and expectations?	Assessment	
	Is there a (perceived) power and knowledge imbalance? Why? How	Is there a (perceived) power and knowledge imbalance? Why? How	Is there a (perceived) power and knowledge imbalance? Why? How	Dependence	How do perceptions of dependence affect negotiations and contract terms?

	does it affect the process?	does it affect the process?	does it affect the process?		
				Shared codes and language	What is the role of shared codes and language in overcoming knowledge differences?
Product: Finalized Contract	What is included in the contract? What is not? Why?	What is included in the contract? What is not? Why?	What is included in the contract? What is not? Why?	Network Configuration: density, connectivity, hierarchy	Are these specified in contract? What other factors determine these?
				Communication	Specification in contract? What other factors determine this? Effect on social capital and effect of social capital?
				Shared codes and language	What is the role of shared codes and language in negotiation and contract finalization?
				Definition/ closure	How much is achieved? Effect of obtaining higher versus lower level of definition?
Operational-ization/ Management	How is the "relationship" operationalized, developed and maintained?	How is the "relationship" operationalized, developed and maintained?	How is the "relationship" operationalized, developed and maintained?	Shared codes and language	How important are shared codes and language? How do these develop?
	What is the influence of the contract in this process?	What is the influence of the contract in this process?	What is the influence of the contract in this process?	Appropriable organization	How much of transfer of routines is possible?
				Ties	
	What are the factors necessary for a successful relationship?	What are the factors necessary for a successful relationship?	What are the factors necessary for a successful relationship?	Trust	Centrality of trust? Interaction with other relational dimension elements?
				Norms	How do these develop? What are the most common?
				Obligations and expectations	Are these met? How can low expectations be overcome?

				Identification	Is similarity in cultures promoted purposefully by one party? What is the effect of this identification?
				Communication	What is the effect of communication on social capital creation and consequent effect on intellectual capital creation?
				Length/age of relationship	What is the effect of age of relationship on social capital creation and consequent effect on intellectual capital creation?
				Definition/ closure	What is the effect of definition/closure on social capital and consequent effect on intellectual capital creation?
				Dependence	What is the effect of dependence on social capital creation and consequent effect on intellectual capital creation? Perception of undue dependence?
Evaluation: Ongoing	What are the monitoring procedures?	What are the monitoring procedures?	What are the monitoring procedures?	Assessment	What is the effect of social capital in the creation of intellectual capital; i.e. technology, etc?
Evaluation: Final	What are the benefits achieved? What are the problems/risks? How is success defined?	What are the benefits achieved? What are the problems/risks ? How is success defined?	What are the benefits achieved? What are the problems/risks ? How is success defined?	Assessment – economic satisfaction (equity), non-economic satisfaction	What is the effect of assessment on the reciprocal relationship between social capital and intellectual capital? Level of change of different elements of social capital
				Negative capital	Negative consequences of social capital – how, when…

The table above highlights a number of interesting issues, but only specific issues related to the primary research question of how social capital contributes to the outcome of the applications outsourcing arrangement are addressed in this study[3]. Specifically, this study looks at how clients and vendors create and maintain their dyadic relationships and whether there is evidence of the influence of social capital in the relationship. In addition, this study also examines and how social capital contributes to the combination and exchange of resources between the client and vendor organizations to create a product or service that can support the business needs of the client organization. Factors that contributed to the acquisition of social capital as well as those that constrain such development are identified. Additionally, following the notion of the bi-directional structuring of social capital and intellectual capital, the study also examines how the processes of "social capital development" and "development and delivery of the product of the IS applications outsourcing project" interact and shape one another over time.

4.5 Conclusions

In this chapter, the theoretical framework that forms the basis of this research was presented. This theoretical framework links the concepts of social capital and intellectual capital and suggests that the presence of social capital promotes the creation of intellectual capital. Previous research has suggested that the relationship plays a significant role in the outcome of the outsourcing arrangement. The theoretical framework developed in this chapter will be used to examine how the relationship contributes to the development and delivery of the IS application in applications outsourcing.

---

[3] That is, issues such as vendor's entry into the market or the superiority of one business model over the other will not be discussed.

Chapter 5
RESEARCH APPROACH

5.1 Introduction

In previous chapters, the research questions and the theoretical framework of this research have been discussed. The purpose of this chapter is to describe the research methodology, the assumptions guiding that methodology, and the research design. In choosing a research methodology, the primary goal is to ensure that it will address the research questions. Since the focus of this research is to study a social phenomenon, the client-vendor relationship in applications outsourcing, a qualitative research approach, specifically the case study method, is employed in this study. As Trauth (2001) states, "…what one wants to learn determines how one should go about doing it" (Trauth, 2001; page 4). The suitability of this research method for the research problem is the starting point for the discussion in this chapter.

The debate on the merits and applicability of different research approaches (positivist/interpretive/critical) has brought much attention to the paradigmatic divide between the approaches. The goal of the third section of this chapter is not to recapitulate this philosophical debate, but to make explicit the philosophical assumptions that guide this research. These assumptions also determine the criteria for evaluating the research and this is the topic of section four. Research design issues including unit of analysis, site selection, and choice of respondents are explained in the next section. The chapter concludes with a discussion of the final stages of the research – the coding and interpretation of data, and reporting of the results.

5.2 Suitability of the research method

The three most favored methods in qualitative research are case study method, action research, and ethnography (Myers, 1997). Practical considerations forced the selection of case study over the other two qualitative methods - ethnography and action research. Given the goal of studying both offshore and domestic outsourcing projects and the long-term duration of each outsourcing contract (the shortest outsourcing contract in this study lasted nine months), it would have not been possible to conduct an ethnographic study. Similarly, action research would not have been feasible; gaining access is itself arduous, implementing change in these organizations would have been impossible. Besides the consideration of feasibility, other factors also supported the use of the case study method; those are discussed in the following paragraphs.

The research primary objective in this study is to examine how the presence of social capital in the client-vendor relationship facilitates the work processes to produce desirable outcomes in applications outsourcing. A second and related objective is to examine how differences in national cultures would affect the development of social capital in the client-vendor relationship. When the research questions are framed as "how" questions requiring explanatory answers, the case study approach is the most suitable (Benbasat et al, 1987). The case study helps describe relationships that exist in reality and capture reality in detail, thus providing rich explanations for the phenomenon under study (Cooper, 2000).

The relationship between the client and vendor organizations develops over time, through the repeated interactions necessary for the completion of the outsourcing project. To obtain an understanding of how social capital facilitates these interactions, it is necessary to track the evolution of the relationship. Thus, this research is processual, following definitions by

Pettigrew (1992) and VandeVen[1] (1992); in particular, it follows the third definition of process from Van de Ven, as a sequence of events that unfold over time. As Yin (1993) recommends, a qualitative approach like the case study is appropriate when the focus is on processes rather than structures and on dynamic rather than static phenomena.

Further, Benbasat et al (1987) and Yin (1993) recommend the use of the case study method when the phenomenon of interest is complex and cannot be studied outside the immediate context. Given that the nature of the outsourcing project and the organizational culture and history of the client and vendor could influence the development of the relationship and the outcome of the outsourcing project, it is appropriate to use a case study approach in this research.

5.3 Philosophical Assumptions

While case study methods could follow the interpretivist, positivist, or critical tradition, the case study method applied in this research follows the interpretivist tradition. Within the interpretivist paradigm, it is assumed that knowledge of reality is gained through "social constructions such a language, consciousness, shared meanings, documents, tools and other artifacts" (Klein & Myers, 1999; p. 69). It is acknowledged that even in the same setting, participants may have different experiences and the researcher needs to interact closely with the subjects to obtain their perspectives. This can be contradicted with the positivist perspective that asserts that the researcher would be able to capture and describe an objective reality that is independent of the researcher and the measurement tools. The critical perspective assumes that reality is socially constructed, similar to the interpretivist perspective; however, the goal in critical research is to bring about social change through critique of the existing social conditions.

Since the interpretivist tradition subscribes to the view that the world around us is socially constructed, it follows that understanding of a phenomenon is best obtained by analyzing the subjective accounts of the phenomena that can be obtained from conversations with participants, documents recording the phenomenon, and other shared artifacts (Klein & Myers, 1999; Luthans & Davis, 1982). However, the interpretivist does not take the extreme stance that nothing exists outside of human cognition; observations are "inevitably mediated by theoretical preconceptions" (Astley, 1985; p. 497) that facilitate understanding of the phenomenon. It is this understanding that enables the researcher to provide explanations for the phenomenon witnessed in the setting.

To obtain accounts of the phenomenon, the researcher interacts with the participants to produce a meaningful interpretation of the phenomenon. This researcher-subject interaction may alter the participant's perceptions and explanation of the phenomenon (Klein and Myers, 1999). This interaction is necessary to gain meaningful insights, and is valid in so far as the objective is to make sense of a specific setting by interpreting the recollections of a specific set of participants (Lacity, 1992). However, this specificity opens interpretive research to the criticism that generalization is not possible in interpretivist research. Proponents of interpretive research argue that generalization from sample to population is not the goal in interpretive research (Yin; 2003). The intention is to understand the phenomenon and "abstract the essences" (Sanders, 1982; p.357) and relate those to "ideas and concepts that apply to multiple situations" of a

---

[1] The first definition of process provided by Van de Ven is the same as that applied by Mohr* (1982), where process logic is used to explain why an independent variable exerts a causal influence over a dependent variable. The second definition of process is as a "category of concepts of individual actions."

* The differences between variance and process theory are described in detail in Mohr (1982).

similar nature (Klein and Myers, 1999; p. 75). The theoretical framework is a sensitizing device that assists the researchers in this endeavor.

The theoretical framework plays "the role of a skeleton" to which the "flesh of empirically contentful concepts can be added to construct mid or low range concepts or theories about the empirical field under investigation" (Kelle, 1997). This theory base, emergent, or existing, enriches the researcher's capability to interpret and present the data. Kelle (1997) states that the "theoretical preconceptions" which the qualitative researchers use to structure their data are quite different from the theoretical concepts that the hypothetico-deductive researchers formulate prior to their data collection and analysis. Kelle refers to the theoretical preconceptions of the qualitative researchers as "heuristic concepts", which serve as implicit lenses for the observation of the empirical world.

5.4 Evaluating research

The traditional concerns of reliability and validity are associated with positivist research and cannot be transferred directly to interpretivist research. However, the objectives of these rigor-enhancing concepts are equally important for all research. These objectives are consistency, truth value, applicability, and neutrality. According to Gergen and Gergen (2000), a focus on these objectives brings the issues of ethics and epistemology together. In line with these objectives, Guba and Lincoln (1989) have recast the positivist understanding of these objectives in interpretivist terms. Table 5-1 provides an overview of the association and comparison between the objectives in the two traditions.

Table 5-1: Objectives and evaluation metrics of research

Research Objective	Objectives for Positivist Research	Objectives for Interpretivist Research
Truth value: Is the research believable?	Internal/Construct Validity: The items used to measure the concept form a single, coherent whole. Content validity: The measure covers the range of meaning included in the concept.	Credibility: Descriptions or interpretations of human experience are so faithful to the experience that people having the experience immediately recognize it from the way the researcher describes them.
Consistency: Are conclusions of research consistent with evidence?	Reliability: Another researcher can get the same results on repeated tries.	Dependability: Another researcher can clearly follow the 'decision trail' you used and arrive at the same or comparable conclusions.
Applicability: Is the research useful or valuable to others?	External Validity/Generalizability: The measurement of the concept actually measures what you intend it to.	Transferability: Findings can fit contexts outside this specific study. The results are transferable to other similar situations and contexts.
Neutrality: Is the research unbiased?	Objectivity: The researcher maintains the proper distance from the subject to avoid biasing the research.	Confirmability: When dependability, credibility and fittingness are established.

While works like Guba and Lincoln's (cited above) clarified the objectives for qualitative research in the interpretivist tradition, it was the publication of Klein and Myers' principles for interpretive research in 1999 that provided IS researchers with clear criteria to judge their qualitative work. Drawing on hermeneutics[2], Klein and Myers identified seven principles for the conduct of interpretivist research (see Table 2). In essence, these principles ensure that the research follows one of the key principles of biblical hermeneutics that "an application of truth may be made only after the correct interpretation has been made."[3]

Klein and Myers' principles also serve as guidelines to researchers embarking on empirical research. When entering the field, *mindful* adherence to these guidelines will ensure that the research is "plausible and convincing." As Klein and Myers further note, it is up to the researcher to "exercise their judgment and discretion in deciding whether, how, and which of the principles should be applied" (p.71).

Table 5-2: Principles for the conduct and evaluation of interpretive field studies (Klein and Myers, 1999)

Hermeneutic circle	The whole consists of the shared meanings that emerge from the interaction between researchers and participants.
Contextualization	The researcher needs to see people as the producers as well as products of history and the description of the historical context should be reflected in the research report.
Researcher-subject interaction	The researcher needs to recognize that participants can also be interpreters and analysts. Participants are interpreters as they alter their horizons by the appropriation of concepts used by researchers and they are analysts so far as their actions are altered by their changed horizons. In addition, the researcher should keep in mind that pre-conceptions about participants will affect the construction, documentation, and organization of the material.
Abstraction and generalization	The researcher needs to relate interpreted data to abstract categories and unique instances to ideas and concepts that apply to multiple situations. Theoretical abstractions and generalizations should be carefully related to study details as they were experienced by researcher, so that it is clear how the researcher arrived at the theoretical insights.
Dialogical reasoning	The researcher should compare theoretical preconceptions to what emerges from data. The researcher should make the historical intellectual basis of the research as transparent as possible to the reader and self.
Multiple interpretation	The researcher should be sensitive to possible differences in interpretations among participants
Suspicion	The researcher should be sensitive to possible biases and distortions in the narratives of the participants.

It can be seen that the traditional concerns of reliability/consistency and validity/truth value are addressed in Klein and Myers' principles. For instance, when the interpretive researcher makes clear how the understanding of the phenomenon emerged from the interactions between the researchers and the participants (principle of the hermeneutic circle), explains any intellectual bias in the research (principle of dialogical reasoning), and carefully reconstructs the

---

[2] Hermeneutics is the theory and practice of interpretation, a discipline that has evolved from the analysis of the Bible.
[3] A. Virkler. (1995). Hermeneutics: Principles and Processes of Biblical Interpretation. Grand Rapids, MI: Baker Book House

study details in the research document (principle of abstraction and generalization), concerns of dependability (equivalent to the concepts of reliability/consistency; see Table 1) are met. Interpretive researchers ensure the credibility or truth-value of their research by providing rich and adequate descriptions of the cases and including quotations from interview transcripts to support their assertions; this is what the principle of abstraction and generalization advocates. Similarly, the goal of applicability or transferability (in qualitative terms; see Table 1) can also be achieved by following the principles of dialogical reasoning and of abstraction and generalization. As Klein (2005) notes, it is no surprise that the principle of abstraction and generalization is the one most used by interpretive IS researchers; the principle speaks most intimately to the traditional objectives of research. Last but not the least, applying the principles of dialogical reasoning and suspicion will ensure the neutrality of the interpretive researcher.

Reflection on the process and findings of research is an integral part of qualitative research; the completed research will be evaluated using these same guidelines. This self-assessment is included in the last chapter.

5.5   Research Design

Research design is defined by Easterby-Smith et al. (1991) as "the overall configuration of a research study, including specifications about what kind of evidence is gathered from where, and how such evidence is interpreted in order to provide good answers to the basic research question(s)". The following sections deals with these pragmatic considerations of data collection and analysis.

5.5.1   Data Collection:

5.5.1.1 Unit of analysis

Since the goal of this research is to determine how the client-vendor relationship contributes to the outcome of the outsourcing arrangement, the "relationship between the client and the vendor organization" is the unit of analysis[4] in this research. Lee and Kim (1999) and Goles (2001) also use 'relationship' as the unit of analysis in their studies on the significance of the relationship in the IS outsourcing context.

5.5.1.2 Interview Questions

Different aspects of relationship management and success were identified from the literature review, as described in the previous chapters. A list of questions that addressed these aspects was created for the interview. The questions and other information that needed to be obtained from the organizations were typed up to create the interview protocol (Creswell, 1998). The protocol for the client and the vendor were similar, except for the initial set of questions aimed to capture background information about the organization and the project. The protocol is included in the appendix.   Besides representatives from client and vendor organizations, consultants were also invited to participate in the research project. The same issues were dealt with in the interviews with the consultants.

Interviews started with general questions as noted in the protocol. However, some respondents would start the conversation with their own views on the topic, often answering many of the questions before being asked. The interviews were conducted in an open and semi-

---

[4] Research on inter-organizational relationships in other disciplines has also used the relationship as the unit of analysis; for example, Mohr and Spekman (1994).

structured manner, and the interviewees were free to interject their comments or expand on issues they thought were important. Therefore, the protocol is only indicative of the questions that were discussed during the interview. Weiss (1995) contends that this is the right choice in interviews for qualitative studies. If the interviewer sticks to the protocol with "standardized precision", the information obtained will be "fragmentary, made up of bits and pieces of attitudes and observations, and appraisals" (page 2). Instead, the interviewer should make it clear to the respondent that "it is their full story we want" (page 3). To obtain such rich and in-depth data, the interviewer should encourage the respondent to share freely and should ask for examples and clarifications as necessary. In fact, Weiss states that only "interviews that sacrifice uniformity of questioning to achieve fuller development of information could be properly called qualitative interviews" (page 3). Most individuals responded to these questions without reluctance and consideration of the time limit for the interview. However, the researcher took care never to over-stay the agreed-upon time limit without the consent of the respondent.

Interviews were conducted face-to-face and via telephone. Totally, sixty interviews were conducted with representatives from client, vendor, and consultancy organizations[5], of which thirty-four were face-to-face interviews. Eighteen interviews were conducted with client representatives, fifteen with domestic vendor representatives, twenty with offshore vendor representatives, and seven with consultants. The majority of the offshore vendor representative interviews were conducted at the offshore vendors' offices in India; a few were conducted over the telephone since it was not possible to schedule some of the interviews while the researcher was in India. On average, the interviews lasted one and a half hours. No difference was noted between the average duration of face-to-face interviews and telephone interviews; however, the longest interview was a face-to-face interview (slightly more than 3.5 hours). In face-to-face interviews, respondents would sometimes show and share documents related to the applications outsourcing project. One advantage of telephone interviews was that it could be conducted at any time convenient to the respondent, often increasing the chance of getting the individual to agree to the interview. Even some respondents from local organizations asked that their interviews be scheduled as a telephone interview while they were traveling; for instance, one respondent took the call while waiting for a connection flight at an airport.

Whenever possible, with the permission of the respondents, interviews were recorded. There were a few cases when the respondents did not wish to be recorded on tape. In such cases, every effort was made to ensure that the notes were as complete as possible.

5.5.1.3 Case Selection

The case site selection process was defined by a combination of factors. First, there are writings on qualitative research advising the researcher on the number of cases that should/could be included in a research project. This counsel on number of cases balances the fact that case studies (dealing with multiple cases) can result in large volumes of data (Miles and Huberman, 1994) with the need to obtain rich data. While Miles and Huberman state that there are no clear rules for the number of cases to be included, different recommendations for the number of cases appear in writings on qualitative research. For example, Miles and Huberman suggest an upper limit of fifteen cases while Eisenhardt (1989) recommends four to ten cases. The goal in picking the number of cases is not to reach a preset number, but to identify enough cases to get as complete an understanding of the phenomenon as possible.

---

[5] Details on the respondents appear in Sections 5.5.1.3 and 5.5.1.4

An additional and inevitable problem in the completion of all research, but particularly in qualitative research due to the greater time commitment required of participants, is access to sites and participants. Access to organizations is extremely difficult, as has been noted by many researchers previously (for e.g. Buchanan et al, 1988; Lacity, 1992); in fact, Lacity mentions that pre-established contacts are often necessary to obtain access. Thus, the selection of sites had to be determined by pragmatic considerations of which organizations and which participants would allow access. However, care was taken to meet that the organizations and participants meet three basic considerations determined by the research objectives as discussed below.

One, The outsourced project needed to be in the area of applications outsourcing. The selection of organizations was not restricted by industry type, organizational size or location.

Two, Since the relationship between partnering organizations needed to be studied, it was also ideal if data could be obtained from representatives of client and vendor organizations on the same applications outsourcing project.

Three, Only management personnel involved in the day-to-day management of the project would be able to provide the information needed to understand how the relationship developed.[6]

Three groups of organizations had to be included in this study: client organizations, domestic vendors, and offshore vendors. Information about the respondents and organizations that participated in this study is available in Appendix 3. Of the sixty interviews conducted, thirty-three interviews were conducted with ten client-and-vendor pairs[7], half of those being client-offshore vendor pairs. The ten pairs of clients and vendors assume additional importance in this study because in those cases, perspectives on the relationship were captured from both organizations. Compared to the cases where an interview was conducted with only one organization in the client-vendor dyad, these paired interview sets provide insight into relationship properties such as shared meaning and differences in perception. These ten client-vendor pairs (in Table 3) are thus the basis for the stories presented in the next chapter (Chapter 6), while the rest of the interview data is used only in the cross-case analysis (Chapter 7).

Table 5-3: Client and Vendor pairs

Case #	Client			Vendor			Total number of interviews
	Organization name	Number of interviews	Position in organization	Organization name	Number of interviews	Position in organization	
1	Montezuma	3	2 Project Executives, 1 IT Manager	Apollo	1	Project Executive at client site	4
2	Chickasaw	1	Technology Director	Zeus	2	Client Executives	3
3	Glacier	2	Project Executive, IT Manager	Hercules	2	Associate Partner, Client Manager	4

[6] This condition is discussed in more detail in Section 5.5.1.4
[7] Where the interviews were with representatives from client and vendor organizations working on the same applications outsourcing project.

4	Haleakala	1	Project Manager	Athene	2	Project Executives	3
5	Bluestone	1	Project Executive	Vesta	2	CEO; on-site manager at client site	3
6	Haleakala	1	Project Manager	Durga	1	Vice President	2
7	Ozark	1	Vice President	Brahma	2	Vice President, Project Manager	3
8	Redwood	1	IT Manager	Shiva	2	Client Manager, Senior IT Manager	3
9	Tallgrass	2	Project Leader, Business Development Manager	Satya	2	Client Managers	4
10	Denali	1	CEO	Vishnu	2	Client Manager, Technical Specialist	3

Access to interviewees was obtained through and telephone and email solicitations. Personal contacts were used to identify and contact interviewees. Additionally, using a combination of print sources (Corporate Yellow Book published by Leadership Directories, Inc.) and online sources from university and local public libraries (Mergent Online, Business & Company Resource Center of Thomson Gale, and Reference USA of InfoUSA), a list of information systems executives with their contact information was created. When different sources are used, one can cross-check the veracity and currency of the information. In addition, news reports on outsourcing in business journals and online sources were scanned to identify individuals to contact. Initially, blind letters were mailed to practitioners. These letters of solicitation (Appendix 2) described the project, assured confidentiality, and invited the recipients to participate in the research project; these were not successful. At this point, email messages and telephone calls were used to contact IS executives. The same letters of solicitation were sent as attachments with all email messages – the initial messages and the messages sent once contact was established via telephone. More than three hundred email messages were sent out, and one hundred and forty telephone calls were made. Attesting to the difficulty of gaining access via cold calls, this high volume of solicitations only resulted in an additional twenty-eight interviews. In some cases, the initial contact at an organization arranged for additional interviews with members of the same organization and/or the partner organization.

Offshore vendor organizations in India, Philippines, Ireland, and Russia were invited via email and telephone to participate in the study. Unfortunately, none of the organizations except those in India could be convinced to participate in the study. Thus, only offshore applications outsourcing vendors from India were interviewed for this study. While this selection was dictated by accessibility, it should be noted that currently India dominates the IS offshore outsourcing market. In the area of software outsourcing, India leads with annual growth of more than 40 percent over the last decade. Besides the appeal of reduced cost, availability of a large pool of software developers educated in English makes India an attractive location for offshore outsourcing (Rajkumar and Dawley, 1998; Rajkumar and Mani, 2001).

5.5.1.4 Respondents

Lacity and Willcocks (2000) recommend that when studying the "dyadic customer-supplier" relationship perspective, the focus of research should guide the researchers in identifying the specific stakeholders within the client and vendor organizations who have the greatest impact on that specific aspect. The research questions that were addressed in this study could only be answered by individuals who were responsible for the management of a specific outsourcing relationship. Though this was not known with certainty before entry into the field, it became clear soon after entry into the field. Some of the top-level executives could not provide the level of detail and insight into an outsourcing relationship; they could only provide an overall picture of the organization's outsourcing policies and expectations. Similarly, IS employees who were lower in the hierarchy did not have a complete picture of the overall relationship. In most cases, respondents from these two groups (top-level executives and operational level employees) suggested that the interviews be conducted with the outsourcing project executive. With the difficulty in gaining access, it was decided to focus on the individuals who would provide the most information. As Sanders (1982) notes, "in-depth probing of a limited number of individuals…who can give reliable information on the phenomena being researched" is more important than having a large number of interviews (page 356). So, after these first few experiences, it was made clear to the organizational representatives who were contacted to set up the interviews that the interviewee needed to be with the individual in charge of managing a specific outsourcing relationship.

One notable demographic characteristic of the respondent group was gender; of the sixty people interviewed, only eight were women. While this does not have any bearing on the study, it is a representation of the male dominance in IS management (Philipkoski, 2005).

The respondents were assured of confidentiality and voluntariness in responding to the interview questions. The respondents were given copies of the Human Subjects Consent form, which detailed their privileges as participants in this research. Even with such assurances, there were a couple of cases when the respondents were a bit reticent during the interview. In one case, a respondent declined to answer questions on future dealings with the partner, in some ways a revealing answer in itself. In another case, the respondent was not willing to provide details on the project. However, in most cases, respondents answered questions in detail and provided additional information. Some of the respondents provided copies of documents such as service level agreements, company reports, and presentations they had given on outsourcing.

5.5.1.5 Interview Data and Other Documents

All of the interviews were transcribed, either from the tape or written notes when the interview was not recorded. The transcribed notes form the field text and are the primary data records for this research. In a few cases, the respondents had to be contacted again via email for clarifications and additional questions. As an additional means of clarification, the contents of the interviews and possible interpretations were discussed with knowledgeable individuals including a senior researcher and three practitioners. One of these practitioners was known to the researcher previously and works for an outsourcing consultancy firm. While the other practitioners (a consultant and a vendor firm representative) were not previously known to the researcher, they were very interested in outsourcing and this research project and initiated meetings with the researcher after the first interview to discuss outsourcing-related issues. As Trauth (1997) notes, discussing and checking with individuals more knowledgeable than the researcher about the phenomenon ensures consistency in research.

Besides the interview data, news reports and case studies on the outsourcing projects were collected from various sources including journals and organization web sites. For example, in the Chickasaw-Zeus case, an academic case study that detailed the initial years of the outsourcing project was available.

5.5.2 Data Analysis

"Qualitative research is endlessly creative and interpretive" (Denzin and Lincoln, 1998; p.30). The field text that includes all the transcribed interviews, documents, and notes needs to be interpreted to produce a text that makes sense to the reader. Lacity and Janson (1994) describe several methods for text analysis in qualitative studies. The interpretivist approach of intentional analysis was noted as being "particularly appropriate for the study of transcribed interviews" (p. 151). In this approach, the researcher seeks to understand the phenomenon based on the "interaction of parts with the whole, while continually elaborating the context of the text" (Kronick and Silver, 1992). As Danke, Shank, and Broadbent (1998) comment, "the strength of analysis in case studies derives from the strength of the exploration of the phenomenon based on interpretation of the data" (p. 285).

Researchers planning to perform intentional analysis on text data go through a series of steps (Lacity and Janson, 1994; Sanders, 1982). First, the researcher describes the phenomenon as revealed in the transcripts of the interviews and texts. The second step is to identify the themes that are present in the texts. The third step involves "development of noetic/noematic[8] correlates" (Sanders, 1982; p.357) through a reflection upon the emergent themes from the previous stage. The goal of the final stage is to "abstract the essences" (Sanders, 1982; p.357) through continued reflection on the themes. The following paragraphs discuss this process in more detail as applied to this research.

In the first step, stories of the participants' experiences are reconstructed using the participants' recollections of the phenomenon under investigation, as recorded in the field text. While seemingly superficial, these stories serve the important purpose of introducing the reader to the facts of the phenomenon. As previously mentioned, ten such stories are presented in Chapter 6.

In the second step, the data is analyzed to identify themes, the "commonalities present between and within narratives" (Sanders, 1982; p.357). These themes are identified based on their significance to the phenomenon, not on the basis of a word count. In this process, the researcher is guided by the research objectives, the theoretical framework, and the data. Stepping through the data, the researcher looks at every sentence and asks "What does this sentence or sentence cluster reveal about the phenomenon or experience being described?" (van Manen, 1990; p. 93). In this study, this in-depth examination of the field text was accomplished by coding, where each line of the text is read and assigned a code or a label with a specific

---

8 An objective statement of behavior constitutes a noema. A subjective reflection of the objective statement constitutes a noesis.

62

meaning (Miles and Huberman, 1994). The coding scheme and the use of qualitative software for attaching these codes to the data are briefly described in the following sections. The process of coding allows the researcher to "notice relevant phenomena, collect examples of those phenomena, and find commonalities, differences, patterns, and structures" (Basit, 2003; p.144). The coding process helped segment the field text into meaningful pieces (Tesch, 1990); the segments of text from the different interviews related to each case that were coded/labeled similarly were then put together to assemble all the comments in a case about a particular aspect. Based on this "decontextualization" and "recontextualization" (Sabherwal, Hirschheim, and Goles, 2001; Tesch, 1990), the ten stories are supplemented by a discussion of the insights provided by the theoretical framework.

The third step focused on capturing the "what" and the "how" of the research participant's experiences. Reflecting on the emergent themes from the data, the researcher is able to recreate how the participants perceive the reality of the phenomenon under study and identify meaningful commonalities across the different cases. This cross-case analysis offers a form of generalizability – not in the statistical sense of the term, but in strengthening the understanding of the phenomenon. This conforms to Klein and Myers' principle of abstraction and generalization, which exhorts researchers to relate interpreted data to abstract categories and unique instances to ideas and concepts that apply to multiple situations. Chapter 7 contains this analysis, an integrative comparison of the findings from all the cases.

In the fourth step, the findings from the analysis are translated into implications for researchers and practitioners. The "abstraction of essences" (Sanders, 1982) provides insights into the phenomenon studied that "transcend the context of the study" (Lacity, 1987). This is a fitting topic for the last chapter of the dissertation, Chapter 8.

5.5.2.1 Coding Scheme

Miles and Huberman (1994) recommend that codes should be related to the theoretical framework, rather than being a random collection of categories. An initial set of codes was developed based on the social capital framework presented in Chapter 4. This set includes terms such as "trust", "shared understanding", and "dependence." These initial codes were used to organize the field text in a first reading; rereading and additional interpretation led to addition of other codes. For example, "certification (such as CMM)", "perception of outsourcing," and "cost focus of the IS organization" were considerations in some of the cases; these were added to the coding list. A complete list of codes appears in Appendix 4.

5.5.2.2 Use of Atlas/ti Software

Atlas/ti, a computer-aided qualitative data analysis software package, was used in the indexing of the data. While Atlas/ti is a complete tool for data analysis, its use in this research is limited to tagging the data with the codes. The design of this particular tool matches the interpretive approach to data analysis; it has been developed based on principles of grounded theory generation, a very data-driven approach. There are two modes of data analysis within Atlas/ti: the textual level and the conceptual level. The textual level focuses on the raw data and includes activities such as text segmentation, coding, and memo writing. In the conceptual level, framework-building activities such as interrelating codes, concepts, and categories to form theoretical networks can be conducted (Muhr, 1997). In this study, the use of Atlas/ti was restricted to the textual level, purely indexing of the data with the codes (described in the previous section). A snapshot of the Atlas/ti screen is included in Appendix 5.

While Atlas/ti does not help do anything that cannot be done manually, the principal advantage of using such a program is that it simplifies and speeds the mechanical aspects of data analysis. "The thinking, judging, deciding, interpreting, etc., are still done by the researcher. The computer does not make conceptual decisions, and does not dictate which words or themes to focus on or which analytical step to take next. These analytical tasks are still left entirely to the researcher" (Tesch, 1991). Lee and Fielding (1991) comment that computers will benefit qualitative researchers, making their work easier, more productive, and potentially more thorough. Rich insights available from the cases can be obtained only from thorough immersion into the transcripts for the cases (Sabherwal, 1999a); such immersion is enabled by tools of this type.

5.5.3   Reporting

"Writing and composing the report brings the entire study together" (Creswell, 1998; p. 167). When we write research reports, we strive to organize the text in a manner consistent with the emphasis of the research approach (Van Manen, 1990). Van Manen suggests five different methods for structuring research reports; these five methods are not mutually exclusive. One may write thematically, with each section of the report related to a theme identified from the study. An alternative is the analytical presentation in which reconstructed stories of the phenomenon under investigation are followed by examination of the emergent themes that the set of narratives reveals. One may proceed exemplificatively by describing the phenomenon and then presenting variations of the phenomenon. An exegetical structure requires the researcher to compare the findings of the current research with existing theoretical knowledge. An existential report uses the existentials of temporality, spatiality, corporeality, and sociality as interpretive guides to explain phenomena.

The report of empirical research presented in the next three chapters is organized analytically and exegetically. As can be readily seen, the stories presented in Chapter 6 follow the analytical structure. The ensuing discussion on the insights provided by the theoretical framework in the following three chapters fits in the exegetical category.

5.6   *Summary*

This chapter briefly presented the research approach adopted for this study. The suitability of a qualitative case study approach in the interpretive paradigm for this study is established and the evaluation criteria for such research are discussed. Details about various aspects of the research design were also discussed. This sets the stage for the discussion on the empirical work in the following chapters.

Chapter 6

CASE DESCRIPTIONS

6.1 Introduction

"In the social sciences, there is only interpretation. Nothing speaks for itself. Confronted with a mountain of impressions, documents, and field notes, the qualitative researcher faces the difficult and challenging task of making sense of what has been learned...This may also be described as moving from the field to the text to the reader. The practice of the art allows the field-worker-as-bricoleur[1] to translate what has been learned into a body of textual work that communicates those understandings to the reader...They are the stories we tell one another. This is so because interpretation requires the telling of a story or a narrative that states "things happen this way because"..." (pp. 313-314: Denzin, 1998)

This chapter presents the *stories* of ten applications outsourcing projects and the client-vendor relationships in those projects. The goal in this stage of the analysis is determine what insights the theoretical framework will provide on each relationship. Using the elements of the framework, the case descriptions will explain how the social capital in the outsourcing relationship affected the outcome of the outsourcing arrangement.

The following sections of this chapter present the descriptions of ten client-vendor relationships. These descriptions have emerged from an examination of the data obtained from the research participants on their experiences with an outsourcing arrangement. Each case description follows the format outlined in Table 6.1.

Table 6-1: Case Description Format

1	Introduction
2	The Outsourcing Project
3	The Client-Vendor Relationship
4	Through the "Social Capital" Lens
5	Case study conclusion

The introduction provides a brief description of the companies involved and the individuals who participated in the research. The second sub-section provides information about the outsourcing project. With this background information, the reader will be able to appreciate the story of the client-vendor relationship presented in the third section. In constructing these stories from the transcribed field texts, no attempt was made to make inferences from the data. However, following Klein and Myers (1999), it must be understood that these stories are a product of the interpretation of reality created by the researcher and participants during the interviews. Further, the selection of events for the case was guided by the theoretical framework. As mentioned in Chapter 5, for the ten cases presented in this chapter, representatives from client and vendor organizations contributed to the description of the relationship. So, scripts from different individuals with experience and knowledge of the relationship were available for each case and aided in creating a description of the outsourcing project and the relationship.

---

[1] A qualitative researcher is viewed as a bricoleur or a professional handy person who uses the tools of his or her methodological trade and whatever strategies are at hand to understand the phenomenon in question

In the fourth section, an analysis of the relationship and its outcomes are presented. To assist in this analysis, the social capital framework (described in Chapter 4) was used. This fourth section supplements the story in the previous section with a discussion on how the concepts from the theoretical framework provide insight into the outsourcing relationship and its impact on the outcomes of the outsourcing arrangement. This section starts with an examination whether the elements of the three dimensions of social capital – structural, cognitive, and relational – are present in the relationship to understand if social capital is manifest in the relationship. This is followed by a discussion on the conditions contributing to the development of social capital. Finally, the effects of the social capital on the outcome of the outsourcing project are discussed. Each case description ends with a conclusion that synopsizes the insights from the story and the theory-based interpretation.

Of the ten cases presented in this chapter, the first five present descriptions of relationships of client and vendor organizations based in the U.S. and the remaining five deal with clients based in the U.S. and vendors based in India. The cases are sequenced in the 'order of diminishing returns'; starting with the first case which provides the richest insights, each successive case augmenting our understanding of the phenomenon through use of the theoretical framework.

6.2 Case 1: Montezuma and Apollo

The story and discussion in this case description focus on the client-vendor relationship in the context of an SAP implementation project. While initially this appears like a textbook case of "outsourcing done right", the story is fascinating because of the unexpected outcome. The case analysis highlights the impact of different dimensions of social capital on the outcome of the outsourcing project, and in particular, the relational dimension.

6.2.1 Introduction

This case involved two large organizations based in the United States. The client, Montezuma, is an energy company that is engaged in worldwide exploration and production of crude oil and natural gas, as well as domestic refining, marketing and transportation of petroleum products. Headquartered in the south central part of the United States, this organization has oil and gas exploration and production activities in the continents of North America, Europe, and Africa. Active in more than a dozen countries, with production in nine, Montezuma has grown through partnerships and mergers.

The vendor, Apollo is a large technology company that provides information technology services, software, systems, products, financing and technologies; in the words of the research participant from Apollo, they "do almost everything." Apollo has been in the information technology business for a long time, and has a solid reputation in the industry. Apollo has more widespread operations than Montezuma and has offices in every continent of the world.

Four individuals were interviewed to obtain the details of this outsourcing arrangement: two executives and an IS manager from Montezuma who were responsible for the outsourcing project and the project executive at Apollo. The two Montezuma executives, Jim and Bob, had been involved in the management of the outsourcing project from its very inception in their organization. This is a unique situation; usually, the outsourcing contract negotiation team hands over to the operational team once the contract is finalized. In Bob's words,

"Unfortunately, those people (the negotiation team) wander away or they walk off or whatever and leave. The front-line people are left to deal with whatever was negotiated, whether they know what they are talking about or not. Montezuma, in this case, had continuity – that is, Jim and I, we get to live with the results (of the negotiation)."

So they were able to offer in-depth and interesting information about the client-vendor relationship.

Table 6-2: Interviewees in the Montezuma-Apollo case

Name of interviewee	Organization	Position	Duration of interview	Taped?
Jim	Montezuma (Client)	Project Executive	3.25 hours	Yes
Bob	Montezuma	Project Executive	1.5 hours	Yes
Jack	Montezuma	IS Manager	45 minutes	No
Tom	Apollo (Vendor)	Project Executive	1.5 hours	Yes

On the other hand, the IS manager at Montezuma, Jack, was not able to add much to the discussion on relationship management; his comments were more narrowly focused on interactions he had with the operational staff from Apollo. This difference in foci was to be expected; while examining the factors affecting the client-vendor relationship, Goles (2001) also noted that the breadth and depth of perceptions of managers at strategic and operational levels in the organization about the same issues were different.

Another interesting fact about the interviews at Montezuma was the difference in orientation between the two Montezuma executives. In his comments and descriptions, Jim came across as a more relationship-oriented person. In fact, he mentioned that one of his primary roles is that of "relationship manager," while Bob introduced himself as a "project executive." Contact with Jim was established through a personal contact; he arranged the interviews with Tom and Bob. All interviews took place at the Montezuma office. The interview with Jack took place while waiting for Jim; he was interested in the objective of the research and started to talk about his opinions on the project. When asked if he would like to contribute, he agreed immediately. However, Jack was not comfortable with the interview being taped and also watched closely as notes were taken during the interview.

The Apollo executive, Tom, is the on-site project executive for this project. He took charge in the second year of the project after the first project executive from Apollo quit that organization. So Tom was not familiar with the events in the very early stages of this project. Additionally, he would not have been part of the contract negotiation team at Apollo. Apollo has different teams for each function associated with outsourcing, such as responding to the RFP, negotiating the contract, and project management.

6.2.2 The Outsourcing Project

The outsourcing project involved application development, hosting, and support including the help desk support for the SAP environment of the client organization, Montezuma. The initiative for SAP was part of an IS blueprint that was created at Montezuma with involvement from all business units and stakeholders.

Montezuma's IS infrastructure has to support more than ten thousand users distributed across its various locations, and was supported by a strong internal IS organization. However, over the years many different systems were in use within the organization. Some of the systems had been developed independently at different offices because of urgent need for certain applications. The result was that various applications were being implemented in different and incompatible ways in parts of the organization. Further, since Montezuma had grown through a number of mergers, acquisitions, and joint ventures, it had inherited many different environments and systems. It was this combination of events that necessitated the development of the IS blueprint. One of the strongest recommendations in the blueprint was a move towards standardization. Another related one was the deployment of an enterprise resource planning system, for which they selected SAP. Other recommendations included initiatives for knowledge management and formation of communities of practice. In Jim's words, "the IT blueprint has brought about a lot of change in the last two to three years."

A defining characteristic of Montezuma's IS organization was its strong customer focus. The IS organization was structured so that the end-users' needs could be met efficiently and satisfactorily. Client representatives, who could "relate to the business needs of the users and understand the technical side", functioned as the interface between the end-user and the more technical IS workers. Jack took pride in the fact that he and his colleagues were able to foresee and meet customer needs, so that "they (the end-users) did not even realize that they were there." As an example of the attention given to customer demands, Jack described an earlier infrastructure outsourcing initiative. In that project, desktops were being replaced with the goal of having a standard image across the organization. However, individual clients were promised that they would have any software they previously had on their new machines as well. According to Jack, this was a response to clients' discontent and anxiety about losing control over their desktops. This strong focus within the IS organization towards satisfying customers became a bone of contention for the operational level employees in the IS organization, an issue on which they found fault with all outsourcing initiatives. It is also not a surprise that the IS staff feels uncomfortable; the new initiatives have introduced many changes in the organization. Blaming outsourcing for some of the resultant issues is a natural reaction to these changes.

The IS blueprint did not speak explicitly of outsourcing; in fact, Jim's comments reveal the organization's attitude towards outsourcing.

"Also hidden in this document (the IT blueprint), I say "hidden" because the culture of the company did not embrace the notion of outsourcing; the "O" word was not used in the document; instead it had some kind of code-speak of "externally leveraging resources," or something. I don't remember what it was called, but there was some phrase like that."

The initiative towards outsourcing which started internal to the IS organization finally had buy-in at the top levels of the organization. The feeling was that an external party could

"... extend their knowledge and expertise in these areas (to Montezuma). They can apply industry-leading best practices. For them, these are core competencies." (Bob)

There was still dissent from the lower ranks of the IS organization. As Jim explained about a meeting organized to explain the decision,

"I am the devil incarnate to some people, how could you consider outsourcing, this critical function to the evil empire of Apollo, how could you, you know go over to the dark side... I was tempted to go out and buy a tee-shirt with a big bull's eye on the front because I knew, it's like how could you do this, Jim, how could you do this."

However, at the meeting, the IS management explained that it was not possible for Montezuma's IS organization to do what Apollo could.

"We did develop a straw man base case, business case – for us to do it internally, this is what it will cost and it was at best a guesstimate ... it was not for Montezuma to invest in technologies we had no experience with, and frankly could not leverage. I mean these companies are large that do this, they have the commercial leverage, technical leverage... By the time I got down to the what we did and how we did it, I had a number of people come up to me afterward and say, oh ok." (Jim)

Montezuma decided to go ahead with the SAP implementation using a third-party provider. Fortunately, the project did not have a major human resources dimension since no employees were let go; a few were reassigned to other areas.

6.2.3 The Client-Vendor Relationship

Once the green light for outsourcing was received, the IS organization at Montezuma moved quickly to the process of vendor selection. From industry dialog and by reading the reports from "the Forresters and Gartners of the world", Montezuma quickly realized that they would need help in structuring the project. Therefore, they brought in Cicero, a consulting firm based in the same region as Montezuma. Montezuma engaged external legal counsel besides their internal counsel. The negotiation team at Montezuma also internal representation from its IS, financial, audit, commercial purchase, and human resource departments and subject matter experts on security and telecommunications. Thus, Montezuma was well prepared for the initial selection and negotiation processes.

Cicero has a standardized process for the whole vendor selection and contract negotiation cycle. Montezuma followed this process on "a very aggressive schedule," according to Jim. While the typical process for vendor selection and contract negotiation and agreement for a project of this nature can take anywhere from eight months to a year, Montezuma was able to complete all the steps in this process in a three month time period. As is customary, the RFI[2] was sent out first to a short list of around ten vendors to gauge their capabilities and interest in taking up the project. With the responses from the RFIs in hand, this list was culled down to three. Before and after the RFP[3] distribution, Montezuma and each of the three vendor organizations had several meetings to clarify issues and exchange additional information. Once the proposals were received, Montezuma picked their first choice in a matter of two weeks. The primary factor in choosing the vendor was not cost. As Jim explained,

"Our goal, our overriding goal was not to reduce cost; that sounds terrible, I know. Cost was clearly a concern, but the overriding concern was that we needed to guarantee success, to have the cheapest SAP failure. We wanted to have a successful SAP implementation – that was paramount. Our selection was with the company that we felt would give us the best guarantee of success."

Their number one pick was Apollo, a leading provider of IS services globally. The negotiation team at Montezuma then informed Apollo that they would negotiate the deal.

---

[2] Request for Information
[3] Request for Proposal

"We're going to negotiate with you for the next week, and we're still in a competitive situation, and if we like the progress--basically, we told them that the deal was yours to lose. But, you have to be nimble."

The consultant from Cicero was skeptical that Apollo would agree to Montezuma's demands. In fact, the consultant told Jim, "You're asking the elephant to learn the hula. And this elephant can't dance." However, the consultant was proved wrong – he ended up having to buy dinner for the Montezuma negotiation team – and Montezuma and Apollo signed the contract three weeks from the date the proposals were in. From Jim's comments regarding this last stage of the negotiation process, one can notice a certain gleeful satisfaction that Montezuma was able to pull off the deal they wanted with a company as established as Apollo.

Apollo, being well-versed in the outsourcing bidding and contract negotiation process, had teams and structures in place to manage the process. A five-year contract with options for two one-year renewals was signed, making it potentially a seven-year contract. As soon as the contract was finalized, Apollo was able to mobilize the resources necessary for the project immediately from their SAP hosting center in Kentucky and the SAP application development centers in Illinois. Interestingly, the person responsible for the hosting environment lived in North Carolina; however, the IS executives at Montezuma realized this only after a few months into the project. As Jim remarked, "They are truly a virtual company" and had such excellent capabilities so that the client did not perceive "any difference."

The haste with which the negotiation process was completed had its negative repercussions also. There were oversights and errors in the contract, which had to be fixed using amendments. However, the errors were dealt with fairly by both organizations. For instance, during the final negotiations it was agreed that Apollo would be responsible for the telecommunication lines in the event of a disaster recovery scenario. This was not reflected in the contract; in fact, there was contradictory language in the contract on this issue. This was quickly amended since both parties saw the contract as a "reflection of what they had agreed on at the personal level", according to Jim.

The day-to-day contract management and governance on the project rests with three individuals: Jim, Bob, and Tom. Cicero consultants are not involved in this stage and Jim and Bob are learning how to manage on the job. As Bob comments, "We were babies, we truly were." All three of them characterize the relationship between the organizations as "a marriage", where those involved "have to work it out and make it work." The contract is "the framework within which you work, within which you frame solutions and compromises." However, the relationship is of paramount importance; "…the whole outsourcing thing does boil down to people and relationships" (Tom). As Bob adds, "there are a lot more dimensions to relationship management than the contract. This was explained to us at length by the industry pundits and the people who helped us through the outsourcing…" The three of them agreed that over-reliance on the contract would hurt the relationship. Supporting that sentiment, Jim remarked, "You can almost chart the frequency of reference to the contract as an indicator of a problem with the relationship."

Yet, this is business and their ultimate goals are different as Bob clearly summed up in his comments:

"We exhibit different behaviors – his is revenue and mine is delivery. In the simplest sense, it is the same because he generates revenue by providing the service delivery and they are a strategic partner for us, but my job is in a management sense is to extract as much value as I can from the investment I am making. Their objective is continued revenue stream and supplemental opportunities... mine is excellence service delivery...there is a subtle difference there..."

This attempt to focus on the relationship may also be because it is impossible to include everything in the contract. As Jim explains, "we were shooting at a moving target. We were developing an application, an entire suite of applications..."

Apollo has processes in place for the management of the operational stage; additionally, Cicero's recommendations for governance were worked into the contract. Formal communication happens through reports and meetings, which are identified in the contract. There is a monthly steering committee meeting with representatives from both organizations "to review all activities and discuss issues." If there are major changes to be made in the contract, consultants are also included in these meetings to ensure that the changes adhere to good business guidelines. Monitoring of the progress of the project is done by tracking milestones and deliverables and monitoring service levels. Beyond this, Apollo is contractually required to have a means to assess the satisfaction of the user community. This is done using a third party, who surveys the organization and provides the results. Apollo views these assessments as chances to show the organization that they "value the judgment, not just from the people we interact with, but from the user organization as a whole." The results are discussed at the monthly steering committee meetings and the quarterly review meetings.

Besides participating in the formal meetings, Jim, Bob, and, Tom, meet informally every week to discuss issues associated with the outsourcing project and come to a common understanding on the evaluation of the completed work and the progress of the project. Issues such as scope changes in the contract and execution problems are resolved in this manner. To incentivize the project management executives in both organizations to work together and ensure the success of the project, the compensation system has been changed. A major part of the compensation for all three executives is tied to the success of the project. Thus, Tom has a vested interested in meeting Montezuma's objectives, while Jim and Bob are committed to making sure that Apollo has all the information they need to meet these objectives. Additionally, staff on both sides are incented by bonuses they would receive if service levels and other project goals are met.

Overall, Jim and Bob are satisfied with the progress on this applications project in terms of the monetary savings and service quality. Though a three level escalation procedure for conflict resolution is included in the contract, they have not had to use it. However, not all parties in the organization agree on the progress on the project and there is some dissatisfaction in the ranks, which stems from the culture of Montezuma's IS organization. This is reflected in the comments from Jack, the IS manager.

"I think they need to be work more closely with the IT people in (Montezuma) to understand what the client needs are...I know in our earlier structure, we had people like myself called client representatives. My job is to understand my client and ... we (the IT staff at Montezuma) were very customer oriented and like I said, it could well have been that customer service wasn't (Apollo)'s biggest concern. They were focused on cost and time and all that kind of stuff. I feel the difference because I am very customer oriented and their focus may have been completely different."

Separately, while answering a question on satisfaction with the vendor, Jim commented on the same issue:

> "Our internal expectations, or culture, whatever you want to call it, our expectation was, just to give you an example... at our helpdesk-if the phone rings, to get that person productive by the time he hangs up the phone. So, that was our customer expectation. And we felt that it was a prudent expenditure to put senior people on phones, again, to get the person back up and running quickly and to encourage them to call quickly rather than try to solve the problem themselves. The situation we have with Apollo is different. They have order takers, and if a monkey can solve a simple problem and I can type in a few words, a few key words, then the knowledge base pops up an answer. They don't know SAP. That's probably going to lead to dissatisfaction. That's a scenario that our fellow IT people point to."

Another area of dissatisfaction for both Jim and Bob was the lack of innovation from Apollo. They had expected innovative ideas from a company like Apollo and they had not received as much as they had expected. Thus, while the project was proceeding satisfactorily with all contract requirements were being met and some service levels were even exceeded, there is still dissatisfaction in Montezuma.

Towards the end of the second year of the project, Montezuma decided to outsource "another chunk of its applications". However, Apollo was not chosen for this project. Bob explains the decision on this latest outsourcing initiative:

> "They (Apollo) could not put together a compelling case and perhaps one of the criticisms I have of them at the end of the day is that they were inflexible..."

Without mentioning this specific comment to Tom, the issue of flexibility was raised during the conversation. He answered that they were meeting all of Montezuma's needs and had the capabilities to accommodate whatever changes they required. When pressed further about how open they would be to such changes, he replied:

> "We don't let the contract stop us from doing the right thing; it does not restrict us."

Yet the relationship has changed, and they all sense it. Bob sums up the nature of the relationship at this time.

> "I guess the relationship has changed because they get tired of the same drum being beaten, perhaps not, but I suspect the changes are because we know where we are coming from; they know that they are not going to get anything more out of us."

Losing that additional opportunity is a sore point for Tom.

> "I feel dissatisfied because we have not leveraged that into a significant increase in business - we didn't get the new contract, so that affects me personally too."

6.2.4 Through the "Social Capital" Lens

Having presented the background and the story of the outsourcing relationship, the focus now turns to analysis of the field text using the social capital framework.

6.2.4.1 Social Capital in the Montezuma-Apollo relationship

The determination of the presence of social capital in the relationship is made by examining whether the different elements of the three dimensions of social capital are manifest in the relationship. The structural dimension of social capital refers to the ways in which members of each organization gain access to members of the other organization with desired sets of knowledge or other resources. The cognitive dimension includes resources promoting shared representations and interpretations, such as a shared language. The third dimension, the relational dimension, is the set of elements that define the quality of the relationship: trust, norms, meeting expectations and obligations, and identification.

6.2.4.1.1 *Structural dimension: Access patterns and appropriable organization*

The contract lays out the structure for communication and interaction between project participants in both organizations. It defines the levels and periodicity of access different individuals in both organizations will have. The contract also determines the format communication between the organizations should take and to whom all such information will be distributed. As explained by Jim,

> "In our governance model, we've got--it's a 3-layer model ...we've got a daily operating function, kind of at a microscopic level. At the next level, we have monthly review meetings...it's much more formal. In addition to this, we have, officially, I think our contract calls for quarterly, but we're doing it semi-annual, where we have executive briefings, executive review meetings."

This structuring of interaction patterns through the contract is a common feature in all ten cases.

In the original conception of the term by Coleman (1987), "appropriable organization" refers to the notion that voluntary organizations formed for one could be deployed for other purposes, and thus be a valuable resource in other settings. The links between individuals and their patterns of behavior could be transferred from one setting to the other. In the business context, "appropriable organization" refers to the notion of roles and associated functions defined for one project can be transferred easily from project to project, and helps in mobilizing the resources necessary for the completion of the project. Apollo, for instance, had experienced and capable negotiation and operations teams. The negotiation team, according to Bob, had "a wide and in-depth experience in negotiating" contracts and so is able to proceed through negotiations with "celerity and certainty". Within four weeks of signing the contract, Apollo started providing services to Montezuma. Thus, appropriability of routines and structures creates the efficiencies of scale that enables outsourcing vendors to provide technically excellent services to their clients and be profitable. Apollo's operations team enacts the roles that they know have been successful in the past and employs routines that will enable the combination and exchange of resources. Client organizations look to vendors to bring in these routines; in many cases, client organizations have emphasized the contract to the detriment of planning the post-contract work. As Jim says, "we spent more time negotiating and discussing our prenuptial than we talked about how the marriage was actually going to work." Thus, it is Apollo's experience in these matters and the appropriability of their routines that enable the project to move quickly into the operational stage.

However, in light of the comments of inflexibility raised by Jim and Bob, this element of the structural dimension needs to be examined deeper. While using and reusing organizational structures provides efficiencies, it may also serve as a barrier to flexibility. In discussing inflexibility, Bob had given the example of how the yearly audits had to be structured the way Apollo wanted it done, which was not in line with how the IS organization at Montezuma conducted the audits. Thus, even when Apollo had information that their routines did not match that of their client, they were not willing to change their routines, thus creating feelings of dissatisfaction. Even though Tom says that they "do not let the contract restrict them", they remain wedded to their routines.

6.2.4.1.2 Cognitive dimension: Shared understanding

In the negotiation of the contract, Cicero facilitates the exchange between Montezuma and Apollo. Montezuma, not familiar with all the processes involved in the process depends on Cicero to bring them that expertise. Since Cicero has vast experience in this area, their guidelines and mechanisms (such as the yellow pad sessions) are able to facilitate a common understanding and agreement on contract terms. Even the errors on the contracts are handled non-acrimoniously based on the mutual understanding that developed from this exchange.

During the project, the staff from Apollo and Montezuma have to interact to complete the project. There is a feeling among the Montezuma IS staff that Apollo staff are only interested in their own ends and do not care too much for the input of the IS staff.

> "They (Apollo staff) need to work more closely with the IT people to understand what the client needs are." (Jack)

While the IS organization at Montezuma does not have experience with SAP, and are not directly involved in the SAP implementation, they feel that Apollo should be interested in obtaining information on the "way things are done", the information systems practices, at Montezuma. This perceived absence of sharing, in turn, could actually reduce the quality of the access provided by the IS. Yet, since the IS management is aware of the negative feelings about the outsourcing project, they motivate the staff to provide the necessary resources by rewarding them with monetary bonuses when objectives are met.

However, there have been no major problems reported in the project, according to both Jim and Bob. In their interactions, the two of them and Tom work together to build a common understanding of the requirements and progress on the project. The shared representations of the goals and evaluation schemes for the project which have been developed during the initial stages, along with a common understanding of business management practices helps reduce ambiguity and induce agreement where differences exist. Such shared language and codes are especially useful where the expectations and the views may be different because of varying goals, as in this case.

6.2.4.1.3 Relational dimension: Trust, norms, obligations & expectations, identification

When two organizations come together, there may be high initial levels of trust due to the security inherent in the guarantees of the contractual documents. Montezuma feels that they have a "contract with a bite" and that Apollo will not be able to terminate for any other reason than non-payment. However, as the organizations interact over time, experiential trust becomes more important. Even though Montezuma and Apollo executives claim that the other organization is a good partner, there is a lack of trust. For instance, Bob comments:

> "…we keep tight reins, intellectual and architectural reins over technical components that Apollo brings - it keeps them honest, it ensures we have got the probe in the system, watching carefully …" (Bob)

Even though they feel they have worked out a fairly equitable contract, they still do not seem to trust Apollo completely. Trust is central to the development of norms such as commitment and collaboration. In an environment where there is a lack of trust, these norms will be absent stunting the growth of the relationship and blocking the development of trust. This lack of trust may partly rise from the fact that Montezuma perceives themselves as highly dependent on Apollo.

Norms determine a range of expected behaviors in the exchange situation. When such norms develop consensually due to trust in the partner, the organizational members are more likely to adhere to such norms. However, behaviors can be modified by other means; reward and punishment are natural determinants of behavior. At Montezuma's behest, Montezuma and Apollo together have instituted a compensation system that they believe will ensure the commitment of the members of both organizations to the success of the outsourcing project. Tom explains that he is committed to meeting the goals set by Montezuma because of this compensation scheme

> "My compensation is tied to the success of this project, as is the compensation of my colleagues at Montezuma. So I have a vested interest in meeting Montezuma's key objectives."

However, it has been shown that the norm of commitment developed through monetary means – calculative commitment – does not beget trust (Caniëls and Gelderman, 2004).

One of the other issues that Montezuma has with the outsourcing relationship is the lack of flexibility. From Apollo's perspective, Montezuma's determination to engage them in negotiations and force concessions before finalizing the contract, even though they came in with the lowest bid would not have set the stage for norms of openness and flexibility. Additionally, Tom sees a lack of effort on Montezuma's part to understand and care for what Apollo wants also.

Jim and Bob are aware that the vendor had long-term expectations, as evidenced by Bob's comments that Apollo's "objectives are continued revenue stream and supplemental opportunities." However, Montezuma does not award the next project to Apollo, making it a difficult situation for Tom. He feels that there has not been enough recognition for the work that has been done. When questioned about the reliability of Montezuma, he comments on the expectations from an outsourcing arrangement, and how that has not been met.

> "There always has to be a willingness to work together and rethink what we had both (Apollo and Montezuma) wanted out of it in a situation like this."

Thus he feels that there has been a lack of interest on Montezuma's part to fulfill their obligations.

Jim is not even sure that a true cultural compatibility exists between the two organizations.

> "I'm not sure I would agree (that there is compatibility in corporate cultures). I do think it's an alignment of the culture between Montezuma and the face that Apollo puts. Apollo's culture could be contrary to what I'm saying right now" (Jim)

His comment reveals that he does not yet have an understanding of what Apollo's culture is. Where such knowledge of the partner is missing, it is not possible to develop a feeling of oneness and similarity in cultures.

6.2.4.1.4 *Is social capital present in the Montezuma-Apollo relationship?*

The structural dimension of social capital is important in providing members of both organizations access to resources and information to complete the project. The levels and timing of access are part of the contractual terms and ensures that this dimension is present in the relationship. With the help of the consultant, Cicero, Montezuma is able to engage with Apollo during the negotiation process and craft a contract that is fair to both parties. During the outsourcing engagement, Apollo is able to perform the services specified in the contract; Jim and Bob are satisfied with the cost-efficiency they have gained from this outsourcing project. Yet, the quality of the relationship suffers; the elements of the relational dimension are not fully evidenced in the relationship: trust is low, norms of flexibility and commitment are low, some expectations have not been met, and the identification could be a sham. Thus, the presence of structural and cognitive dimensions is evident, but that of relational dimension is not completely evident. In the next section, the discussion focuses on the factors that determine the nature of social capital present in the relationship.

6.2.4.2 Factors that promote social capital in the Montezuma-Apollo relationship

The Montezuma-Apollo relationship is young; it is only in the second year of a possible seven year contract. The age of the relationship contributes to the quality of the partnership; it contributes to a deeper understanding of the partner and the development of enduring ties. Montezuma and Apollo have not had a chance to develop such strengths. In fact, it appears that the firms are in a period of disenchantment with the relationship after the initial period of euphoria. Dealing with these issues together could strengthen the relationship, if such actions contribute to the development of common understanding and trust.

Another factor that could contribute to the development of social capital is a high level of definition in the contract and supporting documents. When there is a high level of definition, these documents will include clear specification of the tasks to be completed and the involvement required from both organizations. This promotes openness and sharing of information between the organizations, because clear parameters have been set of activities related to the project. When such detail is absent, the organizations have to go back to the negotiation table. As Bob explains,

> "The devil is in the details…it is …rightly or wrongly and somewhat uniquely… and this was related to us afterwards but… It took an incredible amount of effort, yet in hindsight we didn't do justice to what needs to be done. we could have got more from some tighter definitions in the contract that we subsequently wrestled with and in that great sort of negotiating game to and fro that we probably conceded some issues that came back to haunt us and later."

This was partly due to Montezuma's lack of experience and partly due to the haste with which they completed the process. Due to these oversights, they have to negotiate scope changes, with Montezuma insisting what they are asking for is within the initial scope and Apollo insisting that this would result in extra costs.

Open and continued <u>communication</u> between the organizations also aids in the development of social capital by promoting the development of positive attitudes about the partner. Such communication will help overcome organizational biases and avoid accumulation of grievances and potential conflict. Communication mechanisms at different levels have been instituted for the project. Besides the meetings at the three levels, many documents are developed and exchanged during the project using mutually agreed formats. In addition, the project management executives spend considerable time developing a rapport. As mentioned before, this occurs both through formal (contract-specified) and informal avenues.

> Informal communication is important; every week I spent at least 1 hour with key customer contacts. We talk about anything we want to talk about, there is no specific agenda. (Tom)

> Informal communication is more important than formal. But you cannot do one and not do the other. Formal communication makes it legal and informal communication makes it work. (Bob)

With the informal communication, all three of them expect to build an enduring personal relationship that will help them solve "problems at the human level." However, such personal rapport cannot overcome every problem in an outsourcing relationship, because some issues are more deep-seated within the organization and beyond the scope of the personal relationship.

One such issue that is adversely affecting the development of social capital in the Montezuma-Apollo relationship is the perceived imbalance in <u>dependence</u>. Dependence between organizations involved in an inter-organizational relationship is inevitable. However, when one party perceives themselves as being more dependent, they will be wary and watch out for opportunistic action of the other party, even when there is no such motive. Jim and Bob both feel that Montezuma is more dependent in the relationship, due to two reasons. One, Apollo is such a huge player in the outsourcing market that losing Montezuma as a customer would not have any major repercussions for them; two, Apollo is their sole provider in the applications area and they do not have any in-house expertise in SAP.

> "We've got all our eggs in one basket right now. We hope to change that, and we're going to have a second provider here soon, but still, for us to change is huge" (Bob)

> "It's impossible for us to leave, extremely painful for us to leave." (Jim)

Tom's appraisal of the situation is also the same. He says, "we are not dependent on them...they are dependent on us." The inflexibility that Montezuma believes is in the relationship may stem from Apollo's knowledge that they have more power in the relationship.

There are conditions within the contract to protect both parties. Talking about benchmarking, Jim explains how it would allow them to help to adjust to changing conditions. He continues

> "...even though we've got this long-term relationship, we've got a hammer, if you will, a baseball bat we can use with them."

This comment comes as a surprise since both Jim and Bob have stressed the importance of the relationship, but now talk in terms of 'clobbering' them. Thus it seems that Montezuma does not believe in the relationship, and may have been just paying lip service to those ideas. Apollo knows that it is a powerful organization and does not feel a pressing need to develop social capital. To develop social capital in the relationship, there should be a knowing intention to do so; both parties should recognize the benefits from social capital and desire the benefits and commit to activities that promote social capital.

The personal rapport between the project executives, who are the boundary spanners, also contributes to the development of social capital in the relationship between the organizations. As Adler and Kwon (2002) state, "the reality of organizations is shaped by the constant interplay" at different levels – individual, business unit, and the organization. This is recognized by all three executives; Jim's and Tom's comments corroborate that.

> "At the end of the day, it comes down--and this sounds very callous--it comes down to 2 people: the primary person on both sides of the fence and if there's chemistry between these people, and if they have the respect and knowledge of their organization in how you get things done. I think that if you fail to establish a relationship on the personal level, I think the relationship is doomed" (Jim)

> "People are important, the whole outsourcing thing does boil down to individuals and relationships. Relationships between companies last longer than that between people. Company reps have to be clear that they can make or break the relationship; they are the people who span the boundaries, so to speak." (Tom)

Jim and Bob believe that part of the reason the project has done well is that both of them have been involved in the project from the inception; in addition, they "sit in all the time" in all the meetings and make sure they are in all the communications loops. Bob mentions that this continuous involvement is very important to both of them. Naturally, they have been upset by the fact that the first executive from Apollo, with whom they had started the project, had left.

> "And our project executive decided to retire from Montezuma, from Apollo, actually… But, that's a significant change, especially if--you know, the foundation that I laid is we like to operate on a human level. Now, the good news is that the replacement is certainly not a clone, but a close approximation of the person, reasonable approximation. So, it's different. Um, but, I think that--again, when you operate on a human level, that's probably the most significant change you can make. To me, you know, that was huge."

Tom also senses this uneasiness and thinks there may be a benefit in bringing a new person in his place. Thus, while there is talk of "focusing on the relationship, going to lunch, and playing golf", the personal rapport between the executives is not all that it could be.

A final factor that promotes the growth of social capital in the relationship is the involvement of external parties. Consultants like Cicero have a methodology to help and facilitate the engagement process and to create a shared cognitive scheme for the two organizations. When asked what they would recommend to organizations considering outsourcing, Jim and Bob commented on the benefits of having a consultant hold their hands during the initial period.

To maintain the social capital in the relationship, it is necessary to "reassess and reevaluate the relationship so that it does not become stagnant". According to Bob, "it is the same as in a marriage; you have to spend time reestablishing wedding vows." Revealing his dissatisfaction with the relationship, Tom comments:

> "You have to revitalize the relationship, bring in new ideas - sometimes that involves getting people from outside."

To avoid getting stuck with non-productive practices, it is necessary to continuously monitor if both organizations are able to meet their expectations from the relationship. Such assessment will be seen as a "sign of caring for the other party" and will promote the development of social capital in the relationship.

6.2.4.3 Social capital facilitates the combination and exchange of resources in the Montezuma-Apollo relationship

The theoretical framework suggests that social capital provides facilitating conditions for the combination and exchange and resources necessary for the project. The structural elements of social capital provide the access necessary for the exchange of resources in the outsourcing situation. It ensures that <u>access</u> to the right levels and departments are allowed to complete the project as planned. Further, the structures and processes that have been put in place ensure that information reaches the right person quickly.

"Money is a great incentive for a shared vision" (Bob). Besides the contractual terms and penalties, the compensation system that is built into the contract rewards the executives and the staff on meeting the outsourcing milestones is a <u>motivator</u> to ensure the give-and-take necessary in the outsourcing relationship takes place.

> "My counterpart from Apollo, he has a very hefty part of his salary at risk subject to our customer satisfaction. His primary purpose is to make sure that we're delighted and happy with their services. And he has a substantial part of his personal compensation at risk if he fails to deliver that." (Jim)

> "My incentive, my remuneration – and Jim's - is based on the performance of Apollo and we have made their incentive based on Montezuma's and in that way we have tried to force them into the same space, but…SLA[4]s do the same, they are penalized for failure - if they do not make the SLA levels, they are penalized …but so am I … So I have every interest in making sure they are successful." (Bob)

In addition to the bonuses, Montezuma has used the "spot reward program from (their) money pool" to Apollo employees directly. Thus, in addition to the <u>value anticipated</u> by the organizations from completing the project, employees in both organizations anticipate personal gain from the relationship, another condition that promotes the exchange of resources between the organizations for the completion of the project.

<u>Combination capability</u>, the ability to recognize the value of a piece of information and assimilate it, requires the use of shared language and codes by the two organizations. Since the employees at Apollo have access to the IS staff at Montezuma, they are able to interact using a common vocabulary of technical terms. Similarly, the executives and their bosses are able to communicate in the common language of technology and business management. Combination capability is dependent on prior experience and knowledge of the subject as well. Montezuma is struggling to assimilate all the new information; part of the problem is that Montezuma has no experience with this technology. In an environment that supports the development of elements of the relational dimension, particularly trust, norms of cooperation, and identification, the sharing and the presence of elements of the relational dimension would aid the organizations in this exchange. As we have already seen, this is a problem in the Montezuma-Apollo relationship. Jim recognizes this:

---

[4] Service Level Agreements

"We have got some cultural change to get our head around and it is happening. It hasn't been that easy. We would like to think that we are continuing to do business, but it hasn't stopped as a result of the outsourcing. There is certainly pent-up demand from the user community, we are trying to find how that pent-up demand should be scheduled, prioritized, and handled."

6.2.4.4 Assessment: Satisfaction

While formal service measures such as milestones and deliverables are required for assessing the progress of a project, a subjective evaluation of satisfaction is a commonly accepted measure of the success of an outsourcing project and determinant of the future of the relationship. All contractual terms are being met and there have been no major glitches in the project; so, Jim, Bob, and Tom are satisfied with the overall progress of the project. The points of dissatisfaction for Montezuma are the lack of innovation and the perception of inflexibility. Given the image of Apollo, Jim and Bob had expectations for innovation. However, they feel they are not getting that, and Bob attributes this to Apollo's lack of interest in doing so.

"I thought there would be more. I guess on an expectation scale, with the image of Apollo... I guess they would counter with the statement you didn't buy the gold solution, you bought the brass solution."

Regarding innovation, Tom offers this rebuttal:

"Cost-cutting is always the #1 priority for a client. They say that innovation is important, but it is a mindset. If they viewed IT as a competitive weapon and innovation as a differentiator, then maybe they would be willing to outsource at same cost as their expenses. As long as they do not view IT in that manner in the organization, innovation is a challenge."

However, he wants to "drive innovation into this environment" and is thinking of ways to do that. He also feels that if Montezuma has such expectations, they should "say they want more." Thus, there is a lack of shared vision about achieving innovation. Tom's comments are actually reflective of the manner in which IS is viewed at Montezuma.

"We (the IS organization) are viewed in the value chain as bringing in "no value" (gestures quotes) and so at the end of the day there was no compelling reason to build an empire of resources supporting a new system."

This is a problem faced by many IS organizations (Bashein and Markus, 1997) and this negative perception affects the functioning of the IS organization. All their activities are measured by two yardsticks – whether the required outcome has been achieved and whether it contributes to the credibility of the organization. Having to focus on these internal issues, Jim and Bob sometimes has not been able to provide Apollo with the affirmation that they would like. As Tom comments, "we have done good work here, we better (emphasizes) be recognized." However, this "good work" does not translate into additional opportunities for Apollo. This is a loss for a vendor, because they feel that the efforts they have expended and the learning that has occurred needs to be leveraged into extended contracts and future opportunities. When this does not happen, vendors feel they are not able to leverage the learning that has happened during the relationship and there was not enough "pay back from the investment."

6.2.5   Case study conclusion

From the examination of this case using the "social capital" framework, it is seen that only two of the three dimensions of social capital are present in the relationship. The structural dimension is a given in these situations of contractual governance, providing access and mechanisms for interaction. The technical and business knowledge of both organizations and the business environment contributes to the development of shared interpretations, establishing the presence of the cognitive dimension. Due to perceptions of inflexibility in the manner Apollo is handling the project and dependency imbalance in favor of Apollo, the relational dimension of the relationship does not develop. Yet, the cognitive dimension supported by the structural dimension facilitates the combination and exchange of resources necessary for this project. Given the experience of Apollo in projects of this nature, they are able to implement tried-and-tested methods in completing the requirements for the project. However, lack of important relational elements such as trust and commitment leave both parties somewhat dissatisfied with the other as a partner, even while they recognize the others' good qualities. Montezuma is appreciative of Apollo's process discipline and Apollo sees Montezuma as a refined partner.

Given the emphasis paid to the human element in discussions with the three executives on the management of the outsourcing project, it seems strange that such a "disconnect" has happened. One of the reasons for this disconnect may be the focus of the Montezuma executives in ensuring credibility for the IS organization. Jim mentions that one of the drivers for the recent changes in the IS organization is that they were "looking for credibility." Seeing this project as an opportunity to prove themselves to the organization, they wanted to ensure that the project would "meet the goals of the organization quickly". This haste is seen in all phases of the project – the selection process, the negotiation process, and the transition process. However, this does not give them time to build up trust and other elements of the relational dimension in the relationship with Apollo, particularly given their lack of experience in the outsourcing arena. This problem is compounded when the first Apollo manager leaves. Additionally, the IS management at Montezuma want the project to be cost-effective, since they are under pressure to reinvent the IS function as a leaner and more effective organization. Anxious about the possibility that they would not be able to control the Apollo elephant, they use the contract as a "whip-hand". Thus, even while they were espousing relationship ideals, their actions are geared towards a different goal. Tom's comment sums it up: "And if you don't do enough caring and feeding in the relationship, then it goes sour." And "sour" relationships do not lend themselves to supporting extended business opportunities.

6.3   Case 2-Chickasaw and Zeus

This second case presents the story of a long-lasting outsourcing relationship between two organizations. This case is interesting because this outsourcing arrangement has not only withstood major changes in the client and vendor organizations, but also disagreements that almost forced the cancellation of the contract. The client and vendor organizations have been able to get through rocky periods and "out of divorce court" to come to an agreement to work together for a "win-win proposition." The focus in this case is on the cognitive dimension of social capital and the impact of communication on the development of social capital.

6.3.1   Introduction

This case also involves two very large organizations in the United States. The client, Chickasaw is a major United States airline company, with its headquarters in south central

United States. Incorporated in 1985, the flies to 127 domestic and 101 international destinations and offers additional connecting service through alliances with domestic and foreign carriers. As of December 2003, the company operated 579 aircraft.

The vendor, Zeus, has been in IS services for a long time and is a leading provider of information technology and business process outsourcing services today. Zeus also operates out of south central United States. Incorporated in 1962, Zeus has grown into a global organization with offices in every continent, and is a major competitor of Apollo, the vendor in the first case. Unlike Apollo, Zeus does not have a hardware division, and is in the business of providing managed services alone.

Table 6-3: Interviewees in the Chickasaw-Zeus case

Name of interviewee	Organization	Position	Duration of interview	Taped?
Bill	Chickasaw (Client)	Technology Director	3.5 hours	Yes
Cindy	Zeus (Vendor)	Client Executive	1.25 hours	Yes
John	Zeus	Client Executive	2 hours	Yes

Three individuals were interviewed to get information[5] about the Chickasaw-Zeus deal. Bill, the Technical Director at Chickasaw, has been with the organization since 1984, long before the organization considered outsourcing. Chickasaw first outsourced to Zeus in 1991, and Bill has been involved with the outsourcing arrangement since then. Today, he is the key person in charge of the outsourcing arrangement for Chickasaw and has "ownership of the contract."

Two client executives at Zeus agreed to share their experiences on this outsourcing arrangement. One of them is Cindy, the client executive who is currently in charge of the applications outsourcing for this outsourcing arrangement. Cindy has been with this account since its inception, but has been the lead executive for this account for just the past four years. Cindy suggested that an interview also be conducted with John, since he often represented Zeus at conferences and could explain Zeus' views on outsourcing and experiences with outsourcing. The Chickasaw and Zeus executives also agreed to be available for clarification; short conversations and email exchanges were conducted with Cindy and Bill to clarify the answers to some of the questions[6].

6.3.2 The Outsourcing Project

At the time it was first signed in 1991, Chickasaw's agreement with Zeus was the largest outsourcing agreement in the world and the first major outsourcing relationship in the airline industry. The ten-year contract required that Zeus provide data processing, systems development, system integration, hardware and software maintenance, telecommunications voice and data network services, and other telecommunications services to Chickasaw.

The primary motive behind the outsourcing arrangement was cost reduction, made even more urgent by the fact that Chickasaw had to file for bankruptcy protection in 1990. There was also the recognition that Chickasaw needed to focus on their core business and did not need to

---

[5] Besides the interviews, information on the Chickasaw-Zeus relationship was obtained from a case prepared at the University of Texas in 1996 that details the first few years of the outsourcing arrangement.
6 These were not counted as interviews, since these were just follow-ups to the original interview.

82

expend energy to build expertise in areas where other organizations could do much better than them. Thus, virtually all to Chickasaw's IT was outsourced to Zeus. However, the agreement provided Chickasaw some flexibility; it also stipulated that Chickasaw could use other vendors where Zeus could not provide services because of lack of expertise or geographical presence and that Zeus would provide the necessary interfaces and support in such situations.

6.3.3   The Client-Vendor Relationship

Once Chickasaw made the decision to outsource, it went through a long and rigorous process to ensure that "all the kinks were worked out" of the relationship. Chickasaw's negotiation team had representation from all divisions within the organization and included external advisors. Zeus, being an established outsourcing vendor, has its own internal consulting service, and they use the services of that division when they need additional counsel on an outsourcing contract. The two primary components of the resulting contract were the Master Agreement and the Services Agreement. The Master Agreement laid out the general terms for the relationship and the Services Agreement included all the details of the resources that were to be provided and the levels and metrics for the provision of those resources. The goal was to lay out these specifications as completely and concisely as possible, so that not only were the requirements in terms of the services were clear, but also the responsibilities of different groups in the organization.

In the early periods of the contract, Chickasaw was very cost focused due to their bankrupt status. The focus of the outsourcing arrangement was on maintaining the legacy systems to extract solid performance from those systems, an area that was Zeus' forte. With Zeus providing considerable value to Chickasaw under the terms of the contract and lavishing attention on them as one of their largest customers, Zeus and Chickasaw established a productive and "happy" relationship. Zeus consolidated Chickasaw's four data centers into one central location and updated the operating environment, building on the efficiencies that an organization of their size and nature were able to provide. Chickasaw's technology division was reduced to a staff of just twenty-five from the several thousand that served the organization before.

Things changed in the mid-nineties when a new management team took over Chickasaw and was successful in rebuilding the organization and making it profitable. Chickasaw started to move away from an absolute focus on cost to where they were willing to invest in technology to produce benefits that they desired. Zeus found themselves dealing with a new management team, with whom they would have to build new relationships and prove the benefits of the outsourcing arrangement to. Further, as Bill explained, with the changes in the management team at Chickasaw, there is less first-hand knowledge of the contract and its terms. This lack of understanding creates tension between the organizations.

"In the five years after it was signed, only one person from Chickasaw who sat at the negotiating table remained with the airline and only two senior managers who lived through the outsourcing process were still here. With each generation of new people there is not only less first-hand knowledge of the contract but greater resistance to adopting it as it stands."

Chickasaw's expectations have changed and they started expecting newer and innovative technology and ideas from Zeus. Chickasaw was moving towards client/server architecture, while the nature of the original agreement with Zeus revolved around the mainframe infrastructure and the associated approach to business. Within Chickasaw, there is a growing dissatisfaction towards Zeus. Many feel that Chickasaw could manage things on their own much better, though some of the senior people realize that there it is nearly impossible to bring everything back in after a total outsourcing project. As Bill explains,

> "The time and expense bring back everything in from the outsourced environment is substantial – we could buy an airplane with that money."

For Zeus, the Chickasaw account was becoming unattractive, since it was turning out to be non-profitable. This was partly due to the way the contract was structured relative to Zeus' internal organization. To service an account, the Zeus client executives purchase services from internal service providers. As Bill explains,

> "I could contractually buy a service from you in my account for less money than you could buy it from you internal service provider. So, you were in a world of hurt. And, of course, Zeus looks at the accounts: Are they profitable? "No, we're losing money.""

This lack of profitability affected the way Zeus viewed the account. They were not willing to place competent people on the account.

> "I didn't get the cream of Zeus crop. They had to drag people: "I don't want to go to that damn place. That's a bad account.""

Bill now knows that the Zeus client executive in charge of the Chickasaw account at that time portrayed Chickasaw as an uncooperative and unprofitable account.

> "We're not cooperative, we won't pay the damn bill, we're always yelling, we're always asking for thing we're not entitled to, and it took 6 months before there was a real realization at senior levels of Zeus that the problem wasn't quite as they depicted it."

However, once the Zeus management realized the problem lay with the client executive, they changed out the team. By then, the relationship had deteriorated and Chickasaw was considering leaving the account. The Zeus management realized that "not only were they going to lose the business, but they were going to lose it for reasons that weren't what they were being told," (Bill) and they decided they wanted to save the account, especially since this was a "big account". Chickasaw decided to look around for other vendors, but finally decided to stay with Zeus.

> "We spent the late part of '98, '99 dating six other vendors. And when we got done, you might say we all went to a marriage counselor and figured out that we're better off married than divorcing and looking for a new bride because in fact, when you got through everything else, they were still the best deal in the entire town." (Bill)

When they got back together, the Chickasaw executives and the Zeus executives made every effort to clear up all the misunderstanding. They met many times giving both sides a good chance to communicate all the problems they had and create a more equitable agreement, given the changed circumstances. Bill recounts the events that followed.

> "And they also had a chance to air all their grievances, and it wasn't one-sided; there was unhappiness on the other side, too in terms of the contract and in the way they were used was more favorable to us, somewhat unfair to them, and they were used that way. So both sides had these rubs and these sores, that had built up to a point where it was almost a love-hate relationship, more hate than love." (Bill)

So, they worked together for almost six months "very seriously and hard to make sure that everything that would upset both sides was thoroughly laid out on the table and looked at and assessed" and amended. The resulting agreement addressed the concerns of both sides "fully and equitably", according to Cindy, "and *they* have a better relationship today than what *they* had."

The changes in the outsourcing arrangement were not limited to rewriting the terms of the agreement. Chickasaw went from a total outsourcing situation to a selective outsourcing situation where they have in-house programmers doing the distributed systems and web-based applications development for the company. Demonstrating the strength of the Chickasaw-Zeus relationship, Cindy comments that "this is a positive move." Still, they have more have more programmers outside than inside today. Zeus has over a thousand people working on the applications outsourcing project for Chickasaw, of which more than half are dedicated resources for the project.

The outsourcing management teams at both firms depend on the relationship to manage the account, even though they have a more complete contract now. "A lot is unsaid" in the contract, according to Cindy. John elaborates:

> "The contract is like a prenuptial agreement. It's the kind of thing that when you look at it you hope you never have to look at it again; …you know it is just something you have to do and you know when you are done no matter how much time or care you have put in it there are going to be situations that fall into the gray line of the contract anyway. Hopefully you have a relationship where both sides will try to do what is fair when those unexpected situations occur; if you have that I think you are fine. The contract has very little to do with the day-to-day operations and management of the services. Again I think the best analogy is the prenuptial agreement 80-90% of what you talk about is what will happen when you split up. 20% is what will happen when you are supporting or operating the deal so you hope you don't ever see or talk about 80-90% of what you put in the contract to begin with."

It is a unanimous belief that open communication is the backbone of a good outsourcing relationship. Cindy elaborated the role of communication in the relationship. When both organizations are willing to come to the table and negotiate "where things are not written in black and white in the contract," the account will be more successful. Communication also clarifies the "metrics to be used to measure the performance and compliance of the two organizations."

Today, both organizations view their relationship as one of "mutual understanding and respect." Neither organization sees a power imbalance; while Chickasaw is dependent on Zeus for their IS needs, Chickasaw is also one of Zeus' larger accounts. All parties, the management of the account on both sides and the end-users in Chickasaw are happy with the progress of the outsourcing deal.

6.3.4 Through the "Social Capital" Lens

Having presented the background and the story of the outsourcing relationship, the focus now turns to analysis of the field text using the social capital framework.

6.3.4.1 Social Capital in the Chickasaw-Zeus relationship

As in case 1, the determination of the presence of social capital in the relationship is made by examining whether the different elements of the three dimensions of social capital are manifest in the relationship.

6.3.4.1.1 Structural dimension: Access patterns and appropriable organization

The structuring of interaction patterns through the contract is a common feature in majority of the cases described in this chapter. Chickasaw and Zeus have a three-tier communication structure set up, similar to the Montezuma-Apollo engagement. In addition, they have other routine sessions that provide both organizations insight into activities related to the project in both organizations. One of these is a weekly meeting of the key personnel from both organizations who are responsible for the outsourcing engagement, two from Chickasaw, and three from Zeus. At this meeting, issues are brought out into the open; according to Bill, many things are discussed at those weekly meetings that could not be said elsewhere.

Just like Apollo, Zeus also has structures and routines that are developed in a "highly disciplined environment" that Cindy characterizes as "neurotic in terms of its adherence". These forms of appropriable organization are a characteristic of all established vendors. Additionally, John explains that "if you go with Cicero[7] or someone like that, they bring a project methodology and a process that gets you from the beginning of this process to the end." Clients and vendors can adopt these methodologies in their outsourcing engagement.

6.3.4.1.2 Cognitive dimension: Shared understanding

One of the things that define the renewed relationship is a focus on shared understanding. Given their past history, "mutual agreement on expectations is a very big one" in this relationship. Cindy further elaborates:

> "We need a definition of what defines success; it has to be agreed on by both parties. If you don't know what it is A+ job is, how can you do an A+ job? There needs to be an understanding on how and the way to measure performance between the two co operations."

As in the Montezuma-Apollo case, interactions are channeled through the key people, ensuring that there are individuals in both organizations who know all the details about the outsourcing arrangement. Bill believes that one of the reasons that they have been successful is that he "essentially manages and owns the contract." Working with his counterparts in Zeus, he is able to establish a shared vision regarding the expectations from the project and the activities that need to be completed for the project. These have also been recorded in the new service level documents that came out of the re-negotiations. As Bill explains,

> "When we wrote our contract, I think it is 21 pages of services that they give us. And there are 67 pages of standards against 21 pages of services. So what we've done is set all our expectations…on whatever I need relative to the services that are provided. And over here, it says how often they are required to do that, what the timeframes are, and all that other stuff. So, if you built in the expectations, if you're clear about the expectations, you're clear about what's required. You have to know your vendor, you have to make sure he understands your business, there has to be a mutual understanding as to how

---

[7] A consultancy firm

you're going to contribute to each other's success, and then you have to make sure that everybody understands that you guys are going to make this work."

6.3.4.1.3 *Relational dimension: Trust, norms, obligations & expectations, identification*

"Start with trust. There has to be trust by the customer that they have chosen a partner or service provider that they believe can do the services." (John)

This trust is a central part of the relationship and it is fostered by "consistent delivery on the part of the both organizations on mutual expectations." The difficult times that the organizations have come through have made them realize the value of trust and the importance of not violating that trust. Trust is developed when both parties feel that the other party will not act opportunistically; Bill understands that the vendor may be tempted to behave opportunistically.

"They have a contractual obligation to reduce my spend, but they are selfishly motivated to increase my spend, and we understand that dichotomies are out there and that conflict is there. So we know when people sort of lean one way or the other they are not meeting their internal goals."

To avoid such problems they have set up mechanisms for open communication, one of them being a governance sub-committee. On the Zeus side, the sub-committee includes the client executives for the different outsourced areas; there are three client executives including Cindy on this sub-committee. Bill and his assistant represent Chickasaw on the sub-committee. Bill explains:

"We have a little governance sub-committee that meets once a week right now. When we get to once a month we got some friction. In that room we can say whatever we want, anyway that we want. So we are blunt and to the point…we use names"

Such frank discussions promote openness and an awareness of the needs of both organizations. Instead of looking for solutions in the "lines of the contract", in these discussions they identify areas that are critical to the organizations and commit to "making it work". This also creates an environment of flexibility and cooperation for both parties. Chickasaw management understands that resources at Zeus may sometimes not stretch to cover all their needs. In such cases, Zeus and Chickasaw will work together to find solutions or Chickasaw may try to find an external solution. However, Chickasaw choosing another external vendor for an activity is not a threat to the Chickasaw-Zeus relationship, as Bill explains:

"And he (Zeus) decides that he wants to improve the service level, get me a price break, and keep it or say, "I can't really do any better. That's a minor thing with me. Why don't you give it to them (another vendor) and be happier with them?" So, we (Chickasaw and Zeus) keep our relationship, we work together, and I'm not going to go below what gets them (Zeus) in trouble…he (Zeus) is always my vendor of choice, so I don't do things behind his (Zeus') back, and we have tremendous flexibility in our relationship."

This openness, flexibility, and commitment to the relationship have developed because both parties saw the benefits of being in the relationship and try to deal with each other fairly. In each interaction they try to understand the concerns of the other organization as well.

"It stresses not doing positional negotiation, but in fact looking at the concerns of both parties and formulating solutions to those concerns in the contract that meet both parties' concerns so instead of being on the opposite side of the table and negotiating with somebody you just go "here are our concern, here are your concerns lets get on the same side of the table we can formulate a solution that meets both!" So it's a working together vs. working against each other approach."

Both organizations are thus aware of the expectations of the other organization and hold a shared expectation that the relationship will continue for a long time. Cindy believes that Chickasaw is meeting its obligations to Zeus; this sentiment is reciprocated by Bill in his evaluation of Zeus' dealings with Chickasaw. Chickasaw and Zeus "see themselves as one" (Nahapiet and Ghoshal, 1998; p256), working together towards a common goal.

6.3.4.1.4 *Is social capital present in the Chickasaw-Zeus relationship?*

The Chickasaw-Zeus relationship is marked by the presence of all three dimensions of social capital, though there have been periods in the past where some of the elements of social capital were missing in the relationship. In the initial stages of the relationship, there was shared understanding and the organizations were working towards developing the elements of the relational dimension of social capital. However, with the changes in Chickasaw accompanied with the changes in management, there is a rift between the organizations, a lack of understanding compounded by absence of trust and commitment to the relationship. When the two organizations assessed their relationship, they realized that they want to save the relationship. So, with the help of external mediators, they entered into re-negotiations. During the prolonged negotiation period, both organizations invested time and effort to ensure that the second time around there was a common understanding about the goals and processes of the outsourcing arrangement. It is also seen that the key players have invested time and effort in ensuring mutual trust and commitment in the relationship.

6.3.4.2 Factors that promote social capital in the Chickasaw-Zeus relationship

One of the striking factors of the current Chickasaw-Zeus relationship is the determination of the parties to "make it work." Using an analogy that is used frequently to explain the outsourcing relationship, Bill explains:

"I always characterize it as an old-fashioned Roman Catholic marriage. Divorce is not authorized... So, you better go into it to make it work. And both sides better work their butts off to make it work because you are going to be in it forever."

Their long history together has made each organization aware of the "tolerance levels" of the other organization, and has helped develop a comfort zone for them to complete their interactions in without fear of undue repercussions or opportunistic behavior. Thus, the age of the relationship contributes to the development of social capital in the Chickasaw-Zeus relationship. This can be contrasted to the Montezuma-Apollo relationship, where both organizations have not had time to develop awareness of the "tolerance levels" of the other party and end up with an unsatisfactory relationship.

As a sidebar, it is worth noting the frequent use of the marriage analogy in explaining the outsourcing relationship. While many of the interviewees (in the organizations in this case and others) also equated marriage to a relationship, Bill has hit the nail on its head when he characterizes it as "an old-fashioned Roman Catholic marriage." In an old-fashioned Roman Catholic marriage, family elders meet, discuss, and finalize the marriage contract, sometimes after acrimonious discussions on dowry and wedding expenses. The two individuals who have to live out the contract have little to say in this phase and often do not know what to expect – but they have to make it work. Similarly, in many outsourcing arrangements, the negotiation teams with representation from different departments of the organization meet and finalize the outsourcing contract. In the operationalization stage, the outsourcing management teams from both organizations have to forge a relationship and complete the project, often overcoming the acrimony of the negotiation stage and trying to decipher the various clauses in the contract – which may exactly be why many of the interviewees mentioned that they do not delve into the contract in the operationalization stage.

Another factor that contributes to the development of social capital in the relationship is the high level of definition in the contract and supporting documents. Both organizations have taken care to include clear expectations of the requirements of the outsourcing arrangement in the amendments to the contract that were the result of the round of re-negotiations. Both parties now realize that this definition and structure are essential to avoid problems in the relationship. This is evidenced by Cindy's comment:

> "There are always assortments of contention in any given moment in a contract; so it goes back to having the structure and place that allows for the resolution of those items."

The importance of communication is emphasized by all parties involved. Chickasaw and Zeus executives believe that the shared understanding is facilitated by the communication schemes they have in place. Cindy comments that this is necessary to avoid problems similar to those that developed earlier in the relationship, especially as "expectations change every time the business environment changes" and communication is essential "to raise new issues and to try to drive out areas of gray space."

The role of the boundary spanners in enabling communication is evidenced in the Chickasaw-Zeus case. When problems first developed in the outsourcing relationship, it was compounded by the filtering in the reports of the previous client executive. This also sheds light on the bi-directional relationship between social capital and communication. Communication can develop social capital; but when elements of social capital such as shared understanding and commitment are reduced, it will affect the communication between the organizations – not so much in the amount of communication, but by distorting the communication between the organizations.

Zeus encourages their executives to build relationships with their counterparts in the client organization. John explains that this is considered a responsibility of the client executive at Zeus:

> "In addition to the standard governance – the three-tier hierarchy[8] – regular scheduled meeting and reports and all things like that – I would have the primary responsibility to set up a relationship beyond just a business relationship with one or two customers and every key customer on our account has counterparts that they were signed to do a relationship management job."

Further, Cindy contends that the interaction patterns between the parties are based more on the "agreement between the executive operating teams for the two companies" rather than on any

---

[8] Operations people meeting on a daily or weekly basis, then client executives meeting on a monthly basis to go over service levels and projects and overall status, and then there is top management meetings that occur quarterly.

formal agreements in the contract. Given this focus on relationship building, informal communication is also considered very important.

> "The informal communication is pretty much how you build and maintain the relationship. Also you will find out before issues become problems you know areas of concern that you can address before they blow up." (John)

Cindy also mentions the importance of attending corporate events, where one can "understand your customer...and how things get done in a corporation." Among the interviewees for this research, this attention and effort on relationship-building was unique to Chickasaw and Zeus. Though this question was raised many times when people talked about informal communication, respondents stated that their interactions were limited to their counterparts. It is probable that the near-separation has made both organizations aware of the need to understand each other and stay connected at different levels.

In the Montezuma-Apollo case, the imbalance in dependence created problems in the relationship. With Zeus and Chickasaw, under the renewed agreement, all parties concur that the dependence is mutual. This mutuality actually promotes both parties' openness and commitment; it ensures that obligations and expectations are met. Both parties try hard to find common ground in their dealings, exchanging information that will be beneficial to both parties. Thus, the increase in elements of social capital in the relationship binds the two organizations closer and increases their dependence on the other.

This satisfying state of affairs can be contrasted with the events that transpired before the negotiations. Having completely outsourced their IS to Zeus, Chickasaw is irritated by the seeming indifference to their needs. Just as in the Montezuma-Apollo case, this causes problems in the relationship, and it is compounded by broken ties between the boundary spanners, causing the relationship to fray to the point of being severed. Yet, with the efforts of external parties and by addressing issues that they became aware of through their assessments of the outsourcing arrangement and the inter-organizational relationship, they were able to mend their differences and continue to work together.

The current satisfaction with the relationship also has a lot to do with the personal rapport between the project executives. Both organizations recognize that "you have to have the right people" (John), since "relationships with each account manager takes on a different look" (Cindy). The boundary spanner should be "somebody that can pitch your company psychology and the way you do business, but will respond and partner with *the partner organization* in the way they want to work" (Bill).

6.3.4.3 Social capital facilitates the combination and exchange of resources in the Chickasaw-Zeus relationship

The theoretical framework suggests that social capital provides facilitating conditions for the combination and exchange and resources necessary for the project. In this case also, the structural dimension of social capital provides the access necessary for the exchange of resources in the outsourcing situation. The trust and the norms of cooperation and commitment increase the sharing of information between the organizations.

Chickasaw and Zeus are motivated by the mutual benefits they can receive. Chickasaw "gets all the expertise of a Zeus", which Bill believes is not something he could have had in-house. Zeus wants to be successful in this relationship because failure of such a large account would "hit the Wall Street Journal" (Bill) and ruin their reputation. So both organizations are "mutually motivated to make both sides work". Bill believes that this brings his organization and himself credibility within the organization, while reducing his workload. As he explains:

> "I have got experts running a main frame and I don't have to worry about the budget. I am used to having… we used to have 5 data centers for goodness sakes – in-house and it was a full time job with a big staff to take care of it all. I got one guy to yell at now – the guy who is responsible for Zeus managing the damn thing."

Cindy also believes that beyond the completion of the outsourcing arrangement, there is value derived from the outsourcing arrangement; Zeus has a continuing relationship with Chickasaw and they are "investing in the future together." To be able to work together towards common goals, the organizations need to be able to identify and assimilate information required for the outsourcing arrangement. The social capital in the relationship, particularly the shared understanding, enhances the combination capability required for them to do so. As Bill states, Chickasaw is able to "leverage the greater collective innovation of Zeus" to bring innovation in IS to Chickasaw and have been able to become leaders in the application of technology in the airline industry.

6.3.4.4 Assessment: Satisfaction

Chickasaw and Zeus are both satisfied with their current relationship, because of the "equitable terms" (Cindy) of the outsourcing arrangement and also because they are both able to achieve the goals for this outsourcing arrangement and provide future benefits for each other. The presence of all three dimensions of social capital not only ensures that the goals of the current outsourcing arrangement are met, but also that the organizations will plan to work together in the future.

Assessment serves an even more important purpose when things do not look so rosy. It was the continual assessment of the outsourcing arrangement that goes on at different levels that alerted the organizations to the fact that there were serious issues to be addressed in the outsourcing arrangement.

6.3.5 Case study conclusion

Chickasaw and Zeus have had a long but tumultuous relationship. In the initial stages of the outsourcing arrangement, because of the attention given to developing an agreement on the requirements and measures, shared understanding and agreement on obligations and expectations develop between the organizations. However, as the situation within Chickasaw changes and many of the key people leave Chickasaw and are replaced by less competent people at Zeus, the shared understanding that existed between the two organizations of the goals of the outsourcing arrangement is lost. It is interesting to note how distortion in communication contributes to this situation. The relationship falters and the organizations are ready to breach the contract. With the help of external mediators and the remaining links, the organizations re*define* the outsourcing arrangement re-establish a common understanding.

The organizations are satisfied with the progress with the amended agreement. The relationship is rich in social capital and facilitates the combination and exchange of knowledge that is necessary for the development and delivery of the services defined in the outsourcing agreement. The current relationship is viewed as equitable and providing benefits for both organizations. Keeping in mind the benefits that can be derived from a long-term relationship,

Chickasaw and Zeus are careful to pay attention to developing elements of social capital in the relationship. As Bill puts it,

"You should put the same amount of time and attention into this that you would if you want to get married, you know. You don't marry on lust; you marry pragmatically on building a relationship. Some people do, but those are the ones that fail."

6.4 Case 3- Glacier and Hercules

. This case description presents the story of an inter-organizational relationship where forethought and planning build a collaborative environment where three organizations – the IS organization within Glacier, Hercules and another vendor work together in a multi-party alliance to serve the IS needs of Glacier. The focus in this case is on the structural dimension and the role of assessment in the development of social capital.

6.4.1 Introduction

Glacier is a large publicly owned chemicals company headquartered in the north-eastern part of the United States. Glacier has more than twenty business units and its operations are spread all over the world, making the provision of information technology and services to the organization challenging. Following a review by an external consultant, Glacier's IS organization trimmed a good percentage of its spending and was viewed as being extremely capable within the organization. However, changes in the organization prompted another hard look at IS spending and the IS management realized that there was a "compelling requirement for greater variability in our supplying of IT services", which the IS management believed could be better met by external providers. Therefore, Glacier formed an alliance with two major vendors, one of which was Hercules. The other was Minerva; though a representative from Minerva was interviewed, that person was not involved with the Glacier account. Both organizations continue to compete against each other for new business from Glacier.

Hercules is one of the world's leading technology services organizations and has operations world-wide. It is considered a leader in the area of application outsourcing, and is able to offer clients quality services by virtue of establishments in various parts of the world.

Table 6-4: Interviewees in the Glacier-Hercules case

Name of interviewee	Organization	Position	Duration of interview	Taped?
Vicki	Glacier (Client)	Project Executive	1 hour	No
Anna	Glacier	IS Manager	1.5 hours	No
Mike	Hercules (Vendor)	Associate Partner	50 minutes	Yes
Dave	Hercules	Client Manager	1.45 hours	Yes

Contact with Glacier was made through a cold call that was picked up by the Vice President – Information Systems of Glacier. After a brief conversation, he suggested that Vicki be contacted to provide information on Glacier's outsourcing experience. Vicki agreed to the interview and asked that the interview protocol be sent to her so that she could study it. She was very concerned about confidentiality even though she was assured that all information would be confidential and firms would only be identified by pseudonyms. She still chose not to elaborate on few of the questions related to the structural dimension of social capital as well as on the selection of the vendor. This is understandable given that Glacier is managing a concurrent relationship between two vendors. Anna was an IS manager at Glacier (she no longer works for the company) and was contacted through a personal contact. Given her position in the organizational hierarchy, she was not able to shed light on all aspects of the relationship, but had interesting insights into changes at the operational level and how that would affect the perception of the outsourcing within the client organization.

Mike and Dave were willing to talk about everything but the specifics of the contract, given Hercules' competitive position with Minerva. Mike is one of the top executives at the center that runs the SAP system. Dave's responsibilities are more "functionally focused and involve supporting the application layer of the software".

The Glacier-Hercules-Minerva alliance was among the first in the chemicals industry and has received some attention in the media, particularly in journals dealing with issues of interest to this industry. A couple of these articles, one in *Chemical Week* and one in *Chemical Reporter* were also examined to understand how the positioning of the Glacier-Hercules dyad in the Glacier-Hercules-Minerva triad could have affected the decisions that were made related to the management of the relationship.

6.4.2 The Outsourcing Project

The IS alliance was formed in the latter part of the 1990s, with the responsibility for the IS services for Glacier being split between the three organizations. The move for outsourcing came from the Vice President of IS at Glacier. Glacier IS management approached the problem of convincing the employees of the merit of outsourcing in a similar manner as the Montezuma IS management (in case 1). They got comparative information on the cost-efficiencies of doing it in-house versus getting a vendor to provide the service before addressing the employees.

The outsourcing arrangement involved displacement of a majority of the Glacier IS employees; more than seventy percent of the IS employees were transferred to Hercules and Minerva. The remaining IS employees are responsible for the "stewardship and architecture of the company's IT operations." Under the original contract terms, Hercules was responsible for the applications in manufacturing and production planning systems, while Minerva was responsible for the infrastructure and all the other applications work in North America, and all the applications work in the other locations.

A few years down the road, Glacier decided to invest in an enterprise resource planning system. Glacier chose SAP and initially started the project in-house. Later, Glacier management decided that it would be better to have an external organization handle this project. Even though both Hercules and Minerva were working with Glacier, they also had to bid along with other vendors for the project and Hercules got responsibility for Glacier's ambitious SAP rollout.

Under the contract, Hercules will implement the ERP system within a year of signing the contract, and then take on support and maintenance of it for a six-year term. As in the previous two cases, internal and external lawyers, outsourcing consultants, management of IS and other departments were involved in the crafting of the contract. Hercules would function as the systems integrator to lead the implementation of the SAP software, across Glacier's global operations. Glacier management believed that this would help them achieve better business results with SAP while controlling the IS spending because of the project discipline and accountability that can be expected from Hercules.

6.4.3   The Client-Vendor Relationship

The IS management at Glacier investigated the outsourcing option in-depth before they started the process. Through these investigations they found that while multiple-vendor deals offer many challenges, they can lead to greater overall efficiency because of the competition between the organizations. However, it would be a mistake if the client organization set up the two vendor organizations to compete with each other in an antagonistic manner. Since the Glacier IS management knew that they would be juggling with interfacing between two organizations that normally are competitors, they knew that they had to put in place measures that would build a cooperative relationship between all three organizations; as the VP – IS of Glacier commented, "all three organizations (Hercules, Minerva, and Glacier IS organization) share the stewardship of IS" at Glacier.

Glacier put in a lot of work at the front end of the outsourcing arrangement to ensure that the outsourcing arrangement brought the desired results. As Anna observes:

> "Typically what you see here is that these type of arrangements will take up to any year or more to put in place where you are actually working together and developing the relationship and writing up the contract – what we call shaping the deal… there's a lot of upfront work that goes into one of these before you actually go sign a contract or transition the work."

Based on recommendations from consultants, the Glacier IS organization redefined their needs so that they could be clear about the services they needed to obtain from vendors. They made the decision to retain IS employees who would interface with the other departments and ensure that the needs of those departments were met. In the selection process also, Glacier sought the advice of external consultants. As mentioned above, experts from within and outside Glacier were involved in the contract negotiations.

Glacier signed separate contracts with each of its alliance partners and manages the alliance on its own. Usually in these multiple vendor situations, client organizations tend to choose a primary vendor who manages the other contract relationships for them. While Vicki believes that "a lot in the contract is left to the interpretation" it is clear Glacier has processes in place to manage both vendors. For instance, they have a "standard problem ticket format" so that issues can be tracked and resolved between the different organizations without trouble. They have established a team that manages the alliance, keeping track of the progress and measuring performance against metrics to recommend modification of contract terms as necessary. As part of the internal management of the outsourcing arrangement, one team focuses on communications making sure the employees of the organization are aware of the benefits from the outsourcing arrangement. The team also tracks and documents the progress of different outsourcing initiatives and Glacier has retained an external consultancy organization to track customer satisfaction and assess the benefits from outsourcing.

It is within the context of this well-performing alliance that Glacier decided to outsource its SAP implementation. Though Hercules had to bid against Minerva and a handful of other vendors to bag the contract, Mike believes that their ongoing relationship tipped the scales in their favor. He believes that though the usual path to these contracts is through the RFP process, it is "better if you learn about it through some type of relationship, so that you know what is going on and can bring solutions to them." Glacier sees Hercules as having a greater strength in the applications arena; further Hercules' win preserves the balance in the alliance. Glacier is satisfied with the outsourcing arrangement since they are able to reduce the variability in spending while increasing the flexibility in meeting business needs and access to new technologies and business solutions.

Hercules is also satisfied with the progress of the outsourcing arrangement. There is a feeling of shared responsibility for the IS needs of Glacier and they believe they are meeting the needs of Glacier. David comments that some of the metrics are more outcome-based in terms of the effectiveness of meeting a certain target than measuring "the impact on the bottom line, the impact it (an activity) has on the business." The contract is important in the management of the outsourcing arrangement; however that does not determine the day-to-day management of the contract.

> "The contract should be the boundary, let's say a ball park you should play in. But if you're constantly pulling out your contract and saying section 12 says I can't do this type of thing - that is not going to work." (David)

> "The relationship should be driven by a win-win type of thinking. Mutual respect, integrity, openness, honesty – those types of things will get you a lot further than being well versed on the contract and what it says. You ought to know those things but you ought to look at it as the spirit of the deal."

Both of them believe they have built up a collaborative relationship with Glacier wherein they are treated fairly and are able to fulfill their obligations to Glacier; they also see opportunities for future growth with Glacier.

A major factor in the success of this dyad (and the alliance) is the attention and importance given by Glacier to managing the relationship in a collaborative yet competitive manner. The VP – IS of Glacier belongs to an invitation-only IS think tank restricted to IS executives of the world's largest corporations. This group is a forum for exchange on IS governance and related issues. Additionally, Glacier has continued to rely on the expertise of consultancies and research groups, who have studied a number of these outsourcing arrangements and culled the best practices from these experiences.

6.4.4 Through the "Social Capital" Lens

Having presented the background and the story of the outsourcing relationship, the focus now turns to analysis of the field text using the social capital framework.

6.4.4.1 Social Capital in the Glacier-Hercules relationship

As in the previous cases, the determination of the presence of social capital in the relationship is made by examining whether the different elements of the three dimensions of social capital are manifest in the relationship.

6.4.4.1.1 Structural dimension: Access patterns and appropriable organization

The structuring of interaction patterns so that access is made available to the right people on both sides, whether through the contract or by less formal mutual agreement, is a common feature in all ten cases.

Anna observes that one of the problems with outsourcing is that "they may not have good processes in place, procedures in place to solve problems and it becomes a problem for these companies" when they have to deal with a vendor. However, in dealing with an established vendor like Hercules, Glacier does not run into that problem. Vicki comments that Hercules' "service delivery model overall was very attractive to us from an execution point of view" and the fact that Hercules could appropriate it to provide the services that Glacier requires is a clear benefit for Glacier. As she explained, Hercules could leverage its global service delivery centers to implement and maintain the ERP system for Glacier. Given the time frames and delivery targets of the project, this ability to "follow the sun" is important.

Glacier also has identified routines and procedures for interactions during the outsourcing arrangement, based on consultant recommendations; these are documented and further refined based on assessments as they go through the outsourcing arrangement. Thus, the access routines and patterns for interactions are refined and strengthened during the course of the outsourcing arrangement, with the goal of using it in the later stages of the outsourcing arrangement and in new outsourcing initiatives.

6.4.4.1.2 Cognitive dimension: Shared understanding

Like in the previous cases, all parties agree that a shared understanding is necessary so that the organizations can work towards common goals efficiently. David comments on importance of facilitating a shared understanding:

"If you don't do that (develop a shared understanding) you are going to be killed. If you are just kind of there, then you won't be there very long, so you better understand what's going on. It is an outsourcing relationship and you'll never be part of the company, but if you do it (develop a shared understanding), you will have the opportunity to be more like part of the company and you can integrate like they feel like it's a partner relationship."

Glacier IS management, as managers of the alliance, made sure that a shared understanding of the goals of the project as well as a shared agreement on the process exist. Guidelines for the outsourcing process have been developed by the alliance management team. Anna notes that these guidelines helped avoid the problem of having to deal with incompatible management procedures across the different organizations. Glacier has a document that condenses the legal terms of the document and defines each organization's responsibility; this document also ensures clear understanding of the roles of the three organizations in the outsourcing arrangement and a shared vocabulary in their communications with each other. Vicki notes that newsletters, bulletins, and case studies also allow the three organizations to share what is going on within the business. Besides the usual communication mechanisms like the meetings and interactions at different levels[9], these help maintain agreement among all parties.

6.4.4.1.3 Relational dimension: Trust, norms, obligations & expectations, identification

Vicki listed the attributes necessary for the success of the outsourcing relationship: trust, flexibility, delivering on expectations and meeting obligations. Trust is built through tools that make the process transparent to all parties. For coordination between the organizations, Glacier has standardized reporting and tracking tools; these ensure consistency and transparency in the dealings between them and Hercules (as well as Minerva). Mike also comments on the importance of trust in the relationship:

---

[9] Similar to the three-tier hierarchy in Montezuma-Apollo and Chickasaw-Zeus cases

"It has to be a relationship where one, you got trust and two you understand, because they are essentially giving you a piece of their business to run and they have to have the trust that you are going to want to run it, better than what they are capable of doing it. Then, you are going to be around long enough and that you are not going to go away. So, it's a definitely a big decision on their part. They have to have, they have to have, this is the right thing to do, and they trust you that you will be there."

Norms of commitment, flexibility, and cooperation are important in the relationship and exist in the relationship, according to Dave; he explains:

"It almost has to be a give and take, you scratch my back and I will scratch yours. I mean there are times where Glacier will come and ask for things and we will do them even though it's not in the contract, or we'll tell, we'll ask things in Glacier, that they'll do for us. Because of the nature of the relationship, it is not completely defined in the contract, at least in this case as I see it."

When asked about what distinguishes their vendor from other vendors, Vicki responded, "They have a culture and customer focus that is similar to ours (Glacier's)." She also believes that similarity in organizational culture, work patterns, and project discipline existed between them and the vendor even prior to the outsourcing arrangement, and working together has strengthened these qualities.

6.4.4.1.4 Is social capital present in the Glacier-Hercules relationship?

It is clear that all three dimensions of the social capital are present in the Glacier-Hercules relationship. The relationship is built on structures that promote the elements of the cognitive and relational dimensions of social capital. These structures are not completely laid out in the contract, but have evolved and become accepted as the organizations work together.

6.4.4.2 Factors that promote social capital in the Glacier-Hercules relationship

As in the Chickasaw-Zeus relationship, the longevity of the relationship has contributed to its strength. There has been no discord here; rather, the relationship has grown rich in social capital due to the effectiveness of the interactions between the parties. As David notes, "the relationship is built by both you (the vendor) and the client over time. It is not just something that happens. It takes work on both parts." It can be seen that the leadership in this relationship-building effort is taken by Glacier; a comment attributed to a member of the alliance management team says it better:

"People say that outsourcing is like a marriage, but it isn't. It starts out like a relationship between a parent and a teenage child. How strict are you going to be? Only after years of maturation does the relationship take on characteristics of matrimony."

This comment presented by the Glacier alliance team member can be contrasted with the comments of interviewees in the Montezuma-Apollo and Chickasaw-Zeus cases. In those cases, the interviewees alluded to marriage as an appropriate metaphor for the outsourcing relationship. When emphasizing the importance of the outsourcing relationship, Mike from Hercules also repeats this commonly held view of the outsourcing relationship as a marriage, "It's like a marriage almost, it's a big deal." The different view that the Glacier manager presents may be because while Montezuma and Chickasaw were each dealing primarily with a single vendor, Glacier has to deal with two vendors who are fighting for bigger pieces of the pie. The comment is also indicative of Glacier's determination and commitment to guide and grow the relationship and an awareness that this building process will take time.

Vicki believes that Glacier's efforts are paying off and that the relationship "has gotten better over time" since both parties have developed a mutual understanding and the Hercules has "learned Glacier people, culture and business processes."

Glacier has made sure that all parties know what is expected of them by providing for a high level of definition in the contract and supporting documents. This started as an internal process within Glacier to ensure that their requirements were defined clearly. Additionally, Hercules has their own tools to ensure that the reports are comprehensive and it is clear how service level agreements have been met and problems have been resolved.

As can be expected in an outsourcing arrangement where so much care has been paid to the details, reporting mechanisms and procedures have been specified in the contract, so that communication needs of both organizations are met. However, as Dave explains, as the organizations proceed through the project "you may end up finding, we need to a little bit more here around communications. So your communication patterns will tend to change based on what's going on in the business." Mike commented on the differences in the communication patterns as the relationship progresses.

> "Initially, probably there is a lot more face to face because you are getting to know each other. Once, that relationship is formed, it will naturally, go to phone calls or emails, but it doesn't, face to face, it never goes away. But, initially it's a lot more face-to-face, get to know each other, make sure everything's in place, or a routine of what you interact on."

As in the previous cases, informal communication is considered very important. Dave comments:

> "A lot of the important communication happens informally. What I mean by that is that a lot of times you are going to have a side bar discussion, a one-on-one discussion with some individual, perhaps very frank open type of communication – in which you are willing to say things you would have never gone into a meeting room full of people and say publicly…you really need both, and that doesn't mean you shouldn't be open and frank in those formal meetings. I think that kind of goes back to the relationship you develop; you may be more willing to say something one-on-one than you would at an open session because you might not have a good relationship with everyone in there."

Thus, there is emphasis again on the personal rapport between the project executives. As in previous cases, everyone recognizes that if the individuals functioning in these boundary spanning roles leave the organization, it would affect the relationship between the two organizations and the performance of the outsourcing arrangement.

Looking at the situation from an operational level, Anna believes that the organization "who went outside for help" is more dependent. However, Vicki does not consider that there is a dependence imbalance since both organizations understand the objectives of the outsourcing arrangement, David and Mike believe that Hercules is more dependent in the relationship. Mike comments:

> "The customer is always right; so we have to do whatever, within reason to keep the client happy."

David elaborates on this:

> "That is an interesting question. You would like to think it's somewhat equal so I am going to give you a wishy-washy answer. I think it goes both ways – certainly I am dependent. The clients are important and if I would lose my clients I would lose my job, so there's a certain amount of dependency on them from us. And certainly the client depends on us to deliver and keep their systems running. So if I had to say who's more dependent I would have to say I am probably more dependent and the reason I say this is that it is probably easier for them to find another service provider than for me to find another client. If they decide to make a change they might still have 20 guys lined up at their door."

However, these disparate views on dependence do not appear to affect the Glacier-Hercules relationship. Unlike in the Montezuma-Apollo relationship, the organizations have developed the relational dimension of social capital in their relationship that allows them to work together in a satisfactory manner.

6.4.4.3 Social capital facilitates the combination and exchange of resources in the Glacier-Hercules relationship

The theoretical framework suggests that social capital provides facilitating conditions for the combination and exchange and resources necessary for the project. As in previous cases, the structural elements of social capital provide the access necessary for the exchange of resources in the outsourcing situation. Both organizations are motivated by the mutual benefits they can receive and anticipate value from future opportunities to work together. Hercules also sees additional benefits, since Glacier serves as a reference for them as well.

> "From Hercules's standpoint, Glacier is also a very good reference. When we talk to other clients, that is what you look for in this type of business – you want to have somebody who your perspective client can go and talk to, and they are very good about that. I think from Glacier's perspective we have consistently delivered this a service that meets or exceeds that have no contract, also has driven down their cost as well."

Hercules' absorption of Glacier employees ensures that there is a high level of combination capability in their interactions. Glacier employees who have been absorbed by Hercules go through a training process that "acculturates" them to the new organizational culture. Thus, these employees are versed in the codes and language of both organizations enhancing the combination capability required for the exchange and combination of resources between the two organizations.

6.4.4.4 Assessment: Satisfaction

Even before outsourcing, assessment played an important role in the management of information systems at Glacier. It was an assessment by an external consultant firm that alerted Glacier to the fact that their IS spending was almost double the industry average. Assessment continues to play an important role in the management of the outsourcing relationships as well. Besides their own evaluations of the vendor through metrics that have been agreed upon, Glacier hires external consultants to measure the satisfaction of the user community with the outsourcing arrangement. Glacier is satisfied with the outcome of its outsourcing arrangements; Vicki agrees that it is an equitable outsourcing arrangement and identified additional sources of satisfaction with the arrangement as "the flexibility and good faith from the vendor". When problems are identified, those are addressed by Glacier and Hercules together, "without any finger-pointing" since both parties agree upon the goals of the outsourcing arrangement and have faith in each other.

Hercules is also satisfied with the outsourcing arrangement. They "look to the longer-term contracts because these guarantee you of some sort of recurring revenue, year after year so we don't have to resell that consulting business every year." With Glacier, they have been able to increase the scope of the original contract, even though they still have a lesser share of the total outsourcing contracts at Glacier. Glacier also provides referrals for them, another business-building opportunity. Hercules also believes that the relationship that they have built provides them with a knowledge base from which they can pitch innovative solutions to Glacier. Summing up, Mike says:

> "I think we are very satisfied with it, the relationship. It's a relationship where it's open, we understand what Glacier expects, and they understand what we expect."

However, Dave feels that satisfaction is only a temporary thing and this assessment is a means for identifying the next challenge.

> "If you ever get satisfied, you're on dangerous grounds because things are always changing. Business environments are always changing. So you should strive each year for a new challenge. If you get comfortable, or satisfied then there going to become dangerously close to losing the contract, so I am really never satisfied."

Both organizations use assessment effectively, not as a means of proving a point, but as a way to continuously build the relationship. Thus, assessment contributes to the development of the social capital in the relationship, which, in turn promotes continued ease and efficiency of exchange.

6.4.5   Case study conclusion

This case description exemplifies an outsourcing arrangement where both parties recognize the benefits of social capital and continuously strive to promote the presence of elements of social capital in their relationship. A unique aspect of this case is the use of assessment to drive the relationship and ascertain the benefits from the outsourcing arrangement. Glacier and Hercules are able to attain the goals of their outsourcing arrangement and secure long-term benefits for both from the relationship: additional business opportunities for Hercules and a continuing reduction in cost and increased flexibility in provision of IS services for Glacier.

6.5   Case 4- Haleakala and Athene

.While in the previous three cases the client and vendor organizations were large organizations, the vendor in this case, Athene is a SME[10], which has been in existence for just three years. Athene is trying to establish itself and the management of Athene is glad to have won a contract from a large client like Haleakala. Athene is keen on maintaining a relationship with Haleakala, and is aware that to achieve that goal they need to meet Haleakala's needs on this project and establish a relationship with Haleakala. The focus in the case is on the three dimensions of social capital and how those develop during the outsourcing arrangement resulting in the desired positive outcomes for Athene.

---

[10] Small and Medium Enterprises

6.5.1 Introduction

Haleakala is a global provider of technology products and services to consumers and businesses. Their offerings span information technology infrastructure and storage including personal computing devices, and services including maintenance, consulting and integration and outsourcing. Their products and services are available worldwide. Haleakala is well-versed in outsourcing; the value of IS outsourcing contracts that Haleakala is currently servicing exceed ten billion dollars.

In comparison, Athene is a very small organization, established by an entrepreneur of Indian origin. Its annual revenue amounts to seven million dollars and it is a niche player specializing in SAP implementation, business intelligence, and data warehousing. Unlike Haleakala, Athene's range is limited to the southern United States and its headquarters is in Texas. At the time of the interviews, Athene had about five clients; Haleakala was their first major customer.

Kathy is a project manager at Haleakala; she was assigned to the project to "reassess and identify any changes that need to be made" at the end of the first year of the project. She was not involved with the initial stages of the project. Her role requires her to evaluate the outsourcing project and she has been collecting information from the individuals involved with the project and examining documents produced during the first year of the outsourcing engagement.

Though Mike is a senior executive at Athene, he is deeply involved in the coordination and management of the project since it is one of their first and major projects. Mike comments on the importance of the first major customer:

> "We realized was that we did not have any brand value. Secondly, we did not have resources that the big companies have. Finally, looking at other successful (outsourcing vendor) companies, we found that they had GE or Citibank as their first and main customer and built their business on this base."

They are trying to emulate the success of other outsourcing companies who built their business based on the success of their first outsourcing contract with a large client. In follow-up calls after the first interview, Mike talked about the progress of the outsourcing arrangement and the growth of Athene.

Kurt has been working on the Haleakala account for Athene. He has worked on major outsourcing contracts before joining Athene and brings his experience in the field to this growing organization.

Table 6-5: Interviewees in the Haleakala-Athene case

Name of interviewee	Organization	Position	Duration of interview	Taped?
Kathy	Haleakala (Client)	Project Manager	1.25 hours	Yes
Mike	Athene (Vendor)	Vice President	1.5 hours initially; three follow-up telephone calls of about 45 minutes duration.	No (The interview could not be taped due to

				technical problems)
Kurt	Athene (Vendor)	Project Executive	45 minutes	Yes

6.5.2 The Outsourcing Project

A strong business focus and technical expertise has sustained continued growth at Haleakala; it is a large organization with over a million employees working at more than four hundred locations around the world. The decentralized organizational structure at Haleakala has encouraged autonomy in operations within its business units, and the organization depends on the informal network for knowledge transfer and project management to a great extent. This dependence on informal networks can be a problem in managing an external vendor, as can be seen in this case.

The outsourcing project involved enhancements and support for the software that is used for management and operational reporting needs in one of Haleakala's largest business units. The software includes twelve data warehouse applications running on multiple technologies worldwide, partly a result of the autonomy vested in the business units. This work is being outsourced to a number of vendors, of which Athene was one. Athene starts off with a small part of this work, and is managing the project out of its office in Texas. Kathy comments on the work that Athene is doing: "This project is complex because the environment and the infrastructure (at Haleakala) are pretty complicated and a lot of applications are linked together." At the time of the interviews, the project has been going on for fifteen months.

6.5.3 The Client-Vendor Relationship

Athene's goal is to meet Haleakala's needs "in the bestest manner possible" (Mike) to obtain additional business opportunities from Haleakala. With this initial project, they are therefore eager to establish themselves as a preferred vendor for Haleakala. They believe they have the technical and management expertise to do this project. Based on their examination of the growth of other outsourcing companies and the changed in the outsourcing industry, they have decided to focus on selected areas so that they can establish a reputation as a leading provider in those areas. The management is also committed to educating itself. They regularly attend industry conferences and have established relationships with leading researchers in the area of outsourcing.

The Athene team is committed to doing things right. Mike and Kurt are in charge of the management of the project, with a number of their employees dedicated to the project. Their plan is to put into practice the knowledge they have amassed about outsourcing and establish a long-term relationship with Haleakala. They have established a management hierarchy to deal with the needs of the outsourcing arrangement and have structures in place for internal reporting and documentation. At the start of the project, Haleakala organized a training session for the Athene team to familiarize them with the project. Mike believes that this training equipped them well to deal with the challenges of this project. .New members who join the Athene team are provided with the same training internally (at Athene) by individuals who attended the initial training. The Athene team is thus well-prepared to meet any challenges in the Haleakala engagement.

On the Haleakala side, while there is an overall manager for the outsourcing arrangements, there has not been a counterpart to Kurt dealing with Athene. In managing the outsourcing arrangement, the Haleakala staff applied the same informal networking approach that was used internally. Kathy explained:

"Until now it's been very informal, if people had issues or whatever they would talk to someone they knew usually"

While the Athene staff met any needs and resolved any problems that were brought to their attention, with this informal approach, they were not meeting all the needs of the user community at Haleakala. There has been a lack of monitoring of the progress and changes in requirements. Kathy has been brought to fill in this role and she feels that there is a better fit between the staffing compositions of both organizations now.

Kathy explained that her role was to "look at the overall processes and see where we need to make changes, what needs to be improved." She was reluctant to commit that this was due to any specific problems with the outsourcing arrangement, but from other comments she made it appeared that there was some dissatisfaction with the way things were progressing, though not directly with the service from Athene. For instance, when asked if there was a shared understanding between the organizations regarding the goals and processes of the outsourcing arrangement, she replied: "Yea, I think so now." In many of her responses, she contrasted what had been going on before she started on the project with changes she had initiated. However, she was reluctant to elaborate on the reason behind these changes, beyond mentioning that the management of the business unit recognized the need to reassess the processes associated with the outsourcing arrangement. Kathy mentioned that her primary goal is to improve the process for feedback from Haleakala to Athene and she has started holding weekly review meetings including the vendor representatives to "review processes and bring new processes in (for feedback)." Haleakala has noted the responsiveness and willingness of the vendor to meet their requirements and has determined that the problem does not lie with the vendor, but in the absence of mechanisms to provide feedback to the vendor. Thus, even though there is a belief within Haleakala that there could be more value derived from the outsourcing arrangement, there is an appreciation of the vendor and their work ethics.

The Athene team has not noticed anything amiss with their progress on the project. They make use of the informal networks within Haleakala to keep track of the requirements and believe they have been successful in meeting the needs of Haleakala. While they are glad to be involved in the weekly meetings and comment that it is easier to keep track of the requirements, Mike asserts that this has not changed Haleakala's work or management of the project.

"They had some internal changes going on and there was some change in the interactions after that, but we were meeting their requirements all the time…we did not hear anything different."

Kathy believes that the review process and formal feedback structures she has put in place would help Haleakala obtain greater benefits from the outsourcing arrangement.

During the first interview, Mike mentioned that Haleakala is planning to outsource the complete application management work as one contract and that Athene would be bidding for the project. Haleakala is facing challenges in managing its internal systems because of the complexity associated with the various systems spread across various locations. There is a push for standardization and control within the organization and the Haleakala IS management has decided that it would be better to have one organization manage the support needs and enhancements for these applications worldwide.

The relationship that Athene was able to establish with Haleakala convinced the Haleakala IS management to award the contract for the support and enhancement of the complete set of management and reporting software worldwide to Athene. This achievement in competition with large and established vendors like Zeus and Minerva was a source of gratification for the Athene team. Kurt and Mike repeated comments that they had heard from the Haleakala team:

"Athene's willingness to be flexible and work with us allows Haleakala to have a partner, not just another consulting agency."

"The whole team has a "can do" attitude which is what is needed to be successful."

Meanwhile, Athene's success in the outsourcing arena captured the attention of an international software solutions provider based in India looking to expand its reach in the United States. Seeing the synergies between their areas of expertise, this organization acquired Athene, making Athene a fully-owned subsidiary of the Indian outsourcing organization. This is an advantage for Athene, since it now has offshore resources to back up its service offerings. It was also agreed that Athene would retain the company name since it had built up a reputation that was associated with the name.

In a follow-up telephone call, Mike disclosed that the delivery model for the project had been changed to a "global software development and support model that could provide speed of development and at the same time provide significant cost reductions for future development and support efforts." A major challenge was to transition all applications knowledge to the global team within a very short period of time. Using a model that involved teams in the US and India working in coordination leveraging the time difference between the locations, Athene is able to meet the software needs of Haleakala's business unit and provide 24X7 support.

6.5.4 Through the "Social Capital" Lens

Having presented the background and the story of the outsourcing relationship, the focus now turns to analysis of the field text using the social capital framework.

6.5.4.1 Social Capital in the Haleakala-Athene relationship

As in previous cases, the determination of the presence of social capital in the relationship is made by examining whether the different elements of the three dimensions of social capital are manifest in the relationship.

6.5.4.1.1 *Structural dimension: Access patterns and appropriable organization*

Initially, the Athene team has to rely on informal networks for access to the user community within Haleakala. They are able to forge ties with individuals in Haleakala and provide the services that are required with minimal formal feedback. It appears strange that an organization as experienced in outsourcing as Haleakala would not have the necessary structures in place to manage their outsourcing contract, and would use informal networks to manage the contract. However, once the Haleakala management realized that they were not getting the benefits they expected from the outsourcing arrangement because of this lack of attention to ties between the organizations, they assigned a support manager to the outsourcing arrangement.

With this new position, Haleakala has put in place a link between the two organizations and the means to provide feedback to Athene. Kathy's responsibilities include reviewing and implementing changes in the processes associated with managing the outsourcing arrangement:

> "…management processes, are they working properly, do we need to make any changes there, our escalation processes – overall, how we assign items and taking a look at our documentation – whether it is up to date and if not how to get to it up to date and find out what kind of tools the support folks need and information and they may need from us."

Kathy also mentioned that these changes she was making were based on guidelines that are documented within the organization, which has considerable experience in outsourcing, both as client and vendor. As mentioned before, Mike agrees that the changes have made it easier for them to get information from Haleakala. These structural changes in the management of the outsourcing arrangement facilitate enhanced access and improved communication between the organizations.

One of the changes Kathy has instituted is to make sure that she gets included in all communication between the organizations.

> "In the last couple of months, I have been doing this, getting copied on all correspondence. If there is any backup on what the customer needs, and if I see things that they are not stating correctly or they're not quite correct, I send them feedback as to how they can make that better."

This approach is similar to that taken by the management in the previous cases and the practices that Athene has adopted. When information is channeled through key individuals responsible for the management of the outsourcing relationship on both sides, it reduced the possibility of issues being missed or dealt with inconsistently.

There is also a better match between the structures in place in Haleakala and Athene, as Kathy commented:

> "I think now that they have made it a more dedicated focus on my part, the support manager, I think it (the fit between the organizations in terms of managing the outsourcing arrangement) is improving. I think on the outsourcing side, I think they probably have the right people in place, they probably have had from the beginning, I guess, because these are the same people they started with."

Kathy's comment on the structures that Athene has in place is correct; however, Athene management relies on its contacts in the informal network, so that they could "feel the pulse of the user community" (Kurt). Such informal communication has been found to be more effective than formal channels, because it often provides information that would otherwise have been unavailable and helps reduce misunderstandings (kraut et al, 1990). Athene's affinity and reliance on these informal channels can be easily traced to their determination to earn a good name at Haleakala and build a relationship. Mike puts it in simple terms:

> "We had structures in place – but we wanted them to be happy. That was the most important thing." (Mike)

6.5.4.1.2 Cognitive dimension: Shared understanding

As mentioned in section 6.4.3, the lack of mechanisms within Haleakala to monitor the project inhibits the development of shared understanding about the goals of the project. Even though Athene is willing to bend over backwards to meet the needs of Haleakala, lack of feedback prevents them from doing that, even though they are not aware of that. Kurt's comment evidences this unawareness:

"We felt pretty comfortable dealing with the applications – the training session really helped us. If there were problems, we addressed it as we went along. The client never indicated any dissatisfaction to us. We met the standards."

This is a risky situation for both parties. The vendor due to no fault of theirs is unable to provide the services at the level the client expects. However, the fact that there were no murmurs of dissatisfaction (according to interviewees from both Haleakala and Athene) indicates that Athene was able to understand the applications and deal with the user requirements; their expertise in this particular area enables them to identify and use the information available from Haleakala.

Kathy understands that meeting the requirements of this project would be a challenge for any environment since the applications environment at Haleakala is quite complex. She would have liked to have had more opportunities for bringing Athene up to date on the requirements of the Haleakala user community.

"If had been in there, probably I think we would have done training sessions more regularly. But we had a training session and then just sort of let it go. But I think there probably should have been some updates – a like even orally or whatever to make sure that everybody was up to date and understood our applications and things, so that's probably one thing I'll be looking at changing and implementing something like that."

She has started conducting formal surveys and gathering comments, which gets reviewed at weekly meetings with the vendor representatives. Thus, a shared understanding about the goals and the progress on the project is being created now. Kathy also commented that this process has been easy to manage because "they (Athene) have been willing to do whatever we want them to do for improving." When asked if they felt that Haleakala feedback had helped them to improve, Mike was a bit offended.

"I think we were meeting their requirements. They had some internal changes going on and there was some change in the interactions after that, but we were meeting their requirements all the time…we did not hear anything different."

6.5.4.1.3 *Relational dimension: Trust, norms, obligations & expectations, identification*

Athene's desire and commitment to building the relationship has paid off dividends. Even though Haleakala realized that they were not getting the benefits they expected, they realize that the vendor is willing to provide those benefits. This trust is very important in ensuring the continuity of the relationship. Mike explains how trust needs to be built up at different levels:

"Most important is the trust, trust in terms of openness, in terms of intention, in terms of interaction. That is really important; I think that is the single most important thing. And second is the ability to deliver on promises. That is also part of trust but I would just emphasize it is a bit more. The first is trust in terms of character; the second is in terms of performance."

Kurt elaborates on the second form of trust:

"Most important is doing whatever you commit, whatever timelines you give, the most important is to be on time and deliver what you said."

Kathy comments that there needs to be trust at two levels – at an organizational level and at a personal level between the management personnel in both organizations.

"I think you need to have the trust between the primary players to continue the communication and everything and you also have to some level of trust and confidence from the end-users that are going to be calling the outsourcing folks to seek support or whatever."

The Athene management repeatedly mentions the importance of flexibility, commitment, and cooperation in the outsourcing process. As Mike explains "we are doing it for their goodwill and we want to make them happy and we want to make them come back to us." The Athene team does not have any complaints about the Haleakala account; they believe they have been treated fairly and the Haleakala team will meet their obligations fairly. However, asked about the changes that have taken place recently, Kurt explains that while there should be a willingness on the part of the vendor to accommodate reasonable changes, the client should understand that there are obligations that they should meet.

"Most often we have to show the flexibility we are open to these changes, you can come back and tell us whatever you want; we will do it for you. And I think that openness, uh, allows you-- it helps you better, you know, when you sit down to talk about scope changes…If you've committed to a project, there are certain things the client also has to do to keep the project on track. And they're outside the control of the consultant. And, I think that's where very early in the project you establish your change control process that you're going to use and if--and that's handled through change control--if the client is supposed to, for example, order a piece of hardware or a piece of software and they have to order it by a certain date so that you have it delivered in time so as not to impact the project negatively. Uh, they have to understand that if they don't get that ordered in time, there's a project impact, and that's going to cost them."

As in previous cases, the vendor Athene has expectations of scope enhancement and continuity. They see this project and the opportunity to establish a relationship as a big chance. And, the results of this initials project are as Athene desired as they are awarded a bigger contract.

While Kathy feels that the cultures of Haleakala and Athene are "different, because they are much more structured," she does not have any problems in the interactions with the Athene team. The Athene team has been able to connect with the Haleakala community and the two organizations work together towards the completion of the project.

6.5.4.1.4 *Is social capital present in the Haleakala-Athene relationship?*

It is the efforts of the Athene team that contribute to the development of the relationship between the two organizations initially. Though admittedly there was a lack of shared understanding in the initial stages of the project regarding the expectations from the project, the elements of the structural dimension and the relational dimension developed in the relationship. While the commitment of the Athene team and their ability to gather information even in the absence of formal communication from Haleakala prevented the failure of the project, the Haleakala management soon realized that they were not getting the maximum benefit from the outsourcing arrangement. Kathy was brought in to manage the project for Haleakala, and identify and change processes that were necessary to ensure that the outsourcing arrangement met its objectives. Since these change processes were handled openly, involving Athene also in the review sessions, the cohesiveness and trust in the relationship increased. Thus, through Kathy's efforts, currently the relationship appears to be rich in all three dimensions of social capital.

6.5.4.2 Factors that promote social capital in the Haleakala-Athene relationship

The relationship between Haleakala and Athene is fairly young, but Athene and Haleakala have been able to demonstrate their commitment to the relationship. It is true that longer relationships give both parties many chances to interact and build "trust and norms of cooperation" (Nahapiet and Ghoshal, 1998; p. 257), but in this case, those have been built up between the organizations by their actions in this relatively short period of time. The willingness of Athene "to do whatever it takes to keep the client happy" has contributed significantly to this strong relationship.

The definition in the contract regarding the requirements of the project and the governance structures was sufficient to sustain their activities, according to Mike. However, neither Haleakala nor Athene refers to the contract for the day-to-day management of the relationship. The Athene management believes that the elements of the relational dimension of social capital such as trust, commitment, and "the compatibility between organizations" are the most valuable in a relationship. Kathy also seems to be of the same frame of mind. When asked if the change processes she was implementing were within the scope of the contract, Kathy responded: "I haven't actually looked at the contract really in depth." Thus, while the clarification of the requirements enhances the satisfaction of both parties with the outcome of the outsourcing arrangement, such improved clarity in this case appears to come from the shared understanding that is developed between the user community and Athene and between Kathy and the Athene representatives. Even the review meetings and feedback processes initiated by Kathy have been developed in consensus with the user community and Athene, and not directly from the contract.

Neither party views the other as highly dependent on the other. Kathy believes that the client is "generally more dependent," though in this case she believes that this will not lead to any opportunistic behavior. Kurt believes that there is dependency for both parties:

"I think it's equal in different ways. You know, the client is looking on us to provide the project management experience and the technical experience. We're looking for the client to provide the business knowledge and the understanding of their customers and their internal culture. And so, we're both dependent on each other for different things. I guess I would say it's equal."

Mike clarifies this view and puts it on a timeline:

"Early on, you are dependent because as you try to start to develop a system, you need information from the organization. You need more information from them than they need from you. In later stages of the project, as you're starting to roll out deliverable components, it's the other way around."

In these assessments of dependency, the focus remains on the exchange between the parties and not on the availability of alternate vendors or the size of the organization. As in the previous two cases, this acknowledgement of mutuality strengthens the relationship between the organizations, promoting the exchange of the knowledge resources necessary at different stages for completing the project.

All three executives agree that the <u>personal rapport between the project executives</u> is important. The relationship between the two organizations is "ultimately is a reflection of the management team of the two organizations." (Mike). Mike also comments that these key players have to be willing to play different roles; in his words: "I have to be a CIO to DEO (data entry operator)." This statement once again reflects Athene's commitment to the relationship, which does not go unnoticed by the Haleakala management. As Kathy comments: "The whole team has a "can do" attitude which is what is needed to be successful."

6.5.4.3 Social capital facilitates the combination and exchange of resources in the Haleakala-Athene relationship

The theoretical framework suggests that social capital provides facilitating conditions for the combination and exchange and resources necessary for the project. The four conditions are access, anticipation of value, motivation, and combination capability. While initially there were no formal structures in place to provide <u>access</u>, Athene's capabilities and commitment to providing the services that Haleakala needs help overcome this hurdle. They are able to use the informal network at Haleakala and rely on informal communication to obtain the information needed to complete the project. Naturally, the weekly review meetings and improved communication processes extends this access and ensures complete and timely information. Both organizations <u>anticipate value</u> out of the outsourcing arrangement. For Haleakala, this anticipation is based on the trust in Athene's capabilities and reliability; Athene is also convinced that Haleakala will meet its expectations reliably. This assessment is based on Haleakala's reputation as a large and established organization with considerable experience in outsourcing. Further, Athene is <u>motivated</u> by the expectation that this exchange will bring additional business opportunities with Haleakala and that Haleakala would serve as a reference account for them. Both these expectations were realized later, according to Mike. The completion of the project also contributes to the goals of standardization and control at Haleakala. Finally, the agreement on the processes for the outsourcing arrangement and the common technical vocabulary enhance the <u>combination capability</u> necessary for the exchange and combination of resources in the outsourcing arrangement.

6.5.4.4 Assessment: Satisfaction

Both organizations are satisfied with the progress of the outsourcing arrangement. Kathy rates Athene's "willingness to continue learning, a willingness to take on new ideas and suggestions, willingness for open communication" as contributing to this satisfaction. She believes that the services they are getting "has improved the last few months" and will continue to do so. Athene management believes that they "have a good working relationship where we can talk out things" and that the client will fulfill their obligations. They are reasonably certain that the social capital that has built up in the relationship will provide them the additional business opportunities they are looking for.

6.5.5   Case study conclusion

In this case, the relational dimension of social capital is the most significant. In the absence of formally defined ties and processes between the organizations to provide feedback, the determination of the vendor to develop the relational elements of social capital carry the outsourcing arrangement. The client feels some dissatisfaction initially because of lack of proper internal management, but has trust in the willingness of the vendor to meet the requirements and adapt to their needs, once those needs are communicated. This commitment to the relationship pays off for the vendor in the form of continued business opportunities. This can be contrasted with the Montezuma-Apollo relationship, which was rich in the structural and cognitive dimensions, but lacking in the relational dimension and ends with the vendor not receiving the new contract. Thus, this case lends support to the view that the relational dimension contributes more to a continuing relationship than the other dimensions of social capital.

6.6 Case 5- Bluestone and Vesta

In this case description, the focus is on a relatively small outsourcing project, the development of a software package for a software company, Bluestone. Bluestone has outsourced the development of its core product to Vesta, and the success or failure of this outsourcing arrangement could have a major impact on Bluestone. The focus in this case are on the core of the framework, the relationship between the three dimensions of social capital and the combination and exchange of resources. In the initial stages, the relationship is not strong and it appears that the project may not be completed successfully. Changes in the management of the outsourcing arrangement reduce some of the friction between the two organizations and the project is nearing completion, though it does not meet all the expectations of the client.

6.6.1 Introduction

The client, Bluestone, is a software company in California, providing software solutions for cashiering in higher education. The company has been in existence for more than twenty years and has about forty employees. In 1988, Bluestone built its first payment processing solution for a university in California; similar installations followed at several universities. In 1992, Bluestone consolidated its operations and focused on developing state-of-the-art systems for payment processing, customer service, and student and accounts receivable functions for higher education. This software package was their core product; they also provided installation and maintenance services for this product.

Vesta is a software solutions provider, also based in California. Vesta was founded in 1992, and is financially backed by a large US marine bunker fuel supplier. Vesta has a staff of over fifty software engineers; their focus has been on application development and testing and migrating existing technologies to new platforms.

Table 6-6: Interviewees in the Bluestone-Vesta case

Name of interviewee	Organization	Position	Duration of interview	Taped?
Mark	Bluestone (Client)	Project Executive	1.5 hours	Yes
Atul	Vesta (Vendor)	Client manager	1.5 hours	Yes
Jay	Vesta	Vice President	1 hour	No

Mark is the head of the engineering team at Bluestone and he was designated as the contact "at a technical level and a business level" for the outsourcing arrangement (Atul). Mark has been at Bluestone for more than five years and has been involved with the outsourcing project since the start. Atul is the client manager for this account from Vesta, and has also been on the project from its inception. Jay is the Vice President at Vesta and was assigned to the project after problems developed in the outsourcing relationship.

6.6.2   The Outsourcing Project

Bluestone has identified a niche market in the financial software for higher education and was one of the market leaders in this area, according to Mark. Three years back, the organization realized that they were losing market share because their product was based on an older technology. They needed to update the software and create an integrated web-based billing, payment, and cashiering solution. However, they did not have the necessary resources in-house; there were only four employees who had the necessary skills. Having determined that it would take too long to develop the product in-house, they decided to look for an external software provider.

"The president of our company (Bluestone) and one of the principals at Vesta knew each other personally," Mark explains how Vesta won the contract. It was later clarified by Jay that he principal Mark refers to is the CEO of the US marine bunker fuel supply organization. Vesta had also completed a couple of "very small projects[11]" (Atul) for Bluestone, with which they had been satisfied. No other vendors were considered for this project, and the project was awarded to Vesta. The contract was "not very rigorous and did not include many criteria that it should have," according to Mark.

Atul describes the events leading to the finalization of the contract. Once it was decided that Vesta would be the vendor, "we went there (to Bluestone) initially, for an analysis, and we went through their product training. We created a proposal of basically how many people will be involved for how many months. We have a rate sheet for our developers; that gives the rate. And we came up with the proposal, and along with the proposal we send the rate sheet, and they signed the contract to go ahead with the project."

6.6.3   The Client-Vendor Relationship

Once the contract was signed, Bluestone employees conducted a more detailed training session on using the current software package for a few of the Vesta employees. The Vesta employees were not familiar with the business environment or the accounting requirements associated with higher education. The training was "very hectic because we had to learn something about the specific accounting tasks because it was an accounting package; it was a full-blown business office. And they went through each module, and that was a very good thing." As part of the training, they also went through the "architectural documents and explained the source code" (Atul). The Vesta staff felt fairly comfortable with the package once the training session was over. Assuming that the new product would just be a re-implementation of existing features on a new platform, they also felt that since there was "an existing code base, *they* could leverage from that." The Vesta staff was also impressed with the Bluestone employees by the end of the training. Atul commented: "Even though they have very few people, they were very knowledgeable in their domain."

This was the first major outsourcing contract for Bluestone and Mark's first experience with outsourcing. Since there was a connection between the president of their organization and a principal of the other organization, they assumed that things would proceed smoothly.

---

[11] Asked about the nature of these projects, Jay explained that these projects involved the installation of computer upgrades, for which they had sent over employees from Vesta to Bluestone for a couple of days.

Additionally, the small pilot projects that Vesta had done for them had been completed smoothly. They did not recommend any additions to the contract that Vesta proposed and had approved their proposal without any changes.

At the time of the interview, the project had been going on for slightly more than a year and there were about fifteen people working on the project at Vesta. Atul explained his view on project administration: "The contract would define the things to be implemented and the scope of the project. Almost all of the projects done by us are defined by the contract. We define the handling of change requests, so that if in the middle of implementation, the client comes with new features, new requirements, we refer to those clauses in the contract, saying these additional features will be included at a different cost and will be added to the contract signed by both parties."

Mark believes that the contract did not serve the needs of Bluestone. In the absence of a plan that structured the interaction between the organizations, it "was not possible to work together." As an example of problems that cropped up, he mentioned occasions when modules were delivered for testing without notice. Bluestone was not prepared to test the modules and the Vesta staff would be upset because Bluestone was holding up the work. In retrospect, Mark comments that he would have liked the contract to be "more rigorous."

The Vesta team proceeded under the assumption that all that was involved in the project was to port the application over to a new platform. Mark agrees that they had only specified that the project was "porting cashtrans[12] to java". However, their expectations were different. As Mark explained,

> "The expectation that we had, what that really means is preparing installer programs that were not needed with the previous versions, help systems…Are we simply taking what exists in the old product and putting it in new technology? We also need to do peripheral work that needs to be done in making the technology useable."

Ideally, these expectations would have been included in the contract. It is clear from previous cases that when organizations define the scope of work and the metrics, it lays the groundwork for the development of shared understanding between the organizations. If such definition is not present initially, communication during the outsourcing arrangement can help the organizations identify and work towards completing the project to the satisfaction of both organizations. The Bluestone staff expected that because of the connection between the top management in both organizations, the communication between the two organizations would not be a problem. However, the communication required for the project had to take place at a different level and representatives from both organizations were dissatisfied with the progress.

With the friction between the two organizations increasing, the problem was escalated to the higher levels, and nine months after the project started, Jay, a Vice-President at Vesta was assigned to oversee the project. Atul was not removed from the project because he had the technical competence and experience for the project. Jay had a different perspective from Atul on the management of the project. He explained:

> "I don't think anyone can define your relationship on a piece of paper. It's almost impossible to, I would say, imagine every situation that's going to arise and then have a remedy defined in a contract. You can do it at a broad level, but, you know, over and

---

[12] This is a pseudonym

about that I think it's the working relationship or the rapport the parties have to develop with each other, the one which really makes or breaks the relationship. It's only a framework."

One of the first things Jay did was to define the patterns for interaction between the two organizations. Things started improving with weekly meetings being set up between Atul and Mark. Other individuals would also be included depending on the information Vesta required or the feedback that Bluestone wanted to provide. Copies of internal reports produced at Vesta are shared with the Bluestone team so that they would be aware of the progress and any problems with the project. Conferencing technology is used to connect the developers at Vesta and the employees at Bluestone so that there could be a clearer understanding of the project parameters. As Atul explained:

"It became more a relationship with over time – it was first a relationship between organizations not individuals. We had one main contact that represented the organization and overtime we met some more of the staff who could explain things and answer questions about the product – exchanging ideas. It certainly changed the relationship. We were able to know what to expect from them. We knew which methods would be successful and what we could ask certain team members. It certainly became a more comfortable relationship."

Mark is also satisfied with Vesta's management of the project because now they had up-to-date information on the project and were not being surprised by developments in the project. However, this was not enough to overcome the problems in the project.

Towards the end of the project, Bluestone realized that they would not get the finished project on time. The Vesta team suggested a solution, as Mark explained:

"At the end of the project – it was good and bad – they suggested we bring one of the lead developers to come here and work on the bugs and get them cleared up. He became our sole support in finishing the project. It was very effective but it was an added cost we weren't expecting – that was the bad part."

Though the project was finally nearing completion to Bluestone's specifications, Bluestone now faces another problem. While they were familiar with the previous product and had provided training to Vesta on the features to be included in the project, they found out that they would not be able to take over the maintenance and support of this new application as they had expected. Their involvement in the development of the product had been minimal except for testing of modules and providing feedback. They found themselves unhappily dependent on Vesta for the maintenance of the product and decided to retain the services of Vesta for ongoing support.

6.6.4 Through the "Social Capital" Lens

Having presented the background and the story of the outsourcing relationship, the focus now turns to analysis of the field text using the social capital framework.

6.6.4.1 Social Capital in the Bluestone-Vesta relationship

As in the previous cases, the determination of the presence of social capital in the relationship is made by examining whether the different elements of the three dimensions of social capital are manifest in the relationship.

6.6.4.1.1 Structural dimension: Access patterns and appropriable organization

Ideally, the contract and supporting documents include plans for monitoring and managing the outsourcing project and communication between the client and vendor organizations, representing the agreement between the organizations on the governance of the project. The absence of such definition can result in confusion about who and where to get information from. This is the problem with the Bluestone-Vesta relationship at the beginning of the project. This problem is not unique to Bluestone and Vesta. During the data collection process, it was noted that when small and inexperienced client and small vendor organizations enter into an outsourcing arrangement, often they proceed based on an agreement on price alone. This naturally leads to problems later and can only be overcome with considerable effort on both sides to build a relationship. Initially, while Atul and the Vesta team are working to their own beat, the Bluestone team is frustrated because they are not satisfied since often they are not able to get information from Vesta on the progress of the project. However, under Jay's direction and with input from Bluestone, the access patterns for the project are specified. More people are brought into the project on the Bluestone side as needed, increasing the access necessary to complete the project.

Bluestone did not have the benefit of any processes they could transfer to this outsourcing arrangement. While Vesta has been in existence for more than ten years at the time of this project, the Vesta team also does not appear to use any proven routines to improve the interaction with Bluestone. Many of their actions seemed to be reactions and stopgap measures to overcome problems, like sending an employee over to the Bluestone site so that the project can be finished.

6.6.4.1.2 Cognitive dimension: Shared understanding

> "A common understanding of goals at both high level and specific level is very important, also to have similar quality standards." (Mark)

Though Mark mentions that the shared understanding of the scope of the project is important, the Bluestone team does not provide any input to the proposal or the contract beyond the training. Later, they find that the project is not progressing according to their expectations. All the features they expected will not be included in the final product. Not only are there scheduling issues causing problems in testing, but also differences between the organizations in their expectations of quality. While Atul thinks that the Vesta team is "more disciplined and quality conscious," Mark says they "found too many bugs in the program than they expected."

Once the teams started meeting regularly, these issues were addressed. As Atul explains:

> "They asked us to give those status reports (internal reports) to them also. They get to know what's happening in the project also. And if there's something going wrong, they'll help us."

Realizing that it is the client's responsibility also to define the requirements of the project, Mark and his colleagues now provide more input. The organizations develop a common understanding of what is necessary in the project, supported by the shared technological vocabulary and the understanding of the product features that was transferred to the Vesta team by the Bluestone team during the training. The problem is that this development of shared understanding of the goals and processes of the outsourcing arrangement of the came a bit too late. While a common technological vocabulary and the prevalent business norms provide the seeds for shared understanding, those alone are not sufficient in an outsourcing arrangement. The project does not get completed on time and Vesta has to place an employee at the Bluestone site to complete the project.

6.6.4.1.3 Relational dimension: Trust, norms, obligations & expectations, identification

Trust is an important characteristic of all successful inter-organizational relationships including outsourcing arrangements. At the start of the cashtrans project, Bluestone views Vesta as a trusted partner because of the connection between the top management of the two organizations and performance on the previous smaller projects. Unfortunately, Bluestone's initial faith in the capabilities and reliability of Vesta does not hold up as evidenced by Mark's statements below:

> "We entered in to this with the understanding that Vesta was very skilled in handling projects, and had the ability to handle the project, but we soon realized that there were many problems – quality, estimates, …What we learned in the end was that we needed to have one of their workers here in our offices to get the project done effectively, which was a disappointment."

Atul did not believe that trust was important in this outsourcing arrangement. His comments again indicate his belief that the scope of the project was completely known to both parties and all that was necessary in the outsourcing arrangement was to write the necessary code and test it.

> "Trust didn't play much of a role here because the client was very knowledgeable in the field; it was not a new project. They knew their features, and it's just a matter of what we tell them about how to implement it, and then how to reengineer it in this new version."

Questioned again about the importance of trust, he said that "trust was there." He bases this assessment on his knowledge of the satisfaction of Bluestone with the small projects they have done before. His assessment is correct, because before the start of the project, Bluestone did believe that Vesta was capable and reliable. Many small vendor organizations use this approach where they use small pilot projects as opportunities to develop the client's trust in their capabilities and a chance to gain larger contracts. The familiarity with Vesta and the connection between the top management of the two organizations persuaded Bluestone to continue their relationship with Vesta.

The two organizations have derogatory comments about the discipline and quality of work in the other organization. These organizations definitely do not identify with each other. Atul comments that the Vesta team was more disciplined and that they had the technical competence to do the job. However, Mark does not agree; he comments on the quality of the work done by Vesta initially:

> "One of the issues we ran into early on was that early releases had many more bugs than expected because the quality of testing that was going on within the vendor organization was not at the same level as we do internally with a product we develop."

While Mark agrees that Vesta was flexible in using extra resources to complete the project, he believes the reason that they had to put in extra resources was because they did not estimate the requirements of the project well.

"If they had done the estimation and requirements analysis properly, this would not have been an issue." (Mark)

This is an assessment with which Atul and Jay concur. However, Atul feels they were also flexible in accommodating the changes that Mark and his team brought in. He comments:

"An example was they asked us to do certain things which were not in the contract, but they asked us to drop some modules which were not in the contract, so we had to balance those."

So, there is some amount of finger pointing going on with both parties blaming the other for the glitches in the project. While Jay believes that the goals of the project can only be achieved through cooperation, he comments that the client has to be reasonable in asking for changes and arguing that different items were included in the scope of the project.

"The customer also has to realize that the vendor also is doing work not for free. You know, the vendor also has to feed their staff and everybody else – they have to pay"

Thus, both organizations view the other as not being flexible or cooperative enough. The initial problems in the outsourcing arrangement have inhibited the development of trust and other elements of the relational dimension in the relationship.

6.6.4.1.4 Is social capital present in the Bluestone-Vesta relationship?

The structural dimension of social capital is important in providing members of both organizations access to information to complete the project. It also defines the interaction patterns between the organizations. In cases of "symmetric incomplete information" (Lin et al, 2004) where the vendor does not have the business knowledge and the client does not have the technical knowledge, it is important to have some mechanism to aid the exchange of knowledge. This interaction is necessary for the development of shared understanding, but does not happen to the extent required in the Bluestone-Vesta relationship. The Bluestone-Vesta case is additionally complicated by the fact that a common agreement for the management of the process also has not been set, and the project appears to be floundering. This leads to misunderstanding and frustration, inhibiting the development of the relational dimension of social capital as well. Thus, it is clear that at the start of the outsourcing arrangement, the Bluestone-Vesta relationship was weak in the three dimensions of social capital.

In the initial stages of the previous case, in the absence of formal feedback structures, we see Athene using the informal network within the client organization to provide satisfactory services to the client. Why is Vesta not able to do the same? A primary reason is Atul's insistence that the Vesta team already knew what they needed to do and their job was to "deliver completed modules." While Bluestone's expectations are that they would be involved in the development of the product, Atul's mindset prevents the Vesta team from communicating with the Bluestone team. In fact, Atul believes that is how software development projects have been managed at Vesta. In the absence of interaction between the two teams, the elements of social capital do not develop in the relationship. These repercussions from the actions of one individual emphasize the importance of the role of the boundary spanner. Additionally, being inexperienced with outsourcing, Bluestone did not realize the importance of setting processes for monitoring and feedback. While Mark comments that the relationship is important, he takes no initiative in planning activities such as joint meetings that would help develop the relationship.

Small and inexperienced clients often make this mistake of letting the vendor completely determine the processes for managing the outsourcing arrangement. While Bluestone's lack of involvement can be ascribed to their inexperience with this project, it is clear that both organizations need to recognize and actively pursue the development of a relationship rich in trust, shared understanding, and other elements of social capital to be able to complete the project satisfactorily. Mark now realizes this mistake. He comments:

> "The client organization needs to take the lead on that (defining the requirements and the processes). The vendor may be able to assist, but it's the client's responsibility to make sure that things will be done right."

Jay's advent improves the situation. Under his leadership, they have been able to put in place procedures for communication between the two organizations leading to the development of a shared understanding of the goals of the project. They are working towards a cooperative relationship, and there is an expectation that problems will be solved together. Atul also notices this change; he comments:

> "There was not enough transparency to the client; that was the ultimate thing, so he wants us to—because we sent our status report to our own people, our own project management, initially, and they asked us to give those status reports to them also. They get to know what's happening in the project also. And if there's something going wrong, they'll help us."

However, there is a lingering feeling of distrust with Bluestone now demanding everything in writing from the vendor. Bluestone feels that they have not been able to derive the expected benefits from the outsourcing arrangement. They are forced to continue the relationship because they have not been able to absorb the knowledge required from Vesta to maintain the product themselves and have become dependent on Vesta. While the two organizations have been able to cultivate some amount of social capital, it is not enough to create a desire in Bluestone to continue the relationship.

6.6.4.2 Factors that promote social capital in the Bluestone-Vesta relationship

While the short and simpler initial projects Vesta had done for Bluestone provided an indication of their capabilities, those had not given them an opportunity to develop a working relationship. However, once they started having weekly meetings under Jay's management, a sense of camaraderie developed between the two teams. Thus, it is not purely the age of the relationship between the two organizations in numerical terms that contributes to the development of social capital. As Nahapiet and Ghoshal (1998) note, social capital develops through exchange. While Atul did not see the benefits of developing a relationship with the client at the start, he agrees that the two organizations are able to work together better now, exchanging and combining their know-how to complete the work. As he explains:

> "It became more of a relationship with individuals over time; it was first a relationship between organizations, not individuals. We know what to expect from them and our communication improved. We know which methods of communication will be successful and what kind of things we could ask each team member and this certainly led to a more comfortable relationship."

Mark now realizes that the specification of requirements of the project as well as the processes for monitoring and interaction between the organizations should have been included in the contract. Many of the problems in this relationship can be traced back to this lack of <u>definition</u>. He recollects that there were "some vague statements about that (the governance of the project) in initial proposal, but they were very brief." With hindsight, his advice to clients is "to establish a shared understanding in meetings and conversation."

Strangely enough, a communication plan was not part of the contract. Vesta's plan was to have meetings as needed. As Atul comments:

"The contract didn't address it at all. Initially we did meetings as needed, but as the project developed we decided that a weekly meeting was important."

These weekly meetings clarified for the Vesta team the functionalities of the 'cashtrans' application. These also helped the Bluestone team realize the constraints associated with implementing this product in a new environment. Additionally, it helped the Bluestone team provide the Vesta team with an appreciation of their business and the expectations of their customers. Once the team members from both side got to know each other through the weekly meetings, informal communication between the teams also improved. Mark comments that the "informal communication helps to relax the tension between the two organizations."

Bluestone feels highly dependent on Vesta, given their limited knowledge of the new software. Vesta also realizes that Bluestone is highly dependent on them. As Jay comments:

"I would say the customer has more at stake because it's not like you can chain the party and make them go through with it And then you've lost your money, you've lost your credibility, you've lost the edge over the market place, you've lost the savings you were going to achieve. So, I think, you know, they have a bigger stake. I mean, the supplier's stake is no smaller, either. You know, supplier also has to make sure that--I mean, if word gets around that you did not do well, that's going to affect your ability to compete in other spaces because you want a defensible client."

He realizes however that the outcome of this project can have ramifications for Vesta as well. However, he realizes that the higher dependency of Bluestone makes it unlikely for them to remove them from the project. As seen before in the Montezuma-Apollo case, perceptions of asymmetric dependence inhibit the development of social capital, particularly the development of the relational dimension.

The <u>personal rapport between the project executives</u>, who are the boundary spanners, is acknowledged as a building block for the inter-organizational relationship. In the Bluestone-Vesta case, Atul's initial attitudes did not sit well with the client. Mark comments:

"Initially, there was just a project manager assigned by the vendor organization and I think it didn't prove to be very effective. It wasn't related to position, but to personal issues. Rather than replace a local manager, they gave the responsibilities to the vice president of the organization and that changed the amount of attention our company got. Having weekly involvement with a person so high up in the organization definitely helped."

Asked what qualifications he thought the project manager should have, Mark lists the ingredients for an ideal project manager:

"…should listen and know enough about technology and the environment they are doing it in…to be able to tell us what's reasonable and what's not reasonable and to be able to suggest better alternatives"

It is also interesting to note that Mark thinks they "got better technical skills once the VP (Jay) was involved," even though Jay acknowledged that the reason Atul was not removed from the project was his technical expertise. Among all the interviewees for this research project, Atul's position that the relationship is not important since all the parameters of the project are known and limited interaction between the teams is necessary to complete the project is an isolated one. Henderson (1990) finds that an IS executive's predisposition in favor of the relationship is necessary for success of the outsourcing project. And it can be seen that the absence of this predisposition in this case creates problems in the development of social capital.

6.6.4.3 Social capital facilitates the combination and exchange of resources in the Bluestone-Vesta relationship

The theoretical framework suggests that social capital provides facilitating conditions for the combination and exchange and resources necessary for the project. In the Bluestone-Vesta case, the structures for communication and exchange between the two organizations have not been defined at the onset of the project. In the previous case of Haleakala and Athene, a similar weakness in the structural dimension is initially noted. However, it did not develop into a problem and obstruct the access necessary for the combination and exchange of resources. This difference between the cases can be attributed to two factors: one, lack of appropriable organization, and two, weak relational dimension of social capital. Later, with the development of some amount of trust and cooperation between the organizations, access becomes easier.

It is clear that Bluestone has expectations of value from this outsourcing project; this software was the bread-n-butter of their organization. The livelihood of the Bluestone team depends on the success of this software in the market and it is essential to have this project completed as planned. As Mark says, "it's in my own interest that I want this to succeed." Vesta treats this just as another development project. They are aware of the possibility of continued opportunities with this client, but do not seem particularly concerned about the eventuality of loss of further business with this client. Part of this complacency may arise from the belief that the relationship between the top management puts them in a position of advantage when bidding for future projects at Bluestone. Many interviewees (not in this case) have mentioned that outsourcing deals are awarded through personal contacts.

With the initial access and communication problems, Vesta does not fully understand the project or Bluestone's business need and see themselves only as porting the application from one language to another. Bluestone has no chance to enhance their understanding of the new environment in which they want to operate. This limited sharing inhibits the assimilation and application of knowledge held by the other party. While the project gets completed finally, the flaws in the software are evidence of this lack of combination capability.

6.6.4.4 Assessment: Satisfaction

In the final assessment, Jay feels that they failed in setting the client's expectations, and thus leaving them with feelings of dissatisfaction.

"You have to set the expectations of the customer correctly. You know, they've to be prepared for it. That's what it is."

However, he feels they have provided value to the customer and sees their decision to continue with them as a testimony to that "value-add." Atul also feels comfortable about the outcome of the project, but Mark has a 'laundry list' of items that have led to his dissatisfaction with the project. Starting from the initial estimates, he feels that the Vesta team did a poor job. He explains:

"I think they did not do a good job estimating the amount of work that would need to go in, so their bid was lower than it should have been, and they did more work that they were expecting. But we had to pay some extra to get the project completely done, which technically shouldn't have had to happen in a fix bid contract."

And as the work on the project progressed, there was further "dissatisfaction because they would choose to replicate something exactly from the old system even if it wasn't most appropriate in the new technology." This dissatisfaction can also be seen as a "failure in assessment" by Vesta. If Vesta had employed some means for assessment, they could have captured the client's dissatisfaction earlier and addressed it. However, this lack of assessment is not surprising, given their inattention to communication.

Part of their dissatisfaction comes also with the realization that they should not have outsourced the development of this application.

"Being a software company, we were outsourcing building our core product, and I think we learned that it is too important a part of our business to entrust to an outside organization. In order to maintain it well and support it for our customer, and customer support was a very important part of our organization and in order to respond quickly to our customers, we felt that the kind of activity needs to be in house so we can make sure we have the greatest knowledge on the product. It was very different from a company that sells stuffed animals and uses an outsourcing company to make a software system for them"

There is no doubt that Mark is right, though late in this realization. A pure outsourcing model was definitely not the best choice here. The organizations would have been well advised to adopt a co-sourcing model, "where the vendor and client collaborate so closely that the vendor can replace or augment the client's IT competencies" (Kaiser and Hawk, 2004). However, based on the account of their interactions, it is not sure that they would have been able to achieve the level of collaboration needed to sustain a co-sourcing relationship.

6.6.5 Case study conclusion

In this case, initially the relationship is lacking in all dimensions of social capital. In fact, one may ask whether a relationship existed between the two organizations. The client is the first to realize that they are in real danger of losing their core product. Goaded by the possibility of failure of the outsourcing arrangement, the client assesses the progress of the outsourcing arrangement and presses for changes in the governance of the outsourcing arrangement. This leads to the development of the elements of the structural and cognitive dimensions of social capital in the relationship. Trust and feelings of cooperation and flexibility still need to grow in this relationship.

Yet, there is a positive sign. The learning about the management of the outsourcing relationship that is evidenced in Mark's statements bode well for the future. Through this experience, Bluestone has developed an understanding of the procedures and mechanisms that could be applied in the management of future projects and even in their continued relationship with Vesta. If Jay also stays on board, through continued interaction, there is potential for social capital to develop in the Bluestone-Vesta relationship.

6.7   Case 6: Denali and Vishnu

The Denali-Vishnu case follows the same path as that of Bluestone and Vesta, except that in this case, the vendor, Vishnu, is an offshore vendor located in India. Just like Bluestone and Vesta, Denali and Vishnu fit into the SME category. As the story unfolds, it can be seen that the similarities do not end there. In particular, the actions of managers from Vishnu and the inexperience of the managers at Denali result in a relationship deficient in social capital. Realizing that the project was teetering close to failure, the two organizations have to make a difficult decision – is it too late to save this relationship? The focus of this case is on how the assessment of the work processes results in a reevaluation of the relationship.

6.7.1   Introduction

The client, Denali, is a national wholesale Internet Service Provider (ISP) based in Oregon. Denali offers Internet service solutions for resale to end-users; thus, Denali's customers are ISPs. Denali provides these customers (ISPs) with a product called Netserve in a Box, software that bundles Windows-based management with all the network facilities necessary to provide the ISP's end-users with Internet access. The product helps Denali's customers activate, bill, and manage ISP accounts. The product is backed by 24/7 support.

Vishnu develops and supports business software applications, serving clients in the commercial software, manufacturing, and marketing and media industries. Founded in 1995, Vishnu is based in Bangalore, India. Similar to Durga (Haleakala-Durga case), Vishnu has established a presence in the U.S. with an office in Boston. One of Vishnu's strengths is in providing solutions to software provider. Vishnu offers software providers a full range of services to support the lifecycle of software products. The organization got their start building and maintaining commercial software applications for software providers and Web-based businesses.

Table 6-7: Interviewees in the Denali - Vishnu case

Name of interviewee	Organization	Position	Duration of interview	Taped?
Todd	Denali (Client)	CEO	1.5 hours	Yes
Santosh	Vishnu (Vendor)	Area Manager – US West	1.5 hours	No
Nath	Vishnu	Manager	45 minutes	No

Todd is the CEO of Denali and is the person responsible for the unique idea of servicing ISPs by providing the software in a box. It was his idea to consider offshore outsourcing when the company decided to develop new software to interface with their customers. At the time of the interviews, the project had been going on for about five months.

Santosh is Vishnu's Area Manager for the western part of the United States. Santosh explains his role in the company: "My role is in client relationship, developing new clients. I cover a large area of the Southwest, including California. On projects where there are no assigned project managers, I also do the project management, meeting with the clients, and all that stuff, too." He has been with Vishnu for about five years now and has been working in the sourcing industry before that. Santosh responded to the email message inviting organizations to participate in this research project.

Nath is a project manager at Vishnu's office in Bangalore. He was not involved in this project, but has worked on several outsourcing projects for clients based in the U.S. Nath's comments are interesting because they shed light on the company's perspective on providing services to US clients.

6.7.2 The Outsourcing Project

It was Todd's idea to develop a software application that would "enable an organization to instantly become an ISP." The idea has been quite successful and according to Todd, Denali now offers "a footprint of over 50,000 dialup access numbers-- a larger dial-up footprint than AOL, Earthlink and MSN combined-- and a vast array of technologies and advantages to the hundreds of ISPs across the country that it serves."

Todd and his partner "made a decision to keep *their* staff small and focused on *their* core competence, which is providing wholesale ISP services." So, when they decided to upgrade and modify "software that *their* customers could use to interface with *their* services, to provide our services to their customers," they had to look to vendor organizations for help. They decided to look for an offshore vendor because of possible cost benefits. After a web search, Todd sent email requests for information to half a dozen organizations. Vishnu stood out among the bidders because "they were very consistent with their follow up and professional. They also were certified CMM level 4, and that helped." (Todd)

When the Vishnu team met with Todd, they extensively discussed the product and the requirements. This "initial discussion was captured in a proposal, and the proposal became the statement of work" (Santosh). This statement of work, according to Santosh, was "pretty well defined" and became part of the contract. This was Denali's first foray into outsourcing, and they decided to use the contract templates in use in the vendor organization, Vishnu. Based on these templates, the "contract terms were hammered out between the two companies" (Todd), and a fixed price contract was finalized for the project.

6.7.3 The Client-Vendor Relationship

Todd was certain that Vishnu would be able to handle this project and meet their requirements as stated in the contract. This initial trust is based on several factors. One is the guarantee provided by the contract, which acts as a safety net in case things go wrong. A second factor is the belief that the high CMM rating will translate to quality in the work completed by the vendor. This trust is bolstered by the initial interactions with the client.

While the client thus confidently awaits the completion of the application and makes plans for the marketing of the product, the vendor is in a quandary. At their first introduction to the product, they vendor representatives had realized that the application needed considerably more work than what Todd suggested. However, they decided not to tell the client about this at the start. The reasoning is that once a relationship has been built up, it would be easier to describe the problems with the project. Santosh explained:

"The code was really bad. I mean, the code was pretty pathetic, and what happened was that we were not completely truthful. I'm usually in the middle. My technology person said that this code has to be rewritten. And what will you do if the client says, "I don't have the money. We have to use the code"? Well, if you're trying to build a relationship, I can say, "Well, this works, and this doesn't work," but at the beginning of the relationship, it's kind of difficult to come up and say that. So, after the relationship is built up, then you can say that. So, at the beginning, even though we knew that the code was not good, we were not very truthful, and so, basically, we told them, "OK, we can do that." And, so, we started the work; it was incomplete; the project had a number of problems."

As the project progresses, the Vishnu team realized that the situation was worse than they had even realized.

"Three months later, we are staring down a bottomless pit. From a quality assurance standpoint, a programming standpoint, the functional areas, there were a lot of problems. There were so many problems…"

However, even before they got to the point where "the relationship was built up" enough to confess to this discrepancy, Todd became aware that there was something not completely right with the progress of the project. He is not satisfied with the "quality of the work and the speed of the work." Though they had agreed upon procedures in place for communication, the Vishnu team was not following these consistently. Santosh explained an additional complication with the project:

"The project manager is actually a soft-spoken, nice person, but he was very reluctant about communicating with the customer. He didn't have the guts to say anything to the customer – to explain even the small bugs in the project."

This was certainly a problem, since the project manager was the only member of the project team who was located in the U.S. All the other team members were in their center in Bangalore, India.

Santosh and the Vishnu team explained to Todd that the application had "so many problems that there was no way that the project could be finished on time." At this stage, an irate Todd sent out an email message to the Vishnu management indicating his displeasure and plans to terminate the contract unless the Vishnu team stepped up their efforts. Santosh describes the email:

"This is your last chance; do this, this, this, or we are going to quit."

The Vishnu team explained to Todd that the application had been so bug-ridden that it was not possible to complete the project as laid out in the contract. Though not completely satisfied with these explanations, Todd decided to continue with Vishnu. Acquiescing to Todd's demands, the reporting system was modified to ensure that "all bugs would be completely visible in the system." The client would be able to see the real progress with the project "in terms of bugs that were being fixed as well as the ones that were fixed." Todd felt that the communications between the two still needed "fine-tuning" and he "started to take a more active role in the management of the project." Todd also realized that the contract now had to be modified to a time and materials contract because of the extensive work involved in completing the application.

Todd is now satisfied with Vishnu's performance on the project. He confessed that he "still has some trust issues" with the vendor and does not feel the vendor is capable of fixing all the problems with the application. He has allocated some of the work to one of his own employees so that the work would be completed on schedule.

Surprisingly, even after the project that they had outsourced offshore for cost savings turned out to be six times more expensive, Todd commented that he would consider outsourcing future projects to this vendor. He explained:

> "Um, there's a reasonable chance. I'd say probably a 60/40 chance in their favor. ... a portion of the 60%, half of the 60%, simple the momentum that we have with this company, and 30% of the 60 that I would weigh in their favor anecdotally, is our satisfaction."

6.7.3.1 Through the "Social Capital" Lens

Having presented the background and the story of the outsourcing relationship, the focus now turns to analysis of the field text using the social capital framework.

6.7.3.2 Social Capital in the Denali - Vishnu relationship

As in previous cases, the determination of the presence of social capital in the relationship is made by examining whether the different elements of the three dimensions of social capital are manifest in the relationship.

6.7.3.2.1 Structural dimension: Access patterns and appropriable organization

Even without the contract, the access patterns in this project are quite clear. With "a small project at a small client, there is one project manager" at Vishnu who will be handling the account, according to Santosh. Todd is the project manager's counterpart at the client organization. Thus, the links between the two organizations for exchanging information on this project is clear.

Without prior experience with outsourcing, Denali does not have any routines or procedures to appropriate for use in the management of this project. Vishnu, on the other hand, has been in the business for about nine years at the time of the project, and has developed procedures and routines that they could use in this project. On their web site, they have a number of white papers and case studies that identify and describe best practices in the management of offshore outsourcing[13]. Nath comments that these documents catch the eyes of clients who search for vendors on the web. With its experience in managing offshore projects, Vishnu has a project team and communications set-up in place immediately after finalizing the contract. This is another aspect of the outsourcing arrangement that impressed Todd.

6.7.3.2.2 Cognitive dimension: Shared understanding

Todd had very high expectations about the project outcome at the beginning, based on the CMM rating and the "India brand" image. Santosh comments on the perception of the India-brand:

---

[13] In fact, it was from a white paper published by Vishnu that was available on the Sourcing Interest Group's web site that the contact information for Vishnu was first obtained.

"The media gives people wrong expectations. I think they either lead people to total exuberance or complete cynicism. Often, people come with all these expectations because Bangalore is the software capital of the world."

Todd was also impressed by the CMM rating, and mentions the rating a number of times during the interview. However, he does not have any familiarity with the model in his organization and has neither seen nor asked for any of the documents produced during the project for compliance with the CMM. Nath comments on this:

"I call the CMM problem. Yes, people are expecting some standard today; it is almost like if you want to join this club, you have to exhibit a certain pedigree. And that status symbol is the CMM rating. I have many problems with the CMM rating. One, people tend to focus too much on these ratings. Small business owners, particularly, are not in a position to use or evaluate compliance with CMM. They are captivated by the CMM rating and believe that this is going to get them high quality work. If they do not provide feedback, you assume that things are going well. When you are working on a fixed price contract, the onus is on you (the vendor) to keep the costs low."

Though Santosh and Nath both separately comment on the importance of managing a client's expectations, the Vishnu team does not make any effort at the onset to understand or set the client's expectations. Instead, they are caught in plans for the subterfuge.

The Vishnu team purposefully hides from Denali the problems with the application and the amount of work to be done. While the comments from Santosh about the creation of the statement of work seem to suggest that there was a shared understanding about the work to be done and the metrics to be met, it is apparent that this is not the case. Thus each organization has its own notion of the work to be done, which differs from that of the other organization. There is also a lack of agreement regarding the measurement of the quality of work, with Todd finding that the vendor's output falls short of his expectations. Vishnu's lack of attention to the quality standards that Denali subscribes to also shows that the Vishnu team does not appreciate the market pressures that Denali faces.

Todd is also aware now that the application as it existed had more problems than he knew. He agrees that some of the confusion has been because of these problems and "takes ownership for that." Todd's willingness to accept the situation instead of placing blame entirely on the vendor helps in creating an environment where both organizations can work towards a common understanding of the task and the processes necessary for completing it.

In the Bluestone-Vesta case, the lack of shared understanding about the content of the application and the communication and monitoring processes for the outsourced project was a result of the vendor's inattention to the clients' needs and the client's inability to articulate their needs completely. Denali and Vishnu also end up in a similar unfortunate situation because the vendor was not completely honest at first. If they had initiated a dialogue to identify the problems and come to an agreement on the work to be done, both parties would have a clear understanding of the goals for the project and their own responsibilities.

Todd brought up another factor that inhibits the development of shared understanding between the two organizations. Variations in accent and word-usage often pose a problem when dealing with offshore vendors, even though Todd contended that this was not a major factor in this case.

"There's been some accent issues, understanding what the developers are saying, just understanding what the words they're using. That is just one variable."

Both parties agreed that open communication is the best means for overcoming these problems. The two organizations worked together to improve the reporting and feedback systems so that a common agreement on the progress of the project can be developed. These communication measures have fostered a shared understanding of the processes that need to be in place to complete the development of the application. This agreement on processes and Vishnu's willingness to abide by the agreement contributes to Todd's belief that the two organizations would be able to work together again, and be better the next time around.

6.7.3.2.3 Relational dimension: Trust, norms, obligations & expectations, identification

Trust obviously is an issue in this case. As mentioned before (Section 6.10.3) , Todd had trust in Vishnu's intent and capabilities because of the guarantees offered by the contract, their high CMM rating, and the professionalism and consistency evidenced in the initial interactions. However, as the two organizations interact, and the issues that Vishnu had concealed were exposed, Todd is anxious about Vishnu's reliability and openness. Through communication, often contentious, the differences between the two organizations regarding required modifications to the software, time schedules, and resource requirements were resolved.

The reasons behind Todd's decision to continue with the project given the vendor's duplicity are captured in this statement:

"I knew they had the capabilities – they were a CMM4 company, and in the initial interactions, they came across well"

Along with Vishnu's commitment to address the problem, the high initial trust in Vishnu's capabilities and professionalism that Todd had carries the two organizations over this hurdle and keeps them communicating and working together. Other researchers have commented on this interesting phenomenon of the persistence of trust in problematic situations as well. Robinson (1996) concluded that trust is not completely erased by a perceived breach of agreement, where the parties had high initial levels of trust. Additionally, dependence may have a role to play in Todd's decision. While the vendor's devious behavior has been exposed in the early stages of the contract, in the case of a small organization like Denali whose business depends on the product it has outsourced, the investments it has made in the outsourcing arrangement may encourage it from continuing with the arrangement. This dependence may have influenced Todd's decision to continue trusting Vishnu. Researchers generally agree that dependence is antecedent to trust (Geyskens et al, 1998).

When Todd realized that the Vishnu team was keeping up with the agreed changes, he felt confident that the project will be completed and that Vishnu will honor its agreement with his organization, Denali. However, Todd had some lingering doubts regarding the openness of the Vishnu team.

"There have definitely been some issues of trust where I've questioned the--I mean, sometimes, when a bug gets resolved we think it should be resolved in 30 minutes or an hour and it takes 3 hours or 6 hours to resolve. You know, I've wondered is that really what's going on? And, are we getting over billed for time?"

Surprisingly, he does not ask to see any of the internal documentation at Vishnu, but again decides to resolve these doubts through communication with Vishnu. The Vishnu team has complete trust in Denali; they believe that Denali will meet its obligations to the vendor. Todd's professionalism and openness in communication has contributed to this trust.

"If he has any issues, he will bring it out to the open." (Santosh)

And Todd also commented that he was determined to raise issues as it happened to avoid those from "snowballing."

Interestingly, when talking about the requirements for a successful outsourcing arrangement, Santosh advised:

"In new relationships, building trust is important; commitment follows from that. At first, you build trust; with repeated interaction, this trust will create commitment."

"Avoid ambiguity about the system requirements, avoid ambiguity about what you can provide, avoid ambiguity about what the system can do. This kind of trust, this kind of openness builds trust and avoids problems later." (Nath)

These comments from Vishnu team members are surprising in view of the stance that Vishnu has taken in this project. Their initial decision not to expose all the problems with the software can be viewed as the act of individuals belonging to a national culture that frowns upon disagreeing with individuals in positions of authority, like the decision-maker in a client organization. After all, India has been ranked very high on the Hofstede's power distance[14] index. However, this decision appears to be more a reaction to the pressures of a crowded market place, since Vishnu plans to disclose the problems to the vendor at a later stage. In the Indian IT services industry, entry barriers for new firms are low because of the current global demand (Krishna et al, 2004). However, an easy entry does not promise continued existence, and a number of firms have gone bankrupt shortly after inception. Naturally, every firm in this service industry wants to get new clients and keep them. With their experience in the offshore outsourcing market and dealing with small businesses, the Vishnu team also realizes that once the project has started, the client would become dependent on them. Santosh evaluates the dependency of the client:

"This particular client, his dependence on us is quite high, since this product has to go to the market, and he had been working on it for some time."

Knowing that it is unlikely the client would terminate the contract once the project has started, the Vishnu team decided to go ahead with the subterfuge. However, they do not plan to carry this deception all the way. They intend to tell the client about the problems, as soon as they have built a rapport with the client. The problem is that the project manager initially did not make the necessary efforts to build this rapport. However, once things were out in the open and smoothed out, the client is satisfied with the vendor's commitment to the project and flexibility in handling the project. Todd remarked:

"They've put their best foot forward. Once they found out that this wasn't working, they were willing to come forward and figure out some kind of common ground and use the necessary resources."

With increased involvement in the project from Todd also, the vendor is also assured that the client will provide them with the feedback necessary to keep the project on track. Satisfied with the progress of the current project, both organizations look to the future.

---

[14] Power distance is a cultural index derived by sociologist Geert Hofstede and indicates a culture's respect for authority.

"You're looking at future growth prospects, the referenceablity of the client; I call it the dependability index of the client. You know, what can you get from the client in terms of future business opportunities, as well as his providing additional references for us." (Santosh)

Todd also has expectations of leveraging the learning from this project, which is a reason that he may work further with the vendor. As a small business owner, he would particularly like to keep a lid on costs.

"The overhead involved with changing companies is—I'm reluctant to change companies; that's why I would weight doing another project with them more in their favor because of what we have, because of that momentum."

He has informed the Vishnu management that there are new projects that he may hire them to do, if the outcome from this project is satisfactory.

"We do have other projects coming up that we could hire Vishnu to do, and if their performance in this project could improve even further—and it has improved—if they could improve even further, you know, then, I'd be tickled at that."

6.7.3.2.4 Is social capital present in the Denali - Vishnu relationship?

While the relationship was not rich in social capital at the onset, the development of shared understanding between the organizations regarding the goals of the project and the processes required to complete the project has changed that. Denali is confident that Vishnu will meet its obligations and appreciates their commitment and flexibility in the project. Similarly, Vishnu values Todd's openness and feedback, since he is most knowledgeable about the project. Both organizations are looking forward to a continued and productive relationship.

6.7.3.3 Factors that promote social capital in the Denali - Vishnu relationship

The Vishnu management believed that continued interactions over time would build a relationship rich in social capital that would facilitate the communication of the problems with the project. Unfortunately, Vishnu's plans went awry, with the client discovering that the project was not progressing as well as expected before they were ready for their disclosure. Initially, the project manager was not able to establish a rapport with Todd to smooth out the disclosure either. However, "he (the project manager) woke up after the e-mail, that last call, and he woke up and started interacting with the customer more assertively, and the client has become happy" (Santosh).

With a new determination to solve their problems, the representatives from both organizations "argued their cases and discussed the issues" (Santosh). The two organizations were able to reconcile their differences and arrive at a clear understanding of the requirements through open communication. Open communication, even when contentious, helps develop trust and contributes to the development of norms like commitment and cooperation in the relationship. Similarly, when the requirements are well-defined, it reduces ambiguity and promotes cooperation between the two organizations.

Dependence is a double-edged sword. While the initial maneuvering by Vishnu was based on their belief that Denali's potential dependence on them would lead to inaction, the awareness of this dependence could have forced Denali to resent the relationship and terminate the contract. When organizations, especially small businesses, outsource their core product, they

128

create a situation of asymmetric dependency to their own disadvantage. And when they do not get actively involved in the outsourcing project and leave the management of the project to the vendor, they could dig themselves into a bigger hole. Usually, organizations that have the upper hand in the relationship would be less likely to expend effort to cultivate the relationship. By actively developing all three dimensions of social capital in the relationship, the disadvantaged organization – in this case, the client – can avoid this problem.

6.7.3.4 Social capital facilitates the combination and exchange of resources in the Denali - Vishnu relationship

The theoretical framework suggests that social capital provides facilitating conditions for the combination and exchange of resources necessary for the outsourcing project. Even though the structural ties between the organizations are quite straightforward, the deception practiced by the client limits the sharing of information about the project between the organizations. The problem is compounded by the initial lack of initiative of the client representative and the incapability of the vendor representative to develop a personal relationship. Once the problem is out in the open, the two organizations work together towards the completion of the project, with Todd redistributing the work between his staff and the Vishnu team. Both organizations now have access to the resources of the other organization.

As in all outsourcing arrangements, both organizations anticipate value from the completion of this project. The client is motivated by the potential to expand his customer-base using this product. Both organizations are also looking forward to continuing their relationship to leverage the learning that has happened in this project.

The overlap in knowledge and the shared technical vocabulary help the organizations to combine their knowledge and experience without difficulty. Unlike in the Bluestone-Vesta case, the participants in this case have the advantage that the product that is being developed does not require knowledge of a particular business domain.

6.7.3.5 Assessment: Satisfaction

Currently, both client and vendor are satisfied with the progress of the project. Yet, Todd expressed some dissatisfaction with the results. He explained:

"What we're measuring is quality—what I'm measuring is quality, and effectiveness, their ability to interpret what we're saying and turn it into code. And it is difficult to measure – it depends on them understanding our instructions."

Explaining that this dissatisfaction was not a reflection of the vendor's lack of efforts, he continued:

"Sometimes, their best efforts have not met my expectations".

Nath philosophized about the difficulty of meeting someone's expectations:

"All failure is based on an expectation in the human mind. Yes, you can set service levels, you have to have the system available for this length of time, and yes you do that, but then, the time the system was down that could have been a crucial time for them and so you have failed the client – there is a perception of failure in the client's mind, even if they agree with you that the service levels have been met. I think the fact is that quality standards are different. Take a simple example, for instance – I can ask you, is the car you used today running okay and I can ask the other people who were in the car.

Different people will have different opinions. You might base your answer on whether the car did what it was supposed to do. Other might also consider other aspects – the shock absorber's capability. The things we do are not simple and when they are not simple, the standards and expectations for these can never the same."

Nath's comments highlight the importance of the client and the vendor making their expectations clear at the start of the project and managing the other organization's expectations. Santosh explains how ongoing assessment of the project and communication of the progress and problems can help ensure that expectations are met.

"When you engage the client in a solution discussion, the client is also educated, and his expectations become more realistic."

Indeed, it can be seen that this is the case in the Denali-Vishnu relationship, with Denali accepting responsibility for some of the problems at the start of the project and both organizations working together to create a product that Denali can market.

6.7.4   Case study conclusion

The case thus ends on an upbeat note, even higher than that in the Bluestone-Vesta case. Shaken out of their complacency by Denali's ultimatum, Vishnu made changes in the management of the outsourcing project. Confronted with the problems that they had handed over to Vishnu and failure of the project, Denali also stepped up their efforts to build up a productive and cooperative working relationship. As Suresh sums it up,

"So, basically, we had a relationship that started off kind of OK, but it was shaky, then it actually got really bad, kind of went in the trough, and then we managed to pull it up, and now, it's going pretty well."

6.8   Case 7- Ozark-Brahma

Similar to the last two cases (Bluestone-Vesta and Denali-Vishnu), this case also involves client and vendor organizations who are both SMEs. The client is located in the U.S. while the vendor is based in India.   While in the last two cases the relationship between the two organizations initially floundered with the lack of social capital, this case presents a contrasting picture.   The two organizations have worked together on a number of projects.   Even with the geographical distance and cultural differences, the two organizations have been able to establish a relationship that meets the expectations of both and have grown stronger with each project. The satisfaction with the process and the outcome of each project helps the development of additional social capital in the relationship.   This case demonstrates the bi-directional relationship between social capital and intellectual capital and its creation – in this case, the process and outcome of applications outsourcing.

6.8.1   Introduction

The client organization, Ozark, develops and markets sales, management, and labor-saving tools for the heating, ventilation and air-conditioning (HVAC) industry. Ozark is located in the north-western part of the U.S. and is a subsidiary of a nation-wide organization that provides business training and coaching services to the HVAC industry. Ozark was established to focus on selling the custom hardware products developed by the parent company over the Internet, and to provide custom software for the HVAC industry.

Brahma was founded in 1996 by three individuals who graduated from premier educational institutions in the U.S. and worked with multinational corporations like IBM, Unisys, and Booz-Allen Hamilton. All of them had the opportunity to lead consulting and/or outsourcing projects at these organizations with clients from different countries. At the time of the interview, Brahma had achieved a CMM 4 rating and was shortly to be audited for a CMM 5 rating. Brahma is set up similar to Durga (Haleakala-Durga) and Vishnu (Denali-Vishnu) with an office in California. The development centre is located in a techno park in South India. Like Durga and Vishnu, they focus primarily on meeting the application development and maintenance needs of SMEs.

Table 6-8: Interviewees in the Ozark-Brahma case

Name of interviewee	Organization	Position	Duration of interview	Taped?
Greg	Ozark(Client)	Manager – Software Development	2 hours	Yes
Amar	Brahma (Vendor)	CEO	1.25 hours	Yes
Ajit	Brahma	IT Manager	45 minutes	No

Three individuals were interviewed regarding the Ozark-Brahma relationship: Greg, the manager in charge of software development at Ozark is an HVAC professional and his educational background is in this area. He does not have a background in software development. Amar is one of the founders and CEO at Brahma, and Ajit is a manager at Brahma who had worked on a couple of the Ozark projects.

6.8.2 The Outsourcing Project

At the time of the interview, Brahma has been associated with Ozark as a software outsourcing partner for about three years. For Ozark, Brahma is virtually its development centre. They have developed a number of applications for Ozark including load calculation systems and assessment systems, ecommerce site, and sales force automation tool with handheld device and web interfaces.

6.8.3 The Client-Vendor Relationship

Ozark wanted to develop a range of products for the HVAC industry and establish itself as a leader in providing tools for this industry. Initially, they hired a programmer to develop applications in-house. However, with the organizational management not having expertise or experience in software development, this internal effort fell short of expectations. So, Ozark was looking for an organization which had "talent in software developing" with which they could develop a long-term partnership. Greg explained the plan:

"We are going to discover how each company is going to respond. If you look at it from the relationship angle, it is kind of like dating - do we click, is it worth going forward?"

Ozark chose to find partners through e-guru, a web site that provides links and marketing opportunities to organizations around the world. Braham had already placed a marketing link on that site. Brahma's credentials caught Ozarks's eye. Ozark also identified some other Indian vendors. Ozark sent out a request for information to each of these organizations. With the long-term partnership goal in mind, Ozark interviewed each of the companies who responded. After this round, representatives from a handful of selected companies were brought in to look at one of the products that had been developed internally. Proceeding cautiously, Ozark's plan was to start with a small project requiring the vendor to upgrade this product and thus would help them gauge the organization. Greg commented on the initial interaction with the vendor:

> "We had several companies come in and look at our project, give us an estimate of doing our project, and at that we were looking at them and assessing how they are treating us, the questions they were asking, the communications, could we actually feel they were grasping the ideas."

Brahma's "approach *also* was to start cautiously with a pilot project. And we started off on a small contract – a pilot engagement – first and then it grew from that" (Ajit). Ozark's focus on the inter-organizational relationship is also evident in their lack of interest in CMM ratings. Amar commented: "This particular client was not looking for any CMM rating; he was not very keen on certified ratings, etc."

After the initial meetings, Ozark decided that Brahma would be an ideal candidate. Keeping with the spirit of relationship-building, they entered into a "handshake agreement" (Amar). According to Amar, there was "not much of a contract." He explained the initial legal agreements.

> "The initial document that was exchanged was an agreement to keep each other's intellectual property protection. That is the only kind of legal agreement we entered into. There was no more operational contract, just a handshake agreement. So it was more in terms of protecting an IP creation."

During the initial meetings and the first project, Greg interacted mostly with the project manager at the California office. While the first project was completed "not too much over budget, but past the scheduled time" Greg wanted to interact more closely with the development team in the organization. He felt that many of the problems in the first project happened because of "miscommunication between the salesperson and the programmers." He knew that on future projects were the requirements would be more complex, he needed to interact with the actual development team. In his words,

> "It was very important for me to have access, even to the design, the people that were actually programming, the programmers as well as the design person and not have to go through the salesperson."

This was not a problem for the Brahma management. Explaining Brahma's project management style approach, Amar said "we strive for frequent client interaction and transparency of operations." Greg felt that this closer interaction helped on later projects.

> "It is often hard to communicate when it is translated through the sales person to designer to programmer. By the time it got to the programmer, it was like a rumor. Things were added and left out. Then I was able to get access, and in my case we are working with the developers that are mainly in India." (Greg).

As they went through several projects together, both organizations learned more about each others' work styles and organizational requirements. This learning helped both organizations in their exchanges; Ozark was able to provide the Brahma team with the information they required, while the Brahma was able to translate these requirements into an application more smoothly as time progressed. Occasional disagreements were handled through open communication, with both parties encouraging the voicing of dissatisfaction. Though Brahma lacked knowledge of the HVAC business, through their interactions Ozark was able to provide them information about their company and the environment in which it operates. Together, they have been able to develop a range of applications that Ozark has successfully marketed. In fact, the success of the software products has caught the attention of a national technology and business television show, and Ozark is to be featured on the show in the near future.

6.8.4   Through the "Social Capital" Lens

Having presented the background and the story of the outsourcing relationship, the focus now turns to analysis of the field text using the social capital framework.

6.8.4.1   Social Capital in the Ozark-Brahma relationship

As in case 1, the determination of the presence of social capital in the relationship is made by examining whether the different elements of the three dimensions of social capital are manifest in the relationship.

6.8.4.1.1   Structural dimension: Access patterns and appropriable organization

The access patterns in this case are straightforward. Greg is the point person at Ozark and Amar is in charge of the project at Brahma. One of the associates at their office in California initially acted as the liaison, but in later projects he is taken off the project at Greg's insistence.

Realizing that they did not have the experience to set up the communication plan and monitoring schemes for an outsourcing project, Greg and the Ozark team were looking at the first project as a chance to gain learning and experience. Greg explained:

> "What we were looking for originally was a company that would work for us and we would be responsive and grow together on these projects. We weren't coming in thinking, we wanted that first project to be a huge success and go very well"

Their plan was to learn from this project and create the "appropriable organization" that would help them on later projects. Besides the experience the founders brought to Brahma, the company had gained experience working on applications outsourcing projects over the past years. They also follow the processes prescribed by the CMM model. Thus, Brahma has processes they could use in their engagement with Ozark. These come in useful in their dealings with Ozark. Amar explained:

> "We have learned the best practices while working at our earlier organizations. For instance, I was in charge of a JP Morgan project at IBM – just a small one. And our company only takes small projects, right now we only have the resources to deal with small projects. Our idea is to have a planned growth and structured resources that we can apply to projects again and again. If you look at an Infosys[15], you can see that is one of

---

[15] Infosys Technologies Limited is an India based global IT Services, IT Solutions and Technology Services. With 43,000 employees and revenues of over US $ 1.5 billion, Infosys is one of India's major Information Technology companies.

their strengths – they have developed a good model and instituted processes they can follow and teach their people."

6.8.4.1.2 Cognitive dimension: Shared understanding

The Brahma team realizes that shared understanding must exist at different levels for a project to be successful. While Ozark does not have the programming knowledge, the Brahma team must be able to absorb what The Ozark tem needs. To Ozark this means that they must go beyond simply understanding what the client specifies.

> "We need a business model understanding. We must find out the customers of our customers, because our customer may be doing software development for someone else to use." (Ajit)

> "Understanding each other's organization is very important – otherwise you can't take it through. Knowing each other's organization very well – their constraints and resources – that is important." (Amar)

Given that only some of the employees can visit the client's location in the U.S., these employees play a very important role. According to Ajit, they must "create a proper understanding of what is needed for us and for the client." While they must gather information from the client, they must educate the client on the content and periodicity of information that must be provided to the vendor. Greg also realizes that Ozark needs to be educated. For instance, talking about the testing phase of the system development, he said:

> "I was never a tester and if the design company can develop or help someone like my company develop a testing plan as they go in, it's just going to be a lot smoother. Since them I've kind of learned what I need to do to do testing and the testing, once the initial portion is done the testing is the most important."

Like many successful offshore vendors, Brahma also trains employees on the requisite technologies to ensure that the employees can understand and meet the client requirements. They also aggressively pursue repeat business to leverage the learning that has occurred during previous projects. This learning happens not only through the exchange of information to complete the project, but the sharing of experiences. In this case, as they worked on projects, Greg explained the processes in the HVAC industry to the Brahma team. Greg explained:

> "I try to use a lot of examples because with a lot of things what we are into are manual processes. Another reason being that we have the cultural difference, because homes here, we deal with a product that deals with homeowners in America and they don't quite understand how we are going to interact with those individuals."

As Greg mentioned, the difference in the HVAC industry between India and America does make it even more important that the vendor gets an understanding of the client's business environment and needs through the sharing of experiences. However, this lack of knowledge is not a function of differences in national cultures alone, as seen in the Bluestone-Vesta case. If the project requires specific knowledge of a business domain, the client needs to take the initiative to provide the vendor with knowledge of the processes in that domain, not just the requirements for the software. The vendor also needs to take the time to develop this understanding.

Another problem that clients dealing with offshore vendors often mention is the problem with accents. However, Greg did not see this as a problem. Most of his conversations were with Amar and the liaison in the California office, both of whom had gone to graduate school in the U.S. and worked in the U.S. as well. Greg's interaction with other Brahma employees was primarily through Yahoo Chat.

The Brahma management team also made a conscious effort to avoid the kind of problems that the Vishnu team had. Other interviewees also mentioned how Indian vendors often give false or vague assurances even when they were aware they could not complete the work as promised. Amar and his colleagues were determined to avoid such situations and enforced this rule amongst their employees as well.

6.8.4.1.3 Relational dimension: Trust, norms, obligations & expectations, identification

As in other cases, both organizations valued trust in the inter-organizational relationship. All three interviewees also mentioned that commitment and flexibility contributed to the success of the outsourcing arrangement. Amar mentioned that the availability of qualified professionals locally allowed Brahma to scale up resources as necessary to meet their clients' needs, including that of Ozark, allowing them to exhibit a level of flexibility that vendors in the U.S. would not be able to.

Usually, the client expects the vendor to make adjustments to ensure a fit with the client culture. Ajit commented that this is particularly important when work is being done on-site:

"While working on-site, we must merge with the culture of the organization – so we must prepare the person (who goes for work at the client site). We cannot have an off-shore mindset."

In Greg's opinion, it is possible to "do a lot of projects and have a long-term relationship" only with "the company that can make you feel comfortable." He is not looking for a perfect match between cultures, but for the vendor's awareness and respect of his company's needs and culture.

While the first project was a learning experience, the client and the vendor are now able to anticipate each other's expectations, according to Amar.

"We have understood each other better. There is a trust that is built up, a mutual adjustment. So, by the second phase, they knew what to expect, and we know what to expect, so there has not only been an adjustment and an understanding – we have built something to work together better."

Greg also expected that they would be able to develop a relationship that progressively meets the needs of both parties, and create an "environment of collaboration that would go beyond legal agreements."

6.8.4.1.4 Is social capital present in the Ozark-Brahma relationship?

It is clear that currently all three dimensions of the social capital are present in the Glacier-Hercules relationship. The two organizations struggled on the first project because they had not developed a shared understanding and Ozark had no prior experience with outsourcing. Though Ozark did not have the benefit of "appropriable organization" that could be used in the initial outsourcing arrangement, they were determined to create a repository of best practices to be applied during the course of the outsourcing arrangement ensures that the structural dimension of social capital is completely present in the relationship. Both organizations not only pursue the development of shared understanding regarding the project, but educate each other about their specific domains of expertise. By investing in activities that promote the development of social capital and desisting from those that would inhibit it, they have been able to build "something to work together better" (Amar).

6.8.4.2 Factors that promote social capital in the Ozark-Brahma relationship

Greg expected that "after they (Brahma) get comfortable with us, they should be able to come in and they are going to be able to run our projects more smoothly and give us what we're looking for." The same awareness is behind Brahma's desire to start with small pilot projects. It is clear that both organizations know that it takes investments in inter-organizational exchange over time to develop an environment in which a smooth exchange of knowledge could take place. From Amar's and Greg's comments about the current status, it is evident that the longevity of the relationship has contributed to the development of social capital, and will continue to do so. According to Greg,

> "We know what's going to happen and there's predictability from our side in the future, if they took care of us one time, they will most likely do it again."

While the two organizations did not have a detailed contract, Ozark and Brahma both realized it was important to have clear definition of the task when starting projects. While the failure of any project would be disastrous for Ozark, inefficiencies and delays could also affect their bottom line since these were products they were planning to market. Additionally, as Greg explained, since they were a small company with limited resources, their capability to absorb losses was also limited. The situation was the same for Brahma. Additionally, they were also hoping to build up their reputation in the market on the success of these projects. Amar emphasized the need for definition in requirements:

> "As you know, in a systems development project, the design document is everything, if it's not done well, the projects doesn't go well, if it's done well, the projects goes well"

This definition was developed through communication between Greg and Amar and members of the development team. Greg believes that communication has been the key to success in this outsourcing relationship. Amar emphasizes that communication is even more important in times of crisis. He mentioned that there had been instances of disagreement in the relationship and addressing this through communication had strengthened the relationship.

> "If there is a problem, good communication between each other, even if it is shouting at each other, is necessary. That helps build a trust and comfort between the parties involved. And I think that is one of the things that lasted us through the couple of crises that we had"

The perception of mutual dependence in the relationship encourages trust and cooperation in the inter-organizational relationship. Both organizations admit they are dependent on each other. Amar believes that initially Brahma was at a disadvantage because they had to make considerable investments to get the project started, but Greg does not agree. He comments that they have always been dependent on Brahma because "once we give a target date for the project, we start marketing and if we don't provide, if they can't deliver what we look at is, every potential sale that we can't complete is a loss in capital and consumer confidence."

"The relationships people build, that is the relationship between companies" (Greg). And given that the two organizations, particularly the client, have gone into this outsourcing arrangement determined to develop a long term relationship, both organizations commit to developing that personal rapport. This determination to build a relationship, naturally, contributes to the development of elements of social capital in the relationship.

Greg realizes that the cultural differences between him and the employees of the vendor organization may make it difficult to develop that relationship. He explained that he has made every effort to understand and accommodate their communication and learning styles. He has had no problems communicating with Amar, and commented that "working with one key person through most projects makes the relationship easier on both sides." Amar, similarly, has no difficulty interacting with Greg and other members of Ozark and believes that he has established a personal relationship with them that "strengthens the inter-organizational relationship."

Greg raised an interesting point regarding this capability to develop a personal relationship with the counterpart in the other organization. He believes that this is an important skill that needs to be developed in the employees if firms have to be successful. However, some of it rests in the innate capabilities of the individual. Greg commented:

> "It is ... emotional intelligence, an awareness and understanding of the other person to build a relationship."

Cultural differences between the organizations have not detracted from the development of a "shared understanding or integration of work culture", according to Amar. He explained that the "people who are going over to the client organization are given as much exposure to the culture of the country and as much information about the company as possible." This cultural sensitization minimizes problems in interaction with the client. Additionally, the individuals who are sent from Brahma are "fluent in English and well-qualified." Asked whether he believes that having a domestic vendor would have made the process easier, Greg commented:

> "I don't think that's much of a big deal."

Thus, it would appear that the organizations have been able to overcome any problems due to cultural differences that would have prevented the development of social capital.

6.8.4.3 Social capital facilitates the combination and exchange of resources in the Ozark-Brahma relationship

The theoretical framework suggests that social capital provides facilitating conditions for the combination and exchange and resources necessary for the project.

From experiences with the initial project, Greg knew that it was very important for him to have access to the development team within Brahma directly, and not to the salesperson. Once that was accomplished, "it really made the projects flow much easier" (Greg). Amar also agreed that this direct access was very important in a development project. He explained:

> "We work on that kind of an equation. We do not get in between. We allow direct communication. That way people who are working on the project get to understand the other organization well – constraints, problems, everything."

As in all outsourcing projects, both organizations anticipate value from the completion of the project. This anticipation comes from the belief that the other party will reliably fulfill the obligations that were mutually agreed upon. The vendor is further motivated by growth opportunities – future projects with the client and referrals to other clients.

Ozark wanted a vendor who "could understand our (Ozark's) ideas and then they would be able to put that information into code" (Greg). Beyond technical expertise, this required a commitment by Brahma to understand the client's business. Ozark also had to be taught and be willing to learn what information needs to be conveyed to Brahma so that they could complete this work. Initially, the two organizations faced difficulty in exchanging this information, and the first project did not get completed as planned.

> "We need to successfully convey our ideas to each other to get a program that could actually work and we could actually take out and then market to our customers." (Greg)

Through the efforts of both organizations, they were able to develop such "combination capability" that facilitated the completion of future projects as expected.

6.8.4.4 Assessment: Satisfaction

Both organizations are satisfied with the progress of the outsourcing relationship. With each completed project, the two organizations further their shared understanding and build a closer relationship rich in trust and commitment, increasing the social capital in the relationship between the organizations. This increased social capital facilitates a smoother exchange in the next project, according to Amar and Greg. Thus, social capital increases capabilities for exchange and this exchange offers additional opportunities for developing social capital – the coevolution of social capital and intellectual capital, as suggested by Nahapiet and Ghoshal (1998).

Greg noted one area in which he wished the vendor would improve. He felt that the vendor wanted to start working on the application without spending enough time on the requirements estimation, and should exhibit more patience.

> "We wanted to do what we are currently doing which is the manual system, so if they don't see the manual system, if they don't see what was actually happening, then they would not know whether they are putting together that same product, and I think they have to have a lot of patience. Got to be on the top of their list because if we don't understand, we expect them to slow down and be patient because we are intending to go into a contract and spend a lot of money, so we want to be comfortable, mentally comfortable."

This has not led to any problems in this case and the vendor's work has met the client's expectations. This comment highlights that not only is it important to gain shared understanding but also to demonstrate shared understanding so that the client will be confident in the vendor's capabilities, particularly in custom development outsourcing.

6.8.5 Case study conclusion

> "We have come to expect what is right and they have come to expect what is right. They know that if they commit to a project with us, we will do it as fast as possible with the best results and things like that. They have come to the optimal way of handling us and we also know how to handle them to get things done." (Amar)

6.9 Case 8: Haleakala and Durga

In this case, the client, Haleakala, is a large multi-national firm while the vendor, Durga, is a small firm based in India. This case analysis highlights how attention to relationship management and a joint focus on innovation create a productive outsourcing relationship.

6.9.1 Introduction

The client organization, Haleakala, is the same as in Case 4. In this case, another one of their divisions based in the western part of the United States is the client organization. The vendor organization, Durga, is "basically two organizations"; there are actually two separate business entities functioning as one. One organization is the Silicon Valley based Durga Corp, a company incorporated in the United States, while the other is Durga Systems, a company registered in India. According to the Vice President of Durga Systems, one can look at it two ways: "Durga Corp is the marketing arm for Durga Systems; or the other way around, Durga Systems is the development center for Durga Corp." Durga's expertise is in two areas: developing embedded software for telecommunication devices such as ISDN devices and routers and in client/server computing. The offshore development center is ISO 9001 certified and has achieved CMM level 4 rating.

Table 6-9: Interviewees in the Haleakala-Durga case

Name of interviewee	Organization	Position	Duration of interview	Taped?
Ram	Haleakala (Client)	Project Manager	1.5 hours	Yes
Kumar	Durga (Vendor)	Vice President	2 hours	Yes

Two individuals were interviewed regarding this outsourcing arrangement between Haleakala and Durga. Ram is a Project Manager in a team at Haleakala working on router technology; the applications outsourcing arrangement is between his division and Durga. Kumar is the Vice President of Durga Systems, located in one of the Software Technology Parks[16] in India. Kumar is also coordinating this particular outsourcing arrangement since "it is with a large and valuable customer", though for most projects there are separate project coordinators.

6.9.2 The Outsourcing Project

The objective of the outsourcing arrangement between Haleakala's Internet and Computing Platforms division and Durga was to provide embedded software for a product being developed in this division. Haleakala routinely outsources these types of jobs, where they believe they do not have the skill sets necessary for the task. They have created a list of vendor organizations who have expertise in different areas; many of these organizations have been chosen either because of the proximity of their offices to Haleakala and/or because they "had contacts within Haleakala who recommended them for inclusion on the list" (Kumar).

---

[16] Software Technology Parks of India, called TechnoParks, are high-tech facilities set up under a scheme by the Government of India to encourage development and export of software and IT services.

139

6.9.3   The Client-Vendor Relationship

Durga was one of the organizations on the shortlist of vendors maintained at Haleakala and were invited to bid for the project. A senior systems analyst was sent from India and joined the marketing manager at the Durga Corp office to study the project and understand the requirements for the project. Based on this study, Durga submitted a bid for the project.

Ram explained the selection process within Haleakala.

"Haleakala has published guidelines on these issues – at the higher level, how to select and deal with vendors – published at the corporate level. There were experts involved in that and even the smallest contractor is accepted using that process."

Durga's bid was accepted and they were invited for negotiations. Though Durga had got on the shortlist through personal contacts at Haleakala, Kumar mentioned that Ram and the other individuals involved in the final selection were not directly known to them. At the end of the negotiations, Durga was offered the project. The contract was based on the template used by Haleakala. Durga did not have much say on the contract terms, but these were "standard terms and market prices" according to Kumar.

There are guidelines also for the management of the outsourcing arrangement at Haleakala, but "with this kind of project, once you sign up the vendor, it depends on the project and the manager. It does not really follow the guidelines; it is more of a day-to-day issue" (Ram). This informality is reflective of the Haleakala culture, as was noted in the Haleakala-Athene case. Similarly, Kumar also comments:

"In any client engagement, it (contract) is a written document that has been agreed upon by both parties, so it is an important document – you cannot have an oral agreement. But even with the contract, most of the time you end up doing extra work – it depends on your relationship – you make lots of compromises on top of whatever is written."

Kumar explains how the project was structured with on-site (at the clients' site) and offshore (in India) components.

"Projects are done mostly here and there will be an onsite component. There are two sections (to the online component): for systems study in the initial stages, senior guys will go from here. And also at the end of the projects, for implementation, people will go from India."

The management of the project is also split between on-site and offshore, as Kumar explains:

"For each of these projects, we will have a coordinator or engagement director. He interacts with the client – over the 'phone, and visits the client – this coordinator is in Fremont, CA.   And there will be another person mapped to him, the project manager here. This is to reduce the ambiguity and costs of overseas calls and such."

Both these individuals need to have project management capabilities and technical capabilities as well. Ram concurs, "You need to make sure you staff your (vendor's) organization well – with really knowledgeable people, give them training. Otherwise the client will be swamped with questions." In addition, usually the individuals who are selected for these key positions already have "a similarity in culture from working with US companies."

Haleakala is a very large organization compared to Durga, and naturally Kumar feels that they are more dependent than Haleakala in the relationship and it would not make an impact on Haleakala if they were to cancel the contract with Durga. However, Durga does not have any fear of opportunism. Instead, Kumar feels there" is a lot of give and take" and it is a very satisfying environment to work in because there is "appreciation from the client" and "involvement in developing intellectual property." Ram is also very satisfied with the relationship; he comments that the vendor exhibits "a sense of ownership" regarding the project and "is doing *the* job (they had agreed to)."

6.9.4 Through the "Social Capital" Lens

Having presented the background and the story of the outsourcing relationship, the focus now turns to analysis of the field text using the social capital framework.

6.9.4.1 Social Capital in the Haleakala-Durga relationship

As in previous cases, the determination of the presence of social capital in the relationship is made by examining whether the different elements of the three dimensions of social capital are manifest in the relationship.

6.9.4.1.1 Structural dimension: Access patterns and appropriable organization

Based on the Haleakala-Athene case and the comments of Ram and Kumar, one would not expect much importance to be given to the structural dimension in this outsourcing arrangement as well. However, give given the geographical distance between the two organizations, both organizations pay particular attention to having these structures in place for management of the project

"Even for the day-to-day execution of the project, even for tracking of the project, the costing of the project, the estimation of the project, for higher management it becomes quite easy if you have some processes in place." (Kumar)

Ram also mentioned that it is expedient to have processes in place so that the project can be managed and completed even if the individuals who are working on the project leave or there are changes in either organization. Kumar sees the Capability Maturity Model as serving such a purpose; it "gives *them* a process *they* can follow, particularly by laying out rules for documentation."

6.9.4.1.2 Cognitive dimension: Shared understanding

Both Kumar and Ram agree it is important to establish "agreement on the goals of the project and how it should be done" (Kumar). It is important for the vendor to understand "the client organization's business and even their interactions with the end users" (Ram). Such understanding was fostered in the Haleakala-Durga relationship in the initial meetings where the vendor representatives visit the client organizations and learn about the needs of the client organization for this particular project. As Kumar explains, "we are learning from the client. When they share their ideas with us, we can build on that and contribute to their final product." This promotes a feeling of ownership regarding the project in Durga, a fact that Ram commented on appreciatively.

Ram also believes that agreeing on metrics to assess the output and process of the outsourcing arrangement is necessary for the client and vendor to continue working together harmoniously.

"The metrics should capture the expectations of both parties – see, if there is confusion as to what the metric is to represent, then there is a problem. It becomes difficult to move on. You should be clear about how these metrics are the right metrics, so that if the vendor performs to the metric that is the service you wanted. You do not want to leave the client with a bad taste in the mouth. I agreed to this, so I am stuck with it."

These evaluation issues were also addressed in the initial meetings. Constant email communication between Ram and Kumar also help ensure that this shared understanding is maintained. Thus, the Haleakala and Durga project teams develop and maintain shared understanding during the outsourcing engagement.

6.9.4.1.3 Relational dimension: Trust, norms, obligations & expectations, identification

Ram and Kumar both comment on the importance of trust. Ram comments that trust develops from belief in the vendor's capabilities and reliability and Haleakala is satisfied on both accounts. Kumar adds that "honesty and willingness to sit down and address an issue together" also enhances trust and help build the relationship.

Ram believes that vendors are "willing to commit because they do not have bargaining power" since "they do not want to lose a client like Haleakala." Kumar also asserted that his organization was committed to the completion of the outsourcing arrangement, but explained that it was because the Haleakala team involved them in the development of innovative products and appreciated the work that they did. In fact, Kumar mentioned that one of their expectations was that the client would appreciate the work that they did, and commented that this expectation was being met. Ram and Kumar could not recollect any conflicts; they both said that any disagreements they had were dealt with through "talking it out" and did not involve any escalation processes.

Durga's management team, according to Kumar, is one of their strengths. He explains:

"All of our management team members are post-graduates or PhDs. And all of them have worked in the US as well as in India. People are very familiar with the cultural issues as well as the work ethics of US organizations."

Their representatives are familiar with the nuances of communication in US organizations. Similarly, Haleakala being a multinational organization has many employees of Indian origin as well as employees who have worked in their Indian division. This familiarity is an advantage for both Durga and Haleakala since it significantly reduces the barriers to information sharing. Additionally, their expertise puts them in apposition to identify and assimilate information that is required for the project in the Haleakala environment.

6.9.4.1.4 Is social capital present in the Haleakala-Durga relationship?

The three dimensions of social capital are present in the Haleakala-Durga relationship. The relationship is built on strong commitment to the completion of the outsourcing arrangement, which can be accomplished only by bringing together the expertise of the Haleakala and Durga teams.

6.9.4.2 Factors that promote social capital in the Haleakala-Durga relationship

While the project has been going on only for about eight months at the time of the interview, the two teams have managed to establish a cooperative relationship. The definition of responsibilities in the agreements between Haleakala and Durga and the joint sessions has contributed towards this development of social capital. Haleakala, with its experiences in outsourcing, had defined guidelines and templates for the creation of these documents. The Durga management has also carefully considered the challenges the geographical separation can create and have planned processes to overcome such challenges. One technique they use is maintaining the bridgehead team (Carmel and Agarwal, 2003; Krishna et al, 2004) in California under the name of Durga Corp. Like other offshore vendors, Durga employees in India work extended hours to be available for discussions with the Haleakala employees.

Patterns for <u>communication</u> between the Haleakala and Durga teams were also defined very clearly. Like in many other outsourcing arrangements, communications within the organizations is set up in a channeled manner. Ram explains the set-up in Haleakala:

> "Most of the time we try to channel it (the communication), because we do not want everyone to be bothered by trivial issues. And if there is anything a person is not supposed to handle, they are immediately supposed to pass it up."

Similarly at Durga, Kumar is "kept in the loop for all communications between Haleakala and us (Durga)." The on-site coordinator in Fremont, CA visits the customer weekly, making sure that the customer is satisfied with the progress and communicates that information to Kumar in India.

Haleakala and Durga representatives worked together at the start of the project to define the requirements, processes, and metrics for the outsourced project.

> "We all got together for 10 days at the start – there were presentations, we all had prepared documents that were distributed and discussed. On a project like this, there is significant communication overhead." (Ram)

Such joint sessions enabled the organizations to understand each others' needs and share experiences, developing a shared understanding. It also contributes to the development of feelings of shared ownership of the project and promotes continued and open sharing of information between the teams.

Ram recognizes that small vendors like Durga would perceive themselves as dependent on Haleakala, since they are such a large organization. However, as he explains, "a company like Haleakala won't be squeezing vendors." The project is managed so that there is "some amount of give and take." Thus, potential problems from an imbalance in <u>dependence</u> are avoided and Durga does not feel that they are being forced to commit to terms that are not fair to them. In addition, as in the case of Durga, "main people of the vendor will have Haleakala contacts, so there is some connection there already. There is a relationship going on..."

There is a desire to build a relationship on either side. Haleakala sees the benefit of maintaining relationships with these niche vendors who have expertise in areas where Haleakala needs resources. Durga, as a small vendor, sees the benefit of dealing with an established and stable company like Haleakala, who will meet their financial commitments to them on time. As Kumar explains,

> "Instead of going on an ego trip or hurting each other from the beginning itself, if you get into a mode that you are doing it together"

6.9.4.3 Social capital facilitates the combination and exchange of resources in the Haleakala-Durga relationship

The theoretical framework suggests that social capital provides facilitating conditions for the combination and exchange and resources necessary for the project. The structural elements of social capital provide the <u>access</u> necessary for the exchange of resources in the outsourcing situation. Further the trust and the norms of commitment and cooperation that have developed between the teams opens up access to resources they need to work together and develop new products.

Both firms <u>anticipate value</u> from the completion of the project. The shared understanding of the benefits from the project contributes to this anticipation of value. The success of the product is a matter of pride for Durga as well, since they see themselves as part of the group involved in the development of the product, not as a vendor providing the software alone. The Durga team is <u>motivated</u> by the "feeling of achievement…of seeing something working."

Since the teams have spent time together working on the requirements for the project and sharing information regarding the product, the two teams are able to assimilate the information presented by the other team easily. <u>Combination capability</u>, necessary for the exchange and combination of resources, is enhanced by such shared understanding. Durga has also been able to offer some innovative ideas to Haleakala; Kumar explains that these innovations are the result of Haleakala sharing intellectual property with Durga and asking them for suggestions for improvement. These contributions have not been unidirectional; Durga has learned from Haleakala as well. Kumar comments:

> "It is a question of accepting which is good. If there is a willingness to accept suggestions…you can learn and develop your organization."

6.9.4.4 Assessment: Satisfaction

Both organizations are satisfied with the progress of the project. Kumar believes that the client's satisfaction needs to be managed by setting the expectation levels. Ram elaborates:

> "You have to be very clear about what success is, it should be very well defined. Otherwise, you will have criticisms at the end."

When asked what factors contribute to his satisfaction with the outsourcing arrangement, Ram responds:

> "Cost savings will always be a factor, then timeliness, meeting deadlines…If things slipped, we know there is a problem with the vendor."

Most client organizations look to offshore outsourcing as a way of cutting costs, Kumar agrees. "In fact, that is the logic behind their business model". Kumar thinks that when clients look at the offshore vendor as purely a cheaper alternative, it is not very satisfying for the vendor.

> "If the client is *only* looking at it as a cheap deal, then it is not very satisfying. Some clients give an analogy to the manufacturing in China, Taiwan. Software development – you cannot compare with manufacturing; it is more creative and intellectual level of work. It is not a very tangible thing also…they (the vendor) should be in a position to appreciate it."

Fortunately, Haleakala is in a position to appreciate the work done by Durga and Kumar believes the client appreciates their work. The social capital present in the relationship promotes a cooperative working relationship and provides opportunities for innovation.

The management team at Durga is comfortable working with clients from US organizations. Durga was established with this goal in mind, by engineers from India who had come to US for higher studies and worked in US organizations. Ram's background is similar to that of the Durga management team; he came to the US for graduate work and was hired by Haleakala. The Durga management team does not face any problems with communication or achieving a cultural fit. This fit is also facilitated by the fact that members of the Haleakala team "are comfortable with alliances." Many of them have worked with individuals from various countries since they have been members of teams that included individuals from the different global divisions of Haleakala. For example, Ram mentioned that in a previous project he had been working with Haleakala employees from India and United Kingdom.

6.9.5 Case study conclusion

In this case, it would have been very possible for Haleakala to create an environment where the elements of social capital, particularly those of relational dimension, are not present. The Montezuma-Apollo case highlighted how perceptions of imbalance in dependence can lead to a lack of elements of the relational dimension of social capital. However, recognizing the benefits of social capital, the Haleakala team fosters a relationship with Durga. Haleakala has guidelines in place for the management of the outsourcing arrangement; however, project managers are allowed flexibility in the implementation of these processes. The Haleakala and Durga teams are able to develop a relationship rich in social capital that leads to continued progress of the project and new intellectual property development.

6.10 Case 9: Redwood - Shiva

This case presents the story of two organizations whose attention to the relationship pays dividends in the form of satisfactory outcomes for both organizations. The client, Redwood, is a large utility company requiring an e-procurement solution. Shiva is a large offshore vendor organization based in India. Redwood's decision to outsource the project to Shiva is based "partly on price and partly on capabilities," and Shiva comes through on both accounts. However, this is not a story of labor arbitrage, but of the advantages that any organization can achieve by investing in relationship-management capabilities. The case shows evidence of continued development of all dimensions of social capital due to the continued investments of both parties.

6.10.1 Introduction

The client organization, Redwood, is utility company based in southwest U.S. and is a power provider across the U.S. and in Europe. It is a large multinational ranked among the top 50 in the Fortune 500.

The vendor organization, Shiva, is a fully owned subsidiary of an international engineering and construction conglomerate, and was initially the internal support unit for the firm. It then became a profit center within the firm, and in 1993 started taking on contracts as an outsourcing vendor. Leveraging the heritage and domain expertise of the parent company, its services encompass a broad technology spectrum, including package implementation & support, application development & maintenance, enterprise application integration, data warehousing &

145

business intelligence, infrastructure management services, and strategy consulting. Shiva has development centers in six Indian cities and is headquartered in Mumbai, India.

Table 6-10: Interviewees in the Redwood-Shiva case

Name of interviewee	Organization	Position	Duration of interview	Taped?
Jeff	Redwood(Client)	Project Manager – SAP Team	1.5 hours	Yes
Sarah	Redwood	Director, Contracts Management	1 hour	No
Lal	Shiva (Vendor)	Executive Vice President	2 hours	Partly
Prasad	Shiva	Regional Manager	45 minutes	No
Mathew	Shiva	Liaison Officer	45 minutes	Yes

Jeff was one of the lead managers on the SAP implementation project, and provided the details about the project. Sarah is in charge of Contracts Management for the whole organization and her comments were more general.

Lal is Executive Vice President of Shiva and has been there since the formation of the company as a separate entity; he operates from the company headquarters in Mumbai, India. He talked about the business model of the company and commented on the client from his position as a top level executive at the company. He has also been a regular speaker at many outsourcing conferences and he included a number of general observations on practices in the outsourcing industry in the conversation. Prasad is the Regional Manager for the Southwest region; the Redwood outsourcing arrangement falls under his purview. Mathew is the liaison officer located in Houston, Texas and was instrumental in obtaining the interviews. He was involved in the first interactions with Redwood.

6.10.2 The Outsourcing Project

At the time of the interview, the two companies are nearing the end of the implementation of an e-Procurement solution for Redwood based on SAP EBP[17] 2.0. Redwood decided to adopt SAP EBP 2.0 as an e-commerce procurement engine for the unregulated business, for integrating with Marketplace and also many vendors directly. With this solution, Redwood expected to expand supplier access, reduce costs associated with inventory and procurement, and respond faster to market needs.

Redwood has considerable experience with outsourcing; from initial staff augmentation contracts, they have moved to looking at outsourcing as an opportunity to bring in "innovation and learning." Jeff explains the kind of contracts they are looking at now:

> "We are using a contract where we say, ok, here is the work we need done, tell me how you would do it. And we would listen to two or three different vendors and hear them out and their methodologies and say, ok, we like this one right here. Let's go with it."

Sarah commented that they were looking for partnerships with strategic outsourcing vendors, who she defined as "a vendor who is going to supply you with hardware and/or software to solve

---

17 SAP EBP is an Internet-based procurement system that has been tailored specifically for the purchase of consumable materials

your business problems and run your business differently…they should offer you additional solutions." According to Sarah, "even something as simplistic as a help desk outsourcing arrangement brings new solutions and ways of doing things to your organization."

Being a fairly established vendor, Shiva has a global delivery model to provide the services that Redwood needs. The model defines the division of labor between on-site and offshore resources. With this distributed development model, those parts in the lifecycle that could be done in India or one of our centers are done there and the front-ending ones are done at the customers' site (Lal) .An account manager coordinates the activities required to provide the client with the required services, and sits at the client site managing that relationship. While this client manager is required to keep his eyes and ears open for new opportunities, Shiva's philosophy is that if the relationship is managed well, clients will come back to you. They are proud of their repeat business rate of 'more than 80%'. Besides the account manager, a business development manager also keeps in touch with a client making sure that the client is happy with Shiva's services. The regional manager oversees a number of account managers and business development managers working with the clients in his region.

6.10.3 The Client-Vendor Relationship

Redwood was aware of Shiva before the start of this project. They maintain a list of vendors who fit their requirements, including offshore vendors. For the offshore vendors, CMM ratings were also considered in the selection process, primarily as an elimination tool. Lal commented:

> "You cannot blame anyone for that. Let us say you are getting your house built. You do not care who does the run-of-the-mill stuff. But if you want something special, let's say some special kind of flooring, you would want that to be done by someone who has the qualifications, the reputation. With the CMM, it's the same thing. You are saying that you have processes that have been approved by someone who is an authority, a world-wide accepted authority – it's just common sense."

Shiva believes in building up a relationship with its clients. Mathew explained that "the first part to our business model is that the core value is relationship – we aim to build a long-term relationship." To this end, they start with "high visibility, low risk projects at new client organizations that instill a level of comfort in the client organization and work up to bigger projects." Shiva has had the opportunity to do a 'pilot project' of this nature for another division in Redwood, and they believe this has ensured them a place on the vendor shortlist at Redwood. In fact, Redwood's approach to easing in new vendors is the same. Jeff explained:

> "What we have done is that we start off with small projects with the new vendors. We don't jump in the middle of a multi-million dollar project with a new vendor."

Redwood's decision to pick Shiva for this project was made "partly on price and partly on capabilities" (Jeff). Once, the decision was made, the two organizations proceeded to the next step – the creation of the contract. The purchasing and contracts departments at Redwood were involved in this process and brought in outside counsel to "to be sure that the proper boiler plate language is included in the commercial aspects of the contract" (Jeff). However, echoing the sentiments of many other interviewees and the Shiva management, Jeff also commented the contract is only a legal guarantee that defines the general requirements. In the management of the project, "there are many things that have to go on outside of the bounds of the contract that are really dependent on a relationship."

The two organizations look beyond the contract to the relationship between the organizations, and particularly the relationship between the key people on both sides, to meet the goals of the outsourcing arrangement. This focus on the relationship stems from the realization that it is not possible to include everything in the contract. As Jeff explained:

"We are not building a road, we are putting in a piece of software and you cannot see it or touch it. It is something that runs unseen by anybody, but actually has to deliver something. So, you are defining requirements and you are judging it by delivery, and there is not much you can measure and that makes it very difficult."

They depend on a continuous dialog to make sure that the client's needs are met and that the vendor is provided with all the resources from the client's side to ensure that they can do this. The account manager is responsible for maintaining this interaction from the Shiva side. Prasad explained the role of the account manager:

"You actually build personal relationships with these guys, because finally no sale is made between two companies, it is made between two people. So the two people (the account manager and his counterpart in the client organizations) need to build the relationships, get to know each other well and get to know business well, etc. So there are multiple activities that go on as a part of this relationship building."

Similarly, Jeff explained his role:

"I am ultimately responsible for making it happen. My team manages the project, the cost, schedule and the functionally requirements. We ultimately have to own the deliverable. And we have to be sure that what is developed meets our internal clients' needs. So, there has to be a lot of trust and a lot of very open dialogue. And what we found is you cannot have relationship where you hand everything over a wall and tell the vendor to go to work. You cannot expect that in six months they will hand back a finished product. It does not work that way; there has to be an awful lot of interaction"

As in some of the previous cases (e.g. Montezuma-Apollo), the communication hierarchy, the monitoring patterns, and the metrics are all specified in the contract. With the experience that both organizations brought to the table, these issues were all defined to the satisfaction of both parties. Such experience helped them apply these mechanisms as necessary and supplement those using mechanisms such as informal communication. Jeff owned up that they have had a couple of disagreements at the lower level, and these have been escalated and solved, according to the procedures laid out in the contract. However,

Shiva is a recognized SAP implementation partner and the SAP practice at Shiva has been awarded the Customer Competence Center certification from SAP. Shiva has also experience with large companies in the utilities industry in Europe, Canada, and India. This combination of business domain knowledge and technical knowledge was exactly what Redwood was looking for in a partner. Jeff is satisfied with the services that they are getting from Shiva. Shiva's expectations are also being met as Jeff and Redwood encourages them to use this project as a reference with other clients. As they continue to work together, both organizations build an ongoing mutually beneficial relationship on the strength of tasks well done.

6.10.4 Through the "Social Capital" Lens

Having presented the background and the story of the outsourcing relationship, the focus now turns to analysis of the field text using the social capital framework.

6.10.4.1 Social Capital in the Redwood-Shiva relationship

As in previous cases, the determination of the presence of social capital in the relationship is made by examining whether the different elements of the three dimensions of social capital are manifest in the relationship.

6.10.4.1.1 Structural dimension: Access patterns and appropriable organization

Similar to other outsourcing arrangements between established vendors and experienced vendors, the contract lays out the structure for communication and interaction between project participants in both organizations. It defines the levels and periodicity of access different individuals in both organizations will have. The contract also determines the format communication between the organizations should take and to whom all such information will be distributed. Further, "appropriable organization" in the form of established practices extracted from experiences exists at both organizations. While Redwood does not have much experience in the offshore outsourcing arena, it has considerable experience in outsourcing as well as dealing with workers from other national cultures via staff augmentation. Like other leading offshore vendors, Shiva has developed a global delivery model that incorporates lessons from past experiences and industry best practices and implemented quality processes recommended by institutes like the Software Engineering Institute.

6.10.4.1.2 Cognitive dimension: Shared understanding

A "clear understanding about what needs to be done, how it needs to be done, and agreeing on the metrics" (Lal) is necessary for completing the project successfully. Prasad elaborated on this.

> "I think it depends on the level of clarity we have regarding the requirements. If the requirements are fuzzy and constantly changing, then we have problems with the project. That is an issue we deal with many of our customers. It is mainly because they do not have the discipline to define the requirements well, it's partly because the business is changing rapidly. With this client, they are quite computer literate and we haven't had problems."

Jeff also believes that they have become competent at providing the vendor with enough information as required. He attributes this capability to the growth of computer literacy in the organization.

> "I think we are getting better at defining our requirements as time goes. We are becoming a lot more, globally, computer literate. Our users are a lot more computer literate, so now when we talk to one of our clients, they give better answers than somebody who's going for Big Chief Tablet for the very first time they are going to do something."

Jeff is looking for the vendor organization to bring in solutions based on an understanding of their business environment. He expects them to be innovative, to be a "strategic vendor" in Sarah's opinion.

"They do not do me much good if I have to tell them precisely what to do. They need to add value for their management and their leadership to have invested in there employees, and say "hey, here are some new ways of doing things. We understand the electric business; we understand the gas business - in our case."

Shiva understands that the vendor provides "value-add when he brings in something extra." As the organizations continue to work together, the vendor should try to bring in new ideas. Lal also explained that it is difficult to do that at the very beginning of a relationship. This capability for providing service and innovation comes from learning what the customer wants. To this end, they invest a lot in education and training. Besides training employees in new technology to "keep in step with what is changing in the technology for the customer," Shiva also provides them with skill sets that help them learn continuously on the job. He adds:

"The second thing is that people should have different skill sets –people management skills, communication skills to negotiate with the customer, so we need to train on that too. We have a large investment in education and training."

Shiva management recognizes that cultural differences can create problems in communicating with the client organizations. In their sophisticated and modern facilities in Mumbai, they have training sessions to develop these skills going on continuously. One of the ways in which they keep their recruits abreast of the working environment is by getting employees who have been working at client sites to share their experiences with the classes. They also have in-house classes in diction, where employees are trained to speak in accents from various parts of the world.

6.10.4.1.3 Relational dimension: Trust, norms, obligations & expectations, identification

Trust, flexibility, commitment – these are on the top of every interviewee's list of qualities necessary for a successful outsourcing arrangement. Interviewees in this case also emphasized these characteristics. Jeff's and Lal's comments capture these opinions.

"There has to be trust there has to be an interest in the success of the project. Both companies have to want the project to be successful. And really in most cases both parties have to be willing to go on beyond what they had planned to do, in order to make it successful. Each had to be willing to meet more than halfway." (Jeff)

"Trust is important, like in any relationship, trust is important. That is why we have the annual customer meeting – we get customers in an area to come together and share their experience – about their relationship with us. These are all trust and relationship building techniques. We try to constantly share all info – all project related material- constant trust building." (Lal)

Lal's statement also draws attention again to the attention that Shiva pays to techniques that will encourage the development of elements of social capital in the relationship.

Part of this reliance on trust and other relational elements comes from the knowledge that the contract will not cover every issue in a relationship. Echoing the usual reluctance to have the contract govern the activities during the operationalization of the contract, Prasad commented:

"A contract cannot cover the relationship for the next ten years. It's very rarely we open up the contract after it is signed."

Sarah concurs that "it would be unrealistic in my mind in programming projects to have them (contract) written so specifically that you know the number of days, the precise number of dollars, and the exact deliverables." So, both organizations should accept that changes are inevitable and should take it in a "spirit of give and take" (Mathew). Changes may also be the result of either organization's mistake, as in "items that were poorly defined, or because somebody did not understand the scope magnitude of the project." Jeff's response to such situations is to help out if possible. He described a hypothetical situation as an example: "I have shared in that pain too, where some companies estimated that something was going to be say 50 hours but became 500, because the overall magnitude was much worse than anyone expected. And, we would have agreed to pay for part of that."

"I do not want a company to go broke because they are working for us, but they may not make the profit that they thought they would make if they made a mistake."

This is the reasoning that drives Jeff's approach to changes that could affect the vendor disastrously. This attitude has met with a like response from the vendor. Meeting Jeff's expectations "to be a partner in the process", they "have been flexible with their ability to work with us, to staff as we need to and work with our always changing schedule requirements."

The vendor also does not believe in bargaining when the "chips are down" (Prasad). Technology changes or business changes may force the client to request changes in the outsourcing arrangement, and a vendor looking for an ongoing relationship with the client will not take advantage of a situation like that. Prasad commented that the client had met their obligations fairly. Redwood's readiness to host prospective clients for Shiva and act as a reference has also been a source of satisfaction for Shiva.

6.10.4.1.4 Is social capital present in the Redwood-Shiva relationship?

All elements of social capital are present in the relationship between Redwood and Shiva. These elements are carefully cultivated with the realization that the process of exchange of knowledge and resources necessary for the completion of the applications outsourcing arrangement are embedded in the social relations between the two organizations.

6.10.4.2 Factors that promote social capital in the Redwood-Shiva relationship

In the Redwood-Shiva relationship where both parties are committed to the relationship, the length of the relationship has contributed to the stability of the relationship. In Lal's words, the feeling is "we are married, let us stay married." As discussed before (section 6.8.4.1.2), both organizations realize that clarity in definition contributes to a productive working relationship. This definition starts in the very early stages, according to Prasad. "We give a very structured proposal, which is considerate to our needs and the customer's needs." This document becomes the basis for discussion during the negotiation stage.

At the start of the project, the "number of interactions is high", according to Prasad. He elaborated on the communication pattern used in projects:

"We use all possible forms of communication – e-mail, telephone & v-mail, fax, video conferencing, structured project management reporting, and structured management reporting. We have very defined, structured processes for managing remote projects, for reporting. Every project plan, we would also talk about communication styles and preferences. The reporting frequency is laid out in the contract. Every week we will have a planning meeting; every six weeks we will have an operational review meeting – something like that."

This is supplemented by informal communication, as in other successful outsourcing arrangements. In fact, informal communication is so much the norm that Jeff said he "requires his managers to write reports on a periodic basis." Both organizations agree that communication channels in all forms need to be maintained to develop mutual understanding, trust, and cooperation – elements of the relational and cognitive dimensions of social capital. It would appear that both organizations place more importance on these two dimensions than on the structural dimension.

Perceptions of mutual dependence provide motivation for both parties to develop social capital in the relationship. Jeff explained the stand his organization had taken:

"We have willfully taken the approach to do that with vendors and not with internal resources. My programming staff is a third of what it uses to be."

This has naturally created a dependence on the vendor and Jeff and Sarah both commented that they are interested in the well-being of the vendor and developing a partnership with the vendor. The vendor has also much at stake, because as Prasad commented "no vendor likes to lose a customer."

Both organizations also subscribe to the "policy of small steps" (Sydow, 2003), starting with smaller projects that allow each other to exhibit their credibility. The projects get larger with each engagement, with each project serving as a rung to raise the relationship to stronger and more productive levels.

6.10.4.3 Social capital facilitates the combination and exchange of resources in the Redwood-Shiva relationship

The theoretical framework suggests that social capital provides facilitating conditions for the combination and exchange and resources necessary for the project. The structural elements of social capital, in the form of access patterns and proven practices used in the project provide the access necessary for the exchange of resources in the outsourcing situation. A good example is the escalation procedure used for the resolution of conflict. "Problems and concerns usually bubble up," said Prasad, referring to the escalation procedure that is followed in cases of disagreement. Jeff explained how the escalation procedure has helped them resolve problems.

"We have had some instances of disagreement; typically what happens in an agreement is - especially when you are under a lot of pressure people can get a little dicey with each other. They can get emotional, at a project management level, and that is why the escalation process is there, upon escalation, I have never found an instance where we are not able to prevail and just say, ok lets just get to a rational position on this. So, occasionally that has to happen. But they do not happen that often, honestly."

Following the escalation procedure ensures that individuals with the authority and resources to solve the problem are available.

As in other outsourcing engagements, both Redwood and Shiva anticipate value from the completion of the project. Beyond the rewards guaranteed by the contract, Shiva is motivated by future opportunities that Redwood is completely willing to support. Jeff commented:

"A lot of times with software companies what I have found is, allowing them to use the project as a flagship helps. To have press releases for it, to bring in potential clients and to see the project, things like that. That allows or encourages them to do a really fine job on it, because they want to showcase it. So, I have found that to be very useful. We allow people to come in and allow a vendor to of ours to encourage a potential client to come into our shop and see what we are doing and see the software that that vendor wrote for us. To me that's an easy thing for us to do. We don't mind showing off what we're doing."

By investing in such relationship-building tactics, Redwood can make sure that the vendor is "going to do a fine job on it." Jeff's expectations are that the vendor will be motivated to bring "learn the business and bring new ideas and technology to the table."

Shiva understands that the client will have these expectations and it is necessary to continuously add value to the services they provide to the client.

"If you are not able to do that (innovate) after a while, after a stage in the evolution, then there may be a sense of not dissatisfaction, but there won't be a sense of delight, that they are getting everything from this partner."

The multi-faceted training they provide their employees is intended to help them "learn and understand client perceptions and expectations and identify opportunities to incorporate technology advances into the customer processes" (Prasad).

6.10.4.4 Assessment: Satisfaction

Overall, both organizations are satisfied with the progress of the outsourcing project and the performance of the other on the outsourcing arrangement. As the project nears completion, Sarah commented that the Redwood management is impressed by the technical excellence and the cohesiveness that the Shiva team was able to establish with Redwood.

Shiva periodically monitors client perceptions to ensure client satisfaction with their work. They have implemented tools to evaluate their performance in different client-facing areas and make adjustments based on the feedback.

"We conduct customer surveys every year. These indicate gaps in our people, or our project. Last year for example, the key gap that was identified was in written and oral communication; we were not up to par. So, we addressed that within the company. We use feedback from the customer surveys to create directional changes in the way we interact with them." (Prasad)

Shiva's use of assessment is an example of the constructive role that assessment can play in the development of social capital. Assessment functions as an instrument to continuously improve the services delivered and contribute to the development of social capital.

6.10.5 Case study conclusion

Applications outsourcing is an area where the inter-organizational relationships plays a very important role. In Jeff's words:

"Anybody can make things look great, but the problem with software, is you'll never know it before its too late and everybody's gone. So, it is very much of a relationship type thing."

The case of these two organizations shows that it is a relationship that can be managed to achieve very successful outcomes

6.11 Case 10 – Tallgrass - Satya:

In the previous case, Redwood and Shiva proved that attention to the elements of social capital could not only help achieve satisfactory outcomes in the current outsourcing arrangement, but could also establish the foundation of a symbiotic relationship. In the case of Tallgrass and Satya, we find additional proof for this assertion. Satya, another leading offshore vendor, demonstrates the qualities that have led to the leadership of India in the global sourcing market. Similar to the last case, this case also shows evidence of continued development of all dimensions of social capital due to the continued investments of both parties.

6.11.1 Introduction

The client organization, Tallgrass, is a large U.S. company that manufactures, markets, and sells high-technology components and systems. Tallgrass is the world leader in digital signal processing and analog technologies. It has branches in Europe and in Asia, including one in India. It was one of the first organizations to establish a presence in India, commencing its operations there in the mid-eighties.

Satya, the Bangalore-based vendor organization, is a leading player in the applications development and systems integration business. Outside India, Satya maintains a presence in Taiwan, Japan, and UAE in Asia, UK, Germany, and France in Europe, and in the U.S. For its software operations, Satya has been assessed at CMM Level 5, making it one in a small group of companies currently to have achieved this distinction.

Table 6-11: Interviewees in the Tallgrass-Satya case

Name of interviewee	Organization	Position	Duration of interview	Taped?
Raj	Tallgrass(Client)	Marketing Manager – Audio and Infotainment Business	2.5 hours	Yes
Jason	Tallgrass	IT Manager	1 hour	Yes
Vasant	Satya (Vendor)	Client Manager	1.5 hours	No
Ram	Satya	IT Manager	30 minutes	Yes

Four individuals were interviewed to obtain the details of this offshore outsourcing arrangement. Raj has been with Tallgrass for more than twenty years at the time of the interview. He has worked at various Tallgrass locations in the U.S. and also in Tallgrass centers in Japan and India. Jason is an IT manager at Tallgrass. Though he is not involved in the management of the outsourcing project, he has interacted with the team from Satya on several projects.

Vasant is in charge of the Tallgrass projects for Satya and interacts directly with Raj on the projects. Though he has been with Satya for almost ten years, he has been in his current position with responsibility for the Tallgrass account for just two and a half years. The governance of the outsourcing arrangements between the two organizations are primarily Raj's and Vasant's responsibility. Vasant is an outsourcing practitioner who has a keen interest in the growth and changes in the outsourcing industry. He shared one of the presentations he has given at an industry conference that dealt with the topics of choosing services to be outsourced and the issues to be considered when outsourcing offshore. His answers reflected the though he had given to the subject. Ram works for Satya in India and was able to provide insight into some operational issues associated with the project in the Satya offices in India. He felt that many of the questions were difficult for him to answer since he did not deal with management issues.

6.11.2 The Outsourcing Project

Tallgrass provides silicon chips to its customers to be used in their products like digital cameras and mobile phones. To use these chips for a particular function, system-level algorithms need to be developed. This system development is outsourced to a vendor who has "much more system level understanding than a silicon company will have." Raj gave an example:

> "Like, say, you want to implement something like a video recorder or a camera or a modem, or whatever else it is, the software algorithm that runs this of course is the DSP or other processors. We--our customers will need to get more of a complete solution. Since we can only provide silicon, they will need to get the rest of the solution, which includes the software. So, to make it available to the customers, sometimes we will subcontract some of our third party partners developing other software either directly for us or just develop it, and we will promote it to our customers."

The two options available to Tallgrass, as Raj puts it, is "to hire the expertise to bring it in-house or we can contract it out." The problem with trying to build up the expertise in-house is that they "would never have the critical mass to develop that type of system resources." As Raj concludes, "we will have a delusion of focus and effort." Thus, the primary reason that Tallgrass has decided to outsource this service is the determination to focus on their core competency. Having realized the value of providing the software solution, they do not try to develop it in-house, but look for a competent external provider. The Tallgrass management is also aware that they are creating a situation of dependency here for themselves. As Raj commented:

> "We will always have to rely on the third party developer to support our customers. Actually, that means, you know, with the customer--we don't have complete control over that environment because the customer will start engaging with that third party because they need to get the support from the third party developer, right?"

However, they do not see it as a problem. Raj explained that this awareness helps them manage the relationship between Tallgrass, Satya, and the end-customer of the silicon. In his opinion, "what we need is a mutual agreement that we are all in it together." This sentiment that external providers can be well-used to supplement their internal resources was reflected in Jason's comments also.

> "We will get requests from different marketing or business leaders who are engaged with the customer and what we try to do is quote them how long it will take for us to get to do the work and we very often end up in a situation where we do not have enough resources to complete the work, or we are not the best experts to develop that application and deliver the product."

A couple of the other interviewees (not from the ten cases) had mentioned that they keep the extent of outsourcing a secret from the users within the organization to maintain their credibility. Jason does not feel that this is an issue and said that the role of the IT organization at Tallgrass is "to identify solutions and manage the provision of those solutions, wherever they may come from." Within Tallgrass, there is a clear understanding not only about the role of IT outsourcing and the benefits of outsourcing, but also about the risks associated with outsourcing.

Like many other large organizations with experience in outsourcing, Tallgrass maintains a list of vendors who have the capabilities they need. These vendors are identified through different channels, as Jason explained.

"It is almost always by personal contacts; through industry groups ... I can't think of anyone we have brought in any other way we have met through third parties. In very rare cases, on rare cases, people have brought in companies to present and they maybe unrelated to our personal contacts, but someone else has a contact with that company, who brings them."

Since organizations these days pay considerable attention to ratings like CMM, Raj was asked whether these ratings play a role in the selection of the vendors. Echoing the comment of representatives of many organizations with offshore outsourcing experience that these ratings today serve as an elimination tool, Raj replied:

"Most companies, you know, who are worth anything these days will have an ISO rating."

The vendors that are put on the short list are given a pilot project to assess their capabilities. Raj explained the importance of this evaluation:

"When it comes to developing a system, that's more of a black magic kind of thing; I need to have kind of an idea of the background and expertise in developing particular systems. So, I cannot really farm it out to anybody--carefully evaluate who can develop the product better."

Vasant mentioned that his organization also likes to start with pilot projects, since it gives the opportunity to know the other party better. Having started with a small project three years back, the organizations now have cooperated in several projects that involve the development of embedded software for the silicon that Tallgrass produces.

6.11.3 The Client-Vendor Relationship

The decision to involve a particular vendor in the development of the embedded software for the silicon chips marketed by his division is ultimately made by Raj. Price does not pay an important part in this decision; the focus is on the capabilities of the vendor. Raj and many of his colleagues have visited the Satya development center in Bangalore to see first-hand the processes that are followed there. Even though many offshore vendors commented on the importance of visiting the development center and meeting the individuals who are doing the work for the project, it is very rarely an organization actually spends money on that. Of course, the fact that the Indian office of Tallgrass is also in Bangalore helps.

Vasant explained that when they start the work on a project, they do not wait for the contract. "It takes time to do contracts, and we will personally discuss work, and begin on that confidence." Jason also repeated that starting work without a contract in place is quite common and it happens because it takes time to get it in place. Jason commented that personal contact is important from the very start, even before the project starts, because the project agreement is based on the personal contact, rather than the contract.

The contract is developed by purchasing and legal departments for all these projects, and the work starts without the contract. This can be contrasted with the attention given to contract development at other large organizations like Montezuma and Chickasaw. Even though those companies also claim they do not rely on the contract, the outsourcing project itself starts only after the contract is signed. One reason for this difference may be the size of the project itself. Looking at the Montezuma case, the contract was for ERP implementation for the organization. Similarly, Chickasaw had outsourced quite a large part of the pie, having been involved in a total outsourcing[18] arrangement. The nature of the industry the client organization operates in may also color their view of the vendor. Tallgrass, being a technology company, and more specifically a hardware manufacturer, may see these software companies as complementary resources that are necessary to provide a complete product to their customer. They may view these outsourcing arrangements more as partnership-based development projects, rather than as a provision of service as Montezuma or Chickasaw may view it.

Even after the contract is created, Raj and his team do not rely much on the contract. In fact, Jason mentions that he has never had the opportunity to actually study a contract. Raj commented:

> "I would like to forget it, that the contract exists. It (the outsourcing arrangement) should be based on a relationship, not a legal document. The legal document should be there, of course, as a guarantee."

This is the same comment that has been repeated often. As mentioned in the discussion of the Chickasaw-Zeus case, this view could be because the parties who are required to operationalize the contract are not involved in its development. In the rare case where the individuals involved in the management of the outsourcing project were also part of the contract negotiation, as in the Montezuma-Apollo case, it only served to create a feeling of one-upmanship. Reviewing comments from the various interviewees in both client and vendor organizations, it would appear that there is a tacit agreement that the contract does not have a beneficial purpose in the operationalization stage, except if things go wrong.

Given the importance given to personal relationships at Tallgrass and a similar view at Satya, the communication patterns and the metrics and milestones are decided upon together, apart from the contract. Informal communication is considered very important, and it works well for the projects that Satya does for Tallgrass. One reason that informal communication works well here could be because of the relatively small size of the project. It also does not mean that there is a lack of definition in the requirements or the processes. Both organizations have considerable experience in outsourcing and are aware that these decisions need to be made before the start of the project.

The Tallgrass-Satya relationship meets both parties' requirements and is more than three years old now. As a large multinational organization, Tallgrass is one of Satya's most important clients. Satya has paid particular attention to the needs of Tallgrass, by scaling up resources as needed for Tallgrass projects and making sure that these resources are well-trained. They maintain their own training center in Bangalore also. Vasant commented how over the past years they have become involved in additional applications.

---

[18] All or most parts of the IS function of a company are outsourced to an external vendor. This involves large sums of money and risk (Apte et al, 1997).

"The Tallgrass project gets driven out of TI, India- we touch almost all aspects – chip design, verification, validation application development- we do everything."

Recognizing the learning that has taken place in these projects and the strong inter-organizational and inter-personal relationship, Tallgrass has established a competency centre at Satya's software development center in Bangalore, manned by Satya engineers. Satya has earned the status of a select-partner company, and has been given access to tools that were previously available only to Tallgrass engineers. This additional access will help Satya "provide more value-add to Tallgrass and contribute innovative ideas."

6.11.4 Through the "Social Capital" Lens

Having presented the background and the story of the outsourcing relationship, the focus now turns to analysis of the field text using the social capital framework.

6.11.4.1 Social Capital in the Tallgrass-Satya relationship

As in previous cases, the determination of the presence of social capital in the relationship is made by examining whether the different elements of the three dimensions of social capital are manifest in the relationship.

6.11.4.1.1 Structural dimension: Access patterns and appropriable organization

The constitution of the structural dimension in this case is the same as in the Redwood-Shiva case, and therefore is not discussed again.

6.11.4.1.2 Cognitive dimension: Shared understanding

The emphasis given to the cognitive dimension of social capital is also similar to that in the Redwood-Shiva case. As Raj commented:

"There has to be some common language, something in common so that we have a common goal in understanding and a willingness to work together to reach that goal."

Satya management understands the need for a common language to promote a shared understanding. They also train their employees in communication skills and English usage at their more extensive training facilities in India. Even though all their recruits have completed their education with English as the medium of instruction, it is often necessary to modulate the accents and refine their use of the language. Additionally, it is necessary to train these recruits to understand the American accents.

Satya also trains their recruits in the latest technology related to embedded software and digital signal processing so that they are able to meet the requirements of Tallgrass. Some of this training is in collaboration with Tallgrass, though Vasant could not divulge the details of that agreement. He briefly commented:

"Large clients like TI, Cisco, and Nortel would agree to take fresh graduate engineers and jointly train them with the vendor- that is the investment these large clients make - because of a long term vision."

Another strategy that Satya has adopted is to recruit individuals who have worked at Tallgrass and would like to work in Bangalore. One of their job postings for systems analyst includes a line that reads "Desirable: Experience of working with *Tallgrass*."

6.11.4.1.3 Relational dimension: Trust, norms, obligations & expectations, identification

The importance of trust between the two organizations in applications outsourcing arrangements was emphasized by the interviewees in this case as well. Trust is initially based on reputation (Jason) and on the credentials of the other organization (Ram).

> "As far as how we build up trust, it is through really mutual respect and history, and there's nothing like having success in the past." (Jason)

Initial trust is often formed based on such publicly available signals. Trust in the relationship evolves as interactions happen during the relationship. While actions that demonstrate flexibility and cooperation can increase trust, Raj cautions that deviousness can destroy the relationship.

> "If I say, "Look, I only have hundred thousand dollars for this project, if we can not do this; the project dies. And I understand it is going to cost you 115 thousand dollars, ..." and if the vendor trusts me to be able to help them to cover the costs or give them additional--you know, additional ways to fund this, then--usually, there are things you can do – you need to work out those things. But, if I play games, it will always come back to haunt you...I also have to understand the additional burden that I will put on the vendor financially if I ask him to do things they had not planned to. So, I have to be more willing to be flexible."

Vasant also reiterated the importance of demonstrating a concern for the other party. He added:

> "I'm sure you hear this over and over again, aim at a win-win situation, not a win-lose situation. Even if the other party is in a jam, you better step in to help them so they can also win, not just you can make more money. When those kind of situations develop, that becomes just a failure."

Vasant and Raj are both satisfied with the commitment and flexibility the other organization had demonstrated in this relationship. Vasant and his team understand the pressure the client feels to put a product to market during the short "window of opportunity," and they are committed to helping the client meet their goals. As Vasant commented, "A sense of belonging sets in." This is due to the "involvement and participation" that the client encourages among the vendor employees. Thus, norms of commitment, flexibility, and cooperation have developed in the Tallgrass-Satya relationship.

Vendor representatives in other interviews have mentioned that one of their expectations is that the client would accept and appreciate the technical suggestions they bring in as potential improvements and not imagine these suggestions are the vendor's way of bringing in scope changes and gaining additional revenue. Vasant and his team appreciate the acceptance and respect that the Tallgrass employees have for the suggestions that Satya brings in. They also have expectations that they could learn from Tallgrass, an expectation that is being met with the joint training session and the establishment of the competency center in Bangalore. Part of the learning is just "process knowledge or domain knowledge," (Vasant) which is useful to other customers as well. Tallgrass anticipates that Satya will bring these innovative ideas to the table, and that it should become easier for them to do so as their association continues.

The organizations have tried to understand each other's culture. Responding to a question on the importance of cultural compatibility, Raj commented:

"Companies have characters just like people do, right? And the company characters may not match. Our companies, the way we operate, the company culture, may not match with the contractor's company's culture. That will lead to an uncomfortable relationship and experience for the future. That's not something I can put on paper...I don't think you can do anything to make sure the culture matches. You have to--most important to make sure you understand the difference in the culture. Understanding of the difference in the culture so that won't lead to a misunderstanding later on is more important."

The shared training and the employment of Tallgrass ex-employees by Satya are ways to enhance that understanding of cultural differences. Even given the turnover experienced by Indian IT services organizations, Vasant claimed that many of their employees have "worked with a single customer for 1-3 years," further leveraging the learning and familiarity that have developed during interactions.

6.11.4.1.4 Is social capital present in the Tallgrass-Satya relationship?

It is clear that all three dimensions of the social capital are present in the Glacier-Hercules relationship. The relationship is built on structures that promote the elements of the cognitive and relational dimensions of social capital.

6.11.4.2 Factors that promote social capital in the Tallgrass-Satya relationship

The knowledge that the inter-organizational relationship provides the basis for working together and the predisposition to create that relationship are necessary to develop the elements of social capital in the relationship.

'From a practical point of view, the contract becomes less important because if I ever have to rely on a legal document to get my results, I'm in trouble; because the moment I have to rely on a legal document to get a result, that means something has gone wrong in the relationship. Unless there is a very good working relationship between the vendor and the supplier, the product will not be successful.'

Realizing that the relationship is important, the two organizations invest in activities that contribute to that relationship. Interaction is important to create the "sense of belonging" that Vasant says exists in this relationship. The Satya and Vishnu teams meet together once a week. Ram also mentioned that just "hanging out" with the employees from the other team helped build camaraderie. Raj and Vasant have also developed a personal relationship because both of them believe that it adds to the inter-organizational relationship and ensures that resources are devoted to this project in the partner organization. Raj explained:

"If you have a very good personal relationship, regardless of the company culture, basically develop a champion inside the company for you. That champion will fight for your cause, and he's more likely to take ownership to make sure the product is successful. So that's why developing that personal relationship is more important."

With such awareness, every interaction of the organizations over time has contributed to increased mutual understanding and development of trust and other elements of the relational dimension of social capital. Acknowledging the importance of continuity and stability of the social structure in developing social capital (Nahapiet and Ghoshal, 1998), Satya ensures that employees remain on the same account for extended periods of time.

160

It also helps that the two organizations have a clear understanding of "what is expected" (Vasant) at the start of the outsourcing project. The clarity in the project agreement that is developed by the individuals involved in the management of the project in both organizations ensures that "a common level of expectations is set between both parties" (Vasant). This definition of the task and processes required to complete the task enables specification of access patterns (element of structural dimension) and contributes to the development of expectations regarding how each party will behave in the relationship.

As in all other cases, communication contributes to the development of social capital as well. Jason and Ram both explained how formal communication is channeled through one key person within the organization to ensure consistency. Plans to keep this individual abreast of every communication between the two organizations may not always work, but it is commonly agreed that all communication going from one organization to the other needs to be copied to this individual. Besides this formal communication, both organizations depend on informal communication, particularly to handle problem situations.

> "In a formal communication, especially when it comes to negative news, it's very difficult to communicate through formal channels; it's much easier to communicate through informal channels and take actions to avoid some bad situations if it's communicated early enough." (Vasant)

Timeliness in communication is also very important to avoid problems from getting out of control.

> "It's usually that companies when they don't tell you early enough and they wait until the very last moment to communicate a very bad news, it almost always leads to a disaster." (Raj)

Both organizations see each other as mutually dependent. Raj had acknowledged the dependency of his organization in this arrangement because they do not maintain these resources in-house and have handed over those to the vendor. Since Tallgrass is a very large organization with specific needs and Satya has invested in assets to meet their needs, losing that account would be disastrous for Satya as well. Vasant commented that it is important to keep the relationship where it does not "tilt towards win or lose on either side," so that the relationship is successful in the long run. In their research on partnership quality, Lee and Kim (1999) concluded fears of asymmetric dependence eroded the quality of the relationship in information systems outsourcing.

While Raj acknowledged that cultural differences do exist between Indian companies and U.S. companies, it is not an issue in this case. Raj is of Indian origin as are many of the engineers in the Tallgrass team.

6.11.4.3 Social capital facilitates the combination and exchange of resources in the Tallgrass-Satya relationship

The theoretical framework suggests that social capital provides facilitating conditions for the combination and exchange and resources necessary for the project. In previous cases, the discussion in this section has focused on the four conditions of access, anticipation of value from completion of the project, potential to appropriate value for oneself, and combination capability. From the favorable progress of the story thus far, it can be concluded that these conditions exist in the Tallgrass-Satya case also.

Given the complex nature of the projects, both organizations recognize that there should be "continuous interaction to determine what is doable and what is not doable" (Raj). For knowledge transfer to take place, the two teams should be able to function as one, where the vendor team "becomes a virtual customer organization" (Vasant). In his words, "You are dealing with intellectual capital here. So the engineers on both ends should have a sense of belonging." This sense of belonging and joint action does take place in the Tallgrass-Satya relationship. Vasant commented that customers include Satya engineers "as part of their team." Members of the client team encourage the participation of the vendor team "in all aspects of the chip production process – chip design, verification, validation application development" (Vasant).

> "The customer is very receptive, I would say. They say our engineers are part of their team- that any idea that comes to you, even if it sounds stupid to you, just write to us." (Vasant)

6.11.4.4 Assessment: Satisfaction

Tallgrass' and Satya's relationship have progressed to a mutually beneficial situation. Satya has attained a preferred status with Tallgrass and the assurance of a continued revenue stream. Tallgrass has a partner devoted to developing complementary products for the chips it develops, which fits with its plan to focus on its core competency. Both organizations' expectations are being met.

Similar to the case of Redwood and Shiva, monitoring mechanisms are used in a constructive manner to correct problems and set processes back on the right track. Vasant explained:

> "We have a set of feedback forms that we periodically issue to customers; incorporate that into our process- it is kind of a self correcting mechanism- it happens at all levels-we tell the customer about the corrective action based on the feed back forms."

6.11.5 Case study conclusion

Like the story of Redwood and Shiva, the case of Tallgrass and Satya is an exemplar of the application of the social capital in an applications outsourcing arrangement. As in the case of Shiva, Satya also invests in resources that will build up its capabilities and reputation as an offshore vendor. Knowing that the outcome of the operationalization stage rests in the strength of the relationship between the two organizations, the managers on both sides guide their teams to outcomes that are positive for all

6.12 Epilogue

Thus we have ten cases, each telling a story of two organizations in the throes of outsourcing. Some proceed steadily along the path to achievement of outcomes (e.g., Case 10: Tallgrass – Satya) some flounder (e.g., Case 5: Bluestone – Vesta). Participants in some relationships perceived dependence as a potential threat and reacted to create a relationship lacking in the relational dimension of social capital (e.g. Case 1: Montezuma – Apollo), while others were able to overcome larger imbalances in dependence and build a successful relationship (e.g., Case 8: Haleakala – Durga). Some used communication to overcome problems in developing social capital (e.g. Case 7 – Ozark – Brahma), while others suppressed information (Case 6: Denali – Vishnu) or distorted information (Case 2: Chickasaw – Zeus) and inhibited the development of social capital.

The stories of outsourcing relationships convince us that social capital is necessary for the completion of the outsourcing project and to support a long-term relationship. Yet, even when convinced of the need for social capital, some are unable to develop it. What supports the growth of social capital in these relationships, what inhibits the growth of social capital? Based on the ten different stories, what insights can we obtain about these relationships and the challenges faced in the operationalization stage of applications outsourcing? This is the purpose of the next chapter, where we examine the themes revealed in the stories.

Chapter 7
CROSS-CASE ANALYSIS

7.1   Introduction

In the last chapter, ten stories of inter-organizational relationships in the context of applications outsourcing arrangements were presented. Each story was accompanied by an examination of the relationship through the 'social capital' lens to reveal whether social capital was present in the client-vendor relationship and how the presence (or absence) of the elements of social capital affected the outcome of the outsourcing arrangement. The next step is to conduct an analysis across the cases to "see processes and outcomes across many cases, to understand how they are qualified by local conditions, and thus to develop more sophisticated descriptions and more powerful explanations" (Miles and Hubernman, 1994; p. 172).

Accordingly, the first task in this chapter, and the topic of the next section (7.2), is an examination of the experiences of the organizations in the ten cases in the last chapter to determine meaningful commonalities among the ten cases that would help answer the question "How does social capital contribute to the performance and outcome of the applications development outsourcing arrangement?"

In the next section (7.3), the different factors that affected the development of social capital are discussed. Four of these factors are suggested by the theoretical framework of this research; these are perceptions of dependence, communication, age of the relationship, and definition of the project parameters. An examination of additional themes that emerged from the data completes the third section of the chapter. This thematic analysis complements the exegetic analysis in the previous section.

In the last section (7.4), the development of social capital in offshore outsourcing relationships is examined. This section addresses a secondary question raised in this research, which was whether the cultural and geographic distance between clients and vendors would make a difference in the development of social capital in the client-vendor relationship.

7.2   The Role of Social Capital in Outsourcing Relationships

Each case description in the previous chapter showed how social capital present in a client-vendor relationship affected the achievement of outcomes in applications outsourcing. Each case had its special and unique characteristics. In this section, based on the understanding of the local dynamics of each of those cases, an explanation that transcends particular cases is developed.

A comparative overview of the ten cases is presented in tables 7-1 and 7-2. The characteristics of the participant organizations, the outsourcing project, and the outcome in the ten cases are shown in table 7-1. The clients and vendor organizations are classified as large or small and medium organizations. Doney and Cannon (1997) found that organizational size was a factor affecting the development of trust in inter-organizational relationships. The vendors are classified as domestic or offshore vendors, based on the location of their headquarters. Previous studies in IS outsourcing have found that offshore outsourcing is more problematic than domestic outsourcing. Domestic vendors are based in the U.S.; all offshore vendors in this research are based in India. Only organizations undertaking applications outsourcing projects were considered in this research; yet, there were differences in this characteristic as well. Some organizations were outsourcing implementation of ERP modules, while some organizations were outsourcing the development of software that was unique to their business (e.g., embedded software for digital signal processing chips). Requirements are uncertain on the latter type of projects, leading to task uncertainty and greater risks (Barki et al, 1993; Kraut and Streeter, 1995). Van de Ven et al (1976) found that in cases where task uncertainty is high, the parties preferred to rely on relationship-based exchanges rather than formal rules. Thus, the nature of the project may also determine the role of the relationship in the outsourcing project.

Other factors that may affect the client-vendor relationship have been identified in inter-organizational and IS outsourcing research. Lacity and Hirschheim (1993) commented on the role of consultants in driving the interactions during the outsourcing arrangement. Lacity and Willcocks (1998) highlighted the importance of organization's experience with outsourcing in identifying practices that lead to success. It has also been noticed that when client organizations pursued a selective outsourcing approach rather than a total outsourcing approach, there is a greater chance of achieving the desired outcome (Apte et al, 1997; Lee et al, 2000). The importance of personal relationships between the boundary spanners in the organizations in the development of inter-organizational relationships has been acknowledged in inter-organizational research (e.g., Brass et al, 2004; Doney and Cannon, 1997; Sydow, 1998). Consequently, changes on boundary spanners may also affect the relationship between the organizations (Sydow, 1998). This key role of the boundary spanners was noted in many of the cases also. Thus, the degree of outsourcing (total to selective), experience with outsourcing, presence of consultants, and personal relationships between the managers in the client and vendor organizations were also considered as contextual factors[1] in the examination of the ten client-vendor pairs.

From Table 7-1, it can be seen that no two pairs of organizations in this research were alike. Some clients were new to outsourcing, while some had been involved with the same partner for a number of years. Some clients undertook total outsourcing, treating the outsourcing vendor organization as their development center, while some outsourced just one activity. Some vendor organizations were comparable in size and geographical spread to the multinational organizations they provided services to, while some operated out of an office in a technology park halfway across the world. Of the activities that were outsourced, some were standardized projects, while some were very specialized. Given such qualifying conditions for the sequence of events that defined each outsourcing relationship, surfacing a generalized explanation is a tricky endeavor.

---

[1] Admittedly, several other interesting factors – e.g., the use of multiple suppliers, the criticality of the application outsourced, and the role of internal legal team – have not been included in this list. It is a limitation of this research that data on these issues could not be collected for every organization.

Table 7-1: Participant Organizations

	Case 1: Montezuma - Apollo	Case 2: Chickasaw- Zeus	Case 3: Glacier- Hercules	Case 4: Haleakala – Athene	Case 5: Bluestone – Vesta
Client	A large energy company that is engaged in worldwide exploration and production of crude oil and natural gas. Also domestic refining, marketing and transportation of petroleum products.	A major United States airline company, with its headquarters in south central United States	A large publicly owned chemicals company	A global provider of technology products and services to consumers and businesses	A small software company in California, providing software solutions for cashiering in higher education
Vendor	A large technology company that provides information technology services, software, systems, products, financing and technologies."	A leading provider of information technology and business process outsourcing services	A leading technology services organization	A small organization, specializing in SAP implementation, business intelligence, and data warehousing	A small software solutions provider, also based in California
Project	Application development, hosting, and support including the help desk support for the SAP environment	Data processing, systems development, system integration	SAP rollout	Enhancements and support for the software that is used for management and operational reporting needs in one of Haleakala's largest business units. Custom applications development.	Custom applications development, specialized. Update the applications software the client markets and create an integrated web-based billing, payment, and cashiering solution

166

	Case 6: Denali – Vishnu	Case 7 : Ozark - Brahma	Case 8: Haleakala – Durga	Case 9: Redwood – Shiva	Case 10: Tallgrass – Satya
Client	A national wholesale Internet Service Provider (ISP) - a small company	A small organization that develops and markets sales and management, tools for the heating, ventilation and air-conditioning (HVAC) industry	A global provider of technology products and services to consumers and businesses	A large utility company	A large U.S. company that manufactures, markets, and sells high-technology components and systems
Vendor	An offshore provider based in India - SME	Niche offshore provider meeting the application development and maintenance needs of SMEs	Niche offshore provider meeting the application development and maintenance needs of SMEs	Large offshore vendor organization	A leading player in the applications development and systems integration business
Project	Custom applications development. Upgrade and modify "software that the client's customers could use as interface to enable provision of services to the client's customers' customers	Custom applications development, specialized	Custom applications development, specialized	E-procurement solution (SAP EBP 2.0)	Embedded software, specialized

		Case 1: Montezuma - Apollo	Case 2: Chickasaw- Zeus	Case 3: Glacier- Hercules	Case 4: Haleakala – Athene	Case 5: Bluestone – Vesta
Context	**Total or Selective sourcing?**	Selective outsourcing; first applications outsourcing project. Plans to do more	Moved from total to selective outsourcing. Majority of work is outsourced	Selective outsourcing. This particular project is "very large scale." Value not disclosed.	Selective outsourcing	Total outsourcing. Product is core product marketed by client.
	First project vs. ongoing project for this pair	First outsourcing project. It is also the client's first outsourcing project in the applications outsourcing area.	Ongoing relationship. Outsourcing has changed from total to selective, including custom application development	Ongoing relationship. Client outsources projects based on competitive bidding to one of two major vendors	First project.	First project. It is also the client's first outsourcing project in the applications outsourcing area.
	Perspective on outsourcing in client organization	Not favorable. Outsourcing seen as a last effort to maintain the credibility of the IT organization.	Strongly supported. Vendor organization seen as an extension and complementary resource to internal IT organization. Admits that previous total outsourcing arrangement was not beneficial to client organization.	Strongly supported. Vendor organization seen as an extension and complementary resource to internal IT organization. Acknowledges that this requires change in management of IT.	Outsourcing is an accepted reality in this large organization with different departments/divisions having several outsourcing projects.	Outsourcing seen as a necessary evil due to lack of internal resources.

		Case 6: Denali – Vishnu	Case 7 : Ozark - Brahma	Case 8: Haleakala – Durga	Case 9: Redwood – Shiva	Case 10: Tallgrass – Satya
Context	**Total or Selective sourcing?**	Total outsourcing. Product is integral to client's business	Total and sole-sourcing. Products are marketed by client.	Selective outsourcing	Selective outsourcing	Selective outsourcing. Majority of the work for this line of products is done by this vendor.
	First project vs. ongoing project for this pair	First project. It is also the client's first outsourcing project of any type.	Ongoing relationship. The client has never used any other vendor for applications outsourcing.	Ongoing relationship	Pilot projects completed by vendor for client. First major project. The vendor is on client organization's preferred vendor list.	Small pilot projects completed by vendor before starting major projects. The vendor is on client organization's preferred vendor list.
	Perspective on outsourcing in client organization	Outsourcing recognized as the cost-saving and efficient option since the organization is unwilling to commit scarce resources to this project.	Internal resources are not available and the client wants to focus on core competency. Client is clear about what they want to achieve through outsourcing.	Outsourcing is an accepted reality in this large organization with different departments/divisions having several outsourcing projects.	Outsourcing is an accepted reality in this large organization with different departments/divisions having several outsourcing projects. Maintains a select list of vendors with which they would do business.	Outsourcing is an accepted reality in this large organization with different departments/divisions having several outsourcing projects. Vendors are seen as extensions of the organization.

169

		Case 1: Montezuma - Apollo	Case 2: Chickasaw- Zeus	Case 3: Glacier- Hercules	Case 4: Haleakala – Athene	Case 5: Bluestone – Vesta
Context	Pre-existing personal relationships at the start of first project	None	None	None	None	Yes, between top management Not between outsourcing managers in client and vendor organizations
	Change in boundary spanners	Yes	Yes	No	No	Addition of VP to vendor management team
	Consultants	Yes	Yes	No	No	No
Outcome		Project is completed as per contract, but the outcome is not satisfactory for the client. The vendor loses next contract with client and is not satisfied, either.	Initial projects are completed satisfactorily. Changes in the management of the client company require a refinement of the contract	Satisfactory progress for client and vendor.	Satisfactory progress for client and vendor.	Client is dissatisfied with project progress, but believes that the learning that has occurred can be used in additional projects.

		Case 6: Denali – Vishnu	Case 7: Ozark - Brahma	Case 8: Haleakala – Durga	Case 9: Redwood – Shiva	Case 10: Tallgrass – Satya
Context	**Pre-existing personal relationships at the start of first project**	None Vendor is selected off a web site by client	None	Yes	No	Yes
	Change in boundary spanners	No; vendor manager had attitude change	No	No	No	No
	Consultants	No	No	No	No	No
Outcome		Client is dissatisfied with project progress, but believes that the learning that has occurred can be used in additional projects.	Satisfactory progress for client and vendor. Vendor functions as client's offshore development center providing products that the vendor has been able to market successfully.	Satisfactory progress for client and vendor.	Satisfactory progress for client and vendor.	Satisfactory progress for client and vendor. Vendor is preferred partner for client

The examination of the characteristics of the outsourcing relationships in table 7-1 shows that in three cases (case 1: Montezuma-Apollo, case 5: Bluestone-Vesta, and case 6: Denali – Vishnu) the outcomes were not satisfactory. In the Montezuma-Apollo case, the client perceived the vendor as being inflexible and not exhibiting enough concern for the client's needs, even though the project was progressing as specified in the contract. The vendor, Apollo, in turn felt that the client had not come through on the vendor's expectations of continued business even though they had done "good work at Montezuma." In the Bluestone-Vesta and Denali-Vishnu cases, the clients are dissatisfied with the progress on the projects. The clients feel that they have been forced to continue with their respective vendors because the vendor did not provide them with the requisite quality services in the initial stages of the projects.

In the other cases, the client and vendors have been able to align their goals and work together to achieve those goals. Both parties (client and vendor) understand that the goals of the partner (client or vendor) organization would be different, but proceed with concern for the others' needs. This mutuality ensures cooperative behavior from both organizations.

What sets the three cases (Cases 1, 5, and 6) apart from the others? One commonality highlighted in Table 7-1 is that all three projects were first projects for these three client-vendor pairs. It was also the first applications outsourcing project for these clients. While agreeing that experience would be a plus[2], it would be unreasonable to argue that alone would lead to the failure of projects. In the case of Haleakala and Durga, this is the first outsourcing project for this client-vendor pair. The client was experienced with outsourcing, but one of the anchors of the relationship was the strong motivation to build the relationship[3] evidenced in the behavior of the vendor team. Similarly, the client and vendor interviewees in Ozark-Brahma[4] talked about the attention they paid to the relationship at the start of the relationship, realizing the impact that the relationship would have on the outcome of their project.

Another noteworthy commonality for the three organizations is the biased attitude towards outsourcing. According to Jim, the "O word" was not even used within Montezuma and the outsourcing project was pushed through with the goal of regaining the credibility of the IS function. At Bluestone, the project was outsourced because resources were not available in-house; however, there is also the perception that this decision was made based on the personal relationship between the top management at the client and vendor organizations. While the Denali management chooses to outsource their project to focus on other work, there is also ambivalence towards the outsourcing choice. Todd, the manager at Denali, voiced comments whether it would have been better from a business standpoint to develop in-house resources. These views towards outsourcing may affect the expectations and evaluations of experiences from outsourcing.

A more compelling explanation for the experiences of the different organizations may be obtained from the analysis of the data using the theoretical framework. The social capital framework developed by Nahapiet and Ghoshal (1998) posits that social capital supports the development of conditions necessary for the combination and exchange of knowledge. They

---

[2] This would provide support for the argument that time is required to build up social capital in the relationship. However, longevity of the relationship alone does not determine its success.
[3] Under the standard rational model, it is assumed that all actors are similarly motivated by self-interest. However, in an arrangement with another party, this self-interest could lead them towards opportunistic behavior or the building of a relationship that would lead to the attainment of achievements for both parties.

[4] Brahma was Ozark's first and only vendor.

contend that social capital is necessary when the knowledge to be transferred is complex and sticky. They identify three dimensions of social capital: structural, cognitive, and relational dimensions, and different elements for each dimension[5]. The annotations in the cells in table 7-2 show how the different elements of the three dimensions of social capital were exhibited in the ten cases[6]. Going down the columns in table 7-2, one can assess whether the elements of the different dimensions of social capital were present in a client-vendor relationship. Moving across the rows, the reader can notice the similarities and difference between the cases in the development of an element of a dimension.

The social capital framework suggests that the presence of the elements of the three dimensions of social capital (first column in table 7-2) creates facilitating conditions for the combination and exchange of knowledge. These conditions are access to information held by the other party, anticipation of value from combining knowledge, assurance that some of this value can be appropriated by oneself, and the capability to combine and assimilate knowledge. These facilitating conditions are particularly important in cases where the knowledge is complex and not easily transferable, as is the case in applications outsourcing. In cases where a dimension is weak or absent, facilitating conditions for the exchange will not be present leading to an unsatisfactory outcome. The theoretical framework also emphasizes the recursive relationship between social capital and the knowledge exchange processes and outcomes it supports. Comments on this aspect of the theoretical framework are included in the last row of table 7-2.

While the characteristics of the organizations and the nature of the projects in the three cases are different, through the application of the social capital theoretical framework, *a* plausible explanation can be found for the differing experiences of the client-vendor pairs. Through a review of how the different elements of social capital were developed in different cases and how these elements supported or inhibited the presence of facilitating conditions, an explanation for the success of some client-vendor pairs and the failure of others is put forward, following table 7-2.

---

[5] The three dimensions and their composite elements are presented in Table 4-1 (Chapter 4)

[6] Other factors may affect the relationship; however, only aspects included in the theoretical framework have been highlighted in this table. In section 7.4, data-emergent themes that are not a part of the framework are discussed.

Table 7-2: Cross-case Summary

	Case 1: Montezuma - Apollo	Case 2: Chickasaw-Zeus	Case 3: Glacier- Hercules	Case 4: Haleakala – Athene	Case 5: Bluestone – Vesta
Structural: Ties and configuration	Three-tier interaction pattern defined in contract establishes links between members of both organizations. Inter-personal relationships also developed between project managers. Change in vendor manager causes uneasiness in relationship between top managers.	Three-tier interaction pattern defined in contract establishes links between members of both organizations. Inter-personal relationships also developed between project managers. Formal and informal access established.	Three-tier interaction pattern defined in contract establishes links between members of both organizations. Inter-personal relationships also developed between project managers. Formal and informal access established.	Initially, there is a lack of structure for interaction from client side. This is compensated through informal channels. Client also develops formal patterns for interaction, once this deficiency is realized	Lack of interaction between client and vendor is initially a big hurdle in this case. Stems from lack of personal rapport between the client and the vendor representatives. Once this deficiency is realized, the configuration is changed.
Structural: Appropriable organization	Vendor brings in routines and procedures from previous engagements. The inflexibility in use of these routines, probably due to vendor's perception of advantage in an asymmetric relationship creates problems. The client is new to applications outsourcing and does not have 'appropriable organization' to use in the project. They use routines recommended by consultants in initial interaction.	Over the years, both client and vendor have developed 'appropriable organization' to be used in their projects together.	Client is cognizant of the risks in managing relationships with two large vendors. Client documents and creates 'appropriable organization' to use in this and further arrangements. Vendor has 'appropriable organization' to bring to project.	Vendor has studied best practices of outsourcing vendors and tries to apply these, but gives primacy to developing informal relationships. Client is experienced at outsourcing, but initially does not appear to use 'appropriable organization', though it does so later on (see note above)	Client is new to outsourcing; has no 'appropriable organization'. Vendor does not use 'appropriable organization' for relationship management.

Case 6: Denali – Vishnu	Case 7 : Ozark - Brahma	Case 8: Haleakala – Durga	Case 9: Redwood – Shiva	Case 10: Tallgrass – Satya	Comments
Interaction between client and vendor is defined, though not satisfactory for the project. The problem is compounded by the ineptitude of the vendor representative in developing a personal relationship.	Client and vendor work together to develop interaction patterns that will provide access that is necessary for the projects	Interaction between client and vendor representatives takes place at both informal and formal levels.	Interaction between vendor and client defined. Interpersonal relationships also developed. Formal and informal access established.	Interaction between vendor and client defined. Interpersonal relationships also developed. Formal and informal access established.	Usually at least some ties are developed through formal means. Informal ties developed during project. When ties are not defined at the start, it creates difficulties in developing the other dimensions of social capital. While this element of structural dimension does not directly contribute to the knowledge transfer beyond providing access, it is a necessary condition for developing other elements of social capital. [7]
Client is new to outsourcing; has no 'appropriable organization', but realizes that such routines need to be developed. Vendor has 'appropriable organization' it uses very successfully to impress the client - this pays off in terms of trust in competence.	Client is new to outsourcing and does not have in-house 'appropriable organization', but tries to apply best practices from industry. Vendor has 'appropriable organization' culled from founders' experiences, CMM, etc	Client and vendor both have processes they have identified from previous engagements and through deliberation within the organization. In addition, vendor uses CMM.	Client and vendor both have processes they have identified from previous engagements and through deliberation within the organization. In addition, vendor uses CMM.	Client and vendor both have processes they have identified from previous engagements and through deliberation within the organization. In addition, vendor uses CMM.	As an element of structural dimension, appropriable organization can be used to improve access through the reuse of tried and tested routines. Appropriable organization creates efficiencies when used in a flexible manner. Client organizations see the presence of appropriable organization as an indicator of competence

	Case 1: Montezuma - Apollo	Case 2: Chickasaw-Zeus	Case 3: Glacier- Hercules	Case 4: Haleakala – Athene	Case 5: Bluestone – Vesta
Cognitive: Shared language and codes	Shared business, legal, and IS vocabulary Benchmarking tools for evaluation of benefits	Shared business, legal, and IS vocabulary Benchmarking also used here	Shared business, legal, and IS vocabulary Commonly accepted legal document useful here.	Shared business, legal, and IS vocabulary	Differences in metrics and quality assessments Differences in use of terms (e.g. "porting" means one thing to client, another to vendor)
Cognitive: Shared narratives	Implementation of SAP and associated work - not much sharing of business domain experiences. Client staff feels vendor staff does not welcome that.	Through interaction with client and collocation of vendor staff at client sites, vendor has gathered information on client experiences. Custom development for client done by vendor.	Implementation of SAP and associated work - not much sharing of business domain experiences.	Project involves enhancements for software. Vendor takes initiative at gathering client experiences through informal channels	Business experiences shared in training. After that, there is minimal interaction.

Case 6: Denali – Vishnu	Case 7 : Ozark - Brahma	Case 8: Haleakala – Durga	Case 9: Redwood – Shiva	Case 10: Tallgrass – Satya	Comments
Shared business, legal, and IS vocabulary is possible because client is knowledgeable. However, client does not get involved in initial stages. Client does not understand CMM, but is impressed by it.	Shared business, legal, and IS vocabulary	Shared business, legal, and IS vocabulary	Shared business, legal, and IS vocabulary	Shared business, legal, and IS vocabulary	The shared business and legal vocabulary helps in the definition of processes, metrics to evaluate the progress of the project, etc. The shared IS vocabulary and the use of context-specific terms and models helps establish the goals of the project and the responsibilities of both parties in the project.
The project involves a common business and IS application (management of Internet services). Therefore, very limited sharing of experiences is necessary – according to both parties. However, the vendor needs to understand client's business practices.	Business experiences shared and demonstrated	Members of both organizations work together, sharing experiences.	Vendor expects client to have gained business domain experience	Business experiences shared through joint training	Especially in custom development, it is seen that the vendor organization needs to achieve an understanding of the business domain of the client. This understanding is achieved through a sharing of experiences and stories. These narratives are also used to convey how things are done in each organization

177

	Case 1: Montezuma - Apollo	Case 2: Chickasaw-Zeus	Case 3: Glacier-Hercules	Case 4: Haleakala – Athene	Case 5: Bluestone – Vesta
Relational: Trust	Lack of trust of client in vendor's intent and openness. Vendor feels client is reliable, though.	Trust has developed between client and vendor over time, fostered by consistent delivery and meeting of expectations	Trust built through tools that make processes transparent to all involved.	Client trusts vendor will deliver. Vendor feels client is reliable.	Client has doubts about vendor reliability. Vendor does not have fears of client opportunism. Most interestingly, vendor manager does not feel trust is important.
Relational: Norms	Client and vendor cooperate to achieve outcomes of the current project, though there is a feeling in the client organization that they are required to give more in this relationship. Client manager perceives inflexibility.	Commitment, flexibility, and cooperation fostered.	Commitment, flexibility, and cooperation fostered.	Commitment, flexibility, and cooperation fostered.	Client feels vendor is forced to be flexible due to vendor's own inadequacies at the start. Both client and vendor feel they have been cooperative, but the other has not and there is an undercurrent of antagonism

178

Case 6: Denali – Vishnu	Case 7 : Ozark - Brahma	Case 8: Haleakala – Durga	Case 9: Redwood – Shiva	Case 10: Tallgrass – Satya	Comments
Even though client has doubts about vendor's openness, he is confident about their competence. Vendor does not have fears of client opportunism.	Client trusts vendor will deliver. Vendor feels client is reliable.	Client trusts vendor will deliver. Vendor feels client is reliable.	Vendor uses trust-development techniques such as joint meetings with all clients to show openness. Vendor also ensures that their staff are open about problems. Vendor feels client is reliable - large and established, etc. Vendor empowers managers so that client feels needs will be met expeditiously - this increases trust.	Vendor uses trust-development techniques such as joint meetings with all clients to show openness. Vendor also ensures that their staff are open about problems. Vendor feels client is reliable - large and established, etc. Vendor empowers managers so that client feels needs will be met expeditiously - this increases trust.	Trust is a central concept enabling the development of other elements of the relational dimension. The initial trust of the client in the vendor appears to be based on competence. It is during the exchanges that comprise the project that the parties develop trust based on reliability, openness, and concern. The vendors take the actions of the client during the initial stages as signals of intent and reliability. The factors that affect the development of these bases of trust are perceptions of dependence (related to intent/concern), characteristics of boundary spanners (openness), and delivery (reliability).
Openness and teamwork does not exist, since vendor wants to maintain deception. Given previous experience of deception with this vendor, client is closely monitoring the vendor.	Commitment, flexibility, and cooperation fostered.	Commitment, flexibility, and cooperation fostered.	Commitment, flexibility, and cooperation fostered.	Commitment, flexibility, and cooperation fostered.	In successful cases, the client and the vendor make efforts to ensure that flexibility and commitment are demonstrated.

179

	Case 1: Montezuma - Apollo	Case 2: Chickasaw-Zeus	Case 3: Glacier-Hercules	Case 4: Haleakala – Athene	Case 5: Bluestone – Vesta
Relational: Obligations and Expectations	Client's expectation of innovation not met. Does not meet vendor's expectations regarding future opportunities.	Client aware of vendor's expectation of future business opportunities and willing to meet those. Additionally, client management is willing to work with the vendor's project management team to support their image in their organization. Client's desire for innovation and support with new IT plans are supported by vendor.	Vendor's expectations of future business opportunities assured. Client's expectations that the vendor would provide services as required have been met so far.	Vendor's expectations of future business opportunities assured. Client's expectations that the vendor would provide services as required have been met so far.	Vendor's expectations for future business opportunities are met - however, in this case it has been forced on the client. The client's expectations are that the vendor would support their learning, given that they have had to deal problems in the current project.
Relational: Identification	Lack of compatibility between client and vendor culture in meeting end-customer needs. This lack of compatibility is strongly felt within the client organization. The vendor does not perceive such differences.	No similarity, but compatibility - according to both client and vendor.	Similarity in organizational culture, work patterns, and project discipline exists - according to both organizations. Both organizations feel that they share the same concerns.	Client feels that vendor's organization is more structured. The vendor acknowledges the difference, but is trying to accomplish "being part of the group" through informal relationships	No similarity. No effort to develop compatibility yet.

180

Case 6: Denali – Vishnu	Case 7 : Ozark - Brahma	Case 8: Haleakala – Durga	Case 9: Redwood – Shiva	Case 10: Tallgrass – Satya	Comments
Vendor's expectations for future business opportunities are met. Client's expectations are that the vendor will accommodate their requirements in future projects, given that they have had to deal with problems in the current project.	Client aware of vendor's expectation of future business opportunities and willing to meet those. The client's IS needs and desire for innovation are supported by vendor.	Vendor's expectations for future business opportunities are met. Client's expectations are that the vendor would bring innovative ideas beyond the scope of the contract, and this is met.	Client aware of vendor's expectation of future business opportunities and willing to meet and promote those. Client's expectations are that the vendor would accommodate any changes or problems the client may have. The client is willing to do the same.	Client aware of vendor's expectation of future business opportunities and willing to meet those, motivating the vendor to perform well in the current project. Client's IS needs and desire for innovation are supported by vendor.	Vendor's expectations: 1, future business opportunities with the same client; 2, referrals from the client or willingness to serve as a reference. For the clients, the expectations include the vendor providing insights on the use of IT even when it is not of benefit to the vendor and identifying other resources when the vendor does not have the resources for a project the client requires. For both parties, the expectations center around both parties being willing to accommodate the other, especially when there is a problem - i.e., 1, an absence of opportunistic behavior by one party in the face of problems of the other. 2, a "flexibility begets flexibility" situation.
No similarity. Compatibility not yet developed.	Similarity does not exist, but client and vendor understand, appreciate, and accept each other's culture. The vendor team feels there has been an integration of cultures.	The client feels that there is similarity because of the personal acquaintances and the similarity in background. Vendor creates similarity by assigning highly qualified expatriates for this complex project. There is a sense of being part of the same team on both sides.	Only an appreciation and understanding of each other's culture is necessary, according to client. The organizations are looking for fit, not assimilation, according to vendor.	Only an appreciation and understanding of each other's culture is necessary, according to client. Vendor hires ex-Tallgrass employees to create identificatio n. There is a sense of belonging together and being on the same team.	While the cultures of both organizations do not need to be the same, there needs to be an understanding of how things are done in the other organization and an acceptance of how things are done in the other organization.

	Case 1: Montezuma - Apollo	Case 2: Chickasaw-Zeus	Case 3: Glacier-Hercules	Case 4: Haleakala – Athene	Case 5: Bluestone – Vesta
Comments	The social capital lens highlights how a long-term relationship is not possible where the lack of relational elements is not present. It shows how dependency can affect social capital.	The social capital lens highlights how distortion in communication inhibited the development of social capital, but how concerted effort by individuals involved helped overcome these problems and develop a shared understanding of the goals of outsourcing. Longest arrangement studied in this research. .	The social capital lens highlights how attention to development of social capital and the use of assessment to drive the development of social capital creates a continuous recursive cycle of social capital and social capital enabled exchange that meets the needs of both parties. This is a multiple vendor situation: parent-child analogy vs. marriage analogy	Using the social capital lens, one can see how the vendor relied on relational elements to develop a shared understanding and meet client's needs. However, this does not cause a problem because of both parties', especially vendor's, commitment to project.	The social capital lens highlights how the absence of the three dimensions of social capital creates an antagonistic situation. However, the client and vendor work on turning around the relationship, accomplishing the completion of the project. Further, the client asks the vendor to continue providing maintenance services.

Case 6: Denali – Vishnu	Case 7 : Ozark - Brahma	Case 8: Haleakala – Durga	Case 9: Redwood – Shiva	Case 10: Tallgrass – Satya	
The social capital lens highlights how dependency may encourage a small client to try to maintain the relationship even in the face of hurdles.	The social capital lens highlights how attention to development of all elements of social capital creates a continuous recursive cycle of social capital and social capital enabled exchange that meets the needs of both parties.	The social capital lens highlights how attention to development of all elements of social capital creates a continuous recursive cycle of social capital and social capital enabled exchange that meets the needs of both parties.	The social capital lens highlights how attention to development of all elements of social capital creates a recursive cycle of social capital and social capital enabled exchange that meets the needs of both parties.	The social capital lens highlights how attention to development of all elements of social capital creates a continuous recursive cycle of social capital and social capital enabled exchange that meets the needs of both parties. Vendor gains preferred partnership status; client establishes competency center with vendor's help.	

The underlined structural dimension of social capital is comprised primarily of elements that ensure that the individuals in the client and vendor organizations have access to the resources in the partner organization. In most cases, these ties are defined in the contract, down to details of how often and at what levels interaction needs to take place. To supplement formal ties[8] and to overcome problems posed by the absence of formal links (e.g. Haleakala-Athene), informal ties are also developed between the organizations. Formal ties are defined between the organizations in the cases of Montezuma-Apollo and Denali-Vishnu, just like all the other cases in this research. The case of Bluestone-Vesta is different; here, this definition is absent. Another element of the structural dimension is the appropriable organization. This set of routines for interaction and management that organizations are able to bring to the new outsourcing arrangement facilitates access between organizations.

In the Montezuma-Apollo case, the scheduled meetings at different levels take place and serve their purpose. The problem here happens with the departure of the original vendor project manager. Though the new project manager is competent, the informal ties that supplemented the formal ties between the key players now become weak. The vendor brings in a set of routines to efficiently start and implement the project. However, when the vendor chooses to stick to these routines even when going against "the way things are done" at the client organization, it creates a perception that the vendor is inflexible. The client staff also believes that the vendor does not encourage interaction and would rather "do things the way they do it everywhere else." There are other cases (e.g., Glacier-Hercules) where "appropriable organization" was applied successfully. The difference was that in those cases the vendor organization invested in building a strong relational dimension and made it clear that they understood and appreciated the nuances of the partner organization's culture.

In the Bluestone-Vesta case, based on the personal relationship between top management on both sides, the development of the core product is handed over to the vendor organization without a detailed contract. Yet this also does not happen in the Bluestone-Vesta case because of the ineptitude of the managers on both sides. The client organization is expecting the vendor organization to implement the interaction processes while the top manager from the vendor side does not see any need for such interaction.

In the Denali-Vishnu case, the contract lays out schedules for communication and deliverables. However, the client is lulled into a sense of complacency by belief in the competency of the vendor. Todd, the manger at Denali, views the CMM certification and the organized routines that the vendor brings in as signals of the vendor's competency. While the vendor would like to keep the client at arm's length to perpetrate the fraud they were pulling on the client, the client does not take any initiative to ensure that the communication schedules set in the contract are met. The vendor manager "does not have strong communication skills" and does not attempt to develop informal ties with the client manager.

When the structural dimension is weak, it reduces the access between the organizations. This is most clearly seen in the Bluestone-Vesta case, where there are no structures in place for interaction between the organizations. It can also be seen to a lesser extent in the Denali-Vishnu case, where the structures are not used. In the Montezuma-Apollo case, the interaction between the organizations continues; the problem is in the quality of the relationship between the

---

[8] This is true in all successful cases

boundary spanners – the openness and closeness that existed between the boundary spanners is not present anymore. This reduces the anticipation of value from the relationship.

In the other seven cases, formal and informal ties are used to various degrees. Both client and vendor organizations use formal ties to meet the legal requirements while they depend on informal ties to manage changes and accomplish their goals. As Kern and Willcocks (2000) show, the initial interactions proceed according to the contract. However, as time progresses, the interactions are defined by the key players themselves. They may change schedules and the mode and content of interaction based on their needs of the project and their evaluations of the partner organization. As time progresses, events may necessitate this departure from the contract, with mutually agreed-upon behavior becoming the means to manage the outsourcing arrangement.

While the primary role of the structural dimension is to provide access, it can affect the development of other dimensions leading to an indirect effect on the other facilitating conditions for the combination and exchange of knowledge. For instance, when the ties are weak, the high level of interaction necessary for the development of the cognitive dimension of social capital would not be present, and it would affect the ability of the organizations to combine their knowledge.

The cognitive dimension of social capital comprises those resources that allow the client and vendor organizations to reach a consensus regarding the task and the process and to use common or shared knowledge to achieve their goals. These resources are common language and codes and sharing of narratives. A pre-condition for such sharing is that both organizations must have such knowledge. This is not technical knowledge alone, but knowledge about the process and the management of the process to achieve desired outcomes.

In the Montezuma-Apollo case, the client retained the services of a consultant for contract negotiation and finalization, but decided to manage the project on their own. By their own admission, the client management believes they have not paid enough attention to how the project should be managed. This lack of preparation and absence of in-house staff trained in SAP reduces their ability to assimilate fully the resources that Apollo has brought in. As Bob puts it, "we have got some change to get our head around" to be able to meet user demands with the new technology. However, the project is completed as per contract specifications because it is a standardized project and Apollo has considerable experience with projects of this nature. This is not the case in Bluestone-Vesta and Denali-Vishnu.

In the Bluestone-Vesta case, the client offers training lessons to the vendor to acquaint them with the features of the product. Stories regarding experiences with the product are shared during these training sessions, and this helps the vendor understand the features of the product. The problem here is that there is no consensus regarding the task and the process. Additionally, the client employees have limited understanding of the new technology platform. The vendor believes that the client wants them to "port" the product to a new platform, while the client sees this as the creation of a complete new product.

In the Denali-Vishnu case, the client is fairly knowledgeable about the technology and the requirements for the final project. However, the client is not as knowledgeable as the vendor is, as they do not realize the problems with the existing software. Believing that the client would be locked-in to the project after the initial investments, the vendor has not revealed to the client the extent of work that needs to be done to accomplish what the client needs. Thus, there truly is no shared understanding between the client and the vendor regarding the status of the project and future requirements.

Thus, in all three cases, the cognitive dimension is weak reducing the ability for the two organizations to combine their knowledge. This lack of shared understanding also leads the clients to evaluate the benefits of combination and exchange differently from the vendor. This anticipation of value that the client has will not be realized because these are not based on a true and complete understanding of the situation. When the expected value is not delivered, it will lead to dissatisfaction.

In the Bluestone-Vesta and Denali-Vishnu cases, the client comes close to terminating the current contract because the performance on the current project itself is poor. However, in the Montezuma-Apollo case, the outsourced project is completed according to contract specifications, though not the satisfaction of the client. The difference in the nature of the projects may explain why given three similar scenarios, the first pair was able to complete their first project even with the problems they had. Unlike in the first case, the projects in the second and third cases involved the development of customized applications, which required the vendor to have an understanding of the client's business domain. The capability to combine of knowledge, which is supported by the cognitive dimension of social capital, is particularly important in these two cases. In the absence of such shared knowledge, the project will not meet the needs of the client.

In successful cases like Tallgrass-Satya, the client and the vendor actively pursue technical and management knowledge and make opportunities to utilize synergistically their distinctive knowledge; for example, Tallgrass and Satya organized joint training sessions for employees. It is important for client organizations to develop an understanding of their responsibilities to complete the project; realizing this, the manager at Ozark (Ozark-Brahma case) educates himself on industry best practices. Another mechanism used by some of the interviewees to encourage business domain understanding was to attend industry conferences together. Stories shared by the client and vendor assist in the discovery of practices in the partner organization.

The relational dimension of social capital comprises of trust, norms, obligations, and identification. The elements of this dimension are developed through the personal relationships between the boundary spanners in both organizations. Trust is the cornerstone of this dimension; it facilitates the development of the other elements of this dimension. Trust between client and vendor organizations has been shown to be important in outsourcing arrangements; this is supported by the evidence in cases in this research also. Norms such as flexibility, commitment, and cooperation are present in successful relationships (see table 7-2). The findings from the research suggest that the client and vendor organizations do not need to identify themselves with each other or see themselves as belonging to the same group. Only an appreciation and understanding of each other's culture are necessary.

In the Montezuma- Apollo case, there was a perception that the vendor would be difficult to manage. This view was also fostered by the comments from the consultants the client hired to guide them through the contract negotiations. As a sidebar, this case highlights how consultants can distort the perceptions in a stage (contract-negotiation) that is even otherwise fraught with uncertainty and distrust. The perception of inflexibility is magnified by the client's belief that they are more dependent on the vendor, a belief that the vendor concurs with. There is trust in the vendor's competence and reliability, but misgivings about their intent and openness. There is a lack of consideration to the expectations of the partner and cultural compatibility does not exist.

In the Bluestone-Vesta case, the vendor (Vesta) manager did not believe that a trusting relationship between the organizations was important. Coupled with the problems in delivery, this creates distrust in the vendors' competence and reliability. The limited interactions and lack of consensus on the project goals do not contribute to a relationship strong in trust and norms of cooperation and teamwork, nor does it help develop cultural compatibility.

In Denali-Vishnu, the client finds out that the vendor had purposefully covered up the fact that the project would not be completed within the time and resource limits set in the initial agreements. The vendor does not plan to keep the vendor in the dark forever; unfortunately for them, the client discovers their duplicity before they could present and explain it to the client. The client feels that the vendor has not honored the agreement and provided the level of services that was expected. As in the previous two cases, the relational dimension is not strong in this case either.

When the elements of the relational dimension are not strong, a relationship cannot continue. In the Montezuma-Apollo case, the client and vendor finish the current project, but acknowledge that the "relationship has become sour" preventing them from working together on the next project. From the last row of table 7-2 (and case descriptions 5 and 6 in the previous chapter), it can be seen that the client organizations, Bluestone and Denali, have decided to continue with their current vendors for maintenance of these projects. In these cases, the client and vendor work together to turn around their relationships. They acknowledge their differences and overcome the problems by making changes in the management of the outsourcing arrangement. The clients do not terminate the project, acknowledging the learning that has happened should be used to their advantage in this and future work.

The elements of the relational dimension are hardest to develop in a relationship[9], resulting only from personal efforts of the project managers. The elements of the cognitive dimension may be supported by a common understanding of business practices, expectations, and technical expertise, which may be developed through training sessions and ensuring that the parties involved have the appropriate background and experience. The elements of the structural dimension can be pre-defined and contractually required. The development of elements of the relational dimension in an inter-organizational relationship happen through the institutionalization of the trust, cooperation and such qualities exhibited by the managers in their interpersonal interactions with their counterparts in the other organization. In successful cases, the managers not only recognize the need for the presence of the elements of the relational dimension, but also acknowledge that their effort is necessary to build up these elements.

In summary, different dimensions of the social capital have different roles to play in the client-vendor relationship during an applications outsourcing arrangement. While the primary function of the structural dimension in the exchange and combination of knowledge in applications outsourcing arrangements is to provide access, it supports the development of the

---

[9] The specification of the configuration of ties that constitute the structural dimension is often part of the contract. It is true that organizations expend considerable resources in the creation of this legal document, especially in high value projects. To ensure that the elements of the cognitive dimension are present, organizations need to identify individuals with the right background and experience. While this may also involve use of organizational resources, it has been pointed out by interviewees that identifying and placing the 'right' individuals as boundary-spanners are difficult because the success of the boundary spanner is determined by the inter-personal dynamics between the boundary spanner and his counterpart in the other organization.

other dimensions of social capital. The shared cognition supported by the elements of the cognitive dimension support the combination of knowledge of the two organizations, the successful accomplishment of which will motivate the organizations to provide added access. The relational dimension supports the belief that the outcome of the exchange would be worthwhile and that benefits would accrue to the organization by being part of the exchange, which would lead to more sharing between the organizations.

The presence of elements of relational and cognitive dimensions in the relationship supports innovation. While the organizations need to be able to combine their knowledge effectively to support innovation, it is the trust and cooperation that develops between the individuals and the organizations that encourages them to bring these ideas to the other party, even with the possibility of being ridiculed or accused of avarice. Following Deutsch's "crude law of social relations", trust and cooperation will induce openness and sharing, even that of "stupid ideas" (Vasant: Tallgrass-Satya case). Galunic and Moran (2000) also found that relational capital developed by sales managers in their organizational network contributed to their capabilities for innovation, while the access they had within the organizational network contributed only to operational performance. While the presence of the elements of each dimension provide the facilitating conditions for combination and exchange, the organizations benefit from the interplay of these dimensions as well.

7.3 Shaping Relationships

In the ten stories related in the last chapter, the influence of factors like dependence and communication on the development of social capital in the client-vendor relationship was noted. This section synthesizes the findings from the ten cases to identify the role of these factors in the development of social capital and thus in the outcome of the applications outsourcing relationship.

In the IS outsourcing literature, dependence has been identified as one of the pivotal forces in the client-vendor relationship (Huang et al, 2004; Lacity and Willcocks, 1998). The level of dependence of one organization on the other can affect the level of social capital in the relationship (Moran and Ghoshal, 1996) and elements of social capital such as commitment (Wu et al, 2004) and trust (Zaheer and Venkataraman, 1995). By facilitating coordination and cooperation for mutual benefit (Putnam, 1995), social capital can also help manage dependence. This bi-directional relationship between dependence and social capital leads to interesting scenarios in different cases.

Communication is essential for building inter-organizational relationships and can enhance the potential for building associations in which effective knowledge exchanges can occur (Dyer and Singh, 1998). IS outsourcing researchers have also pointed to the importance of communication in coordinating tasks (Grover et al, 1996; Koh et al, 1999; Kern, 1997) and in managing knowledge overlaps (Tiwana, 2004) between the client and vendor organizations. It is not just the quantity of communication, but also the quality of communication that matters (Dibbern et al, 2004); the quality of communication contributes to satisfaction with the relationship (Lee et al, 1999). In the ten cases, communication plays a vital role in developing the elements of social capital.

Mere longevity does not suggest a strong and fulfilling relationship for both organizations. However, it takes time to develop the elements of social capital in the relationship. The duration of the relationship also enhances the development of trust and cooperation (Ring and VandeVen, 1992), and shared knowledge (Kotabe et al, 2003).

The definition of project parameters provides the scope for the project, determines the deliverables, and identifies individuals who will interact with the partner organization for the project. The setting of such formal boundaries promotes the development of trust and cooperation (Coleman, 1988; McEvily et al, 2003). It fosters the creation of a common set of norms for behavior among all individuals involved in the project (Uzzi, 1999). The first four sub-sections (7.3.1 to 7.3.4) discuss these four factors identified by Nahapiet and Ghoshal as influencing the role of social capital: dependence, communication, duration of the relationship, and definition of the project parameters.

Definition in the outsourcing project follows from the specifications in the contract. The examination of the role of definition in the development of social capital led to a deeper examination of the role of the contract in the outsourcing arrangement. This is the topic of the fifth sub-section (7.3.5).

For the qualitative researcher, the data tells the story. While the theoretical framework is used to surface a particular understanding of the phenomenon under study, other themes may emerge from the examination of the data. This deductive work complements the findings based on the examination of the data using the theoretical framework. Besides the four factors discussed above (sections 7.3.1 to 7.3.4), assessment and the attributes of boundary spanners also affect the development of social capital in the relationship. Organizations like Glacier (Glacier-Hercules) and Shiva (Redwood-Shiva) use assessment as a tool to identify deficiencies in the relationship and forge stronger links. The characteristics of the outsourcing project managers in both organizations have a defining role to play in the inter-organizational relationship. It is the capabilities and motivation of these boundary spanners that cement the relationship between the organizations. The roles of assessment and of boundary spanners in the development of social capital are discussed in the sixth and seventh sub-sections (7.3.6 and 7.3.7). Two caveats should be noted about these factors[10]: one, these factors are not mutually exclusive, and two, the relationship between a factor and social capital is not solely unidirectional.

7.3.1 Role of *Dependence* in the Development of Social Capital

The question of dependence produced varied responses from the interviewees. Some clients felt they had more to lose in the relationship because their business depended on the outcome of the outsourcing arrangement. Some vendors argued that their revenue stream and existence depended on retaining the client. Some interviewees commented that the dependence in the relationship changed as the relationship progressed. Like a seesaw, it teetered from side-to-side depending on the investments parties made in the relationship. The vendors were more dependent in the relationship at the start of the outsourcing project if they had to make considerable investments to get the project off the ground. However, once the project was under way, the client would become more dependent since the client organization's resources are also tied into the relationship. Others tried to bring in an element of future returns into this evaluation; if the relationship provided future opportunities for one party and these would be lost by some event in the current project, it would create a dependency for that party.

---

[10] including dependence, duration of the relations, definition of project parameters, and communication

While mutual dependence promotes cooperation and commitment (Gundlach and Cadotte, 1994; Sivadas and Dwyer, 2000), perception of asymmetry in dependence causes dissatisfaction in the disadvantaged party. When both organizations recognize that positive outcomes for one are dependent on the other party also achieving its goal, they invest in the relationship and build social capital in the relationship (e.g. Redwood – Shiva case).

However, if the client is dependent on the vendor, the vendor may not exhibit behaviors that encourage trust and cooperation (elements of relational dimension). This is the case in the Montezuma- Apollo relationship. Apollo does not perceive any dependence on Montezuma, since it is has established its reputation in the industry. On the other hand, inexperience leads Montezuma to fear that they would not be able to manage Apollo's intentions.[11] The lack of symmetry in dependence contributes to suspicion on the part of the more dependent party, blocking the development of trust. This is the stage when trust is most crucial; the client's trust in the intent and openness of the vendor and would have helped the relationship over the roadblock of asymmetric dependence.

Asymmetric dependency can place the vendor at a disadvantage also. However, if the relationship is managed well, distrust and consequent unproductive behavior can be avoided. In the case of Tallgrass-Satya, Satya has made investments to host Tallgrass' competency center at their Bangalore location. Satya is a very small organization compared to Tallgrass and is one of many offshore vendors who could meet Tallgrass' requirements. Through making investments in the relationship themselves and by creating a sense of belonging in the Satya employees, Tallgrass has signaled its trustworthiness to Satya. They have provided access to Satya employees to their knowledge resources and enhanced the shared understanding through joint training sessions.

A similar trusting relationship exists between Haleakala and Durga, an even smaller outfit with less than fifty employees. Haleakala is a large multinational organization with access to resources from any global location. However, in this case both parties reported that they were mutually dependent[12]. Due to efforts of both parties to develop the cognitive dimension of social capital, combination capability that is necessary for the effective exchange and combination of knowledge resources is assured, and the vendor brings "value add" that "is appreciated" by the client. As in the Tallgrass-Satya case, the vendor feels a sense of ownership in the project and is committed to bringing the innovation to the table. An evaluation of these three cases demonstrates the role of dependency in the development of social capital in applications outsourcing arrangements.

In the Bluestone-Vesta and Denali-Vishnu cases, the clients' decision to continue with the current vendors can also be seen as a sign of dependency. They realize that it would take time and resources to get another vendor to the same stage as their current vendors. Besides, they have had a chance to become familiar with the current vendor's practices. Thus considering the costs of removing this vendor from the project and choosing an alternate and educating them to the same level, the clients decide to retain the same vendor. However, both Bluestone and Denali have learnt from the problems they had in the past. Bluestone, for instance, realized that they have to educate themselves about the new technology platform and invested in developing

---

11 It is true that these fears are expressed in comments by Montezuma managers during their interviews. However, these are not views arising from their personal experiences, but from their roles as managers in an organization involved in its first outsourcing project with an established organization like Apollo.
[12] The services that Durga provides to Haleakala are of a very specialized nature

the cognitive dimension of social capital. The Denali management is building up the relational dimension of social capital by implementing measures that foster trust and teamwork.

In summary, dependence is inevitable and necessary when two organizations come together on an applications outsourcing project. It can be seen that dependency exists on a sliding scale. When this dependency can be balanced by the social capital in the relationship, it is beneficial for both organizations since it ensures that both parties will be concerned about the outcome of the relationship. The encouraging note from the tales of pairs like Bluestone-Vesta and Denali-Vishnu is that the management of organizations can invest in developing social capital and thus control the potential damaging effects of asymmetric dependence through investments in social capital.

7.3.2 Role of *Communication* in the Development of Social Capital

Communication is a precondition for the development of social capital (Nahapiet and Ghoshal, 1998). The findings in this research also support that assertion. The cases provide examples of organizations establishing shared understanding through communication (e.g. Ozark-Brahma), overcoming problems of distrust and resolving conflict through communication (e.g. Denali-Vishnu), and meeting expectations of appreciation through communication (e.g. Tallgrass-Satya).

Organizations use both formal and informal channels of communication. Organizations involved in the outsourcing of large projects lay out the formal communication plan in the initial legal agreements. In these projects (e.g. Chickasaw-Zeus, Montezuma-Apollo), a 3-layer communication model appears to be the most popular. The granularity of the information and the frequency of the meetings decrease as we move from the day-to-day operations level to the executive level. The project manager who operates at the middle layer of this hierarchy is the linchpin[13] in the communications between the two organizations. Depending on the size of the project, there may be more than one person in this role. The project managers from both organizations meet bi-weekly or monthly and review progress and compliance and set goals for the next period. At the top level, there are quarterly review sessions. In smaller projects, the communication patterns may be decided on between the managers involved and may not be as structured.

In offshore outsourcing also, the same pattern is noted: large projects require more structured interactions, while in smaller projects the interaction is less formal. Due to the costs associated with managing offshore projects, the vendors may not place all the individuals involved in the management of these projects on-site. Offshore vendors have a pre-defined ratio for the number of people to be stationed at the client location vis-à-vis the number of people working on the project offshore.

In the previous sub-section (7.3.1), it was noted that age of the relationship affected the level of inter-dependence in the client-vendor relationship. Age of the relationship also has an influence on the choice of the form of communication. New relationships require face-to-face meetings and team sessions. As the relationship matures, more of the communication needs can be met using video conferencing, teleconferencing, email, and/or instant messaging technologies.

---

13 These individuals are involved in the day-to-day management of the project and are kept informed of any interactions with the other organization.

Based on the responses of interviewees, informal communication is used widely; after all, as one interviewee remarked, "these are people!" When asked about informal communication, responses were "Oh, Absolutely! There is probably more of that than anything else," "Definitely," "We depend more on informal communication," and similar comments. Informal communication can be more effective than formal channels, though both are essential. Bob (Montezuma-Apollo case) commented, "Formal communication makes it legal and informal communication makes it work." Informal communication works because individuals choose to participate in informal communication and thus they tend to be more open and intimate. Comparing his reliance on formal and informal communication, Dave (Glacier-Hercules case) said:

"Most of the communication happens very formally, a lot of the important communication happens informally. What I mean by that is that a lot of times you are going to have a side bar discussion, a one-on-one discussion with some individual, perhaps very frank open type of communication in which you are willing to say things you would have never gone into a meeting room full of people and said publicly. So you know, I would say a lot of the important discussion happens informally, but the ones that are on record happens in those formal meetings…you may be more willing to say something one-on-one to somebody than you would at an open session because you might not have a good relationship with everyone in there."

During informal communication, particularly in one-on-one conversations, individuals will elaborate or modify what they have to say to address the other person's objections or provide additional explanations to increase understanding. Raj (Tallgrass-Satya case) explained that he used informal communication, preferably in a personal face-to-face session, as a means of avoiding problems, because it is easier to communicate negative information in this manner. Managers also mentioned that handling problems in this informal manner is a way of warning and shielding one's counterpart in the other organization from repercussions that may occur when problems are reported through formal channels. Such actions help build the interpersonal relationship between the managers in the two organizations. As stated before, these interpersonal relationships provide the foundation for building inter-organizational relationships.

The structuring of interaction in outsourcing projects places the responsibility for maintaining communication between the organizations on the shoulders of the project managers, the boundary spanners. Many interviewees mentioned that interactions between the organizations are channeled through these individuals. Kern and Willcocks (2002) also noted the use of designated individuals as interface points between organizations. The number of individuals depends on the size of the project. At the minimum, there is an effort to keep these key players in the loop for all communications between the organizations. This ensures consistency in management and prevents issues from going unnoticed and unresolved.

It is essential to realize that communication, whether it is formal or informal, is driven by each person's needs and agendas. When one's job is creating and maintaining inter-organizational relationships, it is necessary to get an understanding of the organization's needs as well as the needs of the individual who is managing the project. Understanding of each other's needs comes from being persistent in gathering information from different sources within both organizations and putting the pieces together. Cindy (Chickasaw-Zeus) mentioned how she networked within the organization to stay aware not only of the IS needs of the organization[14], but also to determine which individuals in the organization influence the relationship. The conversation with Cindy highlights various aspects of communication: structuring communication, formal versus informal communication, and the importance of networking.

George: Regarding the communication between the two organizations, how are the communications patterns established? Are they defined in the contract?

Cindy: They are not defined in the contract. Some specific reports and measures are called for in the contract. We abide by that, but communication patterns are mainly based on the agreement between the executive operating team for the two companies.

George: So the communication patterns are basically developed during the course of the arrangement?

Cindy: Yes

George: And are these formal communications patterns or informal patterns?

Cindy: Both

George: The people with who you communicate informally - are they the same people with who you communicate formally?

Cindy: In some cases yes, and in some terms, no.

George: Could you give me an example to figure out - what would your interactions be with people in your partner organization?

Cindy: I mean there is a lot to be said for informal networking and that is why corporations have many of these community affairs: PR and network type events and that are necessary especially when there is all this inner change. You get to go outside your normal set of contacts and understand your customers. You get to understand who are your powerbrokers, who are the decisions makers, and who are the influencers and understanding that the power structure and how things are done. Having relationship with the right decision channels and people that influence and direct the path of the relationship is necessary.

Not all communication is about agreement and understanding; communication can create misunderstanding and turmoil in the relationship as well. In the Chickasaw-Zeus case, the communication of inaccurate information by one of the boundary spanners – the Zeus executive – leads to misunderstanding between the organizations. The client, Chickasaw was dissatisfied with the services they were receiving from Zeus and started looking for another provider. Zeus' response during this initial period was negative. Bill (Chickasaw) explained what happened behind the scenes at this time:

"For the first six months that we were doing this, writing the RFP and putting it out, Zeus allowed the account team--that's a normal practice--to do the negotiating. Well, the account team meanwhile had been--because the account manager's success is how well they are getting along with the customer --he is reporting along to corporate headquarters

---

[14] This would be part of the marketing efforts of every account manager from the vendor organization

what? I got a tough customer, they will not pay the bills, they are always screaming about things that are not germane, etc. So, the story at corporate headquarters is that we are just a lousy, tough account. We're not cooperative, we won't pay the damn bill, we're always yelling, we're always asking for thing we're not entitled to, and it took 6 months before there was a real realization at senior levels of Zeus that the problem wasn't quite as they depicted it."

It took some time for the Zeus management to catch on to what was going on. They realized that "they were going to lose it for reasons that weren't what they were being told" (Bill). To maintain his legitimacy at Zeus, i.e. to be seen as capable of managing the account (Levina and Vaast, 2005), he had to attribute the problems to Chickasaw. As a boundary spanner, he is able to filter and translate events happening in the inter-organizational space to members of his organization. His self-serving accounts lead to the creation of misinterpretations of Chickasaw at Zeus (Daft and Weick, 1984). The distortion in communication thus reduces trust and other elements of the relational dimension of social capital in the Chickasaw-Zeus relationship.

In short, both formal and informal communication serves to strengthen the relationship between the client and the vendor organizations. Through complementary use of both channels, organizations build up shared understanding, trust and continued willingness to listen to each other, establishing the bi-directional relationship between elements of social capital and communication.

7.3.3   Role of *Duration of the Relationship* in the Development of Social Capital

The longevity of the relationship could be an indicator of the well-being of the relationship, because it can be argued that organizations will continue to interact with each other only if they perceive the exchange relationship to be beneficial (Lee and Kim, 1999). As the relationship between the client and the vendor ages, they gain deeper and richer impressions of the other organization's capabilities and constraints through the enactment of the cultures and practices of each organization by the organizational representatives.   Many interviewees expressed the view that organizations reach a stable stage through mutual adjustment over time and the relationship has become "more of a relationship between people" (Mark: Bluestone-Vesta). However, while personal ties are important, the ongoing interaction takes an existence separate from that of the people involved. This institutionalization (Hicks, 1999; Zaheer et al, 1998) has been likened to structuration (Sydow, 1999), a concept that was developed by Giddens to explain the agency-structure dichotomy in social sciences. According to these researchers and other researchers who have investigated social capital at the organizational level (e.g., Kostova and Roth, 2002), the constituted structure spans not only those who created it, but goes beyond to span the relationship between the organizations.

Personal ties thus serve to strengthen inter-organizational relationships (e.g.; Tallgrass-Satya, Redwood-Shiva, and Haleakala-Athene). Time also gives organizations a chance to gain the other's forgiveness and trust (e.g. Denali-Vishnu case). It gives organizations a chance to develop clarity and visibility regarding mutual obligations (e.g. Ozark-Brahma case). In the Chickasaw-Zeus case, the longest relationship in this research, the organizations were able to identify each other's "tolerance levels" through long and sometimes contentious interaction. They were able to build on this accumulated history and develop a "better relationship than what *they[15]* had." This sentiment that time had helped develop something better than they started with was expressed by Amar (Ozark-Brahma) also:

> "What we expect from them, we have come to expect what is right and they have come to expect what is right… They have come to the optimal way of handling us and we know how to handle them to get things done. That is the best thing that happened."

While the relationships between the client and vendor organizations in this research support the contribution of age of the relationship to social capital in the relationship, prior research has found contradictory evidence. Lee and Kim (1999) found that the quality of the partnership was negatively related to the duration of the relationship, with later stages characterized by a decreasing commitment and increasing conflict. This finding was inconsistent with previous research (Anderson and Narus, 1990), and Lee and Kim (1999) suggested that the reason for this finding could be that the service receiver was forced to extend the contract due to conditions in the initial contract. The social capital framework offers an alternate explanation. As the relationship ages, embedded practices can obstruct change, preventing appropriate responses to the environment. This could be because the client is now dependent[16] on the vendor to bring in information on best practices, making the "ties that bind into ties that blind" (Powell and Smith-Doerr, 1994 cited in Adler and Kwon, 2002). This would be particularly true in cases where the client has entered into a sole-sourcing arrangement with a vendor and signed a long-term contract.

7.3.4   Role of *Definition* in the Development of Social Capital

When the client and vendor organizations come together in an applications outsourcing arrangement, it is with a specific outcome in mind: the development, enhancement, or maintenance of an application. The clearer the client organization is regarding their expectations for the product or service, the easier it is for the vendor organization to implement the product or service. When these expectations are clearly defined and communicated to the vendor, the client and the vendor can achieve a comfort level in their relationship. The vendor knows what they are accountable for and the client can determine that they are getting what they want. Ideally, this setting of requirements must be done up-front and both parties must come to an agreement on the expectations from the project.

Based on such expectations, tasks to be accomplished during the course of the outsourcing arrangement can be jointly defined. The milestones and deliverables for the project can then be specified in the agreement between the organizations – the contract and/or service level agreements. It is through such specification that these legal documents "provide the framework for the relationship." As Bob (Montezuma-Apollo case) said:

> "The contract sets the initial parameters, but those parameters have to be clear, they give you a base point to talk from. The contract defines the issues we will be discussing and reviewing."

When both organizations meet these commitments and prove their reliability, they instill confidence in the other party regarding their intentions and capabilities. The definition of tasks to be accomplished during the life of the outsourcing project also enables the identification of

---

[15] Certainly, the interactions over time are between people and the interpersonal relationships will be strengthened. However, these individuals are acting as organizational representatives and their interactions determine the quality of the inter-organizational relationship as well.
[16] Social capital in the relationship can increase dependence

members of the organization who should be interacting with the members of other organization and facilitates an articulation of access patterns (Raposa et al, 2003). Training and joint meetings involving these individuals enable the development of a shared understanding.

In the Ozark-Brahma case, the contract does not include enough information. The organizations are facing a situation of "symmetric incomplete information" – where the client and the vendor do not have enough knowledge about each other's domains to develop this definition (Lin et al, 2005). Greg (the vendor principal) and Amar (the vendor principal) jointly develop the routines and procedures for the project, after the organizations have entered an outsourcing agreement. They rely on communication to ensure that a clear understanding of the tasks develops in the initial stages of a project. It is easy to do this since it is a small project and the number of individuals involved is low. This would not be an option in a large project.

When the contract includes clear definition of the goals of the outsourcing project and the means by which these are to be accomplished, it contributes towards a better relationship between the organizations (Kern, 1999). In the absence of clarity of information in the original agreements of the contract, the client and the vendor can develop this clarity through communication. Problems in the outsourcing relationship crop up when the client lets the vendor completely determine the scope and boundaries of the services and the performance levels. This can lead to the supplier providing something that is not agreed upon, as in the Bluestone-Vesta case. In that case, the client ended up paying a premium for the services they had expected they would be getting as part of the initial agreement.

7.3.5 Role of Contracts in Outsourcing Management

While the role of the contract in providing definition and clarity is acknowledged, in the operationalization stage, the contract plays a very limited role. In this stage of the outsourcing lifecycle, where members of both organizations actually work together, individuals avoid reference to the contract. This negativity towards the contract is captured in remarks like "the moment the contract is brought out, the deal is dead." Relationships are seen as the key to outsourcing success. This is the resounding message sent by the interviewees in this research project.

Considering the costs and time associated with developing the contract, this disregard for the contract in the stage where the work is done is puzzling. Comments from interviewees suggest that there may not be enough substance in the contract dealing with the management of the project. John's (Chickasaw-Zeus) comments express succinctly what was mentioned by many interviewees.

"The contract has very little to do with the day-to-day operations and management of the services. Again, I think the best analogy is the prenuptial agreement 80-90% of what you talk about is what will happen when you split up. 20% is what will happen when you are supporting or operating the deal so you hope you don't ever see or talk about 80-90% of what you put in the contract to begin with."

In the absence of such content, the client and the vendor need to work together to establish a different form of contract – the relational contract.

I must say the contract or services agreement is only a framework to do the work, but beyond that it is what happens--how the customer and the supplier, their 2 cultures blend, how they are able to understand each other's, you know, let us say, pains and each other's objectives, and they work together to a common goal. That is really the contract. I mean, you can say in a paper the contract has several clauses, several things defined in it, but that is not it, and it is beyond that. (Jay, Bluestone-Vesta case)

Thus, outsourcing becomes "a relationship management issue, not a contract management issue" (Bill, Chickasaw-Zeus case).

Yet, why is this information not included in the contract? Is it the separation of negotiation team from post-contract management team that results in the non-inclusion of this important information? In fact, a representative from the consultant organization Cicero contended that these jobs – negotiation and project management – need mutually exclusive skill sets.

"The other thing is that there's a very different culture between the people who do deals and the people who manage them. We do these deals that last 6 to 12 months; they are very intense, people work very hard. And in the past what I thought was, 'great, let them do deals and let them help implement and manage the deals and work at a much slower pace for 3 to 6 months. And what we saw over and over again is after about 2 or 3 weeks, they were going crazy; you know, "I need another deal." And I would tell you, on the other side of the coin, those people who are used to managing deals are not good at being creative and doing deals. So, it is a different mindset. So, in most companies, they have people who are used to doing deals or doing actual work. You have very few people who are used to actually managing relationships and managing contracts."

If the dealmakers and the peacemakers do not gather at the same table, if they have different perspectives on this arrangement, then it would not be possible for the contract to include both sets of information. While the dealmakers seem to relish the intense and antagonistic negotiations, the project managers need to develop plans to work together. Given such views, one must also wonder if it is possible to accomplish both at the same time.

Among the ten cases in chapter 6, there was only one case in which the project managers were also involved in contract negotiations. In the Montezuma-Apollo case, the two client project managers were involved in the contract negotiations. However, this does not seem to help in the relationship between Montezuma and Apollo. During the contract negotiations, Montezuma is warned of Apollo's reputation and inflexibility. Montezuma depends on the contract as a safeguard. Their behavior is defensive and as discussed in the case, though they pay lip service to the relationship, they are not willing to commit to a relationship.

Another possible reason for the lack of use of contracts is the incompleteness of contracts. It is not possible to anticipate every change in a document that has to be signed and dried before the project begins, where the project may last a long time[17] compared to the contract negotiation period. As Prasad (Redwood-Shiva) commented: "A contract cannot cover the relationship for the next ten years." Bill (Chickasaw-Zeus) touches on a more nebulous aspect. He believes that contracts cannot capture the expectations of the companies.

"The expectations of the two companies always are different no matter what they have or haven't agreed to in the contract." Bill (Chickasaw-Zeus)

---

[17] In this research project, the shortest contract term was nine months and the longest contract term extended ten years.

Answering the question why contracts were not used, the consultant from Cicero blamed the executives of laziness and not wanting to define the processes in the contract.

> "And the reality is executive management, they want to do deals; they don't want to figure out the rules and responsibilities in the governance processes and doing continuous improvement. And, because they don't, then the company doesn't."

In the case of smaller organizations, he commented that this problem is even more intense where sometimes organizations start outsourcing projects based on CEO to CEO relationships, without so much as a negotiation or discussion of the project.

Using an analogy that was often repeated during the various interviews, Jim (Montezuma-Apollo) commented:

> "An outsourcing contract is a lot like a marriage. It is not bliss all the time. In every relationship, there are times when you have disagreements. But it is trust that carries the day, trust and a commitment to creating a win-win situation. This requires a dialog, an open communication, and a willingness to listen and understand. Over time, this becomes easier, but you have to invest it at the start. It is through this dialog that an alignment of objectives can occur."

The recognition that relationships are necessary and could only be sustained through concerted effort was voiced by almost every individual who was in charge of an outsourcing project. It also speaks to the joint work that is required in the operationalization stage. It also emphasizes the fact that these interviewees are not talking about a sentimental or maudlin relationship between personal managers, but about making the effort to realize an atmosphere in which individuals from different organization can work together, aligning their mutually exclusive objectives so that they can be accomplished simultaneously. The strength of the social capital framework is that it provides a good mechanism for understanding the nature and content of this relationship and thus managing it.

7.3.6   Role of *Boundary Spanners* in the Development of Social Capital

In all the outsourcing relationships chronicled in the last chapter, there were key people whose personal rapport with their counterparts in the other organization was a mainstay of the inter-organizational relationship. These individuals go by different names: project executive and relationship manager (in client organizations), client executive, account manager, and client delivery executive (in vendor organizations). Organizations expect the boundary spanner to build and maintain the relationship. As John (Chickasaw-Zeus) mentioned, Zeus expects its client managers to "build a relationship that is beyond the standard business relationship." Therefore, besides attending formal review sessions and being involved in conflict resolution and escalation procedures, these individuals often set up a regular informal session with their counterpart to build up the personal relationship.

> "Every week I spent at least 1 hour with key customer contacts. We talk about anything we want to talk about; there is no specific agenda. We just focus on the relationship - going to lunch, playing golf. We get time to understand what drives each other." (Tom: Montezuma-Apollo case)

These boundary spanners play a difficult role; they have to represent the needs of their organization without damaging the personal relationship they have built up with their counterpart in the other organization.

Raj (Tallgrass-Satya case) mentioned how he the personal relationship he has with his counterpart motivates him to act as the champion for Tallgrass in the vendor organization. This implies that the boundary manager has to be in a position of sufficient authority in the organizational hierarchy and can mobilize internal resources to support his cause. In the Redwood-Shiva case, Lal noted that they empower their employees so that they have the freedom to make certain decisions on the spot if the client brought up a change request. Perrone et al (2003) found that such role autonomy permits the representatives of an organization to engage in discretionary behaviors that signal their intent and concern, thus enhancing the trust between the representatives, and consequently the trust between the organizations.

In some outsourcing contracts, the clients stipulate in the contract that they would "have a say" in who would be assigned as the person-in-charge from the vendor organization. Bill (Chickasaw) explained his position:

"We have a veto right on each of the key players on the account. And we can declare the key players. We have a right to kick anybody off the account."

The inclusion of this clause in the contract underscores the criticality of this role.

The ability of boundary spanners to span organizations and settings can be a key organizational competence (Levina and Vaast, 2005). Interviewees commented on the qualities that these individuals require.

"One of the success factors is a softer variable – the people you have. It is a combination of aptitude and attitude…life skills. It gives them business insight, cultural insight" (Mike: Haleakala-Athene)

"When I said a minute ago "It was the most important job," you've asked a very good question. I think the qualifications of the client delivery executive (CDE) are now rather formidable. Yes, they have to have technical skills in order to represent the service line; they have to have knowledge of the delivery organization to make sure they are doing what the customer needs, they have to have customer relationship skills in order to best understand what the customer's real requirements are, not just the customer's wants but their needs, they have to have financial skills so they can be responsible for what we call the Cost Model delivering to the budget that the customer neediness expects, they need to be able to take care of the people if there are people assigned to the account. So it is a tough job in the term of the number of dimensions that the CDE has to be good in." (John: Chickasaw-Zeus)

"Some of it isn't necessarily qualifications or points of expertise, it's just personality." (Amar: Ozark – Brahma)

"It is … emotional intelligence, an awareness, and understanding of the other person to build a relationship." (Kumar: Haleakala-Durga)

Thus, the necessary skills for the boundary spanner include technical expertise, contract management skills, communication skills, financial skills, and human resource management. It appears that not only do these individuals have to be a "master of all trades," but have a charming personality to boot. As a sidebar, given the significance of the role the boundary spanner plays in outsourcing relationships, many organizations have developed new job descriptions for these roles. Titled 'relationship managers' or 'sourcing managers', these individuals have to be "part marriage counselor, part quality-control maven, part salesperson and stay focused on business results" (Collett, 2002)

In summary, the boundary spanner's role is critical in establishing and maintaining the inter-organizational relationship. Recognizing that these individuals can make or break the relationship, organizations are paying more attention to who should fill these roles in outsourcing arrangements. Organizations realize that these individuals need a level of role autonomy to be able to establish and maintain the inter-personal and inter-organizational relationships.

7.3.7 Role of *Assessment* in the Development of Social Capital

Before proceeding to discuss the contribution of assessment to the development of social capital, it would be useful to examine what metrics organizations use in their assessment of outsourcing projects. In the review of evaluation of outsourcing in chapter 2, it was noted that success is most commonly measured by satisfaction. In chapter 3, review of inter-organizational research suggested that satisfaction has an economic and non-economic component. The economic basis of satisfaction is related to the goal attainment, while the non-economic satisfaction relates to evaluations of interactions with the partner. Interviewees' comments show that clients and vendors realize that satisfaction involves more than the delivery of the product; however, delivery is a necessary condition for satisfaction, without which all else is moot. Prasad (Redwood-Shiva) explained the components of satisfaction.

"The satisfaction stems from being able to deliver what we have promised, the ease with which the whole thing was delivered, and the value that realized – did they get that thing at the right price and how much of value-add beyond what was asked for in the proposal did we deliver – so all of those things constitute satisfaction."

Thus, in practice, there appears to be three components to satisfaction: delivery of the promised service, the process of delivery, and an additional "value-add." This last part of the assessment, "the value-add", is a difficult measure to satisfy because expectations tend to be difficult, as Bill (Chickasaw-Zeus) explained. The ability to gauge the expectations of the other organization comes only through repeated interactions and sharing – the same steps required to develop social capital in the relationship. Thus, a relationship rich in social capital is likely to provide the value-add that the organizations are looking for.

Interestingly, while answering questions on satisfaction, none of the clients mentioned innovation as a factor in that satisfaction. However, when asked if they expected innovation, they would always answer in the affirmative. Their expectation for innovation was that the vendor would bring in that value-add. For instance, Bob (Montezuma – Apollo case) mentioned that they were looking for "sector knowledge that *the client* cannot acquire on the street or piece together necessarily." Even while expecting this value-add, some clients complained that the vendors often used opportunities for introducing innovation as a chance to increase their revenue stream. Vendors responded that this mindset of the clients often deters them from bringing in new ideas. However, in cases where there was abundance of social capital, e.g. Chickasaw-Zeus, Tallgrass-Satya, and Redwood- Shiva, the vendors believed that they needed to bring in innovation and that it would be appreciated. Their ideas were not met with skepticism, but with acceptance and a belief that it would contribute to the completion of the project. Vasant (Tallgrass-Satya case) explained how the client welcomed "any ideas, even stupid ideas." That this positive mindset to ideas from the other organization occurred in relationships rich in social capital should not be surprising. In relationships rich in social capital, members of both organizations see themselves as belonging to the same group.

If positive assessments are the result of relationships rich in social capital, how can organizations use this awareness to develop social capital? One option is to identify the routines and processes that worked and reuse them in other similar situations. Some organizations use the evaluation as a means to identify what works and what does not work and document the information in a repository that serves as a repository for future outsourcing projects. These documented experiences serve as a source of "appropriable organization" on future projects for these organizations (e.g.; Glacier, Zeus, and Satya). Such experience helps organization identify which resources to deploy in a new project, but only if the organization has been able to internalize and learn from experience (Simonin, 1997). Firms like Glacier capitalize on such capability, a capability referred to by Kale et al (2002) as alliance capability[18].

In successful outsourcing relationships, clients and vendors continuously assess the progress of the outsourcing project. They use this feedback in a constructive manner to correct deficiencies, if any. In the Redwood-Shiva case, Shiva used the feedback from the satisfaction survey they passed out among the user community in the client organization to correct problems with communication, one of the factors that affect the development of social capital.

7.4 The 'Non-Differences' in Offshore Outsourcing

A secondary question posed in this research was whether cultural and geographical distance between the client and vendor, arising from the organizations being based in different countries, made a difference in the development of social capital in the relationship. In this research, half of the client-vendor pairs had offshore vendors from India.

Past research in IS outsourcing has pointed to cultural factors including communication issues (Apte et al. 1997; Davison 2004; Overby 2003; Krishna et al. 2004; Morello 2003; Qu and Brocklehurst 2003; Ramarapu et al. 1997) and superior-subordinate relationship issues[19] (Nicholson and Sahay, 2001), and problems due to geographical distance (Gopal et al, 2003; Herbsleb and Moitra, 2001) and infrastructure differences (Morstead and Blount, 2003; Rajkumar and Dawley, 1998) as challenges in management of offshore outsourcing[20].

National cultures and values contribute to the molding of organizational cultures and thus could lead to differences in practices within the client and offshore vendor organizations. When posed the question on experiencing challenges due to differences in cultures, some interviewees focused on organizational cultures. In today's global world, some believed that organizational culture is more of an issue than national cultures. Jim (Montezuma-Apollo case) responded: "There is almost a greater difference between an Apollo person and OtherCo person." OtherCo is another domestic outsourcing vendor.

---

[18] Alliance capability is defined as "the firm's ability to capture, share, disseminate and apply alliance management know-how and know-why and its ability to embed this in a stable and repetitive pattern of action" Heimeriks and Duysters (2004). Heimeriks and Duysters (2004) suggest that this capability consists of two parts – routines and mechanisms. Routines evolve from the solutions that employees in organizations apply in inter-organizational situations. Mechanisms aid in capturing and codifying these solutions and adapting them to new experiences.

[19] This will not be evident in this set of data because it does not include comments on superior-subordinate communication, but communication between counterparts at similar levels in different organizations.

[20] Some authors (e.g.; Morstead and Blount, 2003) also point to the differences in the legal system as a challenge in offshore outsourcing. This is not an aspect of the client-vendor relationship in applications outsourcing; it is just a part of doing business globally.

Other client representatives commented that there was difference in accent and use of the language. Client representatives in the Ozark-Brhama and Denali-Vishnu case mentioned that differences in accents made communication problematic, especially over the 'phone, in the initial stages of the outsourcing arrangement. However, they did not have any problems with written communication. Differences may show up in the writing style as well, according to Raj (Tallgrass-Satya case):

> "If I have a Korean contractor, sometimes it may appear that they're very rude or using a more aggressive language in the communication, in the written communication. Especially in the global environment if I have contractors from other cultures, I must have a very good understanding of how that culture operates."

However, none of the client representatives commented that the accent or differences in language usage were a hindrance to communication. None of them has had first-hand experience with infrastructure issues affecting communication either, though they had heard of such problems. If there were such hurdles to communication, it could affect the development of social capital in the relationship.

More interesting were the comments that suggested U.S. organizations relied more on contracts than their counterparts elsewhere did. Raj (Tallgrass-Satya case) commented that Japanese organizations would be willing to use "a handshake to seal the agreement." He also noted the difference in the way scope changes are handled:

> "And when--if I'm doing a project and my project is delayed and they have to do some additional things, they will never think about coming to me and asking me for additional--you know, whatever else it is. What they do expect is for me to remember that and reward them based on the relationship."

However, examining the responses from the clients and U.S. vendors in this research project suggests that U.S. organizations also share the same outlook. When Ozark and Brahma started working together, a contract had not been prepared and signed. Talking about scope changes, Jeff (Redwood-Shiva) commented:

> "I have shared in that pain too, where some companies estimated that something was going to be say 50 hours but became 500, because the overall magnitude was much worse than anyone expected. And, we would have agreed to pay for part of that."

Therefore, it appears at least in this set of client-vendor pairs, that there is no difference between domestic and offshore vendors in their view of contracts and relationships.

What would explain these differences in findings from past research? It is highly unlikely that the experiences of these twenty organizations are so different from that of other organizations. The organizations in this research project do not belong to a specific niche; they span a wide range of industries and include large and small organizations. They include organizations experienced with outsourcing as well as first-timers. One possible reason could be that the area of outsourcing that is the context of this study – applications outsourcing – has been going on for well over two decades and Indian organizations have been early entrants into the market and got accustomed to dealing with U.S. clients and vice versa. While differences may have been more pronounced in the past, it is possible that training in vendor organizations has helped overcome issues with accent and interaction skills. Further, many of the offshore vendor representatives have been educated and/or worked in the U.S., as recorded in the cases. Heeks and Nicholson (2004) comment that the Indian diaspora is one of the contributing factors to the success of India as an offshoring destination. Additionally, the client representatives themselves came from different cultures including India.

Thus, it can be concluded that differences that would affect the development of social capital in the client-vendor relationship are non-existent in the client-vendor pairs included in this study. At this juncture, it would be interesting to examine if there is a difference in the presence of the elements of the three dimensions of social capital between the two groups (U.S. client – domestic vendor and U.S. client – offshore vendor).

Examining the elements of the structural dimension of social capital[21]:

The ties and configuration of ties are initially established via formal means in cases involving domestic and offshore vendors. The initial agreement between the organizations includes the specification of these interaction patterns. In large projects, a tiered interaction model is set up between U.S. clients and vendors, whether domestic or offshore. In the cases involving domestic vendors (Montezuma-Apollo, Chickasaw-Zeus, and Glacier-Hercules), this involves a three-tier model with interactions at the operational, project management, and executive levels. In the case of the offshore vendors (Redwood-Shiva and Tallgrass-Satya), the vendors mentioned that they had two managers at the project management level: one to take care of the technical issues and one to handle relationship management issues, with the former reporting to the latter. In cases where the projects are comparatively smaller, the interaction levels may not be formally specified to the same extent.

In both scenarios, organizational representatives, particularly from the vendor side, expend efforts to establish informal ties. In the Chickasaw-Zeus case, Cindy (from Zeus) explained the importance of building networks using different means. The vendor representative in the Redwood-Shiva case echoed this when he talked about using different tools like joint meetings with all project employees, training sessions, and networking events for relationship-building.

Established vendor organizations, domestic and offshore, are able to bring in a set of routines they have perfected through experience and training. This appropriable organization is an attraction for clients as they believe they can benefit from the efficiencies of tried and established routines. .

Examining the elements of the cognitive dimension of social capital[21]:

Domestic and offshore vendors offer training to their employees to ensure they have the resources to complete the projects they take up. Such training ensures that the employees possess the 'shared language and codes' necessary to support the combination capability of the organizations. During the interviews, representatives of offshore vendors emphasized the training[22] they offer their employees.

The large projects examined in this research primarily involved ERP projects. In the other cases that involved custom applications development projects, the clients had to educate the vendors as to the complexities of the business processes that they needed to build into the application. The ease with which this 'sharing of narratives' occurred depended on the

---

[21] Table 7-2 contains a review of the different elements and dimensions side by side.
[22] In many cases, when the interviews were conducted on the offshore vendor's site, they would invite the researcher to tour their training facilities

interaction between the individuals in both organizations. In this research, there were cases where this sharing did not happen; however, it was not a result of the cultural[23] and geographic distance between the organizations.

Examining the elements of the relational dimension of social capital [21]:

Clients and domestic and offshore vendors alike emphasized the importance of trust and norms like flexibility, cooperation, and commitment. There is a common realization that when the partner organization needs to make a change, it should be met with in a cooperative spirit and with the recognition that there will be opportunities for give and take in a relationship. Domestic and offshore vendors used similar tools to build these elements of the relational dimension of social capital: joint meetings at the beginning of the project, attending conferences together with client organization employees, and informal events. While Prasad (Redwood-Shiva case), an offshore vendor organization representative, remarked that he felt that "it was easier for the Accentures and the IBMs because there is a board-member level relationship," senior level executives from his organization did not think "that was an issue anymore," referring to the inroads that offshore organizations are making into the boardrooms of U.S. organizations by hiring top-management level U.S. professionals.

Many clients and vendors do not believe that they need to have a culture that matches that of the other organization; however, everyone agrees that an appreciation of the other organization's culture and compatibility is beneficial. A difference between domestic and offshore outsourcing is that in domestic outsourcing, client employees are often transferred to the vendor. When this transfer occurs, a cultural similarity is achieved. When offshore vendors like Satya and Durga hire individuals who had previously worked with their clients, a similar effect is obtained.[24]

From the above examination, it appears that the purported differences in offshore outsourcing actually turn out to be non-differences. Seen through the lens of social capital, the interactions of the client-vendor pairs involving domestic vendors as well as offshore vendors bared the same elements, and highlighted the same necessity of attending to the relationship.

7.5 Conclusions

In the operationalization stage of applications outsourcing, social capital plays an important role. Managers of outsourcing projects rely on the relationship to manage the applications outsourcing arrangement, relegating the contract to the background as an incomplete and static document. The cross-case analysis shows that it is the social capital in the relationship that facilitates the conditions necessary for the combination and exchange of the knowledge of the organizations in applications outsourcing arrangements. This reliance of the managers on the relationship to accomplish the goals of the applications outsourcing arrangement makes it imperative to understand and encourage the development of social capital in the client-vendor relationship.

---

[23] Refers to national culture.
[24] Apparently, the same effect can be achieved through different means in the domestic and offshore outsourcing situations – one through transfer and the other through hiring. Nevertheless, the result is the same.

Chapter 8
IMPLICATIONS AND CONTRIBUTIONS

8.1 Introduction

The intention of this study was to examine the client-vendor relationship in applications outsourcing to gain a better understanding of the impact of the relationship on the outcome of the outsourcing project. The discussion in the last chapter shows that the 'social capital' framework offers valuable insight into our understanding of the management of outsourcing relationships. While past outsourcing research has held that the client-vendor relationship is important in outsourcing, the theoretical framework has clarified the nature and content of the relationship and its role in the operationalization stage of the applications outsourcing arrangement.

Before discussing the value of the contributions of this research to the research and practice constituencies, it is useful to reflect on two aspects of the research: the theoretical framework and the research process. Such reflection will uncover the limitations of this research, and along with the findings of this research, suggest directions for future research. Following the section presenting these reflections (8.2), the findings of the research (8.3) and the limitations of this research (8.4) are discussed. Implications for research (8.5) and contributions to practice (8.6) complete the chapter.

8.2 Reflections
on the Theoretical Framework and the Research Process

"No theory – which are all, by definition, partial – explains a "phenomenon of organized complexity" fully," wrote Ghoshal (2004; p.86) in his last article, published posthumously in the Academy of Management Review. The application of a single theoretical framework can indeed be considered a limitation of this study. However, the theoretical framework applied in this research integrates three different streams of research in social capital: the structural, the relational, and the cognitive.

Past outsourcing research had identified various attributes of the inter-organizational relationship (e.g., trust, shared understanding) as having a significant impact on the outcome of the outsourcing arrangement. These attributes appear in the framework, categorized under the three dimensions of social capital: structural, relational, and cognitive. By enfolding these different attributes of the client-vendor relationship under the three dimensions of social capital and relating them to facilitating conditions for the exchange between client and vendor, rather than just the outcome of the outsourcing arrangement, it was possible to explain *how* these elements affected the outcome of the outsourcing arrangement.

In evaluating the usefulness of this research framework, one must consider how the application of this research framework fits within current research. The social capital framework rests on the concept of embededdness from Granovetter- that is, economic exchanges are embedded in social networks. The economics theories (e.g.; transaction cost theory, agency theory) that are most commonly applied in understanding IS outsourcing would argue that economic drivers determine the exchanges in outsourcing and the interactions with the market determine the behavior of the firm. In a reversal of logic from that of Granovetter, it could then be argued that the inter-firm exchange and behaviors within the exchange are driven by concerns for economic performance. To put it differently, in outsourcing arrangements, the client and vendor come together due to economic reasons creating social networks, within which their economic behavior is then embedded. So, which came first, the chicken or the egg? A contribution of the social capital framework to understanding the interactions in the operationalization stage of applications outsourcing is the awareness that all economic exchange is ultimately embedded in social connections – that social capital is not a substitute for the contractual or integration mechanisms, but a complementary mechanism to reduce the costs identified through the economic analysis.

As researchers, we would like to single out our phenomenon of study from what else there is, but it is a nearly impossible task. Although elements of the various dimensions of social capital have been identified separately for analytical purposes in the theoretical framework, they are inevitably interconnected in practice and reflections on practice, as Nahapiet and Ghoshal acknowledge. While the inclusion of such entwined concepts provides a greater understanding of the interactions in the applications outsourcing context, it would be beyond the scope of any single project to explore all links suggested by the framework. Elements of different dimensions of social capital, conditions affecting the development of social capital, conditions for knowledge exchange facilitated by social capital – they all simmer together in the cauldron of human interaction to create sweet or sour outsourcing relationships.

Turning to the research approach of this study, a qualitative case study approach in the interpretive paradigm was utilized for this research. Using interviews and other source materials (e.g. articles in industry journals), information regarding outsourcing relationships from multiple participants with various views and experiences was obtained. Every interview contributed to a deeper understanding of the outsourcing process, of the role of individuals in these organizational endeavors, of the embededdness of all economic exchange in social relations.

While more than sixty interviews[1] were conducted in all, it was possible to collect data from only ten client and vendor organization pairs. Some of these cases had similarities, some were unique and different – raising the question of generalizability of the findings. However, as Walsham and Waema (1995) state "the validity of an extrapolation from one or more individual cases depends not on the representativeness of such cases in a statistical sense, but on the plausibility and cogency of the logical reasoning used in describing results from the case, and in drawing inferences and conclusions from those results" (p.151)

In the table below, an examination of the research process based on the seven principles proposed by Klein and Myers (1999) for the evaluation of interpretive field studies is presented. Adherence to these principles would satisfy the traditional requirements of validity, reliability, and objectivity, as described in chapter 5 (section 5.4).

Table 8-1: Assessment of Research using Klein and Myers' Principles (1999)

Principle		Assessment of Application of Principle[2]
1	Hermeneutic circle	*The whole consists of the shared meanings that emerge from the interaction between researchers and participants.* Each case was reconstructed from information collected from different participants. Therefore, review of a case by participants was not possible because individuals may recognize others in the

---

[1] A number of interviews could not be used in the study because matching information was not available from the other organization. For instance, in one case, interviews were conducted with two members from a vendor organization and the researcher was informed at the start of the third that the client was not willing to talk.

[2] A short description of the principle appears in italics in each cell in this column. The paragraph(s) below shows how this principle was applied in this research project.

		case. This would violate the promises of confidentiality and anonymity offered to participants.
		However, to complete the hermeneutical circle of interpretations, the stories were checked with industry participants and other outsourcing researchers. .
2	*Contextualization*	*The researcher needs to examine how the organizational context could have affected the behavior of participants.*
		The impact of contextual factors like dependence between the organizations and the organizations' experience with outsourcing was considered.
3	*Researcher-subject interaction*	*The researcher needs to recognize that participants can also be interpreters and analysts.*
		This is a potential limitation of this study. Information was collected from participants about events that spanned a long period of time. Their own reflection on these events and the outcome of these events may have influenced their responses to the researcher. Another issue (also affects application of principles 5 and 7) was that the participant's awareness of the research questions before the time of the interview may have colored their responses. Many participants had asked for the questions before the time of the interview so that they may prepare their responses. Along with the information from the executive summary sent to the participant, the knowledge of the questions may have primed them to answer in a certain way. By asking for the reasoning behind the participant's answers whenever possible, the researcher tried to overcome this problem.
4	*Abstraction and generalization*	*The researcher needs to relate interpreted data to theoretical framework.*
		The theoretical framework of social capital was used as a sensitizing device in this research. Klein and Myers (1999) comment that when a theoretical framework is identified and applied in a research project, this principle of abstraction and generalization dominates the research project. The data will be viewed through this theoretical lens and the application of the other principles[3] will be driven by the linking of interpreted data to the theoretical framework ("exegesis", as in van Manen, 1985).
		In the previous chapters, the researcher has provided descriptions supported by quotes. The purpose of these rich descriptions is to allow the reader to judge the validity of the kinks established with the theoretical framework.
5	*Dialogical reasoning*	*The researcher needs to be sensitive to contradictions between theoretical preconceptions and what emerges from data.*
		Not all elements of social capital were seen in all cases. Also, see note on principle 3.
6	*Multiple interpretation*	*The researcher needs to be sensitive to possible differences in interpretations among participants.*
		Multiple accounts of the same set of events were obtained from different participants. These accounts helped verify facts, but one cannot corroborate an individual's assessment of the situation. All

[3] Klein and Myers' principles

7	Suspicion	that can be done is to verify that the events that led to this assessment did happen. In some of the cases, published accounts (case studies, newspaper reports, and journal articles) of the outsourcing arrangement were available to verify the events descried by the interviewees. Additionally, the accounts of these relationships were examined by experienced researchers. Two practitioners interested in the research area served as "sounding boards" for the findings of this research.
7	Suspicion	*The researcher needs to be sensitive to possible biases and distortions in the narratives of the participants.* It is possible that managers may like to present themselves as concerned with governance, and may present the worldview regarding these issues. Also, see note on principle 3.

Though one can formally approach principles and criteria for research and examine whether they have been satisfied, the ultimate yardstick for the research is its acceptance in the mind of the reader (Hirschheim, 1985). As Daft (1983) wrote in his primer on organizational research, this 'acceptability' comes from "liking an idea, feeling right about it, and being able to use it to throw light on a previously hidden aspect of the organization" (page 543). The results have to speak for themselves.

8.3 Summary of Findings

This study started with the assertion that relationships were essential to achieving the desired outcomes in applications outsourcing. Unlike other contractual arrangements, outsourcing, specifically applications outsourcing, requires two organizations to work together closely for an extended period so that the vendor may develop and implement an application for the client organization. The complex knowledge exchanges that need to occur for the development of this application create the need for a relationship rich in social capital. Using an extension of the social capital model presented by Nahapiet and Ghoshal, this research examined how the inter-organizational relationship in the operational stage of applications outsourcing facilitates the knowledge transfer that is necessary to complete the applications outsourcing project. The findings from this research were discussed in detail in the previous chapter; a few key findings are emphasized below:

Given the incomplete nature of contracts and the inevitable changes in the business environment and technology, relationships become the key mechanism for managing the processes during the operationalization stage of the outsourcing arrangement. The social capital framework provides a good tool for understanding the nature and content of the relationship.

The key role of boundary spanners in the development of the inter-organizational relationship, and thus in the development of social capital, has been noted by researchers in the area of social capital and in IS outsourcing. This research affirmed the lead roles played by these individuals in building and shepherding a relationship that will support the simultaneous achievement of the mutually exclusive goals of two organizations. Inter-organizational relationships are built on inter-personal relationships, and the rapport between the project managers is critical in achieving the outcome of the outsourcing arrangement. Some argue that 'good boundary spanners are born, not made; it takes a combination of skills and attitude to play this role well.

Inter-organizational dependence, communication, and longevity have implications for the development of social capital in the relationship. Dependence and social capital share a bi-directional relationship. The mutual dependence of organizations in the applications outsourcing situation requires that social capital be developed in the relationship. When the relationship is rich in social capital, the organizations may decide to pursue more work together, increasing the dependence between the organizations. Further, the potentially damaging effects of asymmetric dependence between the organizations can be controlled through social capital. Communication supports the development of social capital by encouraging the development of shared knowledge and trust, and social capital encourages communication. Since social capital is built through exchanges, time is necessary for the development of social capital.

Cultural differences did not appear to cause any additional complications for the client organizations that contracted with offshore vendors. It was seen that the offshore vendors, just like their domestic counterparts, made methodical and persistent efforts to develop all elements of social capital so that the long-distance knowledge transfer could proceed smoothly.

8.4   Limitations

The challenges raised by the data collection process led to many of the limitations with this research project. One of the issues that the researcher encountered on entering the field was the difficulty in gaining access to participants. This limited the number of interviews that could be conducted for each client-vendor pair and in some cases, the amount of time spent with interviewees. The interviews were usually conducted in one sitting lasting on average two hours[4]. However, most interviewees agreed to follow-up telephone calls or email communication to address unanswered questions.

Due to the focus of the research on the operationalization stage, the solicitation targeted executives who were involved in the management of the project in the operationalization stage. The questions in the interview protocol were also geared solely towards issues in the operationalization stage. This excluded the participation of members of the organization who may have a different perspective on the subject. When contacted for interviews, some of the managers excluded themselves because they felt they could not address the issues in the protocol.

Time constraints precluded the collection of additional information that may have been useful in further understanding the development of the client-vendor relationship. For instance, data about the criticality of the outsourced application was not collected. Criticality may have a bearing on perceptions of dependence, a factor that influences the development of social capital. Another aspect on which more data could have been collected is the configuration of the ties between the organizations, part of the structural dimension of social capital. It was not possible to examine the aspects[5] of this concept in depth for two reasons. One, collecting the details on this issue would have taken more time than was available to the researcher. Two, many of the interviewees were reluctant to share all the details of their interactions with the other organization.

---

[4] Some of the interviews were conducted face-to-face and some were conducted via the telephone. There was not much difference in the duration of the interviews between the two methods. One advantage of the face-to-face interviews was that it resulted in additional interviews more often than with face-to-face interviews. Usually, in face-to-face interviews, interviewees agreed to extend the interview time unless they had some pressing business. However, this may also be a result of the interest of the individual in the research also; some interviewees were agreeable to continue the conversation across two or three 'phone calls.
[5] e.g., density, connectivity, hierarchy

The focus was on understanding the development of social capital – not an instantaneous process, but like most social phenomenon the result of multiple interactions over time. Yet, the interviews were conducted at one point in time, and the cases were studied retrospectively. Though this is a common approach in qualitative research, this is a limiting factor on the richness of data. A retrospective account of experiences will be colored by the participant's experiences since the events.

These constraints on the data collection are indeed valid criticisms and are acknowledged as limitations. However, given that the researcher's goal was to capture the interviewees' views on the management of the outsourcing relationship with a prepared set of questions, these issues do not a not a major problem. It was not possible or practical to get the interviewees to devote more time to the project[6].

Another limitation in this research relates to studying culture[7]. At the start of this research, culture was viewed as an artifact of the nation-state as has traditionally been done in IS research (Myers and Tan, 2002). Past research has shown that the location of organizations in different nation-states would result in cultural distance that is manifested in problems related to communication and dealing with authority (Heeks et al, 2002). However, given the type of outsourcing and the sample of offshore vendors in this research, this approach did not work. Applications outsourcing is the leading category in offshore outsourcing, and India has been a popular destination for U.S. organizations looking for applications outsourcing services for more than two decades now. Thus, most representatives for the Indian vendors had studied in the U.S. and/or worked with U.S. organizations previously, giving them a familiarity with the U.S. business environment and culture. Should the representative for an Indian vendor, who has lived and worked in the U.S. for about fifteen years as the local liaison for the Indian organization, be considered a representative of the Indian culture? Compounding this problem was the fact that there were also situations when interviewees from the client organization included U.S. born individuals and naturalized citizens (from India)[8]. Since the research was being conducted at the organizational level, these questions remained unaddressed, and the culture of each organization was equated to the culture of the country within whose boundaries it was located.

All offshore vendors in this research project are from one country - India. While India is the leading offshore destination for applications outsourcing services, it would have been useful to include vendors from other countries as well. Many attempts were made to contact organizations in Philippines, Ireland, China, and Singapore using contact information obtained from web sites and published information. Unfortunately, none of them would agree to interviews.

A final limitation of this research is the use of a single theoretical framework to examine the data. Even though the framework integrates multiple streams of research, it is possible that richer explanations for the phenomenon could have been obtained through use of multiple theoretical lenses.

---

[6] A couple of the interviewees expressed considerable interest in the research topic and met with the researcher a number of times to discuss the findings of the research. These two were independent consultants; their experiences are not included in the case studies in chapter 6.
[7] This is presented as an issue related to the research process since it was access to participants that limited the offshore vendors included in this study to Indian vendors.
[8] In case 10 (chapter 6), Raj and Jason were interviewed from the client organization. Raj is originally from India.

8.5 Implications for Research

In this research, the social capital theoretical framework was applied to understand the interactions during the operationalization stage in the IS applications outsourcing context. Some researchers (e.g. Mahnke et al, 2003) have suggested that in other types of IS outsourcing, e.g. infrastructure outsourcing, organizations do not have to work together as closely to achieve the desired outcome. The social capital framework, by offering a means to examine the nature and content of the relationship, will help assess the importance of the relationship in other types of IS outsourcing as well as IT-enabled services outsourcing and business process outsourcing. Future research can apply this framework to other inter-organizational relationships in other areas, for example, in e-business and supply chain management.

Daft (1983) advocated simplicity in organizational research, "capturing complex notions in single thoughts". However, some notions like inter-organizational relationships are so complex that they can be captured only in multi-faceted frameworks. As noted in the discussion on the theoretical framework (in section 8.2), it may be beyond the scope of a single research project to do full justice to all facets. A useful avenue for future research would be to study separately each dimension (of the three dimensions) and its influence on the conditions facilitating combination and exchange.

The findings from the ten cases in this research show that that social capital provides benefits in client-vendor exchanges. Client-vendor pairs in cases where all three dimensions were strong were successful in ensuring the stability of the relationship and the satisfaction of both parties, while in the cases where some or all dimensions were weak, there was dissatisfaction with the outcome. While these findings suggest that social capital in the relationship is beneficial, the experience of another organization described in the following paragraph sounds a note of caution.

> The representative of an offshore vendor organization[9] who operates in the transportation industry related the tale of his organization's experience with a client organization. The client organization contracted with them for a project of a very specific nature that utilized the competencies of the vendor to its fullest. The vendor organization was delighted with the chance to do this project, since the client was a large multinational. The successful completion of the project would enhance the reputation of the vendor and establish its name as an applications outsourcing vendor in this industry. The project progressed well and the client was satisfied with the outcome. During the course of the exchanges necessary for the project, the organizations established a relationship strong in social capital. "Based on *our* relationship", the vendor representative related, "they (the client) offered us another project. We told them that it was not in our area of competency, but they insisted." Faced with the potential loss of a source of referrals, the vendor agreed to do the project. Consequently, the vendor has had to invest considerable resources to work satisfactorily on this project. The client organization is unaware that they have lost the opportunity to get this project probably done better, while the project is lagging behind schedule.

And herein lies the dilemma of social capital: too much of a good thing is not good. Portes and Sensbrenner (1993) and Adler and Kwon (2002) warn about these negative consequences of social capital, where it leads to an over-embeddedness in the relationship. Duysters and Lemmens (2002) studied several alliances and found that social capital can work against organizations, locking them in relationships past their usefulness. It can result in undue

---

[9] It was not possible to interview the client in this case. Therefore, the experience of this organization was not included in chapter 6.

dependence on the partner as well (Adler and Kwon, 2002). Future research could identify signals that would indicate the possibility of a lock-in in the relationship and how to avoid such unproductive situations.

While Nahapiet and Ghoshal (1998) focus much of their attention on how social capital facilitates the development of intellectual capital, they acknowledge the co-evolution of social capital and intellectual capital and draw a parallel to the notion of structuration[10] (Giddens, 1984). Social capital increases capabilities for exchange and this exchange offers additional opportunities for developing social capital, as long as it does not violate any of the expectations of the parties involved in the relationship. This continuing construction and reconstruction of institutional arrangements hinges on the tacit acceptance by 'knowledgeable agents'[11] that social capital is good. Otherwise, the agency resident in the individuals would impel them to act as change agents and change the existing structure. Future research could examine what qualities these "knowledgeable agents" would need to have to ensure the construction and reconstruction of social capital in the relationship. Such research could focus on individuals occupying the boundary-spanning positions in client and vendor organizations, since it has been seen in this research and others (e.g., Levina and Vaast, 2005) that these individuals primarily drive the creation and maintenance of the inter-organizational relationship.

Following the line of thought that continuing construction and reconstruction of institutional arrangements rich in social capital hinges on the tacit acceptance by 'knowledgeable agents' that social capital is good, it would appear that the lack of use the contract in the operationalization stage is due to a tacit acceptance that the contract does not provide the best mechanisms for governing the relationship. Sitkin and Roth (1993) contend that the formalization of an agreement opens it to question whether the provisions in the agreement are the best. Thus, from the moment the contract is formalized, often by individuals not involved in the management of the outsourcing project, there is distrust in the merits of the contract. This leads to actions that result in the continued erosion of the legitimacy of the contract – many interviewees confessed to not having seen the contract, though the operationalization stage is the stage in which the contract provisions are operationalized. Others contended that referring to the contract suggested that the project was facing problems. Future research could examine the bases for this distrust in the contract and the processes involved in the construction and reconstruction of this distrust in the contract.

Comparing the findings of this research with previous IS outsourcing research that examines the client-vendor relationship,[12] points of convergence and divergence can be noted. This research examined the role of these boundary-spanning individuals in building the inter-organizational relationship, and identified some required competencies of these individuals. Kern and Willcocks (2002) also identify project managers as key interfaces in the outsourcing arrangement. Future research needs to examine the competencies required for these roles as well

---

[10] Giddens' Structuration Theory (1984) attempts to reconcile the agency/structure dichotomy. Giddens puts forwards the concept of duality of structure, the recursive character of social life and the mutual dependence of structure and agency. Structure is both the medium and the outcome of the practices that constitutes social systems. Structure includes rules and resources that guide human interpretation and actions. Thus, structure directs the formation of meanings and beliefs and has the capability to enable and constrain human actions. Yet, structure itself is constructed and reconstructed by the knowledgeable actions of human actors.
[11] In Giddens' theory, individuals are knowledgeable agents. They act with conscious intention and are able to monitor their social actions. Their actions are governed by discursive and practical consciousness. Since human beings are reflexive and recursive in that they understand and routinely observe what they are doing while they are doing it, they could change or retain their status quo.
[12] Five frameworks have examined the gestalt of client-vendor relationships in outsourcing: Willcocks and Kern (1998), Lee and Kim (1999), Kern and Willcocks (2000), Goles (2001), Kern and Willcocks (2002)

as how organizations may empower these individuals to work in the best interests of the organization.

Lee and Kim (1999) find that age of the relationship had a negative effect on partnership quality, whereas the social capital framework suggests that the longevity of the relationship would allow the development of additional social capital in the relationship. However, as was discussed above, it is possible that organizations can be locked into relationships past their usefulness even though the relationship may be rich in social capital. This is a possible explanation for the findings in Lee and Kim (1999). Future research could trace the development of the client-vendor relationship and the changes in social capital elements as the relationship evolves. Future research could also identify the social capital elements that determine the continued success of a relationship and the factors that affect the development of these social capital elements.

Similar to Lee and Kim (1999) and Goles (2001), the findings from this research also seems to suggest that cultural similarity[13] is not a consideration in establishing a successful relationship. Kern and Willcocks (2002) suggest that the organizations 'adapt' to each other's culture over time, making operational adjustments. Yet, they note," the cultures as such remained quite distinctive and separate," offering a clue to the counter-intuitive[14] and confusing findings. As Sarkar et al (2001) suggest there are two aspects to compatibility: operational compatibility and cultural compatibility. While cultural compatibility addresses issues related to norms and value systems, operational compatibility refers to similarity in capabilities and process discipline. Given the conflicting findings of past research, it would be fruitful for new research in outsourcing to address the issue of compatibility by considering these two different aspects.

Prior research has shown 'conflict between client and vendor' is a factor that can affect both the performance and outcome of the outsourcing arrangement (Goles, 2001; Lee and Kim, 1999; Kern and Willcocks, 2000). Uncertainty, contractual stipulations, and suspicion about the profit motive of the vendor can lead to conflict in the client-vendor relationship (Fitzgerald and Willcocks, 1994; Hancox and Hackney, 1999; Marcolin and McLellan, 1998). Conflict affects an organization's perception of the other organization and affects the client-vendor relationship (Lee and Kim, 1999). Future research should examine how conflict affects the development of social capital in the outsourcing relationship.

8.6 Implications for Practice

The findings of this study highlight that the client-vendor relationship is important in applications outsourcing, not only because of the incompleteness of contracts and because of the uncertainty related to business and technology, but also because of the embeddeddness of economic actions in social networks. Admittedly, this is a not a new finding. While it may be argued that there is value in affirming findings from past research, what additional insights can the social capital framework offer to practitioners? The examination of the ten cases suggests that when problems creep in, it is not due to a lack of awareness of the need to build and nurture the client-vendor relationship. The social capital framework suggests that organizations need to

---

[13] Lee and Kim used "cultural similarity: degree of similarity of shared values and beliefs" while Goles used "cultural compatibility: extent to which parties can coexist with each others' beliefs about what values, behaviors, goals and policies are important, appropriate, and right".
[14] Past academic research (Fitzgerald and Willcocks, 1994; Klepper and Jones, 1998; Willcocks and Kern, 1998) and practitioner commentaries have shown that cultural incompatibility can be a problem in outsourcing.

develop the three dimensions of social capital to ensure a productive relationship. The social capital building techniques suggested in the following paragraphs applies to domestic and offshore applications outsourcing[15].

- Structural Dimension: *Resources that help the organizations connect with each other*
  - Access patterns, including communication plans, should be defined at the beginning of the project. In the absence of such definition and/or to complement initial interaction patterns, the project managers should work together to develop those.
  - Large projects require a formal multi-tiered governance model. While this may not be necessary in smaller projects, it is important to identify project managers as key interface personnel for the project in all cases. Many organizations prefer to channel communication through these managers.
  - Project manager(s) should try to develop personal relationships with their counterparts in the partner organization. Participants in this research had weekly meetings with their counterparts, where the discussion did not focus on the project. Others networked within the partner organization, trying to understand the 'pressures and pains' felt by their counterpart. It must be commented that more vendor managers emphasized the importance of developing the personal relationship than the client managers did.
  - The project managers from the vendor organization are usually stationed at or close to the client location. In the case of offshore outsourcing, these managers are called cultural liaisons (Carmel and Agarwal, 2001).
  - When vendors are able to implement tried and tested business models and routines, clients view this as a sign of the vendor's competency. Use of processes based on the CMM model also contributes to this assessment of competency.
- Cognitive Dimension: *Resources that help the organizations achieve a shared understanding of the project*
  - It is necessary to have a clear understanding of the scope of the project before the start of the project. When such understanding is not present, the vendor could work additional man-hours beyond the original agreement and still not meet the expectations of the client.
  - Many of the successful client-vendor pairs used periodic joint meetings of all the staff involved in the project to develop a common understanding of the project. In some cases, these were virtual meetings.
  - In outsourcing arrangements, success in achieving corporate objectives is dependent on people being able to work together for their mutual benefit. That requires communication. Communication in face-to-face meetings is complemented with various communication technologies. Instant messaging is a popular choice among offshore providers.
  - Vendor employees are trained on the technologies used/needed by the client to ensure that the employees understand the client requirements. The client employees also need to have an understanding of the process because their involvement is necessary for the completion of the project.

---

[15] The results may be applicable to other types of outsourcing as well. Applications outsourcing was the context of this study.

- o In custom applications development outsourcing, vendors may not have enough knowledge about the client's business domain. Clients should be willing to share business domain experiences and the vendors should be patient during this learning process. They should also satisfy the vendor that they have achieved this learning so that the client may be confident and comfortable in the relationship. In offshore outsourcing, this may involve placing some of the vendor personnel at the client location to learn the business practices.
- o Additional steps are taken by offshore vendors to facilitate shared understanding. They provide accent neutralization training and writing skills training to employees so that client representatives can understand them easily. They also expose employees to the national culture of the client firm by providing access to media content from that country to facilitate social networking.
- o Regular monitoring and evaluation ensures that the needs of organizations continue to be met.
- o Documentation should continue during the outsourcing project so that practices that worked and did not work can be identified and recorded to ensure that they do not erode from organizational memory

- Relational Dimension: *Resources that help organizational members work together in a cooperative manner*

  - o New vendor organizations entering the market subscribe to the "policy of small steps" (Sydow, 1998) by taking up small pilot projects. These projects establish inter-organizational links and contribute to the development of trust.
  - o Clients agree to let vendors use their project as a reference project and offer to do marketing presentations for the vendors. This demonstrates their concern for the vendors, and leads to closer relationships. This also results in obligations towards the client on the part of the vendor, since they know that such reputational endorsements from clients are needed to create initial trust with new clients.
  - o In domestic outsourcing, client employees are often transferred to the vendor. In offshore outsourcing, vendors try to achieve a similar effect by hiring employees who have worked in the client firm[16]. These employees bring with them knowledge of business practices in the client organization, thereby facilitating compatibility in processes between the two organizations.
  - o Client and vendor organizations look for similarity in operational procedures, not organizational values and beliefs. However, there should be an understanding and appreciation of the other organization's culture.
  - o When client and vendor representatives share information in an open and timely manner[17], it increases the trust in the relationship. This is particularly important when there are problems.

---

[16] This does not happen all the time, since it may be expensive for offshore organizations to hire professionals from other countries.
[17] The consultant in the Montezuma-Apollo case described a recent development in the area of outsourcing management – outsourcing relationship management (ORM) software. ORM software provides the means for tracking and analyzing compliance with service level agreement (SLA) clauses. Their role in outsourcing management starts at the stage of the creation of the SLA. The software includes templates to reduce the time and complexity of creating SLAs. Service levels can be set and monitored automatically through triggering of signals when thresholds are not being met. While this process seems to suggest that the focus will shift to formal contract administration, these tools will provide support for the cognitive and relational dimensions of the relationship. By automating the monitoring process and making sure everyone involved the project has access to the information

Outsourcing managers play a critical role in developing social capital in the inter-organizational relationship. The commitment and motivation of these outsourcing managers are necessary for the development of social capital in the relationship. Organizations recognize the importance of having the right person in this position. In many cases in this research, participants from client organizations mentioned that there is a clause in the contract that allows them to have a say in who the vendor representative will be. These managers must possess a range of skills including technical expertise, contract management skills, communication skills, financial skills, and human resource management skills. To be able to demonstrate their concern for the other organization and earn their trust, these managers need to granted autonomy to make decisions. Organizations need to place individuals with a combination of technical and management skills in these positions and allow them autonomy to perform their jobs to gain the trust of the partner organization.

As organizations engage in more outsourcing deals and outsource more complex jobs (Cohen and Young, Gartner, 2005), it is necessary to ensure that these do not end in failure and disappointment. While social capital in itself is not sufficient to ensure success, it is a necessary ingredient in the outsourcing arrangement to ensure that outsourcing goals are achieved.

8.7 And the moral of the story is...

The concept of 'social capital' has enjoyed a surge in popularity among organizational researchers. This has been fueled by the awareness and interest in understanding how the social embededdness of the firms influences their behavior and performance (Granovetter, 1973). Social capital has been identified as a concept that can add value to the study of these organizational processes (Leenders and Gabbay, 1999) and researchers have suggested that social capital can facilitate knowledge transfer and creation of new knowledge in and between organizations (e.g., Adler and Kwon, 2002; Nahapiet and Ghoshal, 1998; Inkpen and Tsang, 2005).

In this study, social capital was the theoretical lens that helped to understand why some outsourcing relationships failed while others succeeded. The use of the social capital theoretical framework contributed to the understanding of the nature and content of the client-vendor relationship. The moral is that social capital is an interesting and useful lens, which helps in the explanation of these differing outcomes. Thus, the social capital framework helps us to better understand what companies could do to be successful in managing inter-organizational relationships in the applications outsourcing context. This research has also demonstrated the value of social capital beyond that of a vague and catchall concept. Indeed, it has proved to be an insightful framework, which may be applied for understanding interactions in other areas of outsourcing and other domains, such as virtual organizations and e-commerce ventures.

they need, these tools provide transparency and openness in the exchange relationship and may increase the trust between the client and vendor.

Appendix 1
INTERVIEW PROTOCOL

➤ Request permission for recording

➤ Introduction: This research project addresses two inter-related questions - 1, what are the defining characteristics of the relationship between the client and the vendor - how can the desirable elements be created and sustained, while the undesirable elements are avoided, and 2, what is the impact of the relationship on the execution and delivery of the outsourced product or service? Therefore, the purpose of the interview is to obtain your views on the firm's experiences with outsourcing, specifically the management of the outsourcing relationship.

➤ All participants are guaranteed individual and organizational anonymity. If the research is published externally, the firm will be given a pseudonym to ensure the confidentiality of the data collected from the firm.

Business Model/Profile
Please provide a general overview of your organization;
1. number of employees
2. number of locations,
…
IS Organization?
Overview of outsourcing arrangement
For the purposes of this discussion, I would like you to focus on one specific IS outsourcing project and client/vendor.
Could you please give me an overview of this outsourcing arrangement?
1. With whom
2. How long (age of relationship)
3. What functions are included (e.g., systems development, network support, etc.)
And your role...
Why do you consider this an "outsourcing engagement"?
What were the drivers in this outsourcing decision? Who initiated this move towards outsourcing within your organization?
Profiling - Market Orientation
Starting at the very beginning: How did you become aware of your current outsourcing client/vendor? Is that the predominant way?
What were the factors considered in the selection/acceptance of the vendor/client?
Learning? Proximity? CMM/ISO rating?
What was the process?
What were the factors considered in the selection/acceptance of the vendor/client?
Did the decision to outsource affect the credibility of the IS organization?
Contract
What is the form of the legal agreement between the companies?
What were the processes involved in finalizing and crafting the contract? Who all were involved (any external parties?)?

Definition of contract/SLA? How important?

Exit strategy?

Relationship and contract

What is the role of the contract in the management of the outsourcing arrangement?

Would you consider the relationship with your outsourcing partner to be completely defined by the contract? What is left unsaid?

Relationship Management

What are the elements or characteristics of a relationship between the two business organizations that are necessary for the success of an outsourcing arrangement? How do you ensure these characteristics are present?

Capabilities

What are the capabilities that the two organizations should have for the successful execution and delivery of the outsourcing project? How does the presence or absence of the attributes identified above affect these capabilities?

Management structure/ Governance model

What is the organizational structure or staffing composition you employ to manage an outsourcing deal? What is the form on the other side? Is there a good fit?

Key players

Who are the key players? Why are they important? What are their requisite skills?

Communication

How are communication patterns established? Defined in the contract?

What are the technologies used?

Different levels at which interaction take place? Parties involved?

Are these mechanisms formal or informal; structured or unstructured? Contract defined? Developed during the course of the arrangement?

Informal vs. formal - which do you rely on? How important is informal communication? What is preferred? Why? Typical communication pattern? Channeled interaction or interaction between all levels?

Interaction with end users

Is the end user within the organization or not? What is the nature of the feedback from them?

Shared Understanding

Do you believe there is a shared understanding between the two firms about the process of the outsourcing project?

Do you set operational level goals together? How important do you think this is? If important: How do you ensure this understanding is present? What are the mechanisms that are used? Do you have for instance, group training sessions, meetings with both parties,...?

Processes

Re decision-making and implementing of decisions: how is this shared at the operational level? Is the decision-making process integrated into the policies and procedures of your organization? How about in the client organization? Is this process defined or outlined in the contract? Once a decision is made, how is it implemented?

Performance monitoring

How are activities central to the relationship monitored?

How do you establish the extent to which performance-related provisions in the contract are complied with? What mechanisms do you use to do so? Contract-defined?

Aligned with client's/vendor's?

Metrics; benchmarking

Rewards

ORM software?

Are tools for performance monitoring developed together? Implemented by vendor?

Reliability/trust/commitment

How willing are you to use extra resources for the outsourcing project? How about the client/vendor?

Do you feel the client/vendor will fulfill its obligations fairly? Is there evidence of opportunism, how can you deal with it?

Conflict

Have you had instances of disagreement between you and the client/vendor? How are these resolved? Are there formal mechanisms? Is this process defined or outlined in the contract?

Change management

How willing are your organization and the client/vendor to negotiate and implement changes to the outsourcing arrangement? Is this process defined or outlined in the contract, or has it evolved over the course of the outsourcing arrangement?

Was the process developed within your organization? How?

Time

How do you think the relationship has changed over time?

Expectations

What are your expectations from this outsourcing arrangement? Do you believe this has been an equitable relationship - your overall gains have been proportionate to your overall costs?

Economic benefits

Business benefits

Access to technology – resources

Learning - Innovation - How do you get your partner to propose/accept new ideas?

Satisfaction

Are you satisfied with your outsourcing arrangement? What are some of the things that contribute to this satisfaction?

What are some of the things that contribute to any dissatisfaction or unhappiness with the outsourcing arrangement? What would you change if you could? What have you changed?

If there is a chance to work this client/vendor again, would you?

Did you make any adjustments in the current agreement (in any form - pricing, resources allocated, etc) so that this would happen?

Shared Vision/Expectations

Do you believe that the other firm shares the same vision regarding the outcome of this IS project? What are your partner's expectations? Do you think your partner's expectations are being met? How do you find out/know? Surveys, etc?

Unique Characteristics

What do you think distinguishes you from other IS outsourcing vendors/clients? What makes you different?

What do you think distinguishes your outsourcing partner from other IS outsourcing vendors/clients?

Org culture

Does a similarity in organizational culture - work patterns, project discipline, etc - develop between the outsourcing partners? Do you think this is important? Why? Do you actively try to foster such similarity?

Offshore outsourcing

Additional challenges

Dependence

In your opinion, who is more dependent in the relationship - you or the client/vendor? Who has more at stake? How great is the influence of one party over the other? Why?

How much vendor-specific investment has your firm made in the engagement?

Advice

What advice would you give to an organization considering entering an outsourcing arrangement?

Challenges they might face? How could those be overcome? Managing multiple vendors?

Other Options

Backsourcing?

Contacts

Would it be possible for me to talk with one or two of the people within your organization who interact with the client/vendor on a regular basis/have many interactions with the client/vendor?

If you know of anyone else involved in outsourcing who could discuss their experiences with me, could you please let me know/put in a word for me?

Since the objectives of this study can be achieved fully only by talking to both the client and vendor firms involved in the outsourcing relationship, I would also like to obtain from you the contact information for your outsourcing partner.... Interviews similar to that conducted with you will be conducted with the other organization's representative.

Further questions – request permission to email or telephone?

Appendix 2

LETTER OF SOLICITATION

Exploring Outsourcing Relationships:

A Research Project Proposal

EXECUTIVE SUMMARY

In the past decade, information systems outsourcing has seen an explosion not only in quantity, but also in scope. And the prediction is that this growth will continue. Prompted by optimistic expectations of a leaner and more efficient organization, client firms increasingly rely on outsourcing to meet their information systems needs. Vendor firms also have their own expectations when beginning an outsourcing project. They hope to benefit from the project financially as well as in the form of repeat business. However, the reality is that many such well-intentioned outsourcing projects end in failure. The breakdown in the relationship between the client and the vendor has been identified as the primary cause for this disappointing outcome.

Recognizing the prominent role outsourcing plays in today's organizations, the Information Systems Research Center at the Bauer College of Business, University of Houston has initiated a research project aimed at providing additional insight into the nature and impact of the relationship between information systems outsourcing vendors and their clients. Details about the research project are included in the attached abstract. Requirements are minimal, entailing completion of short interviews with members of the organization who are involved in the management of outsourcing projects. We would like to invite you to participate in this project.

All participants are guaranteed both personal and organizational anonymity.

If you have any questions, please contact

Beena George

Department of Decision and Information Sciences,
280 L, Melcher Hall,
C T Bauer College of Business,
University of Houston,   or
4800 Calhoun,
Houston TX 77204-6283
Telephone: 713 743 4735
Email address: bgeorge@uh.edu

Dr. Rudy Hirschheim

Department of Decision and Information Sciences,
290 B, Melcher Hall,
C T Bauer College of Business,
University of Houston,
4800 Calhoun,
Houston TX 77204-6283
Telephone: 713 743 4692
Email address: Rudy@uh.edu

This research project has been approved by
the University of Houston Committee for the Protection of Human Subjects (713-743-9204).

ABSTRACT

Over the past ten years, information systems outsourcing has steadily grown into a mainstream business practice. And the prediction is that this growth will continue. Prompted by optimistic expectations of a leaner and more efficient organization, the management of client firms increasingly rely on IS outsourcing to meet their information systems needs. Vendor firms also come into the IS outsourcing relationship with their own expectations. They hope to benefit from the relationship financially as well as in the form of repeat business. However, the reality is that many such well-intentioned relationships end in failure. The most common meaning of "failure" in the IS outsourcing context is that the contract for the outsourcing project is cancelled prior to completion. A secondary definition includes projects that are delivered eventually, but prove unsuitable for intended purposes or unprofitable for the life of the IS. A third definition is that organizations spend large sums of money to renegotiate their unacceptable contracts. The costs of a failed IS outsourcing project are significant, but are not contained within itself; both client and vendor face additional costs due to lost opportunities. When considering the increasing dependence on IS outsourcing, these problems gain additional significance.

In an IS outsourcing arrangement, clients and vendors establish a stable connection and the initial parameters for their exchanges through the contract. However, both parties have their own expectations about the process and the product, which have to be realized during the operationalization stage, when the actual development and delivery of the product/service occurs. Problems develop at this stage due to a "disconnect" between the client and the vendor, resulting in unmet expectations and poor performance. The ensuing dissatisfaction leads to a lack of commitment and unwillingness to exert effort to maintain the relationship. The stability of the relationship is thus compromised; in the case of IS outsourcing, this results in non-completion of the project, as originally planned. A recent Gartner report points to "the breakdown in relationship between the client and the provider as the cause for most failures in IS outsourcing". While researchers have started to take note of the importance of relationship management in IS outsourcing, very few have examined the interactions that constitute the relationship and the resultant effect on the outcome of the IS outsourcing arrangement.

To address this issue, this research will focus on the exchanges between the client and the vendor. Such an examination will provide a clearer understanding of the process through which the client-vendor relationship develops and how this outsourcing relationship affects the development and delivery of the service or product, and future exchanges. It will raise awareness about changes in the nature of the relationship that can occur over time and provide insights on how IS outsourcing can become more successful to organizations. By examining the relationships closely, it will be possible to identify what works, and what does not, and thus understand how problems can be overcome.

222

Appendix 3

CASE SITE INFORMATION

To ensure the anonymity of the participants, pseudonyms have been used for the organizations.

Table 1: Client Information
Table 2: Domestic Vendor Information
Table 3: Offshore Vendor Information
Table 4: Consultants

Table Appendix - 1: Client Information

#	Name of organization	Industry	Head-quarters	Locations	Year estab-lished	Number of employees	Revenue	Number of interviews
1	**Acadia**	Power tools and accessories, hardware and home improvement products, and technology-based fastening systems	Maryland	Americas, Europe, Middle-East, Asia	1917	23,000	$4.56 billion	1
2	**Bluestone**	Network architectures and advanced software engineering techniques in the financial and agribusiness industries.	California	California, Oregon, Maryland, Florida, New Mexico	1983			1
3	**Chickasaw**	Airline	Texas	Americas, Europe, and Asia	1934	37,680	$8,870 million	1
4	**Denali**	Internet Service Provider	Oregon	Orgeon	1996	15		1
5	**Glacier**	Chemicals (Plastic and Rubber)	Delaware	Americas, Europe, Middle-East, Africa, Asia	1802	55,000	$28 billion	2
6	**Haleakala**	Computers and peripherals	California	Americas, Europe, Middle-East, Africa, Asia	1947	151,000	$82 billion	2

7	**Montezuma**	Oil and Gas	Texas	North America, Europe, Africa, and Russia	1887	27,007	$40 billion	3
8	**Natchez**	Healthcare facilities	Texas	Texas; more than 24 international affiliates throughout Latin America, Europe and the Middle East	1919	8,600	$1.09 billion	1
9	**Ozark**	In-home selling software, management software, and other tools and products for the HVAC industry	Washington	Washington	Mid-nineties			1
10	**Redwood**	Electric Utilities	Texas	Texas	2001	5,293	$6.72 billion	2
11	**Tallgrass**	Semiconductors	Texas	Americas, Asia, Europe, Japan	1930	35,500	$12.58 billion	2
12	**Yosemite**	Academic	Texas	Texas	1972	5,067	$137.8 million	1
13	**Yellowstone**	Medical	Texas	Galveston	1891	14,129	$279.7 million	1

Table Appendix - 2: Domestic Vendor Information

#	Name of organization	Headquarters	Locations	Year established	Number of employees	Revenue	Number of interviews
1	**Apollo**	New York	Americas, Asia, Europe, Middle-East, Australia, Africa,	1924	329,001	$96.29 billion	1
2	**Artemis**	Arkansas	North America	1943	18, 598	$8.25 billion	1
3	**Athene**	Texas	U.S.A, U.K., Germany, Switzerland, Middle-East, India, Japan	1991	1,247	$54.5 million	2
4	**Diana**	California	Europe, Americas, Asia, South Africa, Australia	1959	79,000	$14.8 billion	1
5	**Hercules**	Bermuda	Americas, Australia, Europe, Asia, Middle-East, South Africa	1996	100,000	$13.7 billion	2
6	**Juno**	New York	All fifty states in the United States	1989	23000		1
7	**Minerva**	Texas	Atlanta, Houston, St. Louis, New Orleans	1996	250	$15.10 million	1
8	**Persephone**	California	California, New Hampshire, Alabama; India; China	1996	280	$29.60 million	1
9	**Vesta**	California	U.K., Japan, Singapore, Tokyo, Dubai, Denmark, India	1995	400+	$8.4 million	2

| 10 | **Vulcan** | Texas | Texas | 1981 | 418 | $37.50 million | 1 |
| 11 | **Zeus** | Texas | Americas, Europe, Asia, Middle-East, South Africa | 1962 | 132,000 | $20.62 billion | 2 |

9 of these 11 vendors had a presence in India.

Table Appendix - 3: Offshore Vendor Information

Name of organization	Headquarters	Locations	Year estab-lished	Number of employees	Revenue	Number of Inter-views
Amba	Thiruvananthapuram, India.	USA, Canada, Australia, Japan, UK & Qatar.	1908	250	$20 billion	1
Brahma	California and Kerala, India	Palo Alto, CA; Chapel Hill, NC; development center in Trivandrum, India	1996			2
Durga	California and Kerala, India	Portland, ME; Fremont, CA; Trivandrum, Kerala, India; project offices in Southeast Asia and Europe	1996			1
Gayathri	New Delhi, India	Mumbai, India; U.S.A., U.K., Dubai	1975	3,000	7,636.72 million rupees	2
Hanuman	California and Bangalore, India	North America, Europe, UAE, Asia, Australia	1981	35,229	$1.14 billion	2
Kali	Bangalore, India and New Jersey	San Francisco, Toronto, London, Frankfurt; development facilities in Chennai, Kolkata, Pune, Hyderabad and Bangalore	1994	14,300	$586.7 million	1
Krishna	Kerala, India	Atlanta, GA; U.K.; Switzerland, Dubai, Australia, India	1997			1
Lakshmi	Chennai, India and Michigan	Chennai, Bangalore and Mumbai	1985	4,701	$25.2 million	2
Rama	Kerala, India	India, Bahrain, Europe, Dubai				2
Satya	Hyderabad, India	Bangalore, Thiruvananthapuram, India; U.S., U.K., Canada, Germany, Japan	1989	515	$25.10 million	2
Shiva	Mumbai, India	Chennai and Bangalore;	1997	2,200		2

		development centers across India					
Vishnu	Bangalore, India		1995	180	$17.4 million	2

Table Appendix - 4: Consultant Information

#	Consultant	Headquarters
1	**Aristotle**	San Mateo, CA
2	**Cicero**	Houston, Texas
3	**Euclid**	Louisville, Kentucky
4	**Plato**	Unionville, Connecticut
5	**Pythagoras**	Houston, Texas
6	**Socrates**	Houston, Texas
7	**Thales**	Fremont, California

CODES

SOCIAL CAPITAL DIMENSION: STRUCTURAL
- Access to parties
- Appropriable organization
- Configuration

SOCIAL CAPITAL DIMENSION: COGNITIVE
- Shared understanding
- Alignment of vision
- Difference in goals/common goals
- Shared codes
- Shared language
- Shared narratives
- Consensus/agreement

SOCIAL CAPITAL DIMENSION: RELATIONAL
- Trust
- Norms: Commitment – calculative
- Norms: Commitment – affective
- Norms: Flexibility
- Norms: Coordination
- Norms: Cooperation
- Norms: Conflict resolution
- Identification
- Cultural compatibility
- Obligations
- Expectations
- Opportunism

ASSESSMENT
- Assessment - equity
- Assessment – process
- Dissatisfaction
- Negative capital
- Innovation
- Determinant of success

OUTCOME
- Outcome: long-term relationship

- Outcome: outsourcing project goal
- Outcome: Referrals
- Outcome: Reputation

BACKGROUND INFORMATION
- History
- Background info

MANAGEMENT
- Monitoring: Output
- Monitoring: Process
- Monitoring: Social
- Importance of relationship
- Role of contract
- Management of relationship/governance
- Attention to relationship and management of relationship
- Perceptions of other
- Boundary spanners
- Change management
- Certification
- Exit strategy/termination
- External parties
- Negotiation outcomes

OUTSOURCING
- Offshoring
- Offshoring to India
- Backsourcing

CONDITIONS PROMOTING COMBINATION AND EXCHANGE
- Anticipation of value
- Combination capability
- Motivation for exchange
- Ease of exchange (access)

CONDITIONS PROMOTING SOCIAL CAPITAL
- Definition of job/closure of team
- Communication
- Formal communication
- Informal communication
- Dependence
- Age of relationship
- Other conditions promoting social capital

CAPABILITIES
- Client capability
- Vendor capability

CONTEXTUAL
- Cost focus in IT and outsourcing
- Reason for outsourcing

- Perception of outsourcing
- Perception of IS
- Organizational change
- Organizational culture

Appendix 5

Snapshot of ATLAS/ti Screen

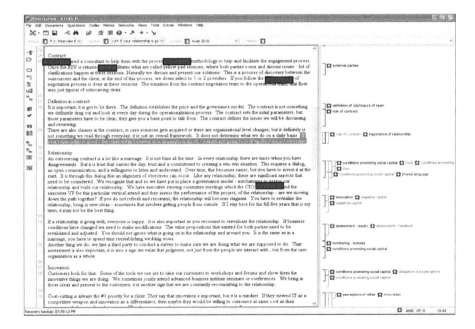

Figure Appendix -1: ATLAS/ti Screenshot

SOCIAL CAPITAL PRIMER

Goals of this review:

1, To do a survey of the social capital research, specifically work based on Nahapiet and Ghoshal's (1998) analysis, from 1998 to 2005

2, To examine articles using NG[1] as primary theoretical lens to determine how NG has been applied.

Social Capital

Introduction

Social capital has a long intellectual *history* in the social sciences. The first usage of the term "social capital" (according to Putnam) in the contemporary sense is that of Lyda J. Hanifan in his work on rural school community centers in the late twenties. He used the term to describe those qualities that color daily interactions. He was concerned with the cultivation of good will, fellowship, sympathy, and social intercourse among members of a social unit. [2]The term was reinvented by Jane Jacobs[3] in the late 1960s in her work on urban life where she emphasized the importance of networks in sustaining urban life. Studying suburban life, social psychologists Seeley[4] and colleagues used the term to refer to the status that individuals accrued because of their group activities. In their research, they examined upscale social clubs. In his early work on disadvantaged communities, Glenn Loury[5] posited that social capital (not human capital[6]) determines an individual's advancement in life.

Current conceptualizations of the term primarily have their roots in the work of Coleman and Bourdieu. The present popularity of the term can be ascribed to Putnam's 2000 work, "Bowling Alone." This review of research is divided into three sections. In the following sub-sections of this section, definitions of social capital, the applications of this concept, the creation of social capital, benefits, and risks from social capital are discussed. In the second section, Nahapiet and Ghoshal's analysis of social capital is presented. The third and last section contains a description of the articles that have applied Nahapiet and Ghoshal's framework.

---

1 Nahapiet, J., and Ghoshal, S. "Social Capital, Intellectual Capital, and the Organizational Advantage," Academy of Management Review (23:2) 1998, pp 242-266.

2 Hanifan, L. J. (1916) 'The rural school community center', Annals of the American Academy of Political and Social Science 67: 130-138.

Hanifan, L. J. (1920) The Community Center, Boston: Silver Burdett.

[3] The Death and Life of Great American Cities, 1961.

4 John R. Seeley, Alexander Sim, and ElizabethW. Loosley, Crestwood Heights: A Study of the Culture of Suburban Life (New York: Basic Books, 1956)

[5]("A Dynamic Theory of Racial Income Differences," in Women, Minorities, and Employment Discrimination, ed. P. A. Wallace and A. LeMond, 1977

[6] Human capital is the collection of capabilities of the individuals required to provide solutions to customers

Definitions of Social Capital

In European social thought, Pierre Bourdieu first used the term "social capital" in 1972 (Turner, 1990). Social capital was defined by Bourdieu as "the sum of the resources, actual or virtual, that accrue to an individual or a group by virtue of possessing a durable network of more or less institutionalized relationships of mutual acquaintance and recognition" (Bourdieu, 1992). Bourdieu sees social processes as being shaped by the economic infrastructure. However, agents are not puppets in these social interactions. They possess their own internalized cognitive structures that they use to deal with the world and thus alter their levels of capital.

Coleman considered social capital to be defined by its function. Social capital was defined as the sum of the processes within and between groups that allow individuals to accrue benefits. Putnam's (1993) definition follows the functionalist slant of Coleman's and explains social capital as the features of social organizations that facilitate coordination and cooperation for mutual benefit. Thus, social capital is the set of expectations for action within a collectivity that affect the goals and goal-seeking behavior of its members. While Bourdieu defines social capital as a fungible[7] property of individuals, Coleman's, and particularly Putnam's usage of the term suggests that social capital is a collective property of the group (e.g., civic spirit) that bestows benefits on the group.

Adler and Kwon (2002) provide a listing of definitions of social capital and the foci of the definitions. Some researchers focus mainly on the relations an actor maintains with others – thus maintaining an external focus. Others focus on relations characterizing the internal structure of the organization, with an internal focus. Bourdieu and Coleman fall in the first group, while Putnam falls in the second. Still others like Pennar (1997) and Woolcock (1998) encompass both foci.

Levels of Analysis

Social capital exists at multiple levels. Organizational researchers (Kostova and Roth, 2003; Peng and Luo, 2000) have addressed this issue by proposing a multiple level approach, a "micro-macro model for social capital formation" (page 16; Kostova and Roth, 2003). This formulation recognizes the fact that relationships and hence social capital are formed at the individual level between members of the organizations participating in the inter-organizational relationship. These individuals act as "boundary spanners" (Zaheer et al, 1998) and it is their continuing interaction that enables the "maintenance and reproduction of this social asset" in the inter-organizational relationship (Lin, 1999; page 32). Information and perceptions about the partner organization are communicated throughout the organization by these boundary spanners, transforming the private social capital that they have accumulated into a "public good" (Kostova and Roth, 2003). Thus even in the absence of direct contacts with members of the other organization, individuals in one organization will form shared perceptions about the other organization based on the interaction of these boundary spanners, thus creating social capital at the organizational level.

Streams of Research in Social Capital

In general, the concept of social capital reflects the fact that members in a social structure are able to secure benefits by virtue of their membership in such structures. There are two predominant conceptualizations of this term in current research. One conceptualization

---

[7] with other forms of capital

235

emphasizes structural considerations and focuses on the value accrued to the individual from being a part of the structure. In this stream of research, the social structure itself is seen as providing value by providing access to information and other resources (e.g. Baker, 1990). Another stream of research emphasizes the relational aspect of social capital (Fukuyam, 1995; Putnam, 1993). Here, social capital is derived from the nature of the relationship, not the structure itself. The relationship is defined by trust and trustworthiness (Tsai and Ghoshal, 1998), obligations and expectations (Coleman, 1990), norms and sanctions (Coleman, 1990), and identification (Hakanson and Snehota, 1995). Relationships characterized by these elements would lead to cooperative behaviors and result in productive outcomes in the form of material benefits for both parties (Nahapiet and Ghoshal, 1998; Zaheer at al, 1998). These conceptualizations are not mutually exclusive. As Adler and Kwon (2002), point out there is an advantage in combining these perspectives. An integrative view in which social capital accrues from the pattern of the linkages and the quality of the linkages is favored by some researchers (e.g., Loury (1992), Pennar (1997), and Woolcock (1998)). Additionally, researchers have looked at cognitive similarity. Portes (1998) argues that common beliefs and shared experiences contribute to a sense of community and solidarity, thus building social capital. Other researchers have identified shared values, common symbol systems, shared assumptions about the world as part of social capital (Adler and Kwon, 2002).

In summary, social capital encompasses many aspects of the social context, such as the "social ties, trusting relations, and value systems" that enable productive behavior (Tsai and Ghoshal, 1998). It comprises both the network and the assets that may be mobilized through that network (Bourdieu, 1986; Nahapiet and Ghoshal, 1998). Social capital can take many forms: structural, relational, and cognitive, but every instance of social capital facilitates activities of units within the structure (Coleman, 1988; Nahapiet and Ghoshal, 1998).

Portes and Sensebrenner (1993) identify another essential characteristic of social capital, stating that "value introjection" is possible because social capital prompts individuals to behave in "ways other than naked greed." Thus, social capital can be understood as "the features of a relationship that bind together the participants in the relationship, enabling them to exchange resources and making it possible to work together in a productive manner."

Forms of Social Capital

The distinction between the three forms of social capital discussed here relate to the nature of ties between the social units (structure).

1. Bonding, Bridging, and Linking

Woolcock (2001) identifies three forms of social capital: bonding, bridging, and linking social capital. Bonding capital links individuals to people in similar situations. The focus is inward and it tends to reinforce identity and create homogenous groups. Bridging social capital links people to individuals in wider social circles (e.g. workmates). Bridging capital generates broader identities. Linking capital ties people in dissimilar situations. For example, it could consist of relationships up and down the economic scale. Putnam (2000) uses the first two forms of capital in his writing. He contends that bonding capital is necessary to 'get by' while bridging capital is necessary to 'get ahead'.

2. Structural Holes

Burt argues that the ties an actor has with others can support or restrain one's actions. To expound his argument, he uses the concept of 'structural holes'. When a connection does not exist between non-redundant actors, a structural hole exists. These holes present opportunities for the focal actor since the actor now can determine who to establish a tie with, and has greater freedom of decision and movement.

3. Weak Ties, Strong Ties

Following Granovetter, Lin (2001) separates ties into weak ties and strong ties. Strong ties bring together individuals with the similar resources while weak ties bring people with dissimilar resources together. Thus, weak ties may be instrumental in achieving goals where access to new types of resources are necessary.

Differentiation of forms of social capital in this manner allows for more clarity in the use of the term, than a general "perfunctory" approach to social capital analysis (Field, 2003).

Applications of the Concept of Social Capital

The concept has been applied in various contexts: For example, Ainsworth (2002) examined the role of social capital in migration patterns and Cechhini and Raina (2002) found that social capital had a facilitating role in the implementation and acceptance of networking technology in an Indian rural community. In organizational research, Kostova and Roth (2003) studied how social capital facilitated coordination between sub-units in a multinational organization, while Kanter (1994) explained how social capital at the individual level facilitated business partnerships.

Information systems researchers have also been intrigued by the concept of social capital. In April 2002, Communications of the ACM devoted an issue to the topic, with the primary theme being the contribution of the Internet and online communities to the development of social capital. Erickson et al (2002) discuss how trust can be developed in online interactions by permitting participants to identify other participants and their activities. Smith also describes a tool for developing trust. This tool can be used in the context of bulletins boards and in Usenet by tracking threads and authors. Other articles in this issue focus on the role of various participants in promoting trust and collaboration. Hiltz and Turoff comment on the role of the teacher in encouraging participation and collaboration in asynchronous learning networks, while Bruckman visualizes a new Internet-enabled learning environment where peers and elders (besides teachers) also facilitate student learning. In a paper similar in flavor to these CACM articles, Oxendine et al (2003) compare two cities' attempts at developing electronic networks and find that the city with more trust and cooperation between its citizens are able to build and sustain a network better than the other. Most of these articles focus on trust. Trust is indeed an essential component of social capital, but it is only one of the elements of social capital. None of these articles captures the depth of the concept of social capital, though they all touch upon the essence of social capital as the "glue that holds networks together" (Preece, 2002; page 38). Portes (1998), among others, attributes the lack of clear definition of the term and its varied and loose uses to Coleman.

Guanxi

Guanxi can be literally translated as "relationship". It describes a personal connection between two people in which one is able to prevail upon another to perform a favor or service or a network of contacts that one can call upon in times of need. In discussions of social capital, particularly those that relate to the Orient, the concept is broached (e.g. Kumar and Worm, 2003)

Gemeinschaft

Tonnies discusses two types of associations: gemeinschaft and gessellschaft. In gemeinschaft, individuals are more concerned about the common good than self-interest. On the contrary, in gessellschaft self-interest takes on predominance. The concept of social capital is conceptually related to gemeinschaft, since in gemeinschaft individuals are regulated by common values and beliefs. Family is cited as an example for the gemeinschaft.

An interesting point is that Tonnies considered the modern business a good example of gessellschaft. However, in discussions on social capital, organizations are seen as social units in which social capital can develop.

Creation and Enhancement of Social Capital

Social capital is created when units within a social system interact with one another (Bourdieu, 1986). In fact, social capital cannot develop without interaction or exchange between the units and will be depleted by the lack of interaction. The exchange and the attendant reciprocity between the units of the social system underlie the creation as well as use of social capital (Bubolz, et al., 1998). It also follows that inter-dependence between the units promotes social capital, since it is this mutuality that will ensure that the units continue to interact and exchange resources. However, dependence is a double-edged sword. It has been noted that when one party feels more dependent on the other, it can lead to the erosion of social capital and of the relationship (Fukuyama, 2000).

Communication between members is an integral part of this interaction and is necessary to develop social capital. Another factor that contributes to the development of social capital, particularly in work settings, is the clarity in the definition of the task for which the group has been formed (Kogut and Zander, 1996). Such clarity delineates the boundaries of the group (Boland and Tenkasi, 1995), within which group members can develop unique codes and means for communication, enhancing the development of social capital. Further, social capital improves with age. Coleman (1990) stressed the significance of the duration of a relationship in the development of social capital.

Value from Social Capital

Social capital acts as a lubricant in relationships, enabling effective governance. It can minimize the transaction costs associated with negotiation and enforcement, imperfect information and layers of unnecessary bureaucracy in relationships. Relationships rich in social capital provide effective governance through commonly agreed monitoring schemes and mutual understanding and trust between parties. High levels of commitment and low levels of opportunism characterize these relationships (Joshi and Stump, 1999). Further, the cooperative behavior that stems from social capital is conducive to the efficient exchange of resources, reducing production costs for the organization.

Social capital affects activities within organizations and its relations with other organizations, across sectors and with society. Social capital promotes greater coordination among individuals and between departments within an organization. As Nahapiet and Ghoshal (1998) show, the organization setting is conducive to the development of social capital and this gives the organization an advantage in the completion of work processes. Similarly as organizations establish stronger relationships with one another and social capital in the inter-organizational relationship increases, they will work together in the future on other business projects beyond the scope of the original project (Kostova and Roth, 2003). However, social capital cannot replace financial resources and technical and business expertise. It only serves as a necessary complement to these resources, ensuring the effective use of these resources.

Negative Capital

Adler and Kwon (2002) sound a cautionary note about the risks associated with social capital. Developing and maintaining social capital in the relationship involves considerable time and effort, which may take away from the work at hand. While positive benefits may accrue from social capital in the initial stages, in the later stages of a relationship embedded practices can obstruct change, preventing appropriate responses to the environment. Strong ties can inhibit opportune action, by causing "organizational inertia" (Portes and Sensenbrenner, 1993) or inducing dependence. This potential for confining and counter-productive outcomes from social capital underlines the necessity for constant monitoring of organizational interactions with partners and the environment. Another negative aspect of social capital is exclusion. People within a social network benefit, while those outside can suffer negative consequences.

Organizational Advantage from Social Capital:
Nahapiet and Ghoshal (1998)

Nahapiet and Ghoshal (1998) build on Ghoshal and Moran (1996)'s critique of market-based theories, particularly, transaction cost theory, where they present the notion of "organizational advantage". Advocating an organizational economy perspective, rather than one based on a market economy, they argue that organizations are not mere substitutes for structuring efficient transactions when markets fail, but possess unique advantages for managing certain economic activities. Applications of transaction cost theory overlook this aspect, and thus are "bad for practice". Transaction cost theory is criticized as a "static theory" applicable only to situations where markets and economies foster the uncontrolled growth of opportunism. Organizations actually have an advantage over markets in that they are able to "leverage the human ability to take initiative, to cooperate, and to learn." When organizations are unable to create an internal environment that is conducive to the generation of trust and commitment, they will fail to achieve those benefits that accrue from cooperation and teamwork. Nahapiet and Ghoshal (1998), in turn, explain how organizations can enjoy "organizational advantage," by employing "social capital" to generate an environment that is conducive to the creation of "intellectual capital."

Social capital and its dimensions:

In Nahapiet and Ghoshal's treatise, social capital is defined as the access and resources available in an exchange relationship. Social capital thus has the potential to influence processes of knowledge creation in exchange relationships. Social capital is "the sum of the actual and potential resources embedded within, available through and derived from the network of relationships" and is collectively owned (page 243).

	Definition of social capital in NG
Focus	Internal and external
Public vs. private	A public good of the group benefiting all members of the group, and can be accessed by any member of the group
Streams of research	Structural, relational, cognitive

Based on a comprehensive review of the previous work on social capital, Nahapiet and Ghoshal (1998) identify three dimensions of social capital: the structural, the relational, and the cognitive. To distinguish between the structural and the relational dimensions, Nahapiet and Ghoshal (1998) rely on Granovetter's (1985) discussion of structural and relational embededdness. The structural dimension refers to the pattern of connections – "who you know and reach and how you reach them." The relational dimension refers to the assets that are rooted in these relationships, such as trust and commitment. While previous researchers have recognized the importance of mutual understanding and sharing of knowledge among parties (Cohen and Levinthal, 1990; Kogut and Zander, 1992), Nahapiet and Ghoshal were the first to specify a separate third dimension of social capital, the cognitive dimension, to include these elements. The cognitive dimension facilitates a common understanding by relying on shared representations and interpretations. Table 1 provides definitions of the three dimensions in Nahapiet and Ghoshal's framework, which elaborated on these concepts in the intra-organizational setting.

Element of framework	Definition
Structural Dimension: Pattern of connections Who you know, how you know and reach them	
Network ties	Links that provide access to resources.
Network Configuration:	Properties of ties between groups that afford the flexibility and ease of information exchange (Density, Connectivity, Hierarchy)
Appropriable organization	"Organization" created for one purpose may provide a source of valuable resources for other purposes
Cognitive Dimension Resources providing shared representations and interpretations, and systems of meaning among parties	
Shared codes & language	Codes organize sensory data into perceptual categories and provide a frame of reference for observing and interpreting the environment. Shared codes provide a common conceptual apparatus for evaluating the likely benefits of exchange and combination. Shared language facilitates communication
Shared narratives	Tools that facilitate the exchange of

	meanings and tacit experience – e.g. stories
Relational Dimension: Assets created and leveraged through relationships	
Trust	Multi-dimensional; indicates a willingness to be vulnerable to another party, arising from 1, belief in the good intent and concern of exchange partners, 2, belief in their competence and capability, 3, belief in their reliability, and 4, belief in their perceived openness
Norms	Shared beliefs of what constitute appropriate behavior; reflects a degree of consensus in the social system. Examples: cooperation, flexibility
Obligations & Expectations	Commitment or duty to undertake some activity in the future
Identification	A group sees themselves as one with another group of people

Definitions of social capital dimensions and elements from Nahapiet and Ghoshal (1998)

Nahapiet and Ghoshal comment that while the separation of social capital into dimensions and their elements is necessary for analytical purposes, inter-relationships may exist among dimensions and within a dimension. For instance, trust, one of the elements of the relational dimension in Nahapiet and Ghoshal's analysis, is necessary for the development of shared norms, which is yet another element of the same dimension. Research has shown that trust is necessary for the development of norms such as commitment (Ganesan and Hess, 1997) and cooperation (Rindfleisch, 2000). It is also possible that a relationship exists between the dimensions of social capital. It is reasonable that without access (an element of the structural dimension), it is not possible to develop the elements of the relational dimension or enhance the elements of the cognitive dimension.

Social capital facilitates the creation of intellectual capital

The primary argument in Nahapiet and Ghoshal (1998) is that social capital facilitates the creation of new intellectual capital8 in organizations, by providing an environment conducive to the combination and exchange of resources. Combination and exchange have been identified as the two processes that generate new intellectual capital at the group level. New intellectual capital is the result of combining the knowledge resources of different individuals and is dependent on the exchange of such resources between the parties. Exchange enables the reallocation of resources, stimulating potentially new and productivity-enhancing combinations of resources. Such combinations can also lead to the creation of additional resources by stimulating the learning and innovation potential of the individuals involved (Moran and Ghoshal, 1999). Thus, following Schumpeter (1934) Nahapiet and Ghoshal note that the resultant new intellectual capital may be created through radical change, producing something

---

[8] Nahapiet and Ghoshal (1998) identified intellectual capital as "the knowledge and knowing capacity of organizations."

that is entirely new, an innovation, or new intellectual capital may be created through incremental change, a combination of existing knowledge, or an enhancement to an existing routine.

The argument is presented in the form of several hypotheses that relate the social, relational, and cognitive dimensions of social capital to conditions that facilitate the processes necessary for combination and exchange. Figure 1 provides a graphical representation of Nahapiet and Ghoshal's arguments. A basic requirement is that the opportunity to combine and exchange resources exists, which is determined by accessibility of resources and is the first condition necessary for combination and exchange. Even if the opportunity exists, individuals may desist from exchanging and combining resources. However, if the individuals feel that something worthwhile may come out of the process, they may feel encouraged to participate in the processes of intellectual capital creation. This anticipation of value is the second condition necessary for combination and exchange. Additionally, the individuals involved in the exchange will be motivated to exchange and combine if they believe that they can appropriate some of the value from the exchange. Thus, a third condition is that, individuals must be motivated to contribute to the process of intellectual capital creation.

However, even if these three conditions exist, lack of ability to assimilate and apply new knowledge may act as a barrier to combination and exchange of resources (Szulanski, 1996). Nahapiet and Ghoshal term the capability to overcome this barrier "combination capability"; this is the fourth condition necessary for the combination and exchange of intellectual capital. Various researchers have studied this phenomenon, recognizing its importance in achieving organizational advantage and acknowledging the "inertness of knowledge" (Kogut and Zander, 1992). For instance, Cohen and Levinthal (1990) applied the label "absorptive capacity" to the critical "ability of an organization to recognize the value of new external information, assimilate it, and apply it".

Nahapiet and Ghoshal emphasize the bi-directional structuring relationship between social capital and the work-process and its outcome: intellectual capital. They include a feedback loop from the creation of intellectual capital to social capital. Social capital enables exchange and the exchange supports and develops social capital in a "dialectical process" (Nahapiet and Ghoshal, p.259), leading to the co-evolution of social capital and intellectual capital.

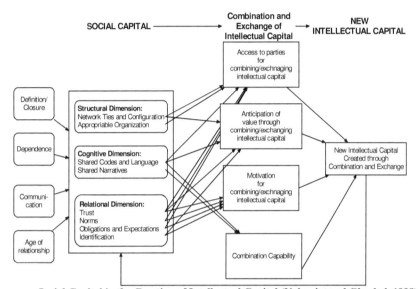

Social Capital in the Creation of Intellectual Capital (Nahapiet and Ghoshal, 1998)

Nahapiet and Ghoshal identify four factors that affect the development of social capital.

One, Age of the relationship: Social capital is built over time. It takes time to produce the stability and continuity necessary for the development of social capital. Therefore, it is more likely that social capital will develop in long-term relationships than in short-term transactions. Additionally, social capital will be valued more in long-term relationships while factors such as price will be valued more in short-term transactions.

Two, Communication: Social capital is developed through frequent interactions. Communication between the parties promotes the development of the cognitive and relational dimensions of the social capital. In many inter-organizational settings, communication patterns and mechanisms are defined by the structures put in place for the inter-organizational project.

Three, Dependence: Another factor that affects the development of social capital is the relative dependence of the people on each other. Social capital is unlikely to develop where there is no reason for either party to be dependent on the other. However, perceptions of asymmetric dependence can negatively affect the development of social capital, especially the relational dimension.

Four, Closure: Definition of task boundaries and teams provides an environment in which trust and norms of cooperation and coordination as well as sharing of codes and language can be developed. Thus, definition or closure aids in the creation of social capital.

About Criticisms of Nahapiet and Ghoshal's conceptualization:

Nahapiet and Ghoshal present a model where the social capital promotes the creation of intellectual capital. Locke (1999), in criticism, argues that social capital cannot be the cause for intellectual capital, and that the relationship should be reversed. Nahapiet and Ghoshal (1998) do not suggest that intellectual capital is created only by social capital. Knowledge can certainly be created and used by single social units. However, where an exchange situation exists, the development of social capital increases the production of intellectual capital, by providing the conditions necessary for the exchange. Bouty (2000) in her research on exchanges between researchers also noted that social capital operates as a regulatory and critical factor in the knowledge exchange process. Additionally, Nahapiet and Ghoshal acknowledge that the creation of intellectual capital can lead to the enhancement of social capital in the relationship. The feedback loop from intellectual capital to social capital in the model is indicative of that relationship (See figure 1).

Research based on Nahapiet and Ghoshal's work:

Judging by the number of articles in academic journals as well as trade journals that use the term "social capital," the concept seems to have a certain appeal to researchers. Nahapiet and Ghoshal's elucidation of the concept of social capital and the identification of its dimensions have attracted considerable attention. In this section, research that apply this conceptualization of social capital are discussed.

Statistics

312 articles that referred to Nahapiet and Ghoshal were identified through examination of articles in various library databases including the AIS electronic library and the ECIS article repository. 217 of these articles were retrieved. Of these articles, only 17 applied the dimensional analysis of social capital from NG. In the remaining articles, propositions from NG were used as support for the arguments developed in those articles. The table in the next section provides examples of how various articles used the NG analysis. In the last section, the 17 articles that used the dimensional analysis are examined in detail.

Articles that have used NG to develop argument in article

Article identification	Use of N&G work
Adler and Kwon (2002)	Pulls together research undertaken in various disciplines on SC and develops a common conceptual framework that identifies the sources, benefits, risks, and contingencies of social capital. Comments on NG also.
Anand et al (2002)	Exhorts that organizational members need to develop SC, but focuses only on cognitive dimension.
Armstrong and Sambamurthy (1999)	Systems of knowing' are structures of interaction among team members
Balijepally et al (2004)	Reviews NG's model and Leana and van Buren's model (includes dimensions of associability (the willingness and ability of participants in an organization to subordinate individual goals and associated actions to collective goals and associated actions) and trust), and

	suggests uses for the concept of social capital in IS research - including outsourcing
Becker (2001)	To deal with dispersed knowledge, social relationships are required
Blyler and Coff (2003)	Discussion on network centrality
Boh (2003), Newell et al (2002), Chae et al (2003)	SC facilitates development of knowledge
Cappelli	Work systems based on teamwork and empowered groups rely on social relationships between employees
Certo (2003)	SC facilitates exchanges
Chellappa and Saraf (2000)	Structural position of an organization in a network determines organizational performance = SC
Ellis (2003)	The network induces both the motive and the entrepreneurial opportunity to secure the benefits of productive relationships in imperfect markets
Fischer and Pollack (2004)	Trust and shared understanding lead to positive outcomes in exchanges between organizational members.
Florin et al (2003)	Ties promote exchange. Context: various relationships that affect venture's ability to accumulate financial capital during its growth stages (before an initial public offering) and its performance during the two-year period after going public
Gold, Malhotra, and Segars (2001)	Technical, structural, and cultural infrastructures that maximize social capital are a necessary for effective knowledge management.
Goodall and Roberts (2003)	NG's analysis is suggestive of how knowledge transfer in organizations is likely to encounter a certain immobility. Friendships and obligations cannot be easily passed from one person to another or from one context to another; norms and mutual identifications in strongly networked groups effect a sort of closure, both to others and to alternative practices.
Gray (2000)	Common language required to integrate complex knowledge
Gray and Chan (2000)	Knowledge has tacit and explicit dimensions
Harvey et al (2002)	Diversity is directly linked to the creation of new intellectual capital

Hillman and Dalziel (2003)	Board incentives and board capital (akin to social capital) affect board member performances
Huang et al (2001)	Support for the importance of trust in cross-functional knowledge exchange
Huysman and Huff (2005)	A social capital analysis should supplement an analysis of the *infrastructure* and *infostructure,* when studying technologies that support group work
Levina and Vaast (2005)	Developing an organizational competence in boundary spanning produces SC
Locke (1999)	Criticism of NG - too much emphasis on "social" - and not enough on individual and objectivity
McFadyen and Cannella (2004)	Goal: to study relationship between social capital and knowledge creation at the individual level. The authors state that they examined the relational dimension (strength of interpersonal exchange relationships) and the structural dimension of SC. "Key facets of the relational dimension of social capital are shared language and experiences, norms and sanctions, obligations and expectations. The structural dimension of social capital is also important, and indicates the degree of "closure," or interconnectedness, among the members of a network" (pg. 736). Measured number of direct relationships (to capture structural dimension) and strength of relationships (to capture relational dimension). The number of relations for a given scientist was the sum of that scientist's coauthors during the previous five years. Strength of relationships measured for each scientist in each year by counting the average number of times that the scientist published with the same coauthor during the previous five years.
Miranda and Kavan (2005)	Context: outsourcing governance. Splits governance into two stages: promissory contract and psychological contract, which applies during the implementation stage. View of SC: SC is part of the structure. Structure is defined as assets that can be utilized by an organization as well as rules and resources. SC provides for combination and exchange of IC resulting in new IC. SC provides the structure for the governance during implementation of the outsourcing contract. Based on NG, three structural elements of control are identified: associations (linkages across inter-organizational

	relationship), affect (opportunism or trust), cognition (extent of common knowledge and shared beliefs, expectations, and understandings). Role of boundary spanners mentioned. Two governance alternatives exist: hierarchy and network. In a hierarchy, associations are few and formal, opportunism exists, and there is discreteness of identities, codes, and understandings. Level of analysis at the psych contract stage appears to be at the individual level, based on limited data analysis included in article.
Molina-Morales (2005)	Gradual knowledge requires the combination of previously unconnected pieces of knowledge, whereas radical innovations are based on novel conceptual distinctions, or novel ways of combining elements that might already have been associated
Nambisan (2002)	Relations serve as the foundation of knowledge development
Newell et al (2004)	No direct use of model, but observes appropriability of organization. Comments on difference between bridging and bonding social capital. NG has bonding perspective. "The 'bridging' view sees social capital as a resource inhering in a social network that can be appropriated by a focal actor based on relations with others in the network (Burt, 1992). Individuals who provide a 'bridge' across divided communities (structural holes) are important, since they play a brokerage role." "The 'bonding' view, by contrast, focuses on the collective relations between a defined group." (page 546)
Osterloh and Frey (2000)	intrinsic motivation to be an undisputed organizational advantage because it lowers transaction cost and raises trust and social capital
Pavlou (2002)	Trust has a causal influence on shared knowledge creation
Preston and Karahanna (2004)	Systems of knowing' are structures of interaction among team members and has three dimensions, of which two are structural and social.
Rowley et al (2000)	Social capital in dense networks can limit a firm's 'openness to information and to alternative ways of doing things, producing forms of collective blindness that sometimes have disastrous effects'.

Schultze (2002)	SC develops in exchange relationships
Smith et al (2005)	Refers to the conditions necessary for combination and exchange identified by NG
Soda et al (2004)	Refers to the notion that shared languages and codes are necessary for information exchange
Sporleder and Goldsmith (2001)	Social capital refers to the composite of contacts, trust and collaboration efficiency that exists within the organization
Subramaniam and Youndt (2005)	SC is the third aspect of IC, along with organizational and human capital. SC is defined as the knowledge embedded within, available through, and utilized by interactions among individuals and their networks of interrelationships.
Teigland and Wasko (2000)	New knowledge created through combination and exchange of knowledge
Tempest et al (2004)	Links the existence of SC within or between organizations to accelerated learning and innovation
Tiegland and Wasko (2003)	The ability to develop the commitment and trust that are necessary for knowledge exchange is difficult to achieve in computer networks. Therefore, the sharing of organizational knowledge through electronic networks is likely to increase the amount of internal information trading within the firm.
von Krogh (2002)	Before knowledge can be shared, individuals must realize the potential for sharing and the benefits involved, and that the cost of identifying opportunities for sharing increases with the size of the organization
Wasko and Faraj (2000)	Knowledge flows best when seekers and experts are considered members of the same community and thus share the same values, codes, and narratives
Wasko et al (2004)	In development of model on knowledge contribution in electronic networks, uses N & G in general terms
Yli-renko et al (2001)	Social interaction, relationship quality, and network ties affect knowledge acquisition in customer relationships of entrepreneurial ventures
Zaheer and Bell (2005)	The process of sharing ideas with innovative alters is likely to generate new knowledge, rather than merely exchanging existing information.

Articles that have applied NG framework as theoretical lens of article

1. Bolino, M.C., Turnley, W.H., and Bloodgood, J.M. "Citizenship Behavior and the Creation of Social Capital in Organizations," *Academy of Management Review* (27:4), Oct 2002, pp 505-522.

Summary	Citizenship behavior within organizations (evidenced as loyalty, obedience, functional participation, advocacy participation, social participation) can contribute to the development of social capital. Since previous organizational research has established that social capital is necessary for the functioning of organizations, this research examines how individuals within the organization through citizenship behavior can contribute to the development of social capital in the organization.
	This article does not present empirical research.
	While the components of dimensions are identified, the elements of each dimension are grouped together in the three propositions that relate aspects of citizenship behavior to the dimensions of social capital.
	1. Social participation will enhance the structural dimension through formation of network ties, changes in configuration, and appropriability of network for other purposes.
	2. Social and advocacy participation will enhance the cognitive dimension through development of shared language and narratives
	3. Loyalty builds trust and liking. Obedience begets trust and liking. Functional participation helps develop liking, trust, and identification since the employees (with high functional participation) would be seen as reliable and competent. Social participation will encourage liking between employees.
	The other two propositions focus on the feedback loop between social capital and citizenship behaviors and the mediating role of social capital in the link between citizenship behaviors and organizational performance.
Definition of social capital	Resource derived from relationships across social units
Structural dimension	The extent to which individuals in an organization are connected, description of patterns of connections among employees, and examinations of the usefulness pf such connections across contexts.
Cognitive dimension	Degree to which employees possess a common language and share narratives
Relational dimension	Affective relationships between employees in which coworkers

		like one another, trust one another, and identify with one another
Comments		While the structural and cognitive dimensions remain the same, the relational dimension has been modified to reflect the affective relationships. Admittedly, these are individual relationships, and the elements that Bolino et al include – trust, liking, and identification – are applicable to individuals. Bolino et al offer that interpersonal attraction enhances group performance by increasing the cohesiveness of the group. In addition, respecting obligations and adhering to norms may be considered part of citizenship behaviors in this context.

Note: Obedience describes employees' willingness to abide by the organization's rules, regulations, and procedures. Loyalty describes willingness to subordinate personal interests for the benefit of the organization and to promote and defend the organization. Social participation describes employees' participation in company affairs and social activities. Advocacy participation describes willingness to offer suggestions, innovating, and encouraging others to speak up. Functional participation describes contributions that exceed required standards.

2. Edelman, L.F., Bresnen, M., Newell, S., Scarbrough, H., and Swan, J. "The Benefits and Pitfalls of Social Capital: Empirical Evidence from Two Organizations in the United Kingdom," *British Journal of Management* (15), Mar 2004, pp S59-S69.

Summary		Social capital has been considered a positive asset in most ˑsearch. While there has been recognition of the negative ffects in recent research, empirical evidence for the same has ɔt been presented. Based on qualitative analysis of data ᵘthered through interviews about the learning that occurred in ʳojects in two organizations in the U.K., vignettes are ˑesented that highlight the beneficial and detrimental effects ˑsocial capital. The authors use NG's analysis along with dler and Kwon's discussion of bridging and bonding social ᵖital.
Definition of social capital		The goodwill available to individuals or groups. Jointly owned resource. Its source lies in the structure and content of the actor's social relations. Its effects flow from the information, influence, and solidarity it makes available to the actor.
Structural dimension	Definition	The ways in which motivated recipients gain access to actors with desired sets of knowledge
	Findings	Changes in the organizations (e.g., restructuring) may result in holes in the network. Relying on these networks for

		access to knowledge may be problematic.
	Definition	Collaborative mechanisms such as narration and joint work
Cognitive dimension	*Findings*	The shared mental models and shared language of the group will enable the sharing of knowledge within the group. However, pursuit of unique models in each group creates barriers to information sharing between groups in the organization.
Relational dimension	*Definition*	Underlying normative dimensions that guide exchange relationship behaviors.
	Findings	When group norms develop from trust and are cooperative, it can create an environment where information is shared freely. However, norms could be counter-productive if they did not provide any reward for individuals who shared. The conclusion is that 'good' norms are productive, but not all norms are good.
Comments		The two cases presented in this article are different. One deals with a construction company. In this organization, regional engineering managers lead a construction team, but the managers network among themselves as well and are able to develop the cognitive and relational dimensions of social capital. Thus, the manager serves as the bridge between the team and the rest of the organization also. In the other case, which deals with a technology company, the senior manager cannot develop bridging capital in the absence of pro-sharing norms and limited access to other groups. This research presents an interesting case where knowledge needs to be shared within groups and across groups. Theoretically, this requires the concurrent examination of the three dimensions of social capital as well as the bridging and bonding nature of social capital.

Note: Bridging social capital refers to the external linkages of groups, while bonding capital refers to the linkages within groups.

3. Hatzakis, T., Lycett, M., Macredie, R.D., and Martin, V.A. "Towards the Development of a Social Capital Approach to Evaluating Change Management Interventions," European Journal of Information Systems (14:1), Mar 2005, pp 60-74.

Summary	Relational issues between business and IT workers during information systems development (ISD) affect the outcomes of ISD. One interventional technique used in organizations is to employ relationship managers (RM).

		Hatzakis et al propose a framework that may be used to evaluate the efficacy of RM. Social capital could have positive impacts on creativity, innovation, decision-making quality, collaboration, and coordination of work since social capital facilitates access to knowledge resources, expectation of value, motivation, and combination capability.
		The elements of the relational and cognitive dimensions of social capital were assessed using an electronic survey and follow-up interviews. The elements of the structural dimension were assessed only using the follow-up interviews.
Definition of social capital		Follows NG
Structural dimension	*Definition*	Pattern of institutionalized connections between actors
	Elements	Ties Configuration
	Findings	Relationship managers played the role of liaison, but did not develop direct communication across groups. The presence of the RM has loosened the bonds between the units.
Cognitive dimension	*Definition*	Highlights the importance of shared representations, interpretations, and systems of meaning among parties. Represents shared language and codes and shared narratives
	Elements	Shared language and codes Shared narratives
	Findings	The RM worked as the intermediary and helped the development of shared understanding in the short-term.
Relational dimension	*Definition*	Ongoing personal relationships that people fulfill
	Elements	Trust and trustworthiness between actors Norms and social sanctions embedded in social conduct Obligations and expectations Levels of identification and perceptions of social identity
	Findings	Effect of RM on development of social capital between units was mixed. Trust and meeting of obligations increased. However, the RM did not foster identification in the long-term. Participants were unaware of the RM's role in norm development, but commented that the RM

		helped avoid conflict.
Comments		Hatzakis et al recommends changes in the framework based on their analysis of RM interventions.
		While NG suggest that configuration affects access, Hatzakis et al find that changes in configuration alter the expectation of value from collaboration.
		NG suggest that the cognitive dimension affects access, expectation of value, and combination capability. In the text of the article, Hatzakis et al suggests the same, though the graphical representation is different. Their findings indicate that motivation to share knowledge was affected by the element of shared codes and language, and shared codes and language affected motivation.
		Different from NG, Hatzakis et al conclude that trust increases combination capability. Their discussion suggests that trust increases open communication, but does not help conclude this.
		Hatzakis et al's effort is different from other work that examines social capital development between groups or within groups, since the focus is not on the acts of the members of the groups but an RM who acts as a bridge between the groups and is not a member of either group.

4. Inkpen, A.C., and Tsang, E.W.K. "Social Capital, Networks, and Knowledge Transfer," Academy of Management Review (30:1), Jan 2005, pp 146-165.

Summary	Organizations are members of various types of networks. This article focuses on 3: intra-corporate networks, strategic alliances, and industrial districts. The goal is not to cover every type of network, but a representative spectrum including the most-researched forms.
	The article examines how social capital dimensions (following NG) affect an organization's ability to acquire new knowledge and facilitate transfer of knowledge in these three types of networks. The outcome of acquisition of new knowledge is the benefit from social capital.
	This is a conceptual article.
Definition of social capital	Aggregate of resources embedded within, available through, and derived from the network of relationships possessed by an individual or an organization.

Structural dimension	*Definition*	Pattern of relationships between network actors
	Elements	Network ties
		Network configuration
		Network stability - defined as change of membership in a network. (Replaces appropriability because it is an important concept and due to space limitations)
Cognitive dimension	*Definition*	Resources that provide shared meaning and understanding
	Elements	Shared goals – degree to which members share a common understanding and approach to the achievement of network tasks and outcomes
		Shared culture – degree to which norms of behavior govern relationships.
		While the definition of cognitive dimension comes from NG, the elements used in this study are presented without reference to NG's elements.
Relational dimension	*Definition*	
	Elements	Focus only on trust because of space limitations and centrality of trust.
Comments		• Discussion on distinction between social capital as a public good and a private good.
		• Organizational social capital is created based on individual social capital. Interactions between managers determine the relationship between the organizations, especially in strategic alliances.
		• In the discussion of development of shared goals, there is a parallel to the discussion of closure in NG.
		• In the discussion on trust, traces of norms and expectations can be noticed.

Note: Intracorporate network consists of a group of companies operating under a unified corporate identity, with headquarters having controlling interest in subsidiaries. Strategic alliance is a group of firms entering into voluntary arrangements that involve exchange, sharing, or co-development of products, technologies, and services. An industrial district is a network comprising independent firms operating in the same or related market segment and a shared geographic locality, benefiting from external economies of scale and scope from agglomeration.

5. Kankanhalli, A., Tan, B.C.Y., and Wei, K.K. "Contributing Knowledge to Electronic Knowledge Repositories: An Empirical Investigation," MIS Quarterly (29:1), Mar 2005, pp 113-143.

Summary	Electronic knowledge repositories (EKR), a part of KM systems, fail due to lack of contributions from users. Cost factors (loss of knowledge power when knowledge is shared, codification effort involved in sharing knowledge), intrinsic benefit factors (knowledge self-efficacy, enjoyment in helping others) and extrinsic benefit factors (rewards, reciprocity potential, image enhancement) are hypothesized to impact contributions to EKR contingent on contextual factors. These contextual factors include three elements from the relational dimension of social capital: trust, norms, and identification. Using data gathered through a survey, hypotheses were tested.
Comments	Though this article does not apply the NG model per se, this article applied some of the elements from the NG model in a context similar to the original NG context – knowledge sharing within an organization and was therefore included on this list. The findings indicate that the context influences the relevance of these elements in determining the extent of knowledge sharing.
	Since knowledge contribution was voluntary in organizations included in this study, norms (that support sharing) did not have a significant impact on knowledge sharing.
	The potential for reciprocity is important when norms that encourage sharing are weak is not important when the norms are strong.
	When trust is high, codification effort will not deter knowledge sharing since contributors believe that they will receive the credit for the contribution.
	If knowledge contributors do not identify with organizational interests, external rewards will not induce them to share knowledge.
	While NG focus on how social capital results in organizational outcomes such as knowledge sharing, this article examines how the costs and benefits associated with knowledge sharing are moderated by aspects of the relational dimension of social capital.

6. Kumar, R., and Worm, V. "Social Capital and the Dynamics of Business Negotiations between the Northern Europeans and the Chinese," *International Marketing Review* (20:3) 2003, pp 262-285.

Summary		Kumar and Worm draw on the concept of social capital to explain how the characteristics of a pre-existing relationship affect the negotiation process and outcomes between two organizations. Based on interviews with respondents from Danish and Chinese firms, this article examines how social capital affects inter-cultural negotiation processes. The findings suggest that the presence of social capital determines the capability of the participants to overcome problems during interaction and reveal differences between the Danes and the Chinese in interactions. Additionally, the study presented findings on Chinese negotiating behavior that contradict past findings, indicating a change in Chinese organizations.
Definition of social capital		Resource reflecting the character of the social relations within the organization realized through collective levels of goal orientation and shared trust. This definition fits with NG's conceptualization of social capital as a resource, but highlights one element each of NG's relational and cognitive dimensions. The authors go on immediately to discuss the dimensions, so it is not clear why this definition was presented.
Structural dimension	*Definition*	Overall pattern of connectivity
	Elements	Mix of factors that constitute the dimension: • Ties • Configuration • Presence of intermediaries And factors that affect the dimension: • Long-term orientation • Amount of socializing • Communicative style – direct or indirect
Cognitive dimension	*Definition*	Focuses on degree of shared understanding among actors achieved through use of similar schematic frameworks
	Elements	Mix of factors that constitute the dimension: • Mutual understanding of goals and objectives • Communication effectiveness – each party's ability to understand the other And a factor that affects the dimension:

		• Similarity in persuasive styles
Relational dimension	*Definition*	Affective bonding among actors
	Elements	Mix of factors that constitute the dimension: • Trust • Obligations • Flexibility (willingness to work together) • Willingness to exchange information freely (The last two could be classified as norms. The missing element is identification. In this cross-cultural situation, the interactional problems arise from lack of identification) And factors that affect the dimension: • Attitude towards time – willingness to devote time to the negotiation. Duration of the relationship is a factor that affects social capital in NG. • 'Face' management – ensuring that one party does not lose 'face' (roughly translates to 'prestige') during negotiations: Could be considered as a specific 'obligation' arising from knowledge of the other party
Comments		While the findings are interesting, this research combines factors that affect social capital with elements of social capital. The authors state that the clusters of elements for each dimension emerged from the analysis of the qualitative data than pre-fixed codes and introduce a listing of elements for each dimension. This is confusing since it is not clear how these elements fit in with the definition and how they fit together.

7. Lee, S.H., Wong, P.K., and Chong, C.L. "Human and Social Capital Explanations for R&D Outcomes," *Ieee Transactions on Engineering Management* (52:1), Feb 2005, pp 59-68.

Summary	An individual's R & D outcomes are influenced by personal capabilities (human capital perspective) and interactions with others (social capital perspective). To explain the latter, the authors draw on NG and related dimensions of social capital to R & D outcomes. Data was gathered from over 1000 employees of R &

		D organizations in Singapore in 1997. R & D outcomes were assessed using perceptions of one's productivity and actual numbers of completed projects. Gender was used as a control variable since it has an influence on research productivity in Singapore. Type of industry (service or manufacturing) was also included as a control variable. Hierarchical logistic regression analysis was used to examine the incremental effect of social capital over human capital.
Definition of social capital		Follows NG
Structural dimension	*Definition*	Overall pattern of connections and linkages that an individual has with others.
		Refers to network ties between individuals. The more ties one has, the better one's access to information.
		Captured as perceived support from superiors, persuading other professionals within organization, keeping others informed, and ties to external parties.
	Findings	Ties to professionals within one's organization was useful to increase productivity, but not ties to external parties.
Cognitive dimension	*Definition*	Resources that are available to an individual from having shared expectations as team members interpret cues in a similar manner, make compatible decisions, and coordinate their actions.
		Captured as shared expectations related to research goals and responsibilities.
	Findings	The existence of shared expectations increased perceptions of productivity, but not actual productivity. A positive bias may exist when one works in an environment where a high degree of agreement exists.
Relational dimension	*Definition*	Nature of relationship with others.
		In a research context, creativity and innovation are important. Informal relationships support innovation and creativity by brainstorming of ideas. The structural dimension is captured by the level of informality in the individual's relationships.
	Findings	Marginal effect
Comments		The authors stayed with the definitions of the dimensions from NG, while identifying an element to capture each dimension. However, it is not clear why

		these alone are chosen. For example, in the relational dimension, trust may be an important consideration in sharing of new ideas, again supporting innovation and creativity.
		One notable attribute of the model is that it focuses on individual level outcomes and not on group level outcomes as in NG. Thus social capital within the group and the individual's human capital are related to individual level outcomes.

8. Lesser, E.L., and Storck, J. "Communities of Practice and Organizational Performance," *IBM Systems Journal* (40:4) 2001, pp 831-841.

Summary		While research has shown that communities of practice (CoP) produce value, the linkage between the social interactions in CoP and the community outcomes has not been well explained. Lesser and Storck posit that communities enable the development of social capital. This social capital enhances knowledge sharing, positively influencing business performance. Data were gathered through interviews at seven companies with functional CoP.
Definition of social capital		Follows NG
Structural dimension	*Definition*	Series of connections individuals have to others.
		Ability of individuals to make connections to others.
	Findings	Recommended mechanisms for developing this dimension:
		Face-to-face meetings
		Leveraging ICTs
Cognitive dimension	*Definition*	Common interest or common understanding of issues facing the organization
	Findings	Recommended mechanisms for developing this dimension:
		Face-to-face meetings
		Discussion boards
Relational dimension	*Definition*	A sense of trust (Lesser and Storck acknowledge that this is only one aspect of the relational dimension)
	Findings	Recommended mechanisms for developing this dimension:

		Development of taxonomies
		Sharing of experiences
Comments		While Lesser and Storck list the elements of the three dimensions as identified by NG, the focus is on the relationships between the dimensions of social capital and business outcomes – decreasing the learning curve, increasing responsiveness to customers, reducing rework, and increasing innovation. The structural dimension provides connections that help locate experts and individuals with similar experiences and find relevant artifacts. The relational dimension supports mentoring and coaching of new employees, willingness to respond to queries, enhancement of reputation, and an environment conducive to brainstorming and testing new ideas. Similarly, the cognitive dimension provides the means to understand rules of the organization and identify important problems and relevant knowledge.

9. Li, L.Y. "An Examination of the Foreign Market Knowledge of Exporting Firms Based in the People's Republic of China: Its Determinants and Effect on Export Intensity," *Industrial Marketing Management* (33:7), Oct 2004, pp 561-572.

Summary		The basic premise of this article is that export market knowledge (knowledge of laws, regulations, norms of foreign market) determine export intensity (percentage of sales exported). Export market knowledge is influenced by the structural and relational dimensions of social capital. Using data gathered from respondents in Chinese firms across various industries, these propositions were tested. Both structural and relational dimensions of social capital have an effect on foreign market knowledge.
Definition of social capital		Follows NG In this study, two forms of social capital have been included: 1, intra-firm structural social capital, 2, inter-firm relational social capital
Structural dimension	*Definition*	Intra-firm structural social capital refers to overall pattern of connections between individuals within a given firm. Impersonal configuration of linkages between people
	Elements	1. Group based decision making

		2. Structural integration within organization (includes mechanisms such as inter-departmental task force, mechanisms for sharing information, etc) These two factors will affect access to knowledge resources within the organization. NG explained that the structural dimension of social capital would affect access, and hence these two factors fit within the structural dimension.
	Findings	Structural integration did not have a significant effect.
Relational dimension	*Definition*	Assets created and leveraged through relationships.
	Elements	Norms of cooperation, dependence, and perceived importance of partner are important in this context since they define the quality of interaction with the partner
	Findings	Norms of cooperation have a negative impact on providing foreign market knowledge. This finding is consistent with past research in this area and emphasizes the negative side of cooperation that fosters groupthink and inhibits gaining additional knowledge.
Comments		In this article, structural dimension was considered at the intra-organizational level while the relational dimension was considered at the inter-organizational level. The definitions of both follow NG. It would seem that in this situation where knowledge is communicated within the group and acquired from external parties, the cognitive dimension providing shared interpretations and sense of meaning would be important. However, the cognitive dimension is not mentioned and the absence of the dimension is not explained.

10. Llewellyn, N., and Armistead, C. "Business Process Management - Exploring Social Capital within Processes," *International Journal of Service Industry Management* (11:3) 2000, pp 225-243.

Summary	This article presents a qualitative study that describes how social capital supports business processes in a service industry. It is proposed that social capital will help smooth over operational problems (unknown service parameters, service failure, etc) by providing a lubricant to reduce friction in the process and enabling the required knowledge transfer and

		coordination.
		Empirical research was conducted in a large telecom company, following a qualitative approach. The interview protocol focused on questions that would reveal the nature of interactions than on specific dimensions and elements.
Definition of social capital		Follows NG
Structural dimension	*Definition*	Network configuration and linkages
	Elements	Configuration
		Favored routes across functional boundaries for communication
Cognitive dimension	*Definition*	Resources used to articulate shared interpretations and systems of meaning among parties
	Elements	Shared customer service ethic – provides a collective rationale for action and a shared way of thinking and interpreting events.
		Shared language – use of common terms
Relational dimension	*Definition*	Interpersonal ties, affective bonds
	Elements	Trust
		Friendship
		Rapport
Comments		Data showed that social capital was effective in dealing with service recovery situations, coping with technology problems, and dealing with emergencies.
		This was one of the first articles reporting the use of the three dimensions of social capital in empirical research. In applying the NG framework, the researchers started with the definitions from NG, but did not use the same set of elements as NG. This is not a critical issue as long as the identified elements show the manifestation of the dimension in the selected context. Such specification would help ensure that the discussion stays focused within the particular context. However, a problem here was the use of different sets of elements in various sections discussing the dimensions.

11. Massimo, M., and Proserpio, L. "Users' Beliefs Towards Technology: A Social Capital

Perspective," European Conference on Information Systems, 2005.

Summary		Past research focusing on social factors in IT acceptance has considered either the network structure or the influence of norms on users. This article proposes a model that combines the above two perspectives along with the quality of network connections. Social capital in the user community can build perceptual congruence toward the technology among users. Massimo and Proserpio employ the social capital framework along with the concept of subjective norms to build the model. The presence of dimensions of social capital will reduce the deviation from perceptual congruence among members of the user community regarding ease of use and usefulness of the technology. The paper presents these arguments, but does not contain empirical work.
Definition of social capital		Resources embedded in a social structure that are accessed and/or mobilized for purposive action
Structural dimension	Definition	Concerns existence of connections among individuals. Refers to the configuration of social ties among individuals. While Massimo and Proserpio focus only on the configuration element of the structural dimension, they have identified three aspects of this dimension for this particular context of technology adoption.
	Elements	Actor centrality – Position of actor in the network structure. An individual in a central position is more accessible to others and hence will be more subject to influence of group members. Relational proximity – Frequency of interaction, repeated interaction Spatial proximity – Geographical proximity
Cognitive dimension	Definition	Attributes that facilitate the common understanding of the social context
	Elements	Shared language and vocabulary
Relational dimension	Definition	Quality of connections among individuals
	Elements	Trust – willingness to be vulnerable to another. When there is trust, the sender will be willing to share information about the system and the receiver can accept the information without verification.

		Interpersonal cohesion – Desire to remain inside the group. An affective relationship among group members, cohesion has a positive impact on communication and will thus contribute to sharing of beliefs about systems
		Identification – Perceive themselves to be members of the same social category. When there is high level of identification, there is uniformity in intragroup opinions and behaviors.
Comments		Within the structural dimension, Massimo and Proserpio assume the presence of ties. They do not include the concept of "appropriable organization," but that would not be relevant in this context. The focus is on elements that would be relevant in a situation where a common agreement has to be reached within the group.

12. Sherif, K., Hoffman, J., and Wetherbe, J. "Can Technology Build Organizational Social Capital: The Case of a Global It Consulting Firm," Americas Conference on Information Systems, New York, New York, 2004.

Summary		Past research on Knowledge Management Systems (KMS) suggests that these KMS aid in the creation and transfer of knowledge. However, it is not clear how KMS create knowledge. The authors posit that KMS enables the development of social capital between the interactants using the KMS and the social capital that enables the creation of knowledge.
		A case study was conducted in an multinational IT consulting firm, which is recognized as a pioneer in knowledge management. The technology used was k-web, a KM tool.
Definition of social capital		Cites Nahapiet and Ghoshal – page 243
Structural dimension	*Definition*	Information channels that connect individuals and units.
	Elements	Includes ties and network configuration. Network configuration refers to density, connectivity, hierarchy, and adaptability of network. .
		Does not mention "appropriable organization."
		The hypothesis is that KMS allows the members of the network to develop a central location within the network.

	Findings	Better connectivity and increased frequency of communication supported by trust and a sense of identity helped the users of k-web establish a "central location" within the network.	
Cognitive dimension	*Definition*	Engages in emerging a shared meaning and a shared understanding of the purpose of the networked community	
	Elements	Focuses on common language and shared stories	
	Findings	Common language emerged through threaded discussions within virtual communities. Experiences were recorded in the KMS	
Relational dimension	*Definition*	Assets created and leveraged through relationships	
	Elements	Includes all 4 elements. Usage of KMS will enable the development of trust by allowing for interaction using discussion boards and chat rooms. Further, such interaction will support the evolution of norms that govern their interaction and will define the obligations of all involved. This will also help establish the community identity.	
	Findings	Trust: k-web helped build trust through a feature that keeps track of use of resources Norms: Norms were transmitted via messages to all members Obligations: Norms created and reinforced obligations (essentially set expectations) k-web also helped build reputation for those who contribute valuable assets.	
Comments		Adds an element to the structural dimension termed adaptability, defined as ability of the network to reconfigure itself. It is not used in the analysis. Does not further the analysis of the social capital dimensions from NG.	

Note: KMS is defined as "a class of information systems applied to managing organizational knowledge…they are IT based systems developed to support and enhance the organizational processes of knowledge creation, storage/retrieval, transfer, and application." (p. 2332)

13. Tsai, W.P. "Social Capital, Strategic Relatedness and the Formation of Intraorganizational Linkages," Strategic Management Journal (21:9), Sep 2000, pp 925-939.

Summary		This article investigates how inter-unit linkages for transfer and sharing of resources between different business units in an organization are formed. Using the concepts of strategic relatedness and social capital, Tsai examine show linkages are created. Data gathered from managers of a large multinational organization via surveys and interviews were analyzed to determine the effects of network centrality, trustworthiness, and strategic relatedness on linkage formation.
Definition of social capital		Relational resources attainable by social actors through networks of social relationships
Structural dimension	Definition	Location in social network – network centrality. Confers access advantages
	Findings	• Has a strong impact on linkage formation • Has a strong impact on linkage formation between strategically related units
Relational dimension	Definition	Trustworthiness
	Findings	• Has a strong impact on linkage formation between strategically related units • By itself, is likely to affect linkage formation (not a strong relationship)
Comments		Limits discussion to these two elements of social capital, and does not even mention the other dimension or the other elements.

Note: Strategic relatedness between two organizations implies that these have prior related knowledge that allows effective utilization of new knowledge.

14. Wang, J. "The Role of Social Capital in Open Source Software Communities," Americas Conference on Information Systems, 2005.

Summary	The success of open source software (OSS) projects depends not only on the characteristics of the individual developers, but also on the characteristics of the community as well. Wang proposes a two-level model that combines these two levels of analysis (individual and community). At the individual level, intrinsic motivation, personal needs and expectations of future returns drive the members of the development

	community to participate in the project. Through the use of the Internet, aspiring developers have the opportunity to participate in the development of OSS. Collective goals motivate them while the ability to exchange information via common codes and schemes enables their participation. This encourages the development of different dimensions of social capital in the community. The social capital of the community determines the outcomes of the project.
	This article only proposes a model (copied below). There is no empirical work.
Definition of social capital	Valuable resources embedded in social ties within a collectivity
Comments	Wang discusses the various dimensions of social capital, as identified by NG. He does not add any element to the list, nor drop any. The discussion follows along the lines of NG since the context of the article is similar to NG's: an inter-group knowledge exchange and combination.

15. Wasko, M.M., and Faraj, S. "Why Should I Share? Examining Social Capital and Knowledge Contribution in Electronic Networks of Practice," Mis Quarterly (29:1), Mar 2005, pp 35-57.

Summary	This article examines why people voluntarily contribute knowledge and help others through electronic networks*. Electronic networks can be viewed as a "network of practice" – a large, loosely knot group of individuals engaged in a shared practice, but who may not know each other or expect to meet f-t-f. In electronic networks, sharing occurs primarily through ICTs. An electronic network of practice (eNoP) is defined as a self-organizing, open activity system focused ona shared practice that exists primarily through computer-mediated communication.
	Researchers in social capital have argued that significant levels of social capital and knowledge exchange will not develop in eNoP.
	The hypotheses related individual motivations and the three dimensions of social capital to knowledge contribution (sheer volume and volume of useful responses) in eNoP.
	Data were collected from members of the eNoP of a

		U.S. legal professional organization. Contributions were not anonymous.
Definition of social capital		Resources embedded in a social structure that are accessed and/or mobilized in purposive action
Structural dimension	Definition	Dense connections
	Elements	Network centrality – more direct ties with others
	Findings	Strongly supported for usefulness and volume of contributions
Cognitive dimension	Definition	Resources that make possible shared interpretations and meanings within a collection.
	Elements	Individual expertise - Mastery of the language
		Experience with applying the expertise - tenure
	Findings	Tenure in field influences volume of contributions
Relational dimension	Definition	Affective nature of relationships
	Elements	Reciprocity – Sense of mutual indebtedness
		Commitment – obligation to engage in future action
		(from past research on eNoP)
	Findings	Commitment has a weak, positive relationship with usefulness. It was seen that commitment was acting as a suppressor variable while reputation and centrality variables were present. Once those impacts are considered, higher levels of commitment predict lower levels of helpfulness – a confusing finding.
		Reciprocity affects volume of contributions negatively.
		In general, the findings provide support for previous research that indicated that the relational dimension of social capital may not develop in eNoP.

*Note similarity to citizenship behavior from Bolino et al.

16. Willcocks, L., Hindle, J., Feeny, D., and Lacity, M. "IT and Business Process Outsourcing: The Knowledge Potential," Information Systems Management (21:3), Sum 2004, pp 7-15.

Summary	Five possible options for sourcing are discussed: Do-it-yourself, management consultancy, outsourcing IT, fee-for-service BPO, and enterprise partnership. Drawing upon the extensive case database these researchers hold, the article presents examples of each and explains how enterprise partnership offers the best possible arrangement for knowledge sharing because of the presence of social

	capital. The authors state that the enterprise partnership model, where a risk and reward sharing partnership is established between client and supplier, is rich in all dimensions of social capital and produces the best outcomes.
Definition of social capital	Follows NG.
Structural dimension	Formal governance networks and a jointly held organization
Cognitive dimension	A competency model that defines seven knowledge-based capabilities is employed in the enterprise-partnership model: service, people, process, technology, environment, sourcing and implementation. These competencies employ distinctive languages and codes. Communities formed for the development of these competencies provide an environment for sharing of narratives.
Relational dimension	In the creation of an enterprise partnership model, the employees are relocated and trained extensively. This effort builds group identity and trust, establishes norms of behavior and performance, and instills a sense of mutual obligation.
Comments	The goal of the discussion is to show that social capital facilitates the knowledge exchange necessary in outsourcing.

17. Ye, F., and Agarwal, R. "Strategic IT Partnerships in Outsourcing as an Distinctive Source of It Value: A Social Capital Perspective," International Conference on Information Systems, 2003.

Summary	This article presents a conceptual model of the contributions of social capital to learning in an outsourcing partnership. An outsourcing partnership involves flows of knowledge and ongoing inter-organizational learning between the client and the vendor organizations. "Partnership" suggests long-term commitment, cooperation, shared risk and benefits*, and other attributes related to participatory decision-making and joint action. NG's social capital framework is used as a "relational lens based on knowledge exchange and learning" that takes place in an outsourcing partnership. Hypotheses are framed relating social capital dimensions to outcomes for the focal firm.
Definition of social capital	Follows NG

Structural dimension	*Definition*	Overall pattern of connections between actors
	Elements	• Resource endowment of partner (size, financial abundance, and diversity (of knowledge?)) • Power asymmetry – The authors state that the nature of the contract can influence the way the organizations interact.
Cognitive dimension	*Definition*	Resources providing shared representations, interpretations, and systems of meaning across parties
	Elements	• Shared vision regarding common goals • Shared mental model – relatedness of knowledge base • The authors comment on the need for shared language, but do not state that as a proposition
Relational dimension	*Definition*	Assets created and leveraged through relationships, and parallel to what was described as behavioral as opposed to structural
	Elements	Trust
Comments		• The expectation of value and motivation and combination capability enter this model as moderating factors. These conditions facilitated the combination and exchange of knowledge in NG. • The definition of partnerships includes the dimensions of the relational dimension, leaving trust as the only element in the relational dimension. • On page 308, Ye and Agarwal state that the strategic partnership "is a form of social capital" for the focal firm. They do not elaborate on this and it is not clear how this is captured in the propositions.

*Note similarity to enterprise partnership model in Willcocks et al. Strategic intent is the motivation to use alliance as an opportunity to learn.

Summary Comments:

• All articles define social capital as a resource. Many restate the social capital definition from NG.

• Levels of analysis: NG social capital model (whole or parts) was used to explain individual level, within group and across group levels, organizational level, and inter-organizational outcomes.

• Public good versus private good: Depending on the level of analysis and the context, social capital is seen as a public good available to all in the collective or as a resource to be mobilized by the individual social unit.

• While a few articles discussed the negative aspects of social capital, many acknowledge the costs and risks of social capital. Most discussion placed social capital in a positive light, following the general approach in this area of research.

- Most articles focused on knowledge transfer and acquisition. This is natural given that NG have established a theoretical connection between social capital and intellectual capital creation and (implicitly) business outcomes (Bolino et al, 2002)

Table listing articles using NG as theoretical lens

Review of genitive and relational dimensions continue on page 276

Article	Context/ Objective	Use of NG	Form of social capital	Structural			
				Ties	*Configuration*	*Appropriable organization*	**Comments**
Inkpen and Tsang (2005)	Three network types: intracorporate networks, industrial districts, strategic alliances. How does social capital contribute to knowledge transfer in these three different networks?		Recognizes social capital as a public good and private good. No empirical work.	X Role of boundary spanners recognized - individual social capital forms the basis of organizational social capital.	X elements of configuration as hierarchy, density, and connectivity affect the flexibility and ease of knowledge exchange through their impact on the extent of contact and accessibility among network members	Replaced with network stability - defined as change of membership in a network. (Owing to space limitations, we focus on facets that are most related to knowledge transfer between network members. (footnote, pg. 152))	
Bolino et al (2002)	How does organizational citizenship behavior characterized by obedience, loyalty, participation contribute to development of SC, which		Individual level	X	X	X	

271

	contributes to org. performance ?						
Sherif et al (2004)	KM systems promote developmen t of social capital, which in turn promotes developmen t of knowledge		Individual level	X	X		
Wang (2005)	Social capital can promote exchanges in the OSS community - conceptual article	Includes all aspects of NG model; no empirical study					
Edelman et al (2004)	Is more social capital better? Studies (quali) within two organization re info access & retrieval, etc		Individual level				General notion of structural dimension providing access
Hatzakis et al (2005)	Does social capital serve as an evaluative mechanism for relationship managers' intervention s? Outcomes looked at were work coordination and	Revised model →	Individual level	X	X		

	creativity & innovation (instead of IC). Case study						
Lesser and Storck (2001)	SC develops in communitie s of practice	Includes all aspects of NG model except appropriab le organizati on; no detailed analysis					
Lee et al (2005)	Beyond individual's own capabilities, social capital also contributes to R & D performance	R & D outcomes are affected by network ties (structural) , informal relationshi ps with others (relational) and shared expectatio ns with others (cognitive)	Individual level	X			
Willcocks et al (2004)	Various outsourcing models	Includes all aspects of NG except appropriab le organizati on - brief discussion. Enterprise partnershi p model rich in social capital.	Organizati onal level.				

273

Li (2004)	In exporting firms, does relational social capital in the inter-firm relationship and structural social capital in the organization contribute to foreign market knowledge?		Organizational level				Group decision making and structural integration mechanisms represent structural dimension
Ye and Agarwal (2003)	How does SC contribute to learning in an outsourcing partnership? No empirical data	SC can be used as a "relational lens based on knowledge exchange and learning" that takes place in an outsourcing partnership	Organizational level				Resource endowment (size, financial abundance, diversity), nature of contract and power asymmetry
Llewellyn and Armistead (2000)	How does SC support business processes in a service industry? Quali. study		Individual level	X	X		Structural dimension evident in reciprocity and flexibility in interaction
Kumar and Worm (2003)	How does SC facilitate the negotiations between Danish and Chinese managers? Quali. Study		Individual level				Pattern of connectivity as seen in network ties; network configurations; intermediaries; and communications configuration and

							socializing.
Tsai (2000)	How do organization al units create linkages for resource exchange?		Unit level - aggregatio n of individual data				
Wasko and Faraj (2005)	How do motivations and social capital at the individual level influence knowledge contribution in electronic networks? Quantitative . Study		Individual level		Network centrality		
Kankanha lli et al (2005)	Social exchange theory is used to identify cost and benefit factors affecting electronic knowledge repositories usage, and social capital theory to account for the moderating influence of contextual factors. Quantitative		Individual level				

	study.						
Massimo and Proserpio (2005)	Previous studies on technology adoption have considered social sanction and social influence, without considering the quality of social relationships. Using SC perspective, link all three.	Propositions developed in the form of dimensions of SC negatively related to deviation from group's perception of usefulness and group's perception of eou.	Individual level		Centrality, relational and geographic proximity		

	Cognitive			Relational				
Article	Shared langua ge & codes	Shared narrativ es	Comments	Trust	Norms	Obligati ons	Identificati on	Comments
			The two facets addressed are shared goals and shared culture among network members. Shared goals represent the degree to which network members share a	X Focus only on trust because of space limitation s and centrality of trust.				

			common understanding and approach to the achievement of network tasks and outcomes. Shared culture refers to the degree to which norms of behavior govern relationships					
Inkpen and Tsang (2005)	X	X		X			X	Included affection as part of relational dimension
Bolino et al (2002)	X	X		X	X	X	X	
Sherif et al (2004)								
Wang (2005)			Cognitive dimension - sharing of ideas through joint work and narration	X	Some norms are good; others not. Norms of conformity, control and compliance can deter innovation			

Edelman et al (2004)	X	X		X	Finding: ROMs actions have no effect on norm developm ent	X	Finding: RMs actions reduces identificat ion	
Hatzakis et al (2005)								
Lesser and Storck (2001)			Shared expectations					Informal relationships with others
Lee et al (2005)								
Willcock s et al (2004)								Cooperation, dependency, and relational importance represent inter-firs relational dimension
Li (2004)	X		Shared mental model and shared vision	X				
Ye and Agarwal (2003)	X	X	Cognitive dimension evident in shared work ethic	X				Also included emotional bonds and friendship Relational dimension evident as trust, rapport, and respect

278

Llewelly n and Armistea d (2000)			Checked for cognitive similarity - mutual understandi ng of each other's goals/objecti ves; similarity in persuasive styles; and communicat ive effectivenes s, i.e. how well do the parties understand each other.	X				Checked for attitudes of the negotiators towards time, their trust perceptions, face management, pattern of information exchange, perceptions of flexibility, and the management of obligations.
Kumar and Worm (2003)				X			
Tsai (2000)			Expertise and tenure in the field		Norms of commitm ent and reciprocit y			
Wasko and Faraj (2005)				X	Norms - "pro-sharing": cooperatio n collaborat ion teamwork openness tolerance		X	
Kankanh alli et al (2005)							
Massimo and Proserpio (2005)							

List of Articles that have cited Nahapiet and Ghoshal (1998 – September 2005):

1. Adam, F., and Roncevic, B. "Social Capital: Recent Debates and Research Trends," *Social Science Information Sur Les Sciences Sociales* (42:2), Jun 2003, pp 155-183.

2. Adler, P.S. "Market, Hierarchy, and Trust: The Knowledge Economy and the Future of Capitalism," *Organization Science* (12:2), Mar-Apr 2001, pp 215-234.

3. Adler, P.S., and Kwon, S.W. "Social Capital: Prospects for a New Concept," *Academy of Management Review* (27:1), Jan 2002, pp 17-40.

4. Adner, R., and Helfat, C.E. "Corporate Effects and Dynamic Managerial Capabilities," *Strategic Management Journal* (24:10), Oct 2003, pp 1011-1025.

5. Alvesson, M., and Karreman, D. "Odd Couple: Making Sense of the Curious Concept of Knowledge Management," *Journal of Management Studies* (38:7), Nov 2001, pp 995-1018.

6. Anand, V., Glick, W.H., and Manz, C.C. "Thriving on the Knowledge of Outsiders: Tapping Organizational Social Capital," *Academy of Management Executive* (16:1), Feb 2002, pp 87-101.

7. Anderson, A.R., and Jack, S.L. "The Articulation of Social Capital in Entrepreneurial Networks: A Glue or a Lubricant?," *Entrepreneurship and Regional Development* (14:3), Jul-Sep 2002, pp 193-210.

8. Andersson, U., Forsgren, M., and Holm, U. "The Strategic Impact of External Networks: Subsidiary Performance and Competence Development in the Multinational Corporation," *Strategic Management Journal* (23:11), Nov 2002, pp 979-996.

9. Andrews, K.M., and Delahaye, B.L. "Influences on Knowledge Processes in Organizational Learning: The Psychosocial Filter," *Journal of Management Studies* (37:6), Sep 2000, pp 797-810.

10. Arenius, P., and De Clercq, D. "A Network-Based Approach on Opportunity Recognition," *Small Business Economics* (24:3), Apr 2005, pp 249-265.

11. Armstrong, C.P., and Sambamurthy, V. "Information Technology Assimilation in Firms: The Influence of Senior Leadership and It Infrastructures," *Information Systems Research* (10:4), Dec 1999, pp 304-327.

12. Arthur, M.B., DeFillippi, R., and Jones, C. "Project-Based Learning as the Interplay of Career and Company Non-Financial Capital," *Management Learning* (32:1), Mar 2001, pp 99-117.

13. Autio, E., Hameri, A.P., and Vuola, O. "A Framework of Industrial Knowledge Spillovers in Big-Science Centers," *Research Policy* (33:1), Jan 2004, pp 107-126.

14. Avrahami, Y., and Lerner, M. "The Effect of Combat Service and Military Rank on Entrepreneurial Careers: The Case of Israeli Mba Graduates," *Journal of Political & Military Sociology* (31:1), Sum 2003, pp 97-118.

15. Bagley, C., Ackerley, C.L., and Rattray, J. "Social Exclusion, Sure Start and Organizational Social Capital: Evaluating Inter-Disciplinary Multi-Agency Working in an Education and Health Work Programme," *Journal of Education Policy* (19:5), Sep 2004, pp 595-607.

16. Baker, T., Gedajlovic, E., and Lubatkin, M. "A Framework for Comparing Entrepreneurship Processes across Nations," *Journal of International Business Studies*

(36:5), Sep 2005, pp 492-504.

17. Balatti, J., and Falk, I. "Socioeconomic Contributions of Adult Learning to Community: A Social Capital Perspective," *Adult Education Quarterly* (52:4), Aug 2002, pp 281-298.

18. Balijepally, V., Mahapatra, R., and Nerur, S. "Social Capital: A Theoretical Lens for Is Research," Americas Conference on Information Systems, New York, 2004.

19. Baron, R.A. "Ob and Entrepreneurship: The Reciprocal Benefits of Closer Conceptual Links," in: *Research in Organizational Behavior, Vol 24*, 2002, pp. 225-269.

20. Baron, R.A., and Markman, G.D. "Beyond Social Capital: The Role of Entrepreneurs' Social Competence in Their Financial Success," *Journal of Business Venturing* (18:1), Jan 2003, pp 41-60.

21. Barreto, C., and Heckman, R. "Understanding Knowledge Sharing Motivators within Knowledge Management Initiatives," Americas Conference on Information Systems, 2004.

22. Batt, P.J. "Examining the Performance of the Supply Chain for Potatoes in the Red River Delta Using a Pluralistic Approach," *Supply Chain Management-an International Journal* (8:5) 2003, pp 442-454.

23. Becerra-Fernandez, I., and Sabherwal, R. "Organizational Knowledge Management: A Contingency Perspective," *Journal of Management Information Systems* (18:1), Sum 2001, pp 23-55.

24. Becker, M.C. "Managing Dispersed Knowledge: Organizational Problems, Managerial Strategies, and Their Effectiveness," *Journal of Management Studies* (38:7), Nov 2001, pp 1037-1051.

25. Becker, M.C., and Zirpoli, F. "Organizing New Product Development - Knowledge Hollowing-out and Knowledge Integration - the Fiat Auto Case," *International Journal of Operations & Production Management* (23:9) 2003, pp 1033-1061.

26. Bhandar, M., Pan, S.-L., Tan, B., and Goh, P.-G. "Roles of Social Capital in Collaborative Is Projects," European Conference on Information Systems, 2005.

27. Bhatt, G.D. "Managing Is Competence for Competitive Advanatge: An Empirical Analysis," International Conference on Information Systems, 2003.

28. Blyler, M., and Coff, R.W. "Dynamic Capabilities, Social Capital, and Rent Appropriation: Ties That Split Pies," *Strategic Management Journal* (24:7), Jul 2003, pp 677-686.

29. Boele, R., Fabig, H., and Wheeler, D. "Shell, Nigeria and the Ogoni. A Study in Unsustainable Development: Ii. Corporate Social Responsibility and "Stakeholder Management' Versus a Rights-Based Approach to Sustainable Development," *Sustainable Development* (9:3), Aug 2001, pp 121-135.

30. Boh, W.F. "Knowledge Sharing Mechanisms in Project-Based Knowledge Work: Codification Versus Personalization," International Conference on Information Systems, 2003.

31. Bolino, M.C., Turnley, W.H., and Bloodgood, J.M. "Citizenship Behavior and the Creation of Social Capital in Organizations," *Academy of Management Review* (27:4), Oct 2002, pp 505-522.

32. Bollingtoft, A., and Ulhoi, J.P. "The Networked Business Incubator - Leveraging

Entrepreneurial Agency?," *Journal of Business Venturing* (20:2), Mar 2005, pp 265-290.

33. Bozeman, B., Dietz, J.S., and Gaughan, M. "Scientific and Technical Human Capital: An Alternative Model for Research Evaluation," *International Journal of Technology Management* (22:7-8) 2001, pp 716-740.

34. Bresnen, M., Edelman, L., Newell, S., Scarbrough, H., and Swan, J. "Exploring Social Capital in the Construction Firm," *Building Research and Information* (33:3), May-Jun 2005, pp 235-244.

35. Brush, C.G., Greene, P.G., and Hart, M.M. "From Initial Idea to Unique Advantage: The Entrepreneurial Challenge of Constructing a Resource Base," *Academy of Management Executive* (15:1), Feb 2001, pp 64-78.

36. Bryant, S.E. "The Impact of Peer Mentoring on Organizational Knowledge Creation and Sharing - an Empirical Study in a Software Firm," *Group & Organization Management* (30:3), Jun 2005, pp 319-338.

37. Burns, A.T. "Dissecting the Black Box: A Knowledge Management System for Transferring Levels of Technical Knowledge," Americas Conference on Information Systems, 2004.

38. Burt, R.S. "The Network Structure of Social Capital," in: *Research in Organizational Behavior, Vol 22, 2000,* 2000, pp. 345-423.

39. Burt, R.S. "Decay Functions," *Social Networks* (22:1), Jan 2000, pp 1-28.

40. Burt, R.S. "Structural Holes and Good Ideas," *American Journal of Sociology* (110:2), Sep 2004, pp 349-399.

41. Cabrera, A., and Cabrera, E.F. "Knowledge-Sharing Dilemmas," *Organization Studies* (23:5) 2002, pp 687-710.

42. Cabrera, E.F., and Cabrera, A. "Fostering Knowledge Sharing through People Management Practices," *International Journal of Human Resource Management* (16:5), May 2005, pp 720-735.

43. Cameron, K.S., Bright, D., and Caza, A. "Exploring the Relationships between Organizational Virtuousness and Performance," *American Behavioral Scientist* (47:6), Feb 2004, pp 766-790.

44. Cappelli, P. "Why Do Employers Retrain at-Risk Workers? The Role of Social Capital," *Industrial Relations* (43:2), Apr 2004, pp 421-447.

45. Certo, S.T. "Influencing Initial Public Offering Investors with Prestige: Signaling with Board Structures," *Academy of Management Review* (28:3), Jul 2003, pp 432-446.

46. Chae, B., Koch, H., Paradice, D., and Van Huy, V. "Exploring Knowledge Management Using Network Theories: Questions, Paradoxes and Prospects," *Journal of Computer Information Systems* (45:4), Sum 2005, pp 62-74.

47. Chae, B., Koch, H., and Van, H.V. "Knowledge Management in Communities and Networks of Practice: Challenges, Issues and Paradoxes," Americas Conference on Information Systems, 2003.

48. Chellappa, R., and Saraf, N. "Standards and Alliances in Non-Standardised Software Industries," Americas Conference on Information Systems, 2000.

49. Choi, B., and Lee, H. "An Empirical Investigation of Km Styles and Their Effect on Corporate Performance," *Information & Management* (40:5), May 2003, pp 403-417.

50. Chou, S.W., and He, M.Y. "Knowledge Management: The Distinctive Roles of Knowledge Assets in Facilitating Knowledge Creation," *Journal of Information Science* (30:2) 2004, pp 146-164.

51. Chuang, S.H. "A Resource-Based Perspective on Knowledge Management Capability and Competitive Advantage: An Empirical Investigation," *Expert Systems with Applications* (27:3), Oct 2004, pp 459-465.

52. Coakes, E. "Knowledge Management - a Primer," *Communications of the Association for Information Systems* (4:14) 2004, pp 406-489.

53. Cooper, L.P. "A Research Agenda to Reduce Risk in New Product Development through Knowledge Management: A Practitioner Perspective," *Journal of Engineering and Technology Management* (20:1-2), Mar-Jun 2003, pp 117-140.

54. Cross, R., Borgatti, S.P., and Parker, A. "Making Invisible Workvisible: Using Social Network Analysis to Support Strategic Collaboration," *California Management Review* (44:2), Win 2002, pp 25-+.

55. Currie, G., and Kerrin, M. "Human Resource Management and Knowledge Management: Enhancing Knowledge Sharing in a Pharmaceutical Company," *International Journal of Human Resource Management* (14:6), Aug 2003, pp 1027-1045.

56. Currie, G., and Kerrin, M. "The Limits of a Technological Fix to Knowledge Management - Epistemological, Political and Cultural Issues in the Case of Intranet Implementation," *Management Learning* (35:1), Mar 2004, pp 9-29.

57. Dakhli, M., and De Clercq, D. "Human Capital, Social Capital, and Innovation: A Multi-Country Study," *Entrepreneurship and Regional Development* (16:2), Mar 2004, pp 107-128.

58. Davenport, S., and Bibby, D. "Rethinking a National Innovation System: The Small Country as 'Sme'," *Technology Analysis & Strategic Management* (11:3), Sep 1999, pp 431-462.

59. Davenport, S., Campbell-Hunt, C., and Solomon, J. "The Dynamics of Technology Strategy: An Exploratory Study," *R & D Management* (33:5), Nov 2003, pp 481-499.

60. Davidsson, P., and Honig, B. "The Role of Social and Human Capital among Nascent Entrepreneurs," *Journal of Business Venturing* (18:3), May 2003, pp 301-331.

61. Day, D.V. "Leadership Development: A Review in Context," *Leadership Quarterly* (11:4), Win 2000, pp 581-613.

62. De Clercq, D., and Sapienza, H.J. "When Do Venture Capital Firms Learn from Their Portfolio Companies?," *Entrepreneurship Theory and Practice* (29:4), Jul 2005, pp 517-535.

63. de Holan, P.M., and Phillips, N. "Remembrance of Things Past? The Dynamics of Organizational Forgetting," *Management Science* (50:11), Nov 2004, pp 1603-1613.

64. De Long, D.W., and Fahey, L. "Diagnosing Cultural Barriers to Knowledge Management," *Academy of Management Executive* (14:4), Nov 2000, pp 113-127.

65. Del Favero, M. "Faculty-Administrator Relationships as Integral to High-Performing Governance Systems - New Frameworks for Study," *American Behavioral Scientist* (46:7), Mar 2003, pp 902-922.

66. Denis, J.L., Lamothe, L., and Langley, A. "The Struggle to Implement Teaching-Hospital

Mergers," *Canadian Public Administration-Administration Publique Du Canada* (42:3), Fal 1999, pp 285-311.

67. Dess, G.G., Ireland, R.D., Zahra, S.A., Floyd, S.W., Janney, J.J., and Lane, P.J. "Emerging Issues in Corporate Entrepreneurship," *Journal of Management* (29:3) 2003, pp 351-378.

68. Dess, G.G., and Lumpkin, G.T. "The Role of Entrepreneurial Orientation in Stimulating Effective Corporate Entrepreneurship," *Academy of Management Executive* (19:1), Feb 2005, pp 147-156.

69. Dess, G.G., and Shaw, J.D. "Voluntary Turnover, Social Capital, and Organizational Performance," *Academy of Management Review* (26:3), Jul 2001, pp 446-456.

70. Dietz, J.S., and Bozeman, B. "Academic Careers, Patents, and Productivity: Industry Experience as Scientific and Technical Human Capital," *Research Policy* (34:3), Apr 2005, pp 349-367.

71. Downing, S. "The Social Construction of Entrepreneurship: Narrative and Dramatic Processes in the Coproduction of Organizations and Identities," *Entrepreneurship Theory and Practice* (29:2), Mar 2005, pp 185-204.

72. Duguid, P. ""the Art of Knowing": Social and Tacit Dimensions of Knowledge and the Limits of the Community of Practice," *Information Society* (21:2), Apr-Jun 2005, pp 109-118.

73. Earl, M. "Knowledge Management Strategies: Toward a Taxonomy," *Journal of Management Information Systems* (18:1), Sum 2001, pp 215-233.

74. Echols, A., and Tsai, W. "Niche and Performance: The Moderating Role of Network Embeddedness," *Strategic Management Journal* (26:3), Mar 2005, pp 219-238.

75. Edelman, L.F., Bresnen, M., Newell, S., Scarbrough, H., and Swan, J. "The Benefits and Pitfalls of Social Capital: Empirical Evidence from Two Organizations in the United Kingdom," *British Journal of Management* (15), Mar 2004, pp S59-S69.

76. Ellis, P.D. "Social Structure and Intermediation: Market-Making Strategies in International Exchange," *Journal of Management Studies* (40:7), Nov 2003, pp 1683-1708.

77. Empson, L. "Fear of Exploitation and Fear of Contamination: Impediments to Knowledge Transfer in Mergers between Professional Service Firms," *Human Relations* (54:7), Jul 2001, pp 839-862.

78. Erikson, T. "Entrepreneurial Capital: The Emerging Venture's Most Important Asset and Competitive Advantage," *Journal of Business Venturing* (17:3), May 2002, pp 275-290.

79. Erikson, T., and Sorheim, R. "'Technology Angels' and Other Informal Investors," *Technovation* (25:5), May 2005, pp 489-496.

80. Erridge, A., and Greer, J. "Partnerships and Public Procurement: Building Social Capital through Supply Relations," *Public Administration* (80:3) 2002, pp 503-522.

81. Falconer, J. "Knowledge Management at a Branchpoint: Will We Ignore the Lessons of the AI Discipline the Way It Ignored the Lessons of Ludwig Wittgenstein?," *International Journal of Technology Management* (20:5-8) 2000, pp 601-632.

82. Fenton, E., Harvey, J., Griffiths, F., Wild, A., and Sturt, J. "Reflections from Organization Science on the Development of Primary Health Care Research Networks,"

Family Practice (18:5), Oct 2001, pp 540-544.

83. Ferguson-Amores, M., Garcia-Rodriguez, M., and Ruiz-Navarro, J. "Strategies of Renewal - the Transition from 'Total Quality Management' to the 'Learning Organization'," *Management Learning* (36:2), Jun 2005, pp 149-180.

84. Ferrary, M. "Confidence and Accumulation of Social Capital in the Regulation of Credit Activities," *Revue Francaise De Sociologie* (40:3), Jul-Sep 1999, pp 559-+.

85. Ferrary, M. "Managing the Disruptive Technologies Life Cycle by Externalising the Research: Social Network and Corporate Venturing in the Silicon Valley," *International Journal of Technology Management* (25:1-2) 2003, pp 165-180.

86. Fey, C.F., and Birkinshaw, J. "External Sources of Knowledge, Governance Mode, and R&D Performance," *Journal of Management* (31:4), Aug 2005, pp 597-621.

87. Fischer, H.M., and Pollock, T.G. "Effects of Social Capital and Power on Surviving Transformational Change: The Case of Initial Public Offerings," *Academy of Management Journal* (47:4), Aug 2004, pp 463-481.

88. Florin, J., Lubatkin, M., and Schulze, W. "A Social Capital Model of High-Growth Ventures," *Academy of Management Journal* (46:3), Jun 2003, pp 374-384.

89. Forret, M.L., and Dougherty, T.W. "Correlates of Networking Behavior for Managerial and Professional Employees," *Group & Organization Management* (26:3), Sep 2001, pp 283-311.

90. Forret, M.L., and Dougherty, T.W. "Networking Behaviors and Career Outcomes: Differences for Men and Women?," *Journal of Organizational Behavior* (25:3), May 2004, pp 419-437.

91. Foss, N.J. "Research in the Strategic Theory of the Firm: 'Isolationism' and 'Integrationism'," *Journal of Management Studies* (36:6), Nov 1999, pp 725-755.

92. Foss, N.J. "Selective Intervention and Internal Hybrids: Interpreting and Learning from the Rise and Decline of the Oticon Spaghetti Organization," *Organization Science* (14:3), May-Jun 2003, pp 331-349.

93. Fowler, S.W., Lawrence, T.B., and Morse, E.A. "Virtually Embedded Ties," *Journal of Management* (30:5) 2004, pp 647-666.

94. Fu, W.Y., and Tsai, H.J. "Impact of Social Capital and Business Operation Mode on Intellectual Capital and Knowledge Management," *International Journal of Technology Management* (30:1-2) 2005, pp 147-171.

95. Gant, J., Ichniowski, C., and Shaw, K. "Social Capital and Organizational Change in High-Involvement and Traditional Work Organizations," *Journal of Economics & Management Strategy* (11:2), Sum 2002, pp 289-328.

96. Geisler, E. "Good-Bye Dodo Bird (Raphus Cucullatus) - Why Social Knowledge Is Cumulative, Expansive, and Nonevolutionary," *Journal of Management Inquiry* (10:1), Mar 2001, pp 5-15.

97. Geletkanycz, M.A., Boyd, B.K., and Finkelstein, S. "The Strategic Value of Ceo External Directorate Networks: Implications for Ceo Compensation," *Strategic Management Journal* (22:9), Sep 2001, pp 889-898.

98. Ghoshal, S., Bartlett, C.A., and Moran, P. "A New Manifesto for Management," *Sloan Management Review* (40:3), Spr 1999, pp 9-+.

99. Gibbons, D., and Olk, P.M. "Individual and Structural Origins of Friendship and Social Position among Professionals," *Journal of Personality and Social Psychology* (84:2), Feb 2003, pp 340-351.

100. Gittell, J.H. "Organizing Work to Support Relational Co-Ordination," *International Journal of Human Resource Management* (11:3), Jun 2000, pp 517-539.

101. Globerman, S., and Shapiro, D. "Global Foreign Direct Investment Flows: The Role of Governance Infrastructure," *World Development* (30:11), Nov 2002, pp 1899-1919.

102. Gold, A.H., Malhotra, A., and Segars, A.H. "Knowledge Management: An Organizational Capabilities Perspective," *Journal of Management Information Systems* (18:1), Sum 2001, pp 185-214.

103. Goodall, K., and Roberts, J. "Repairing Managerial Knowledge-Ability over Distance," *Organization Studies* (24:7), Sep 2003, pp 1153-1175.

104. Gosain, S., Malhotra, A., and El Sawy, O.A. "Coordinating for Flexibility in E-Business Supply Chains," *Journal of Management Information Systems* (21:3), Win 2004, pp 7-45.

105. Gottschalk, P., and Khandelwal, V.K. "Inter-Organizational Knowledge Management: A Comparison of Law Firms in Norway and Australia," *Journal of Computer Information Systems* (42:5) 2002, pp 50-58.

106. Gottschalk, P., and Khandelwal, V.K. "Stages of Growth for Knowledge Management Technology in Law Firms," *Journal of Computer Information Systems* (44:4), Sum 2004, pp 111-124.

107. Gray, P.H. "The Effects of Knowledge Management Systems on Emergent Teams: Towards a Research Model," *Journal of Strategic Information Systems* (9:2-3), Sep 2000, pp 175-191.

108. Gray, P.H. "A Problem-Solving Perspective on Knowledge Management Practices," *Decision Support Systems* (31:1), May 2001, pp 87-102.

109. Gray, P.H., and Chan, Y.E. "Integrating Km Practices through a Problem-Solving Framework," *Communications of the Association for Information Systems* (4:12) 2000.

110. Griffiths, F., Wild, D., Harvey, J., and Fenton, E. "The Productivity of Primary Care Research Networks," *British Journal of General Practice* (50:460), Nov 2000, pp 913-915.

111. Haahti, A., Madupu, V., Yavas, U., and Babakus, E. "Cooperative Strategy, Knowledge Intensity and Export Performance of Small and Medium Sized Enterprises," *Journal of World Business* (40:2), May 2005, pp 124-138.

112. Hall, H. "Input-Friendliness: Motivating Knowledge Sharing across Intranets," *Journal of Information Science* (27:3) 2001, pp 139-146.

113. Hall, H. "Borrowed Theory - Applying Exchange Theories in Information Science Research," *Library & Information Science Research* (25:3) 2003, pp 287-306.

114. Hansen, M.T., and Nohria, N. "How to Build Collaborative Advantage," *Mit Sloan Management Review* (46:1), Fal 2004, pp 22-+.

115. Hardy, C., Phillips, N., and Lawrence, T.B. "Resources, Knowledge and Influence: The Organizational Effects of Interorganizational Collaboration," *Journal of*

Management Studies (40:2), Mar 2003, pp 321-347.

116.   Hargreaves, D.H. "A Capital Theory of School Effectiveness and Improvement," *British Educational Research Journal* (27:4), Sep 2001, pp 487-503.

117.   Harvey, J., Pettigrew, A., and Ferlie, E. "The Determinants of Research Group Performance: Towards Mode 2?," *Journal of Management Studies* (39:6), Sep 2002, pp 747-774.

118.   Haslam, S.A., Eggins, R.A., and Reynolds, K.J. "The Aspire Model: Actualizing Social and Personal Identity Resources to Enhance Organizational Outcomes," *Journal of Occupational and Organizational Psychology* (76), Mar 2003, pp 83-113.

119.   Hatzakis, T., Lycett, M., Macredie, R.D., and Martin, V.A. "Towards the Development of a Social Capital Approach to Evaluating Change Management Interventions," *European Journal of Information Systems* (14:1), Mar 2005, pp 60-74.

120.   Haunschild, A. "Managing Employment Relationships in Flexible Labour Markets: The Case of German Repertory Theatres," *Human Relations* (56:8), Aug 2003, pp 899-929.

121.   Hayton, J.C. "Competing in the New Economy: The Effect of Intellectual Capital on Corporate Entrepreneurship in High-Technology New Ventures," *R & D Management* (35:2), Mar 2005, pp 137-155.

122.   Higgins, M.C. "Changing Careers: The Effects of Social Context," *Journal of Organizational Behavior* (22:6), Sep 2001, pp 595-618.

123.   Higgins, M.C., and Kram, K.E. "Reconceptualizing Mentoring at Work: A Developmental Network Perspective," *Academy of Management Review* (26:2), Apr 2001, pp 264-288.

124.   Hillman, A.J., and Dalziel, T. "Boards of Directors and Firm Performance: Integrating Agency and Resource Dependence Perspectives," *Academy of Management Review* (28:3), Jul 2003, pp 383-396.

125.   Hillman, A.J., and Hitt, M.A. "Corporate Political Strategy Formulation: A Model of Approach, Participation, and Strategy Decisions," *Academy of Management Review* (24:4), Oct 1999, pp 825-842.

126.   Hite, J.M. "Evolutionary Processes and Paths of Relationally Embedded Network Ties in Emerging Entrepreneurial Firms," *Entrepreneurship Theory and Practice* (29:1), Jan 2005, pp 113-144.

127.   Hitt, M.A., Bierman, L., Shimizu, K., and Kochhar, R. "Direct and Moderating Effects of Human Capital on Strategy and Performance in Professional Service Firms: A Resource-Based Perspective," *Academy of Management Journal* (44:1), Feb 2001, pp 13-28.

128.   Hitt, M.A., Ireland, R.D., and Lee, H.U. "Technological Learning, Knowledge Management, Firm Growth and Performance: An Introductory Essay," *Journal of Engineering and Technology Management* (17:3-4), Sep-Dec 2000, pp 231-246.

129.   Hodson, R. "Management Citizenship Behavior and Its Consequences," *Work and Occupations* (29:1), Feb 2002, pp 64-96.

130.   Hodson, R. "Organizational Trustworthiness: Findings from the Population of Organizational Ethnographies," *Organization Science* (15:4), Jul-Aug 2004, pp 432-445.

131.   Hodson, R. "Management Behaviour as Social Capital: A Systematic Analysis of Organizational Ethnographies," *British Journal of Industrial Relations* (43:1), Mar 2005, pp 41-65.

132.   Hodson, R., and Roscigno, V.J. "Organizational Success and Worker Dignity: Complementary or Contradictory?," *American Journal of Sociology* (110:3), Nov 2004, pp 672-708.

133.   Horng, C., and Huarng, F. "Tqm Adoption by Hospitals in Taiwan," *Total Quality Management* (13:4), Jul 2002, pp 441-463.

134.   Huang, J.C., Newell, S., Galliers, R.D., and Pan, S.-L. "Erp and Km Systems: Managerial Panaceas or Synergetic Solutions?," Americas Conference on Information Systems, 2001.

135.   Huang, J.C., Newell, S., Galliers, R.D., and Pan, S.-L. "Intellectual Buy-in and Emotional Buy-In: A Reappraisal of Erp Implementation," Americas Conference on Information Systems, 2002.

136.   Huang, J.C., Newell, S., and Pan, S.L. "The Process of Global Knowledge Integration: A Case Study of a Multinational Investment Bank's Y2k Program," *European Journal of Information Systems* (10:3), Dec 2001, pp 161-174.

137.   Huang, J.C., Pan, S.L., Tsai, Y.S., and Hsieh, M.-H. "The Interrelationships of Managing Knowledge and Organizational Learning: A Case Study of a British Retailer," Americas Conference on Information Systems, 2000.

138.   Huotari, M.L., and Chatman, E. "Using Everyday Life Information Seeking to Explain Organizational Behavior," *Library & Information Science Research* (23:4) 2001, pp 351-366.

139.   Huotari, M.L., and Iivonen, M. "University Library - a Strategic Partner in Knowledge and Information Related Processes?'" in: *Asist 2001: Proceedings of the 64th Asist Annual Meeting, Vol 38, 2001*, 2001, pp. 399-410.

140.   Huysman, M., and Wulf, V. "The Role of Information Technology in Building and Sustaining the Relational Base of Communities," *Information Society* (21:2), Apr-Jun 2005, pp 81-89.

141.   Inkpen, A.C., and Tsang, E.W.K. "Social Capital, Networks, and Knowledge Transfer," *Academy of Management Review* (30:1), Jan 2005, pp 146-165.

142.   Ireland, R.D., Hitt, M.A., and Sirmon, D.G. "A Model of Strategic Entrepreneurship: The Construct and Its Dimensions," *Journal of Management* (29:6) 2003, pp 963-989.

143.   Janney, J.J., and Dess, G.G. "Can Real-Options Analysis Improve Decision-Making? Promises and Pitfalls," *Academy of Management Executive* (18:4), Nov 2004, pp 60-75.

144.   Jarzabkowski, P. "Strategy as Practice: Recursiveness, Adaptation, and Practices-in-Use," *Organization Studies* (25:4), May 2004, pp 529-560.

145.   Jashapara, A. "The Emerging Discourse of Knowledge Management: A New Dawn for Information Science Research?," *Journal of Information Science* (31:2) 2005, pp 136-148.

146.   Johnson, J.P., Korsgaard, M.A., and Sapienza, H.J. "Perceived Fairness, Decision

288

Control, and Commitment in International Joint Venture Management Teams," *Strategic Management Journal* (23:12), Dec 2002, pp 1141-1160.

147.   Johnson, W.H.A., and Johnston, D.A. "Organisational Knowledge Creating Processes and the Performance of University-Industry Collaborative R&D Projects," *International Journal of Technology Management* (27:1) 2004, pp 93-114.

148.   Jones, O. "Manufacturing Regeneration through Corporate Entrepreneurship - Middle Managers and Organizational Innovation," *International Journal of Operations & Production Management* (25:5-6) 2005, pp 491-511.

149.   Joshi, A.W., and Campbell, A.J. "Effect of Environmental Dynamism on Relational Governance in Manufacturer Supplier Relationships: A Contingency Framework and an Empirical Test," *Journal of the Academy of Marketing Science* (31:2), Spr 2003, pp 176-188.

150.   Kankanhalli, A., Tan, B.C.Y., and Wei, K.K. "Contributing Knowledge to Electronic Knowledge Repositories: An Empirical Investigation," *Mis Quarterly* (29:1), Mar 2005, pp 113-143.

151.   Kern, T., and Willcocks, L. "Exploring Information Technology Outsourcing Relationships: Theory and Practice," *Journal of Strategic Information Systems* (9:4), Dec 2000, pp 321-350.

152.   Kim, Y.G., Yu, S.H., and Lee, J.H. "Knowledge Strategy Planning: Methodology and Case," *Expert Systems with Applications* (24:3), Apr 2003, pp 295-307.

153.   King, Z. "Career Self-Management: A Framework for Guidance of Employed Adults," *British Journal of Guidance & Counselling* (29:1), Feb 2001, pp 65-78.

154.   Kinnie, N.J., Swart, J., and Purcell, J. "Influences on the Choice of Hr System: The Network Organization Perspective," *International Journal of Human Resource Management* (16:6), Jun 2005, pp 1004-1028.

155.   Koka, B.R., and Prescott, J.E. "Strategic Alliances as Social Capital: A Multidimensional View," *Strategic Management Journal* (23:9), Sep 2002, pp 795-816.

156.   Kor, Y.Y., and Mahoney, J.T. "Penrose's Resource-Based Approach: The Process and Product of Research Creativity," *Journal of Management Studies* (37:1), Jan 2000, pp 109-139.

157.   Kostova, T. "Transnational Transfer of Strategic Organizational Practices: A Contextual Perspective," *Academy of Management Review* (24:2), Apr 1999, pp 308-324.

158.   Kostova, T., and Roth, K. "Adoption of an Organizational Practice by Subsidiaries of Multinational Corporations: Institutional and Relational Effects," *Academy of Management Journal* (45:1), Feb 2002, pp 215-233.

159.   Kostova, T., and Roth, K. "Social Capital in Multinational Corporations and a Micro-Macro Model of Its Formation," *Academy of Management Review* (28:2), Apr 2003, pp 297-317.

160.   Kristof-Brown, A., Barrick, M.R., and Stevens, C.K. "When Opposites Attract: A Multi-Sample Demonstration of Complementary Person-Team Fit on Extraversion," *Journal of Personality* (73:4), Aug 2005, pp 935-957.

161.   Kuhn, T., and Corman, S.R. "The Emergence of Homogeneity and Heterogeneity in Knowledge Structures During a Planned Organizational Change," *Communication*

Monographs (70:3), Sep 2003, pp 198-229.

162.   Kumar, R., and Worm, V. "Social Capital and the Dynamics of Business Negotiations between the Northern Europeans and the Chinese," *International Marketing Review* (20:3) 2003, pp 262-285.

163.   Laamanen, T. "Dependency, Resource Depth, and Supplier Performance During Industry Downturn," *Research Policy* (34:2), Mar 2005, pp 125-140.

164.   Langley, A., Denis, J.L., and Lamothe, L. "Process Research in Healthcare: Towards Three-Dimensional Learning," *Policy and Politics* (31:2), Apr 2003, pp 195-206.

165.   Lanzara, G.F., and Patriotta, G. "Technology and the Courtroom: An Inquiry into Knowledge Making in Organizations," *Journal of Management Studies* (38:7), Nov 2001, pp 943-971.

166.   Laszlo, K.C., and Laszlo, A. "The Role of Evolutionary Learning Community in Evolutionary Development: The Unfolding of a Line of Inquiry," *Systems Research and Behavioral Science* (21:3), May-Jun 2004, pp 269-280.

167.   Leana, C.R., and Van Buren, H.J. "Organizational Social Capital and Employment Practices," *Academy of Management Review* (24:3), Jul 1999, pp 538-555.

168.   Lee, H., and Choi, B. "Knowledge Management Enablers, Processes, and Organizational Performance: An Integrative View and Empirical Examination," *Journal of Management Information Systems* (20:1), Sum 2003, pp 179-228.

169.   Lee, S.H., Wong, P.K., and Chong, C.L. "Human and Social Capital Explanations for R&D Outcomes," *Ieee Transactions on Engineering Management* (52:1), Feb 2005, pp 59-68.

170.   Lengnick-Hall, C.A., Lengnick-Hall, M.L., and Abdinnour-Helm, S. "The Role of Social and Intellectual Capital in Achieving Competitive Advantage through Enterprise Resource Planning (Erp) Systems," *Journal of Engineering and Technology Management* (21:4), Dec 2004, pp 307-330.

171.   Lesser, E.L., and Storck, J. "Communities of Practice and Organizational Performance," *Ibm Systems Journal* (40:4) 2001, pp 831-841.

172.   Leung, A. "Innovation Diffusion as a Process for Status Attainment," in: *Advances in Consumer Research, Volume Xxix*, 2002, pp. 485-486.

173.   Levina, N., and Vaast, E. "The Emergence of Boundary Spanning Competence in Practice. Implications for Implementation and Use of Information Systems," *Mis Quarterly* (29:2), Jun 2005, pp 335-363.

174.   Li, H.Y., and Atuahene-Gima, K. "The Adoption of Agency Business Activity, Product Innovation, and Performance in Chinese Technology Ventures," *Strategic Management Journal* (23:6), Jun 2002, pp 469-490.

175.   Li, L.Y. "An Examination of the Foreign Market Knowledge of Exporting Firms Based in the People's Republic of China: Its Determinants and Effect on Export Intensity," *Industrial Marketing Management* (33:7), Oct 2004, pp 561-572.

176.   Li, S.X., and Berta, W.B. "The Ties That Bind: Strategic Actions and Status Structure in the Us-Investment Banking Industry," *Organization Studies* (23:3) 2002, pp 339-368.

177.   Lindsey, K. "Measuring Km Effectiveness: A Task-Contingent Organizational Capabilities Perspective," Americas Conference on Information Systems, 2002.

178.   Llewellyn, N., and Armistead, C. "Business Process Management - Exploring Social Capital within Processes," *International Journal of Service Industry Management* (11:3) 2000, pp 225-243.

179.   Locke, E.A. "Some Reservations About Social Capital," *Academy of Management Review* (24:1), Jan 1999, pp 8-9.

180.   Lockett, A., Murray, G., and Wright, M. "Do Uk Venture Capitalists Still Have a Bias against Investment in New Technology Firms," *Research Policy* (31:6), Aug 2002, pp 1009-1030.

181.   Lounsbury, M., and Glynn, M.A. "Cultural Entrepreneurship: Stories, Legitimacy, and the Acquisition of Resources," *Strategic Management Journal* (22:6-7), Jun-Jul 2001, pp 545-564.

182.   Lumpkin, G.T. "The Role of Organizational Learning in the Opportunity-Recognition Process," *Entrepreneurship Theory and Practice* (29:4), Jul 2005, pp 451-472.

183.   MacMillan, K., Money, K., Money, A., and Downing, S. "Relationship Marketing in the Not-for-Profit Sector: An Extension and Application of the Commitment-Trust Theory," *Journal of Business Research* (58:6), Jun 2005, pp 806-818.

184.   Macpherson, A., Jones, O., and Zhang, M. "Evolution or Revolution? Dynamic Capabilities in a Knowledge-Dependent Firm," *R & D Management* (34:2), Mar 2004, pp 161-177.

185.   Malhotra, A., Gosain, S., and El Sawy, O.A. "Absorptive Capacity Configurations in Supply Chains: Gearing for Partner-Enabled Market Knowledge Creation," *Mis Quarterly* (29:1), Mar 2005, pp 145-187.

186.   Maravelias, C. "Post-Bureaucracy - Control through Professional Freedom," *Journal of Organizational Change Management* (16:5) 2003, pp 547-566.

187.   Marion, R., and Uhl-Bien, M. "Leadership in Complex Organizations," *Leadership Quarterly* (12:4), Win 2001, pp 389-418.

188.   Markman, G.D., Espina, M.I., and Phan, P.H. "Patents as Surrogates for Inimitable and Non-Substitutable Resources," *Journal of Management* (30:4) 2004, pp 529-544.

189.   Massimo, M., and Proserpio, L. "Users' Beliefs Towards Technology: A Social Capital Perspective," European Conference on Information Systems, 2005.

190.   Matlay, H., and Westhead, P. "Virtual Teams and the Rise of E-Entrepreneurship in Europe," *International Small Business Journal* (23:3), Jun 1 2005, pp 279-302.

191.   McEvily, B., Perrone, V., and Zaheer, A. "Trust as an Organizing Principle," *Organization Science* (14:1), Jan-Feb 2003, pp 91-103.

192.   McFadyen, M.A., and Cannella, A.A. "Social Capital and Knowledge Creation: Diminishing Returns of the Number and Strength of Exchange Relationships," *Academy of Management Journal* (47:5), Oct 2004, pp 735-746.

193.   Mele, D. "Organizational Humanizing Cultures: Do They Generate Social Capital?," *Journal of Business Ethics* (45:1-2), Jun 2003, pp 3-14.

194.   Merali, Y. "Individual and Collective Congruence in the Knowledge Management Process," *Journal of Strategic Information Systems* (9:2-3), Sep 2000, pp 213-234.

195.   Merali, Y. "The Role of Boundaries in Knowledge Processes," *European Journal of Information Systems* (11:1), Mar 2002, pp 47-60.

196.   Mezias, J.M., and Scandura, T.A. "A Needs-Driven Approach to Expatriate Adjustment and Career Development: A Multiple Mentoring Perspective," *Journal of International Business Studies* (36:5), Sep 2005, pp 519-538.

197.   Miranda, S.M., and Kavan, C.B. "Moments of Governance in Is Outsourcing: Conceptualizing Effects of Contracts on Value Capture and Creation," *Journal of Information Technology* (20:3), Sep 2005, pp 152-169.

198.   Mohrman, S.A., Finegold, D., and Mohrman, A.M. "An Empirical Model of the Organization Knowledge System in New Product Development Firms," *Journal of Engineering and Technology Management* (20:1-2), Mar-Jun 2003, pp 7-38.

199.   Molina-Morales, F.X. "The Territorial Agglomerations of Firms: A Social Capital Perspective from the Spanish Tile Industry," *Growth and Change* (36:1), Win 2005, pp 74-99.

200.   Molina-Morales, F.X., and Martinez-Fernandez, M.T. "How Much Difference Is There between Industrial District Firms? A Net Value Creation Approach," *Research Policy* (33:3), Apr 2004, pp 473-486.

201.   Molina-Morales, F.X., and Martinez-Fernandez, M.T. "Factors That Identify Industrial Districts: An Application in Spanish Manufacturing Firms," *Environment and Planning* (36:1), Jan 2004, pp 111-126.

202.   Moran, P., and Ghoshal, S. "Markets, Firms, and the Process of Economic Development," *Academy of Management Review* (24:3), Jul 1999, pp 390-412.

203.   Morgan, N.A., Zou, S.M., Vorhies, D.W., and Katsikeas, C.S. "Experiential and Informational Knowledge, Architectural Marketing Capabilities, and the Adaptive Performance of Export Ventures: A Cross-National Study," *Decision Sciences* (34:2), Spr 2003, pp 287-321.

204.   Morris, T. "Asserting Property Rights: Knowledge Codification in the Professional Service Firm," *Human Relations* (54:7), Jul 2001, pp 819-838.

205.   Mouritsen, J., Larsen, H.T., and Bukh, P.N.D. "Intellectual Capital and the 'Capable Firm': Narrating, Visualising and Numbering for Managing Knowledge," *Accounting Organizations and Society* (26:7-8), Oct-Nov 2001, pp 735-762.

206.   Mueller-Prothmann, T., and Finke, I. "Selakt - Social Network Analysis as a Method for Expert Localisation and Sustainable Knowledge Transfer," *Journal of Universal Computer Science* (10:6) 2004, pp 691-701.

207.   Nahapiet, J., Gratton, L., and Rocha, H.O. "Knowledge and Relationships: When Cooperation Is the Norm," *European Management Review* (2) 2005, pp 3-14.

208.   Nambisan, S. "Designing Virtual Customer Environments for New Product Development: Toward a Theory," *Academy of Management Review* (27:3), Jul 2002, pp 392-413.

209.   Newell, S., Huang, J., and Tansley, C. "Social Capital in Erp Projects: The Differential Source and Effects of Bridging and Bonding," International Conference on

Information Systems, 2002.

210.   Newell, S., Tansley, C., and Huang, J. "Knowledge Creation in an Erp Project Team: The Unexpected Debilitating Impact of Social Capital," Americas Conference on Information Systems, 2001.

211.   Newell, S., Tansley, C., and Huang, J. "Social Capital and Knowledge Integration in an Erp Project Team: The Importance of Bridging and Bonding," *British Journal of Management* (15), Mar 2004, pp S43-S57.

212.   Nickerson, J.A., and Zenger, T.R. "A Knowledge-Based Theory of the Firm-the Problem-Solving Perspective," *Organization Science* (15:6), Nov-Dec 2004, pp 617-632.

213.   Obstfeld, D. "Social Networks, the Tertius Lungens and Orientation Involvement in Innovation," *Administrative Science Quarterly* (50:1), Mar 2005, pp 100-130.

214.   Osterloh, M., and Frey, B.S. "Motivation, Knowledge Transfer, and Organizational Forms," *Organization Science* (11:5), Sep-Oct 2000, pp 538-550.

215.   Patriotta, G. "Sensemaking on the Shop Floor: Narratives of Knowledge in Organizations," *Journal of Management Studies* (40:2), Mar 2003, pp 349-375.

216.   Pavlou, P.A. "Institution-Based Trust in Interorganizational Exchange Relationships: The Role of Online B2b Marketplaces on Trust Formation," *Journal of Strategic Information Systems* (11:3-4), Dec 2002, pp 215-243.

217.   Pearce, J.L., and Randel, A.E. "Expectations of Organizational Mobility, Workplace Social Inclusion, and Employee Job Performance," *Journal of Organizational Behavior* (25:1), Feb 2004, pp 81-98.

218.   Peterson, S.J., and Spiker, B.K. "Establishing the Positive Contributory Value of Older Workers: A Positive Psychology Perspective," *Organizational Dynamics* (34:2) 2005, pp 153-167.

219.   Pike, S., Roos, G., and Marr, B. "Strategic Management of Intangible Assets and Value Drivers in R&D Organizations," *R & D Management* (35:2), Mar 2005, pp 111-124.

220.   Poesche, J. "Influence of It and the Internet on Production Planning in the Chemical Industry," *Chemie Ingenieur Technik* (72:11), Nov 2000, pp 1294-1303.

221.   Preston, D., and Karahanna, E. "Mechanisms for the Development of Shared Mental Models between the Cio and the Top Management Team," International Conference on Information Systems, 2004.

222.   Puffer, S.M., and McCarthy, D.J. "Navigating the Hostile Maze: A Framework for Russian Entrepreneurship," *Academy of Management Executive* (15:4), Nov 2001, pp 24-36.

223.   Rashman, L., and Hartley, J. "Leading and Learning? Knowledge Transfer in the Beacon Council Scheme," *Public Administration* (80:3) 2002, pp 523-542.

224.   Ravasi, D., and Marchisio, G. "Going Public and the Enrichment of a Supportive Network," *Small Business Economics* (21:4), Dec 2003, pp 381-395.

225.   Ravichandran, T., and Rai, A. "Structural Analysis of the Impact of Knowledge Creation and Knowledge Embedding on Software Process Capability," *Ieee Transactions on Engineering Management* (50:3), Aug 2003, pp 270-284.

226.   Rayalu, R.T. "Behavioral Aspects and Collaboration Technologies for Process

Innovation: A Grounded Theory Approach," Americas Conference on Information Systems, 2005.

227.   Reich, B.H., and Kaarst-Brown, M.L. "Creating Social and Intellectual Capital through It Career Transitions," *Journal of Strategic Information Systems* (12:2), Jul 2003, pp 91-109.

228.   Ridder, H.G., Bruns, H.J., and Spier, F. "Analysis of Public Management Change Processes: The Case of Local Government Accounting Reforms in Germany," *Public Administration* (83:2), Jun 2005, pp 443-471.

229.   Ridings, C.M., Gefen, D., and Arinze, B. "Some Antecedents and Effects of Trust in Virtual Communities," *Journal of Strategic Information Systems* (11:3-4), Dec 2002, pp 271-295.

230.   Rindova, V.P., and Fombrun, C.J. "Constructing Competitive Advantage: The Role of Firm-Constituent Interactions," *Strategic Management Journal* (20:8), Aug 1999, pp 691-710.

231.   Rodan, S., and Galunic, C. "More Than Network Structure: How Knowledge Heterogeneity Influences Managerial Performance and Innovativeness," *Strategic Management Journal* (25:6), Jun 2004, pp 541-562.

232.   Rodgers, W., and Gago, S. "Stakeholder Influence on Corporate Strategies over Time," *Journal of Business Ethics* (52:4), Jul 2004, pp 349-363.

233.   Rodriguez, C.M., and Wilson, D.T. "Relationship Bonding and Trust as a Foundation for Commitment in Us-Mexican Strategic Alliances: A Structural Equation Modeling Approach," *Journal of International Marketing* (10:4) 2002, pp 53-76.

234.   Rothenberg, S. "Knowledge Content and Worker Participation in Environmental Management at Nummi," *Journal of Management Studies* (40:7), Nov 2003, pp 1783-1802.

235.   Rouse, M.J., and Daellenbach, U.S. "Rethinking Research Methods for the Resource-Based Perspective: Isolating Sources of Sustainable Competitive Advantage," *Strategic Management Journal* (20:5), May 1999, pp 487-494.

236.   Rousseau, D.M., and Shperling, Z. "Pieces of the Action: Ownership and the Changing Employment Relationship," *Academy of Management Review* (28:4), Oct 2003, pp 553-570.

237.   Rowley, T., Behrens, D., and Krackhardt, D. "Redundant Governance Structures: An Analysis of Structural and Relational Embeddedness in the Steel and Semiconductor Industries," *Strategic Management Journal* (21:3), Mar 2000, pp 369-386.

238.   Roy, S. "Ok You Are Now an Approved Supplier - but You Still Do Not Get Orders - Understanding the Case of the P-Card," *Industrial Marketing Management* (32:7), Oct 2003, pp 605-613.

239.   Ruona, W.E.A., and Gibson, S.K. "The Making of Twenty-First-Century Hr: An Analysis of the Convergence of Hrm, Hrd, and Od," *Human Resource Management* (43:1), Spr 2004, pp 49-66.

240.   Russo, M.V. "The Emergence of Sustainable Industries: Building on Natural Capital," *Strategic Management Journal* (24:4), Apr 2003, pp 317-331.

241.   Sabherwal, R., and Becerra-Fernandez, I. "Integrating Specific Knowledge:

Insights from the Kennedy Space Center," *Ieee Transactions on Engineering Management* (52:3), Aug 2005, pp 301-315.

242.   Santoro, M.D., and Chakrabarti, A.K. "Firm Size and Technology Centrality in Industry-University Interactions," *Research Policy* (31:7), Sep 2002, pp 1163-1180.

243.   Sapienza, H.J., Parhankangas, A., and Autio, E. "Knowledge Relatedness and Post-Spin-Off Growth," *Journal of Business Venturing* (19:6), Nov 2004, pp 809-829.

244.   Scarbrough, H. "Knowledge Management, Hrm and the Innovation Process," *International Journal of Manpower* (24:5) 2003, pp 501-516.

245.   Scarbrough, H., and Swan, J. "Explaining the Diffusion of Knowledge Management: The Role of Fashion," *British Journal of Management* (12:1), Mar 2001, pp 3-12.

246.   Scheffer, M., Brock, W., and Westley, F. "Socioeconomic Mechanisms Preventing Optimum Use of Ecosystem Services: An Interdisciplinary Theoretical Analysis," *Ecosystems* (3:5), Sep-Oct 2000, pp 451-471.

247.   Schultze, U. "Self-Serve Internet Technology and Social Embeddedness: Balancing Rationalization and Relationships," International Conference on Information Systems, 2002.

248.   Schulz, M. "Pathways of Relevance: Exploring Inflows of Knowledge into Subunits of Multinational Corporations," *Organization Science* (14:4), Jul-Aug 2003, pp 440-459.

249.   Schwartz, R.W., and Tumblin, T.F. "The Power of Servant Leadership to Transform Health Care Organizations for the 21st-Century Economy," *Archives of Surgery* (137:12), Dec 2002, pp 1419-1427.

250.   Shaffer, B., and Hillman, A.J. "The Development of Business-Government Strategies by Diversified Firms," *Strategic Management Journal* (21:2), Feb 2000, pp 175-190.

251.   Shane, S., and Cable, D. "Network Ties, Reputation, and the Financing of New Ventures," *Management Science* (48:3), Mar 2002, pp 364-381.

252.   Sharma, P., and Irving, P.G. "Four Bases of Family Business Successor Commitment: Antecedents and Consequences," *Entrepreneurship Theory and Practice* (29:1), Jan 2005, pp 13-33.

253.   Sherif, K., Hoffman, J., and Wetherbe, J. "Can Technology Build Organizational Social Capital: The Case of a Global It Consulting Firm," Americas Conference on Information Systems, New York, New York, 2004.

254.   Sims, R.R. "Business Ethics Teaching: Using Conversational Learning to Build an Effective Classroom Learning Environment," *Journal of Business Ethics* (49:2), Jan 2004, pp 201-211.

255.   Simsek, Z., Lubatkin, M.H., and Floyd, S.W. "Inter-Firm Networks and Entrepreneurial Behavior: A Structural Embeddedness Perspective," *Journal of Management* (29:3) 2003, pp 427-442.

256.   Smith, K.G., Collins, C.J., and Clark, K.D. "Existing Knowledge, Knowledge Creation Capability, and the Rate of New Product Introduction in High-Technology Firms," *Academy of Management Journal* (48:2), Apr 2005, pp 346-357.

257.   Soda, G., Usai, A., and Zaheer, A. "Network Memory: The Influence of Past and Current Networks on Performance," *Academy of Management Journal* (47:6), Dec 2004, pp 893-906.

258.   Soh, P.H., and Roberts, E.B. "Networks of Innovators: A Longitudinal Perspective," *Research Policy* (32:9), Oct 2003, pp 1569-1588.

259.   Song, S., and Song, J. "Collaborative Electronic Media Usage for Information Sharing: Technology Competence and Social Ties," Americas Conference on Information Systems, 2002.

260.   Soo, C., Devinney, T., Midgley, D., and Deering, A. "Knowledge Management: Philosophy, Processes, and Pitfalls," *California Management Review* (44:4), Sum 2002, pp 129-+.

261.   Spence, L.J., Schmidpeter, R., and Habisch, A. "Assessing Social Capital: Small and Medium Sized Enterprises in Germany and the Uk," *Journal of Business Ethics* (47:1), Sep 2003, pp 17-29.

262.   Sporleder, T.L., and Goldsmith, P.D. "Alternative Firm Strategies for Signaling Quality in the Food System," *Canadian Journal of Agricultural Economics-Revue Canadienne D Agroeconomie* (49:4), Dec 2001, pp 591-604.

263.   Sporleder, T.L., and Moss, L.E. "Knowledge Management in the Global Food System: Network Embeddedness and Social Capital," *American Journal of Agricultural Economics* (84:5) 2002, pp 1345-1352.

264.   Staples, D.S., Greenaway, K., and McKeen, J.D. "Opportunities for Research About Managing the Knowledge-Based Enterprise," *International Journal of Management Reviews* (3:1), Mar 2001, pp 1-20.

265.   Strathdee, R. "Globalization, Innovation, and the Declining Significance of Qualifications Led Social and Economic Change," *Journal of Education Policy* (20:4), Jul 2005, pp 437-456.

266.   Subramaniam, M., and Youndt, M.A. "The Influence of Intellectual Capital on the Types of Innovative Capabilities," *Academy of Management Journal* (48:3), Jun 2005, pp 450-463.

267.   Swan, J., and Scarbrough, H. "Editorial," *Journal of Information Technology* (16:2), Jun 2001, pp 49-55.

268.   Tan, C.W., Pan, S.L., Lim, E.T.K., and Chan, C.M.L. "Managing Knowledge Conflicts in an Interorganizational Project: A Case Study of the Infocomm Development Authority of Singapore," *Journal of the American Society for Information Science and Technology* (56:11), Sep 2005, pp 1187-1199.

269.   Teigland, R., and Wasko, M.M. "Creating Ties That Bind: Examining the Impact of Weak Ties on Individual Performance," International Conference on Information Systems, 2000.

270.   Teigland, R., and Wasko, M.M. "Integrating Knowledge through Information Trading: Examining the Relationship between Boundary Spanning Communication and Individual Performance," *Decision Sciences* (34:2), Spr 2003, pp 261-286.

271.   Tempest, S., McKinlay, A., and Starkey, K. "Careering Alone: Careers and Social Capital in the Financial Services and Television Industries," *Human Relations* (57:12),

Dec 2004, pp 1523-1545.

272. Tempest, S., and Starkey, K. "The Effects of Liminality on Individual and Organizational Learning," *Organization Studies* (25:4), May 2004, pp 507-527.

273. Tencati, A., Perrini, F., and Pogutz, S. "New Tools to Foster Corporate Socially Responsible Behavior," *Journal of Business Ethics* (53:1-2), Aug 2004, pp 173-190.

274. Thompson, M., and Heron, P. "The Difference a Manager Can Make: Organizational Justice and Knowledge Worker Commitment," *International Journal of Human Resource Management* (16:3), Mar 2005, pp 383-404.

275. Tjosvold, D., and Yu, Z.Y. "Goal Interdependence and Applying Abilities for Team in-Role and Extra-Role Performance in China," *Group Dynamics-Theory Research and Practice* (8:2), Jun 2004, pp 98-111.

276. Tsai, W.P. "Social Capital, Strategic Relatedness and the Formation of Intraorganizational Linkages," *Strategic Management Journal* (21:9), Sep 2000, pp 925-939.

277. Tsang, E.W.K., Nguyen, D.T., and Erramilli, M.K. "Knowledge Acquisition and Performance of International Joint Ventures in the Transition Economy of Vietnam," *Journal of International Marketing* (12:2) 2004, pp 82-103.

278. Tsoukas, H., and Mylonopoulos, N. "Introduction: Knowledge Construction and Creation in Organizations," *British Journal of Management* (15), Mar 2004, pp S1-S8.

279. Tung, R.L. "Building Effective Networks," *Journal of Management Inquiry* (11:2), Jun 2002, pp 94-101.

280. Ulhoi, J.P. "The Social Dimensions of Entrepreneurship," *Technovation* (25:8), Aug 2005, pp 939-946.

281. Un, C.A., and Cuervo-Cazurra, A. "Strategies for Knowledge Creation in Firms," *British Journal of Management* (15), Mar 2004, pp S27-S41.

282. Valentine, S., and Fleischman, G. "Ethics Codes and Professionals' Tolerance of Societal Diversity," *Journal of Business Ethics* (40:4), Nov 2002, pp 301-312.

283. Valentine, S., and Fleischman, G. "The Impact of Self-Esteem, Machiavellianism, and Social Capital on Attorneys' Traditional Gender Outlook," *Journal of Business Ethics* (43:4), Apr 2003, pp 323-335.

284. Valentine, S., Fleischman, G., and Godkin, L. "Work Social Agency as a Function of Self-Esteem and Machiavellianism," *Psychological Reports* (93:3), Dec 2003, pp 855-858.

285. Verbeke, W., Belschak, F., and Bagozzi, R.P. "The Adaptive Consequences of Pride in Personal Selling," *Journal of the Academy of Marketing Science* (32:4), Fal 2004, pp 386-402.

286. Viedma, J.M. "Scbs Social Capital Benchmarking System - Profiting from Social Capital When Building Network Organisations," *Journal of Universal Computer Science* (9:6) 2003, pp 501-509.

287. von Krogh, G. "The Communal Resource and Information Systems," *Journal of Strategic Information Systems* (11:2), Jun 2002, pp 85-107.

288. Vyakarnam, S., and Handelberg, J. "Four Themes of the Impact of Management Teams on Organizational Performance - Implications for Future Research of

Entrepreneurial Teams," *International Small Business Journal* (23:3), Jun 1 2005, pp 236-256.

289.	Wang, J. "The Role of Social Capital in Open Source Software Communities," Americas Conference on Information Systems, 2005.

290.	Wasko, M.M. "A Framework for Successful Knowledge Management Implementation," Americas Conference on Information Systems, 1998.

291.	Wasko, M.M. "How Are Knowledge Management Systems Different from Information Systems, and Who Cares?," Americas Conference on Information Systems, 1999.

292.	Wasko, M.M., and Faraj, S. ""It Is What One Does": Why People Participate and Help Others in Electronic Communities of Practice," *Journal of Strategic Information Systems* (9:2-3), Sep 2000, pp 155-173.

293.	Wasko, M.M., and Faraj, S. "Why Should I Share? Examining Social Capital and Knowledge Contribution in Electronic Networks of Practice," *Mis Quarterly* (29:1), Mar 2005, pp 35-57.

294.	Wasko, M.M., Faraj, S., and Teigland, R. "Collective Action and Knowledge Contribution in Electronic Networks of Practice," *Journal of the Association of Information Systems* (5:11-12), Dec 2004, pp 403-513.

295.	Watson, G.W., and Papamarcos, S.D. "Social Capital and Organizational Commitment," *Journal of Business and Psychology* (16:4), Sum 2002, pp 537-552.

296.	Watson, G.W., Scott, D., Bishop, J., and Turnbeaugh, T. "Dimensions of Interpersonal Relationships and Safety in the Steel Industry," *Journal of Business and Psychology* (19:3), Spr 2005, pp 303-318.

297.	Weeks, J., and Galunic, C. "A Theory of the Cultural Evolution of the Firm: The Intra-Organizational Ecology of Memes," *Organization Studies* (24:8), Oct 2003, pp 1309-1352.

298.	Weisinger, J.Y., and Salipante, P.E. "A Grounded Theory for Building Ethnically Bridging Social Capital in Voluntary Organizations," *Nonprofit and Voluntary Sector Quarterly* (34:1), Mar 2005, pp 29-55.

299.	Wheeler, D., Fabig, H., and Boele, R. "Paradoxes and Dilemmas for Stakeholder Responsive Firms in the Extractive Sector: Lessons from the Case of Shell and the Ogoni," *Journal of Business Ethics* (39:3), Sep 2002, pp 297-318.

300.	Widen-Wulff, G., and Ginman, M. "Explaining Knowledge Sharing in Organizations through the Dimensions of Social Capital," *Journal of Information Science* (30:5) 2004, pp 448-458.

301.	Willcocks, L., Hindle, J., Feeny, D., and Lacity, M. "It and Business Process Outsourcing: The Knowledge Potential," *Information Systems Management* (21:3), Sum 2004, pp 7-15.

302.	Williamson, I.O., and Cable, D.M. "Organizational Hiring Patterns, Interfirm Network Ties, and Interorganizational Imitation," *Academy of Management Journal* (46:3), Jun 2003, pp 349-358.

303.	Witt, L.A., and Ferris, G.R. "Social Skill as Moderator of the Conscientiousness-Performance Relationship: Convergent Results across Four Studies," *Journal of Applied*

Psychology (88:5), Oct 2003, pp 809-820.

304.   Woiceshyn, J. "Technology Adoption: Organizational Learning in Oil Firms," *Organization Studies* (21:6) 2000, pp 1095-1118.

305.   Wright, M., Filatotchev, I., Hoskisson, R.E., and Peng, M.W. "Strategy Research in Emerging Economies: Challenging the Conventional Wisdom - Introduction," *Journal of Management Studies* (42:1), Jan 2005, pp 1-33.

306.   Ye, F., and Agarwal, R. "Strategic It Partnerships in Outsourcing as an Distinctive Source of It Value: A Social Capital Perspective," International Conference on Information Systems, 2003.

307.   Yeung, H.W.C. "The Firm as Social Networks: An Organisational Perspective," *Growth and Change* (36:3), Sum 2005, pp 307-328.

308.   Yli-Renko, H., Autio, E., and Sapienza, H.J. "Social Capital, Knowledge Acquisition, and Knowledge Exploitation in Young Technology-Based Firms," *Strategic Management Journal* (22:6-7), Jun-Jul 2001, pp 587-613.

309.   Youndt, M.A., Subramaniam, M., and Snell, S.A. "Intellectual Capital Profiles: An Examination of Investments and Returns," *Journal of Management Studies* (41:2), Mar 2004, pp 335-361.

310.   Zack, M.H. "Developing a Knowledge Strategy," *California Management Review* (41:3), Spr 1999, pp 125-+.

311.   Zaheer, A., and Bell, G.G. "Benefiting from Network Position: Firm Capabilities, Structural Holes, and Performance," *Strategic Management Journal* (26:9), Sep 2005, pp 809-825.

312.   Zahra, S.A., and George, G. "Absorptive Capacity: A Review, Reconceptualization, and Extension," *Academy of Management Review* (27:2), Apr 2002, pp 185-203.

REFERENCES

1. Adler, P.S. "Market, Hierarchy, and Trust: The Knowledge Economy and the Future of Capitalism," *Organization Science* (12:2), Mar-Apr 2001, pp 215-234.

2. Adler, P.S., and Kwon, S.W. "Social Capital: Prospects for a New Concept," *Academy of Management Review* (27:1), Jan 2002, pp 17-40.

3. Ainsworth, J. "Social Capital and International Migration: A Test Using Information on Family Networks," *American Journal of Sociology* (106:5) 2002, pp 1262-1298.

4. Andersen, O., and Buvik, A. "Inter-Firm Co-Ordination: International versus Domestic Buyer-Seller Relationships," *Omega-International Journal of Management Science* (29:2), Apr 2001, pp 207-219.

5. Anderson, E., and Weitz, B. "Determinants of Continuity in Conventional Industrial Channel Dyads," *Marketing Science* (8:4) 1989, pp 310-323.

6. Anderson, E., and Weitz, B. "The Use of Pledges to Build and Sustain Commitment in Distribution Channels," *Journal of Marketing Research* (29:1) 1992, pp 18-34.

7. Anderson, J.C., and Narus, J.A. "A Model of Distributor Firm and Manufacturer Firm Working Partnerships," *Journal of Marketing* (54:1) 1990, pp 42-58.

8. Ang, S., and Slaughter, S.A. "Organizational Psychology and Performance in Is Employment Outsourcing and Insourcing," 31st Annual Hawaii International Conference on System Sciences, IEEE, Hawaii, 1998, pp. 635-643.

9. Ang, S., and Straub, D. "Costs, Transaction-Specific Investments and Vendor Dominance of the Marketplace: The Economics of Is Outsourcing," in: *Information Systems Outsourcing: Enduring Themes, Emergent Patterns and Future Directions,* R. Hirschheim, A. Heinzl and J. Dibbern (eds.), Springer-Verlag, Berlin, 2001, pp. 47-76.

10. Apte, U.M., and Mason, R.O. "Global Disaggregation of Information-Intensive Services," *Management Science* (41:7) 1995, pp 1250-1262.

11. Apte, U.M., Sobol, M.G., Hanaoka, S., Shimada, T., Saarinen, T., Salmela, T., and Vepsalainen, A.P.J. "Is Outsourcing Practices in the USA, Japan and Finland: A Comparative Study," *Journal of Information Technology* (12) 1997, pp 289-304.

12. Armstrong, C.P., and Sambamurthy, V. "Information Technology Assimilation in Firms: The Influence of Senior Leadership and IT Infrastructures," *Information Systems Research*, 1999, p. 304.

13. Arnett, K.P., and Jones, M.C. "Firms That Choose Outsourcing - a Profile," *Information & Management* (26:4), Apr 1994, pp 179-188.

14. Astley, W.G. "Administrative Science as Socially Constructed Truth," *Administrative Science Quarterly*, 1985, p. 497.

15. Aubert, B.A., Dussault, S., Patry, M., and Rivard, S. "Managing the Risk of IT Outsourcing," 32nd Annual Hawaii International Conference on System Sciences, 1999.

16. Aubert, B.A., Patry, M., and Rivard, S. "Assessing the Risk of IT Outsourcing," 31st Annual Hawaii International Conference on System Sciences, 1998, pp. 685-691.

17. Aubert, B.A., Rivard, S., and Patry, M. "A Transaction Cost Model of IT Outsourcing," *Information & Management*, 2004, p. 921.

18. Aulakh, P.S., and Kotabe, M. "Trust and Performance in Cross-Border Marketing Partnerships: A Behavioral Approach," *Journal of International Business Studies* (27: 5) 1996, p 1005.

19. Baker, W.E. "Market Networks and Corporate Behavior," *American Journal of Sociology* (96) 1990, pp 589-625.

20. Barki, H., Rivard, S., and Talbot, J. "Toward an Assessment of Software Development Risk,"

Journal of Management Information Systems (10:2) 1993, pp 203-225.

21. Barthelemy, J. "The Hard and Soft Sides of IT Outsourcing Management," *European Management Journal* (21: 5) 2003, p 539.

22. Basit, T.N. "Manual or Electronic: The Role of Coding in Qualitative Data Analysis," *Educational Research* (45:2) 2003, pp 143-154.

23. Beath, C.M., and Walker, G. "Outsourcing of Application Software: A Knowledge Management Perspective," 31st Annual Hawaii International Conference on System Sciences, 1998, pp. 666-674.

24. Beccerra, M., and Gupta, A.K. "Trust within the Organization: Integrating the Trust Literature with Agency Theory and Transaction Costs Economics," *Public Administration Quarterly* (23:2) 1999, pp 177-203.

25. Bell, C.R. "Intellectual Capital," *Executive Excellence* (14:1) 1997, p 15.

26. Benbasat, I., Goldstein, D.K., and Mead, M. "The Case Research Strategy in Studies of Information Systems," *Mis Quarterly* (11:3) 1987, pp 369-386.

27. Boland, R.J., and Tenkasi, R.V. "Perspective Making and Perspective Taking in Communities Of Knowing," *Organization Science* (6:4) 1995, pp 350-372.

28. Bourdieu, P. "The Forms of Capital," in: *Handbook of Theory and Research for the Sociology of Education,* J.G. Richardson (ed.), Greenwood Press, Westport, CT, 1986.

29. Bourdieu, P. "The Purpose of Reflexive Sociology," in: *An Invitation to Reflexive Sociology,* P. Bourdieu and L.J.D. Wacquant (eds.), University of Chicago Press, Chicago, 1992.

30. Bouty, I. "Interpersonal and Interaction Influences on Informal Resource Exchanges between R&D Researchers across Organizational Boundaries," *Academy of Management Journal* (43:1), Feb 2000, pp 50-65.

31. Brass, D.J., Galaskiewicz, J., Greve, H.R., and Tsai, W. "Taking Stock of Networks and Organizations: A Multi-Level Perspective," *Academy of Management Review* (47:6) 2004, pp 795-817.

32. Brynjolfsson, E. "An Incomplete Contracts Theory of Information, Technology and Organization," *Management Science,* 1994.

33. Bubolz, M., Flora, J.L., Hartanto, F.M., Morgan, S., and Wollcock, M. "Social Capital: Bridging the Disciplines," Social Capital: Bridging the Disciplines, Michigan State University, 1998.

34. Buchanan, D., Boddy, D., and J, M. "Getting in, Getting on, Getting out, and Getting Back," in: *Doing Research in Organizations,* A. Bryman (ed.), Routledge, London, and New York, 1988, pp. 53-67.

35. Bucklin, L.P., and Sengupta, S. "Organizing Successful Co-Marketing Alliances," *Journal of Marketing* (57:2) 1993, pp 32-46.

36. Business Wire "CFOs Say Outsourcing Increases Shareholder Value," 2002.

37. Caldwell, B. "Outsourcing Deals with Competition," in: *Information week,* 1999.

38. Caniëls, M.C.J., and Gelderman, C.J. "Buyer-Supplier Relationship Development - Empirical Identification and Quantification," Open Universiteit Nederland.

39. Cannon, J.P., and Perreault, W.D. "Buyer-Seller Relationships in Business Markets," *Journal of Marketing Research* (36:4), Nov 1999, pp 439-460.

40. Carmel, E., and Agarwal, R. "Tactical Approaches for Alleviating Distance in Global Software Development," *IEEE Software* (18: 2) 2001, p 22.

41. Casale, F. "Outsourcing Institute Overview," The Outsourcing Institute, 1999.

42. Casale, F. "IT Index 2001," The Outsourcing Institute, 2001.

43. Cecchini, S., and Raina, M. "Warana: The Case of an Indian Rural Community Adopting ICT," *Information Technology in Developing Countries* (12:1) 2002.

44. Chenet, P., Tynan, C., and Money, A. "Service Performance Gap: Re-Evaluation and Redevelopment," *Journal of Business Research* (46:2), Oct 1999, pp 133-147.

45. Cheon, M.J., Grover, V., and Teng, J.T.C. "Theoretical Perspectives on the Outsourcing of Information Systems," *Journal of Information Technology* (10) 1995, pp 209-219.

46. Clark, T.D., Zmud, R.W., and McCray, G.E. "The Outsourcing of Information Services: Transforming the Nature of Business in the Information Industry," *Journal of Information Technology* (10) 1995, pp 221-237.

47. Clemons, E.K., Reddi, S.P., and Row, M.C. "The Impact of Information Technology on the Organization of Economic Activity: The "Move to the Middle" Hypothesis," *Journal of Management Information Systems: JMIS* (10:2) 1993, pp 9-35.

48. Cohen, L., and Hughes, D. "Going Global? Offshore Survival Guide at Gartner Outsourcing Summit." Gartner, 2003.

49. Cohen, L.R., and Young, A. "Ten Steps to Mastering Outsourcing," G00135067, Gartner.

50. Cohen, W.M., and Levinthal, D.A. "Absorptive Capacity: A New Perspective on Learning and Innovation," *Administrative Science Quarterly* (35), March 1990, pp 128-152.

51. Coleman, J.S. "Social Capital in the Creation of Human Capital," *American Journal of Sociology* (94) 1988, pp S95-S120.

52. Coleman, J.S. *Foundations of Social Theory* Belknap Press of Harvard University Press, Cambridge, MA, 1990.

53. Collett, S. "Wanted: Outsourcing Relationship Managers," *Computerworld)* 2002.

54. Collett, S. "Wanted: Outsourcing Relationship Managers," *Computerworld* (36:33), 8/12/2002 2002, p 35.

55. Commeiras, N., and Fournier, C. "Critical Evaluation of Porter Et Al's Organizational Commitment Questionnaire: Implications for Researchers," *Journal of Personal Selling & Sales Management* (XXI: 3), Summer 2001, pp 239-245.

56. Constantine, L., and Lockwood, L. "Orchestrating Project Organization and Management," *Communications of the ACM* (36:10) 1993, pp 31-43.

57. Cooper, R.B. "Information Technology Development Creativity: A Case Study of Attempted Radical Change," MIS *Quarterly*, 2000, p. 245.

58. Corbett, M. "Outsourcing Failures," Michael Corbett & Associates, Firmbuilder.com, 2001.

59. Creswell, J.W. *Qualitative Inquiry and Research Design* Sage, Thousand Oaks, CA, 1998.

60. Cross, J. "IT Outsourcing: British Petroleum's Competitive Approach," *Harvard Business Review* (73:3) 1995, pp 94-102.

61. Crutcher, C.A., Walsh, K.D., Hershauer, J.C., and Tommelein, I.D. "Effects of a Preferred Vendor Relationship on an Electrical Component Supplier and Electrical Contractor," Conference of the International Group for Lean Construction, 2001.

62. Currie, W.L. "Outsourcing in the Private and Public Sectors: An Unpredictable IT Strategy," *European Journal of Information Systems* (4:4), FEB 1996, pp 226-236.

63. Currie, W.L. "Organizational Structure and the Use of Information Technology: Preliminary Findings of a Survey in the Private and Public Sector," *International Journal of Information Management* (16:1) 1996, pp 51-64.

64. Currie, W.L. "Using Multiple Suppliers to Mitigate the Risk of IT Outsourcing at ICI and Wessex Water," *Journal of Information Technology* (13) 1998, pp 169-180.

65. Currie, W.L., and Willcocks, L.P. "Analysing Four Types of IT Sourcing Decisions in the

Context of Size, Client/Supplier Interdependency and Risk Mitigation," *Information Systems Journal* (8) 1998, pp 119-143.

66. Daft, R., and Weick, K. "Toward a Model of Organizations as Interpretation Systems," *Academy of Management Review* (9) 1984, pp 284-295.

67. Daft, R.L. "Learning the Craft of Organizational Research," *Academy of Management Review* (8:4) 1983, pp 539-546.

68. Dant, R.P., and P.L., S. "Conflict Resolution Processes in Contractual Channels of Distribution," *Journal of Marketing* (56:1) 1992, pp 38-54.

69. Darke, P., Shanks, G., and Broadbent, M. "Successfully Completing Case Study Research: Combining Rigor, Relevance and Pragmatism," *Information Systems Journal* (8:4) 1998, pp 273-289.

70. Das, S. "A Question of Wines and Bottles? Examining New Technology and Competition between New Technologies." in: *Academy of Management Proceedings*, Academy of Management, 1994, p. 335.

71. Das, T.K., and Teng, B.-S. "Between Trust and Control: Developing Confidence in Partner Cooperation in Alliances," *Academy of Management Review* (23:3) 1998, pp 491-512.

72. Dataquest "Worldwide IT Services Spending to Be $865 Billion by 2005," Gartner, 2002.

73. Davison, D. "Top 10 Risks of Offshore Outsourcing," *CIO Magazine*, 2004.

74. Denzin, N.K., and Lincoln, Y.S. "Introduction: Entering the Field of Qualitative Research," in: *Collecting and Interpreting Qualitative Materials,* N.K. Denzin and Y.S. Lincoln (eds.), Sage Publications, Thousand Oaks, CA, 1998, pp. 1-34.

75. Deshpande, R., and Webster, F. "Organizational Culture and Marketing: Defining the Research Agenda," *Journal of Marketing*), January 1989, pp 3-15.

76. Dibbern, J., Goles, T., Hirschheim, R., and Jayatilaka, B. "Information Systems Outsourcing: A Survey and Analysis of the Literature," *Database* (35:4) 2004, pp 6-102.

77. DiRomualdo, A., and Gurbaxani, V. "Strategic Intent for IT Outsourcing," *Sloan Management Review* (39:4), SUM 1998, pp 67-+.

78. Doney, P.M., and Cannon, J.P. "An Examination of the Nature of Trust in Buyer-Seller Relationships," *Journal of Marketing* (61:2), Apr 1997, pp 35-51.

79. Doney, P.M., Cannon, J.P., and Mullen, M.R. "Understanding the Influence of National Culture on the Development of Trust," *Academy of Management Review* (23:3) 1998, pp 601-620.

80. Duncan, N.B. "Beyond Opportunism: A Resource Based View of Outsourcing Risk," 31st Annual Hawaii International Conference on System Sciences, 1998, pp. 675-684.

81. Duysters, G., and Lemmens, C. "Cohesive Subgroup Formation: Enabling and Constraining Effects of Social Capital in Strategic Technology Alliance Networks," Working Paper 02.07, Eindhoven Center for Innovation Studies, the Netherlands.

82. Dwyer, F.R., Schurr, P.H., and Oh, S. "Developing Buyer-Seller Relationships," *Journal of Marketing* (51:11-27) 1987.

83. Dyer, J.H., and Singh, H. "Relational Advantage: Relational Rents and Sources of Interorganizational Competitive Advantage," *Academy of Management Review* (23) 1998, pp 660-679.

84. Earl, M.J. "The Risks of Outsourcing IT," *Sloan Management Review* (37:3), 1996, pp 26-32.

85. eBusiness_Strategies "Trends, Statistics, and Perspectives," eBusiness Strategies.

86. Eisenhardt, K.M. "Building Theories from Case Study Research," *Academy of Management Review*, Academy of Management, 1989, p. 532.

87. Elitzur, R., and Wensley, A. "Game Theory as a Tool for Understanding Information Services

Outsourcing," *Journal of Information Technology* (12) 1997, pp 45-60.

88. Elmuti, D. "The Perceived Impact of Outsourcing on Organizational Performance," in: *Mid-American Journal of Business*, 2003, pp. 33-41.

89. Erickson, T., Halverson, C., Kellogg, W.A., Laff, M., and Wolf, T. "Social Translucence: Designing Social Infrastructure That Makes Collective Activity Visible," in: *Communications of the ACM*, Association for Computing Machinery, 2002, pp. 40-44.

90. Fitzgerald, G., and Willcocks, L. "Contracts and Partnerships in the Outsourcing of IT," 15th International Conference on Information Systems, Vancouver, Canada, 1994, pp. 91-98.

91. Fontenot, R.J., and Wilson, E.J. "Relational Exchange: A Review of Selected Models for a Prediction Matrix of Relationship Activities," *Journal of Business Research* (39:1), MAY 1997, pp 5-12.

92. Ford, D. *Managing Business Relationships* John Wiley & Sons, West Sussex, England, 1998.

93. Fortgang, R.S., Lax, D.A., and Sebenius, J.K. "Negotiating the Spirit of the Deal," *Harvard Business Review* (81: 2) 2003, p 66.

94. Fowler, A., and Jeffs, B. "Examining Information Systems Outsourcing: A Case Study from the United Kingdom," *Journal of Information Technology* (13:2), JUN 1998, pp 111-126.

95. Fukuyama, F. *Trust: The Social Virtues and the Creation of Prosperity* Free Press, New York, 1995.

96. Fukuyama, F. "Social Capital," in: *Culture Matters: How Values Shape Human Progress,* S. Huntington (ed.), Basic Books, New York, 2000.

97. Gallivan, M.J., and Oh, W. "Analyzing IT Outsourcing Relationships as Alliances among Multiple Clients and Vendors," 32nd Hawaii International Conference on System Sciences, 1999.

98. Galunic, D.C., and Anderson, E. "From Security to Mobility: Generalized Investments in Human Capital and Agent Commitment," *Organization Science* (11:1) 2000, pp 1-20.

99. Ganesan, S., and Hess, R. "Dimensions and Levels of Trust: Implications for Commitment to a Relationship," in: *Marketing Letters*, Kluwer Academic Publishing / Business, 1997, p. 439.

100.   Garbarino, E., and Johnson, M.S. "The Different Roles of Satisfaction, Trust, and Commitment in Customer Relationships," *Journal of Marketing* (63:2), Apr 1999, pp 70-87.

101.   Gergen, M.M., and Gergen, K.J. "Qualitative Inquiry: Tensions and Transformations," in: *Handbook of Qualitative Research,* N.K. Denzin and Y.S. Lincoln (eds.), Sage, Thousand Oaks, CA, 2000, pp. 1025-1046.

102.   Geyskens, I., Steenkamp, J.-B., Scheer, L., and Kumar, N. "The Effect of Trust and Inter-Dependence on Relationship Commitment: A Trans-Atlantic Study," *International Journal of Research in Marketing* (13:4) 1996, pp 303-317.

103.   Geyskens, I., Steenkamp, J.-B.E.M, and Kumar, N. "A Meta-Analysis of Satisfaction in Marketing Channel Relationships," *Journal of Marketing Research (JMR)*, American Marketing Association, 1999, pp. 223-238.

104.   Ghoshal, S., and Moran, P. "Bad for Practice: A Critique of the Transaction Cost Theory," *Academy of Management Review* (21:1), JAN 1996, pp 13-47.

105.   Giddens`, A. *The Constitution of Social Polity* Cambridge, 1984.

106.   Global_Insight "Executive Summary: The Comprehensive Impact of Offshore IT Software and Services Outsourcing on the U.S. Economy and the IT Industry," Information Technology Association of America.

107.   Gold, A.H., Malhotra, A., and Segars, A.H. "Knowledge Management: An Organizational Capabilities Perspective," *Journal of Management Information Systems* (18:1), Sum 2001, pp 185-214.

108. Goles, T. "The Impact of Client/Vendor Relationship on Is Outsourcing Success," UH, Houston, 2001.

109. Goles, T., and Chin, W.W. "Relational Exchange Theory and Is Outsourcing: Developing a Scale to Measure Relationship Factors," in: *Information Systems Outsourcing: Enduring Themes, Emergent Patterns and Future Directions,* R. Hirschheim, A. Heinzl and J. Dibbern (eds.), Springer-Verlag, Berlin, 2001, pp. 221-250.

110. Gopal, A., Sivaramakrishnan, K., Krishnan, M., and Mukhopadhyay, T. "Contracts in Offshore Software Development: An Empirical Analysis," *Management Science* (49: 12) 2003, p 1671.

111. Granovetter, M.S. "Economic Action and Social Structure: The Problem of Embededdness," *American Journal of Sociology* (91) 1985, pp 481-510.

112. Gronroos, C. "From Marketing Mix to Relationship Marketing - Towards a Paradigm Shift in Marketing," *Management Decision* (35:4) 1997, pp 322-339.

113. Grover, V., Cheon, M.J., and Teng, J.T.C. "The Effect of Service Quality and Partnership on the Outsourcing of Is Functions," *Journal of Management Information Systems* (12:4) 1996, pp 89-116.

114. Guba, E.G., and Lincoln, Y.S. *Fourth Generation Evaluation* Sage, Newbury Park, CA, 1989.

115. Gundlach, G.T., and Cadotte, E.R. "Exchange Interdependence and Interfirm Interaction: Research in a Simulated Channel Setting," *Journal of Marketing Research*), November 1994, pp 516-532.

116. Hakansson, H. *International Marketing and Purchasing of Industrial Goods: An Interaction Approach* John Wiley & Sons, Ltd., 1982.

117. Hakansson, H., and Snehota, I. *Developing Relationships in Business Networks* Routledge, London, 1995.

118. Halvey, J.K., and Melby, B.M. "International Outsourcing Transactions," *Managing Intellectual Property* (56) 1996, pp 38-39.

119. Hancox, M., and Hackney, R. "IT Outsourcing: Conceptualizing Practice in the Public and Private Sector," 32nd Hawaii International Conference on System Sciences, 1999.

120. Hancox, M., and Hackney, R. "IT Outsourcing: Frameworks for Conceptualizing Practice and Perception," *Information Systems Journal* (10:3), JUL 2000, pp 217-237.

121. Harris, S., and Dibbern, M. "Trust and Cooperation in Business Relationship Development: Exploring the Influence of National Values," *Journal of Marketing Management* (15) 1999, pp 463-483.

122. Hartmann, E., Ritter, T., and Gemuenden, H.G. "Determining the Purchase Situation: Cornerstone of Supplier Relationship Management," 17th Annual IMP Conference, Norwegian School of Management BI, Oslo, Norway, 2001.

123. Heckman, R.L., and King, W.R. "Behavioral Indicators of Customer Satisfaction with Vendor-Provided Information Services," Fifteenth International Conference on Information Systems, Vancouver, 1994, pp. 429-444.

124. Heeks, R., and Nicholson, B. "Synching or Sinking: Global Software Outsourcing Relationships," *IEEE Software* (18: 2) 2001, p 54.

125. Heeks, R., and Nicholson, B. "Software Export Success Factors and Strategies in Follower Nations," *Competition and Change* (8:3) 2004, pp 267-303.

126. Heide, J.B. "Interorganizational Governance in Marketing Channels," *Journal of Marketing* (58:1), JAN 1994, pp 71-85.

127.   Heide, J.B., and John, G. "Do Norms Matter in Marketing Relationships?" *Journal of Marketing* (56), April 1992, pp 32-44.

128.   Heide, J.B., and Miner, A.S. "The Shadow of the Future: The Effects of Anticipated Interaction and Frequency of Contact on Buyer-Seller Cooperation," *Academy of Management Review* (35) 1992, pp 265-291.

129.   Heimeriks, K., and Duysters, G. "A Study into the Alliance Capability Development Process," 04.21, Eindhoven Centre for Innovation Studies, the Netherlands.

130.   Henderson, J.C. "Plugging into Strategic Partnerships: The Critical Is Connection," *Sloan Management Review*) 1990, pp 7-18.

131.   Herbsleb, J.D., and Moitra, D. "Global Software Development," *IEEE Software* (18: 2) 2001, p 16.

132.   Hicks, A. *Social Democracy and Welfare Capitalism* Cornell University Press, Ithica, 1999.

133.   Hiltz, S.R., and Turoff, M. "What Makes Learning Networks Effective?" in: *Communications of the ACM*, Association for Computing Machinery, 2002, pp. 56-59.

134.   Hirschheim, R., Porra, J., and Todd, P. "The Changing World of the IT Organization: Understanding the Need for Marketing and Relationship Building," Information Systems Research Center, Houston.

135.   Hodgson, G.M. "Evolutionary and Competence Based Theories of the Firm," *Journal of Economic Studies* (25:1) 1998, pp 25-56.

136.   Hofstede, G. *Culture's Consequences* Sage, Newbury Park, 1982.

137.   Holmlund, M., and Tornroos, J.-A. "What Are Relationships in Business Networks?" *Management Decision* (35:4) 1997, pp 304-309.

138.   Hoskisson, R.E., Hitt, M.A., Wan, W.P., and Yiu, D. "Theory and Research in Strategic Management: Swings of a Pendulum," *Journal of Management* (25:3) 1999, pp 417-456.

139.   Huang, R., Miranda, S., and Lee, J.-N. "How Many Vendors Does IT Take to Change a Light Bulb? Mitigating the Risks of Resource Dependence in Information Technology Outsourcing," Twenty-fifth International Conference on Information Systems, 2004.

140.   Huber, R.L. "How Continental Bank Outsourced Its Crown Jewels," *Harvard Business Review*) 1993, pp 121-129.

141.   Huberman, M., and Miles, M. "Data Management and Analysis Methods," in: *Collecting and Interpreting Qualitative Materials,* N.K. Denzin and Y.S. Lincoln (eds.), Sage Publications, Thousand Oaks, CA, 1998, pp. 179-210.

142.   Hui, P., and Beath, C. "The IT Sourcing Process: A Framework for Research," UT - Austin.

143.   Husted, K., and Michailova, S. "Diagnosing and Fighting Knowledge-Sharing Hostility," *Organizational Dynamics* (31: 1) 2002, p 60.

144.   Huston, T.L., and Robins, E. "Conceptual and Methodological Issues in Studying Close Relationships," *Journal of Marriage and the Family*), November 1982, pp 901-925.

145.   Iivari, J., Hirschheim, R., and Klein, H.K. "A Paradigmatic Analysis Contrasting Information Systems Development Approaches and Methodologies," *Information Systems Research*, 1998, p. 164.

146.   InfoWorld "Should Outsourcers Be Part of Your IT Act?" InfoWorld, 2001.

147.   International_Association_of_Outsourcing_Professionals "Facts, Figures, and Findings from the 2005 Outsourcing World Summit," International Association of Outsourcing Professionals, Lagrangeville, NY, 2005.

148.   John, G. "An Empirical Investigation of Some Antecedents of Opportunism in a Marketing Channel," *Journal of Marketing Research* (21) 1984, pp 278-289.

149.   Jones, C. "Benchmarks and Best Practices for Outsourced Software," in: *Software Assessment, Benchmarks and Best Practices,* Addison Wesley Longman, 2000.

150.   Joshi, A.W., and Stump, R.L. "The Contingent Effect of Specific Asset Investments on Joint Action in Manufacturer-Supplier Relationships: An Empirical Test of the Moderating Role of Reciprocal Asset Investments, Uncertainty, and Trust," *Journal of the Academy of Marketing Science* (27:3), Sum 1999, pp 291-305.

151.   Joshi, A.W., and Stump, R.L. "Determinants of Commitment and Opportunism: Integrating and Extending Insights from Transaction Cost Analysis and Relational Exchange Theory," *Canadian Journal of Administrative Sciences-* (16:4), Dec 1999, pp 334-352.

152.   Kakabadse, A., and Kakabadse, N. "Trends in Outsourcing: Contrasting USA and Europe," *European Management Journal* (20:2) 2002, pp 189-198.

153.   Kakabadse, N., and Kakabadse, A. "Critical Review--Outsourcing: A Paradigm Shift," *Journal of Management Development* (19: 8) 2000, p 668.

154.   Kale, P., Dyer, J.H., and Singh, H. "Alliance Capability, Stock Market Response, and Long Term Alliance Success: The Role of the Alliance Function," *Strategic Management Journal* (23: 8) 2002, p 747.

155.   Kampmeier, C. "Intellectual Capital: The New Wealth of Organizations," *Journal of Management Consulting* (10:1), May 1998, pp 61-63.

156.   Kanter, R.M. "Collaborative Advantage: The Art of Alliances," *Harvard Business Review*, 1994, p. 96.

157.   Kelle, U. "Theory Building in Qualitative Research and Computer Programs for the Management of Textual Data," *Sociological Research Online* (2:2) 1997.

158.   Kelly, T. "A Brief History of Outsourcing," Global Envision, 2002.

159.   Kern, T. "The Gestalt of an IT Outsourcing Relationship: An Exploratory Analysis,") 1997, pp 37-57.

160.   Kern, T., and Blois, K. "Norm Development in Outsourcing Relationships," *Journal of Information Technology* (17: 1) 2002, p 33.

161.   Kern, T., and Willcocks, L. "Exploring Information Technology Outsourcing Relationships: Theory and Practice," *Journal of Strategic Information Systems* (9:4) 2000, pp 321-350.

162.   Kern, T., and Willcocks, L. "Exploring Relationships in Information Technology Outsourcing: The Interaction Approach," *European Journal of Information Systems* (11:1), MAR 2002, pp 3-19.

163.   Kern, T., and Willcocks, L.P. *The Relationship Advantage* Oxford University Press, Oxford, 2001.

164.   Kern, T., and Willcocks, L.P. "Service Provision and the Net: Risky Application Sourcing?," in: *Information Systems Outsourcing: Enduring Themes, Emergent Patterns and Future Directions,* R. Hirschheim, A. Heinzl and J. Dibbern (eds.), Springer-Verlag, Berlin, 2001, pp. 513-534.

165.   Kern, T., Willcocks, L.P., and van Heck, E. "The Winner's Curse in IT Outsourcing: Strategies for Avoiding Relational Trauma," *California Management Review* (44: 2) 2002, p 47.

166.   Kim, S., and Chung, Y.-S. "Critical Success Factors from an Is Outsourcing Implementation from an Inter-Organizational Perspective," in: *Journal of Computer Information Systems*, International Association for Computer Information Systems, 2003, p. 81.

167.   Kishore, R., Agarwal, M., and Rao, H.R. "Determinants of Sourcing During Technology Growth and Maturity: An Empirical Study of E-Commerce Sourcing," in: *Journal of Management Information Systems*, M.E. Sharpe Inc., 2004, pp. 47-82.

168.   Kishore, R., Rao, H.R., Nam, K., Rajagopalan, S., and Chaudhury, A. "A Relationship Perspective on IT Outsourcing," in: *Communications of the ACM*, Association for Computing Machinery, 2003, pp. 86-92.

169.   Klein, H.K. "Research Potential of Hermeneutic Field Studies, "Joint Ph.D. Workshop on Information Systems: Louisiana State University - University of Texas at San Antonio - University of Houston, Baton Rouge, LA, 2005.

170.   Klein, H.K., and Myers, M.D. "A Set of Principles for Conducting and Evaluating Interpretive Field Studies in Information Systems," *MIS Quarterly* (23:1) 1999, pp 67-94.

171.   Klepper, R. "The Management of Partnering Development in I/S Outsourcing," *Journal of Information Technology* (10:4), DEC 1995, pp 249-258.

172.   Klepper, R. "Outsourcing Relationships," in: *Managing Information Technology Investments with Outsourcing,* M. Khosrowpour (ed.), Idea Group Publishing, Harrisburg, 1995, pp. 218-243.

173.   Knemeyer, A.M., and Murphy, P.R. "Evaluating the Performance of Third-Party Logistics Arrangements: A Relationship Marketing Perspective," in: *Journal of Supply Chain Management: A Global Review of Purchasing & Supply*, 2004, pp. 35-51.

174.   Knight, D.J. "Performance Measures for Increasing Intellectual Capital," *Planning Review* (27:2) 1999, pp 22-27.

175.   Kogut, B., and Zander, U. "What Firms Do? Coordination, Identity, and Learning," *Organization Science* (7:5), SEP-OCT 1996, pp 502-518.

176.   Koh, C., Ang, S., and Straub, D.W. "IT Outsourcing Success: A Psychological Contract Perspective," *Information Systems Research*, 2004, pp. 356-373.

177.   Koh, C., Tay, C., and Ang, S. "Managing Vendor-Client Expectations in IT Outsourcing: A Psychological Contract Perspective," International Conference on Information Systems, 1999, pp. 512-517.

178.   Kostova, T., and Roth, K. "Adoption of an Organizational Practice by Subsidiaries of Multinational Corporations: Institutional and Relational Effects," *Academy of Management Journal* (45:1), Feb 2002, pp 215-233.

179.   Kostova, T., and Roth, K. "Social Capital in Multinational Corporations and a Micro-Macro Model of Its Formation," in: *Academy of Management Review*, Academy of Management, 2003, p. 297.

180.   Kotabe, M., Martin, X., and Domoto, H. "Gaining from Vertical Partnerships: Knowledge Transfer, Relationship Duration, and Supplier Performance Improvement in the U.S. And Japanese Automotive Industries," *Strategic Management Journal* (24:4) 2003, pp 293-316.

181.   Kraut, R.E., Fish, R.S., Root, R.W., and Chalfonte, B.L. "Informal Communication in Organizations: Form, Function, and Technology," in: *Human Reactions to Technology: The Claremont Symposium on Applied Social Psychology,* I. Spacapan (ed.), Sage, Beverly Hills, CA, 1990.

182.   Kraut, R.E., and Streeter, L.A. "Coordination in Software Development," *Communications of the ACM* (38:3) 1995, pp 69-81.

183.   Krishna, S., Sahay, S., and Walsham, G. "Managing Cross-Cultural Issues in Global Software Outsourcing," *Communications of the ACM* (47:4) 2004, pp 62-66.

184.   Krishna, S., Sahay, S..., and Walsham, G. "Managing Cross-Cultural Issues in Global Software Outsourcing," *Communications of the ACM* (47: 4) 2004, p 62.

185.   Kumar, K., and van Dissel, H.G. "Sustainable Collaboration: Managing Conflict and Cooperation in Interorganizational Systems," *MIS Quarterly* (20: 3) 1996, p 279.

186.   Kumar, R., and Worm, V. "Social Capital and the Dynamics of Business Negotiations between the Northern Europeans and the Chinese," in: *International Marketing Review*, Emerald, 2003, p. 262.

187.   Lacity, M., and Willcocks, L. "Relationships in IT Outsourcing: A Stakeholder Perspective," in: *Framing the Domains of IT Management,* R.W. Zmud (ed.), Pinnaflex Education Resources, Inc., 2000, pp. 355-384.

188.   Lacity, M., and Willcocks, L. "Preparing for Outsourcing: The Core IT Capabilities Framework," in: *Global Information Technology Outsourcing: In Search of Business Advantage,* M. Lacity and L. Willcocks (eds.), John Wiley & Sons Ltd, West Sussex, 2001, pp. 245-280.

189.   Lacity, M., Willcocks, L., and Feeny, D. "Commercializing the Back Office at Lloyds of London: Outsourcing and Strategic Partnerships Revisited," in: *European Management Journal*, 2004, p. 127.

190.   Lacity, M.C. "An Interpretive Investigation of the Information Systems Outsourcing Phenomenon," in: *Decision and Information Sciences*, University of Houston, Houston, 1992.

191.   Lacity, M.C., and Feeny, D.F. "Outsourcing," *Sloan Management Review* (36:4), SUM 1995, pp 6-7.

192.   Lacity, M.C., and Feeny, D.F. "In Search of Europe's Information Technology Leaders: Review of Methods and Empirical Evidence," *Information Systems Journal* (6:2), APR 1996, pp 85-108.

193.   Lacity, M.C., and Hirschheim, R. "Information Systems Outsourcing: Key Issues and Experiences of an Early Adopter," *Journal of General Management* (19:1) 1993.

194.   Lacity, M.C., and Hirschheim, R. "The Information-Systems Outsourcing Bandwagon," *Sloan Management Review* (35:1), 1993, pp 73-86.

195.   Lacity, M.C., and Hirschheim, R. "Benchmarking as a Strategy for Managing Conflicting Stakeholder Perceptions of Information-Systems," *Journal of Strategic Information Systems* (4:2), JUN 1995, pp 165-185.

196.   Lacity, M.C., and Hirschheim, R. "Four Stories of Information Systems Insourcing," UH, Houston, pp. 348-389.

197.   Lacity, M.C., and Hirschheim, R. "Information Technology Outsourcing: What Problems Are We Trying to Solve?" in: *Rethinking Management Information Systems,* Currie and Galliers (eds.), Oxford, New York, 1999.

198.   Lacity, M.C., and Janson, M.A. "Understanding Qualitative Data: A Framework of Text Analysis Methods," *Journal of Management Information Systems* (11:2), 1994, pp 137-155.

199.   Lacity, M.C., and Willcocks, L.P. "An Empirical Investigation of Information Technology Sourcing Practices: Lessons from Experience," *Mis Quarterly* (22:3), SEP 1998, pp 363-408.

200.   Lacity, M.C., Willcocks, L.P., and Feeny, D.F. "The Value of Selective IT Sourcing," *Sloan Management Review* (37:3), 1996, pp 13-25.

201.   Lacity, M.C., Willcocks, L.P., and Feeny, D.F. "IT Outsourcing: Maximize Flexibility and Control," *Harvard Business Review* (73:3) 1995, pp 84-93.

202.   Lambe, C.J., Spekman, R.E., and Hunt, S.O. "Intermistic Relational Exchange: Conceptualization and Propositional Development," *Journal of the Academy of Marketing Science*, Academy of Marketing Science, 2000, p. 212.

203.   Lander, M.C., Purvis, R.L., McCray, G.E., and Leigh, W. "Trust-Building Mechanisms

Utilized in Outsourced Is Development Projects: A Case Study." in: *Information & Management*, 2004, pp. 509-528.

204.   Lee, J.-N. "Is Outsourcing Research Relevant?" Outsourcing Center, 2000.

205.   Lee, J.-N., Huynh, M.Q., Chi-wai, K.R., and Pi, S.-M. "The Evolution of Outsourcing Research: What Is the Next Issue?" The 33rd Annual Hawaii International Conference on System Sciences, Hawaii, 2000.

206.   Lee, J.-N., Huynh, M.Q., Kwok, R.C.-W., and Pi, S.-M. "IT Outsourcing Evolution--Past, Present, and Future," in: *Communications of the ACM*, Association for Computing Machinery, 2003, p. 84.

207.   Lee, J.-N., and Kim, Y.G. "Effect of Partnership Quality on Is Outsourcing Success: Conceptual Framework and Empirical Validation," *Journal of Management Information Systems* (15:4) 1999, pp 29-61.

208.   Lee, J.-N., Miranda, S.M., and Kim, Y.-M. "IT Outsourcing Strategies: Universalistic, Contingency, and Configurational Explanations of Success," *Information Systems Research*, 2004, pp. 110-131.

209.   Lee, R.M., and Fielding, N.G. "Computing for Qualitative Research: Options, Problems and Potential," in: *Using Computers in Qualitative Research,* N.G. Fielding and R.M. Lee. (eds.), Sage, London, 1991, pp. 1-13.

210.   Lee-Kelley, L., and Crossman, A. "Tiptoe through the Tulips: Toward Collaboration in the Network Organization," Telework 2001 Conference, 2001.

211.   Levina, N., and Ross, J.W. "From the Vendor's Perspective: Exploring the Value Perspective in IT Outsourcing," *MIS Quarterly*, 2003, pp. 331-364.

212.   Levina, N., and Vaast, E. "The Emergence of Boundary Spanning Competence in Practice: Implications for Implementation and Use of Information Systems," *MIS Quarterly* (29: 2) 2005, p 335.

213.   Leydesdorff, L. "Luhmann, Habermas, and the Theory of Communication," *Systems Research and Behavioral Science* (17) 2000, pp 273-288.

214.   Liker, J.K., and Choi, T.Y. "Building Deep Supplier Relationships," in: *Harvard Business Review*, Harvard Business School Publication Corp., 2004, pp. 104-113.

215.   Lin, L., Geng, X., and Whinston, A.B. "A Sender-Receiver Framework for Knowledge Transfer," *MIS Quarterly* (29:2) 2005, pp 197-219.

216.   Lin, N. "Building a Network Theory of Social Capital," *Connections* (22:1) 1999, pp 28-51.

217.   Linder, J.C. *Outsourcing for Radical Change* AMACOM, New York, 2004.

218.   Llewellyn, N., and Armistead, C. "Business Process Management - Exploring Social Capital within Processes," *International Journal of Service Industry Management* (11:3) 2000, pp 225-243.

219.   Locke, E.A. "Some Reservations about Social Capital," *Academy of Management Review* (24:1), JAN 1999, pp 8-9.

220.   Loh, L. "An Organizational Economic Blueprint for IT Outsourcing: Concepts and Evidence," 15th International Conference on Information Systems, Vancouver, Canada, 1994, pp. 73-89.

221.   Loh, L., and Venkataraman, N. "Diffusion of IT Outsourcing: Influence Sources and the Kodak Effect," *Information Systems Research* (3:4) 1992, pp 334-358.

222.   Loh, L., and Venkataraman, N. "An Empirical Study of IT Outsourcing: Benefits, Risks and Performance Implications," Proceedings of the 16th International Conference on Information

Systems, Amsterdam, The Netherlands, 1995, pp. 277-288.

223.   Loury, G. "The Economics of Discrimination: Getting to the Core of the Problem," *Harvard Journal for African-American Public Policy* (1) 1992, pp 91-110.

224.   Luthans, F., and Davis, T.R.V. "An Idiographic Approach to Organizational Behavior Research: The Use of Single Case Experimental Designs and Direct Measures," in: *Academy of Management Review*, Academy of Management, 1982, p. 380.

225.   Macaulay, S. "Non-Contractual Relations in Business: A Preliminary Study," *American Sociological Review,* 1963, pp 55-67.

226.   Macneil, I. *The New Social Contract* Yale University Press, New Haven, CT, 1980.

227.   Mahnke, V., Overby, M.L., and Vang, J. "Strategic IT Outsourcing: What Do We Know and What Do We Need to Know?" DRUID Summer Conference 2003 on Creating, Sharing And Transferring Knowledge., Copenhagen, 2003.

228.   Manen, M.V. "Researching Lived Experience: Human Science for an Action Sensitive Pedagogy," State University of New York Press, Albany, NY, 1990.

229.   Marchington, M., and Vincent, S. "Analysing the Influence of Institutional, Organizational and Interpersonal Forces in Shaping Inter-Organizational Relations," in: *Journal of Management Studies*, Blackwell Publishing Limited, 2004, pp. 1029-1056.

230.   Marcolin, B.L., and McLellan, K.L. "Effective IT Outsourcing Arrangements," 31st Annual Hawaii International Conference on System Sciences, 1998, pp. 654-665.

231.   Matthyssens, P. "Getting Closer and Nicer: Partnerships in the Supply Chain," *Long Range Planning* (27: 1) 1994, p 72.

232.   McAlister, L., Bazerman, M.H., and Fader, P. "Power and Goal Setting in Channel Negotiations," *Journal of Marketing Research* (23:3) 1986, pp 228-236.

233.   McCaffrey "Fighting to Write: Global Competition in the Software Outsourcing Industry," Siliconindia, New York.

234.   McEvily, B., Perrone, V., and Zaheer, A. "Trust as an Organizing Principle," *Organization Science* (14:1) 2003, pp 91-103.

235.   McFarlan, F.W., and Nolan, R.L. "How to Manage an IT Outsourcing Alliance," *Sloan Management Review* (36:2), WIN 1995, pp 9-23.

236.   McKnight, D.H., and Chervany, N.L. "What Is Trust? A Conceptual Analysis and an Interdisciplinary Model," American Conference on Information Systems, Long Beach, CA, 2000.

237.   Michell, V., and Fitzgerald, G. "The IT Outsourcing Marketplace: Vendors and Their Selection," *Journal of Information Technology* (12) 1997, pp 223-237.

238.   Miles, M.B., and Huberman, A.M. *Qualitative Data Analysis: An Expanded Sourcebook* Sage, Thousand Oaks, CA, 1994, p. 338.

239.   Mohnot, N. "Why 'India inside' Spells Quality?" Dataquest, 2003.

240.   Mohr, A.T., and Puck, J.F. "Exploring the Determinants of the Trust-Control-Relationship in International Joint Ventures," EURAM 2003, Milan, Italy, 2003.

241.   Mohr, J., and Spekman, R. "Characteristics of Partnership Success: Partnership Attributes, Communication Behavior and Conflict Resolution Techniques," *Strategic Management Journal* (15:2) 1994, pp 135-152.

242.   Mohr, J., and Spekman, R. "Characteristics of Partnership Success: Partnership Attributes, Communication Behavior and Conflict Resolution Techniques," *Strategic Management Journal* (15) 1994, pp 132-135.

243.   Moran, P., and Ghoshal, S. "Markets, Firms, and the Process of Economic Development," *Academy of Management Review* (24:3) 1996, pp 390-412.

244.   Morello, D. "The Organizational Implications of Offshore Outsourcing," AV-21-1610, Gartner.

245.   Morgan, R.M., and Hunt, S.D. "The Commitment-Trust Theory of Relationship Marketing," *Journal of Marketing* (58:3), JUL 1994, pp 20-38.

246.   Morstead, S., and Blount, G. *Offshore Ready: Strategies to Plan & Profit from Offshore IT-Enabled Services* ISANI Press, United States of America, 2003.

247.   Muhr, T. *Atlas.Ti: The Knowledge Workbench* Scientific Software Development, Berlin, 1997, p. 110.

248.   Myers, M.D. "Qualitative Research in Information Systems," *Mis Quarterly* (21:2) 1997, pp 241-242.

249.   Myers, M.D., and Tan, F.B. "Beyond Models of National Culture in Information Systems Research," *Journal of Global Information Management* (10: 1) 2002, p 24.

250.   Nahapiet, J., and Ghoshal, S. "Social Capital, Intellectual Capital, and the Organizational Advantage," *Academy of Management Review* (23:2) 1998, pp 242-266.

251.   Nair, K.G.K., and Prasad, P.N. "Offshore Outsourcing: A SWOT Analysis of a State in India," *Information Systems Management*, Auerbach Publications Inc., 2004, pp. 34-40.

252.   Nam, K., Rajagopalan, S., Rao, H.R., and Chaudhury, A. "A Two-Level Investigation of Information Systems Outsourcing," *Communications of the ACM* (39:7) 1996, pp 36-44.

253.   Natovich, J. "Vendor Related Risks in IT Development: A Chronology of an Outsourced Project Failure," *Technology Analysis & Strategic Management*, Carfax Publishing Company, 2003, pp. 409-419.

254.   Nicholson, B., and Sahay, S. "Some Political and Cultural Issues in the Globalization of Software Development: Case Experience from Britain and India," *Information and Organization* (11) 2001, pp 25-43.

255.   Obstfeld, D. "Knowledge Creation, Social Networks and Innovation: An Integrative Study," *Academy of Management Proceedings*) 2002.

256.   Oliver, C. "Network Relations and Loss of Organizational Autonomy," *Human Relations*) 1991, pp 943-961.

257.   Overby, S. "The Hidden Costs of Offshore Outsourcing," *CIO Magazine*) 2003.

258.   Oxendine, A., Borgida, E., Sullivan, J., and Jackson, M. "The Importance of Trust and Community in Developing and Maintaining a Community Electronic Network," *International Journal of Human-Computer Studies* (58:6) 2003, pp 671-696.

259.   Paun, D.A. "A Study of "Best" Versus "Average" Buyer-Seller Relationships," *Journal of Business Research* (39:1), MAY 1997, pp 13-21.

260.   Peng, M.W., and Luo, Y. "Managerial Ties and Firm Performance in a Transition Economy: The Nature of a Micro-Macro Link," *Academy of Management Journal* (43:3) 2000, pp 486-505.

261.   Pennar, K. "The Ties That Lead to Prosperity," *Business Week*, December 1997, pp 153-155.

262.   Perrone, V., Zaheer, A., and McEvily, B. "Free to Be Trusted? Organizational Constraints on Trust in Boundary Spanners," *Organization Science* (14:4) 2003, pp 422-439.

263.   Philipkoski, K. "Where Are All the Women?" Wired News, 2005.

264.   Portes, A., and Sensenbrenner, J. "Embededdness and Immigration - Notes on the Social Determinants of Economic-Action," *American Journal of Sociology* (98:6), MAY 1993, pp 1320-1350.

265.   Preece, J. "Supporting Community and Building Social Capital," in: *Communications of*

the ACM, Association for Computing Machinery, 2002, pp. 36-39.

266.   Putnam, R.D. "The Prosperous Community: Social Capital and Public Life," *American Prospect* (13) 1993, pp 35-42.

267.   Qu, Z., and Brocklehurst, M. "What Will IT Take for China to Become a Competitive Force in Offshore Outsourcing? An Analysis of the Role of Transaction Costs in Supplier Selection," *Journal of Information Technology* (18:1) 2003, pp 53-67.

268.   Quinn, J.B. "Strategic Outsourcing: Leveraging Knowledge Capabilities. (Cover Story)," *Sloan Management Review* (40: 4) 1999, p 9.

269.   Rajkumar, T.M., and Dawley, D.L. "Problems and Issues in Offshore Development of Software," in: *Strategic Sourcing of Information Systems,* L.P. Willcocks and M.C. Lacity (eds.), John Wiley & Sons Ltd, 1998.

270.   Ramachandran, J., Khorakiwala, H.F., Rao, J., Khera, P., Dawar, N., Kalyani, B.N., and Karki, R. "Indian Companies in Overseas Markets: Perspectives, Patterns, and Implications," in: *Vikalpa: The Journal for Decision Makers*, Indian Institute of Management, 2004, pp. 93-111.

271.   Ramarapu, N., Parzinger, M., and Lado, A. "Issues in Foreign Outsourcing," *Information Systems Management*) 1997, pp 7-31.

272.   Rami Olkkonen, Tikkanen, H., and AlajoutsijaÈrvi, K. "The Role of Communication in Business Relationships and Networks," *Management Decision* (38:6) 2000, pp 403-409.

273.   Rao, M.T. "Key Issues for Global IT Sourcing: Country and Individual Factors," in: *Information Systems Management*, Auerbach Publications Inc., 2004, pp. 16-21.

274.   Raposo, A.B., Gerosa, M.A., and Fuks, H. "Modeling Coordination in Business-Webs," Third IFIP Conference on E-commerce, E-business and E-government, Guarujá-SP, 2003, pp. 549-559.

275.   Reponen, T. "Outsourcing or Insourcing?" Fourteenth International Conference on Information Systems, Orlando, FL, 1993, pp. 103-112.

276.   Rindfleisch, A. "Organizational Trust and Interfirm Cooperation: An Examination of Horizontal Versus Vertical Alliances," in: *Marketing Letters*, Kluwer Academic Publishing / Business, 2000, p. 81.

277.   Ring, P.S., and Vandeven, A.H. "Developmental Processes of Cooperative Interorganizational Relationships," *Academy of Management Review* (19:1), JAN 1994, pp 90-118.

278.   Robinson, S.L. "Trust and Breach of the Psychological Contract," *Administrative Science Quarterly* (41) 1996, pp 574-599.

279.   Rockart, J.F., Earl, M.J., and Ross, J.W. "Eight Imperatives for the New IT Organization," *Sloan Management Review,* 1996, pp 43-55.

280.   Roslender, R. "Accounting for Intellectual Capital: A Contemporary Management Accounting Perspective," *Management Accounting* (78:3) 2000, pp 34-37.

281.   Ross, J.W. "Preparing for Utility Computing: The Role of IT Architecture and Relationship Management," *IBM Systems Journal*, IBM Corporation/IBM Journals, 2004, pp. 5-19.

282.   Roth, K., and Kostova, T. "Organizational Coping with Institutional Upheaval in Transition Economies," *Journal of World Business*, Elsevier Science Publishing Company, Inc., 2003, p. 314.

283.   Rumelt, R.P., Schendel, D.E., and Teece, D.J. "Fundamental Issues in Strategy," in: *Fundamental Issues in Strategy,* R.P. Rumelt, D.E. Schendel and D.J. Teece (eds.), Harvard School Press, Boston, 1994.

284.   Rus, I., and Lindvall, M. "Knowledge Management in Software Engineering," *IEEE Software*), May/June 2002, pp 26-38.

285.   Sabherwal, R. "The Role of Trust in Managing Outsourced Is Development Projects," *Communications of the ACM* (42:2) 1999, pp 80-86.

286.   Sabherwal, R. "Coordination of Remotely Outsourced Software Development: A Comparison of Client and Vendor Perspectives," *MIS Quarterly*) 1999.

287.   Sabherwal, R., Hirschheim, R., and Goles, T. "The Dynamics of Alignment: Insights from a Punctuated Equilibrium Model," *Organization Science* (12:2), Mar-Apr 2001, pp 179-197.

288.   Sabherwal, R. "The Evolution of Coordination in Outsourced Software Development Projects: A Comparison of Client and Vendor Perspectives," *Information & Organization* (13: 3) 2003, p 153.

289.   Saint-Once, H. "Tacit Knowledge: The Key to the Strategic Alignment of Intellectual Capital," *Planning Review* (24:2) 1996, pp 10-14.

290.   Sanders, P. "Phenomenology: A New Way of Viewing Organizational Research," *Academy of Management Review* (7:3) 1982, pp 353-360.

291.   Sarkar, M.B., Echambadi, R., Cavusgil, S.T., and Aulakh, P.S. "The Influence of Complementarity, Compatibility, and Relationship Capital on Alliance Performance," *Journal of the Academy of Marketing Science* (29:4) 2001, pp 358-373.

292.   Saunders, C., Gebelt, M., and Hu, Q. "Achieving Success in Information Systems Outsourcing," *California Management Review* (39:2), WIN 1997, pp 63-&.

293.   Schumpeter, J.A. *The Theory of Economic Development: An Inquiry into Profits, Capital, Credit, Interest, and the Business Cycle.* Harvard University Press, Cambridge, 1934.

294.   Sharma, A. "Professional as Agent: Knowledge Asymmetry in Agency Exchange," *Academy of Management Review* (22:3), Jul 1997, pp 758-798.

295.   Simonin, B.L. "The Importance of Collaborative Know-How: An Empirical Test of the Learning Organization," *Academy of Management Journal* (40: 5) 1997, p 1150.

296.   Sitkin, S.B., and Roth, N.L. "Explaining the Limited Effectiveness of Legalistic Remedies for Trust/Distrust," *Organization Science* (4:3) 1993, pp 367-392.

297.   Sivadas, E., and Dwyer, R. "An Examination of Organizational Factors Influencing New Product Success in Internal and Alliance-Based Processes," *Journal of Marketing* (64) 2000, pp 31-49.

298.   Sivadas, E., and Dwyer, R. "An Examination of Organizational Factors Influencing New Product Success in Internal and Alliance-Based Processes," *Journal of Marketing* (64) 2000, pp 31-49.

299.   Slaughter, S., and Ang, S. "Employment Outsourcing in Information Systems," *Communications of the ACM* (39:7) 1996, pp 47-54.

300.   Smith, J.B., and Barclay, D.W. "The Effects of Organizational Differences and Trust on the Effectiveness of Selling Partner Relationships," *Journal of Marketing* (61:1), Jan 1997, pp 3-21.

301.   Smith, M. "Tools for Navigating Large Social Cyberspaces," in: *Communications of the ACM*, Association for Computing Machinery, 2002, pp. 51-55.

302.   Smith, M.A., and Kumar, R.L. "A Theory of Application Service Provider (ASP) Use from a Client Perspective," in: *Information & Management*, 2004, pp. 977-1002.

303.   Smith, M.A., Mitra, S., and Narasimhan, S. "Information Systems Outsourcing: A Study of Pre-Event Firm Characteristics," *Journal of Management Information Systems* (15:2) 1998, pp 61-93.

304.   Snir, E.M., and Hitt, L.M. "Vendor Screening in Information Technology Contracting with a Pilot Project," in: *Journal of Organizational Computing & Electronic Commerce*, Lawrence Erlbaum Associates, 2004, pp. 61-88.

305.   Sobol, M.G., and Apte, U. "Domestic and Global Outsourcing Practices of America's Most Effective Is Users," *Journal of Information Technology* (10: 4) 1995, p 269.

306.   Sobrero, M., and Schrader, S. "Structuring Inter-Firm Relationships: A Meta-Analytic Approach," *Organization Studies* (19: 4) 1998, p 585.

307.   Souza, R.D., Goodness, E., Young, A., Silliman, R., and Caldwell, B.M. "IT Outsourcing Market Forecast: Worldwide, 2002-2007," Gartner.

308.   Stewart, T.A. "Your Company's Most Valuable Asset: Intellectual Capital," *Fortune* (130:7) 1994, pp 68-74.

309.   Sydow, J. "Understanding the Constitution of Interorganizational Trust," in: *Trust within and between Organizations: Conceptual Issues and Empirical Applications,* L. Christel and B. Richard (eds.), Oxford University Press, 1998.

310.   Szulanski, G. "Exploring Internal Stickiness: Impediments to the Transfer of Best Practice within the Firm," *Strategic Management Journal* (17), WIN 1996, pp 27-43.

311.   Terdiman, R. "Offshore Application Outsourcing," Gartner.

312.   Terdiman, R. "IT Outsourcing Trends," Gartner.

313.   Tesch, R. *Qualitative Research: Analysis Types and Software Tools.* Palmer Press, New York, 1990.

314.   Tesch, R. "Software for Qualitative Researchers: Analysis Needs and Program Capabilities," in: *Using Computers in Qualitative Research,* N.G. Fielding and R.M. Lee (eds.), Sage, London, 1991, pp. 16-37.

315.   Thompson, L., and Fine, G.A. "Socially Shared Cognition, Affect, and Behavior: A Review and Integration," *Personality & Social Psychology Review* (3: 4) 1999, p 278.

316.   Tiwana, A. "Knowledge Partitioning in Outsourced Software Development: A Field Study," International Conference on Information Systems, 2003, pp. 259-270.

317.   Tiwana, A. "Beyond the Black Box: Knowledge Overlaps in Software Outsourcing," in: *IEEE Software*, 2004, pp. 51-58.

318.   Tiwana, A., Bharadwaj, A.S., and Sambamurthy, V. "The Antecedents of Information Systems Development Capability in Firms: A Knowledge Integration Perspective," International Conference on Information Systems, 2003, pp. 246-258.

319.   TPI "Research Suggests Ways to Avoid Outsourcing Disasters," M2 PRESSWIRE, 1999.

320.   Trauth, E. *Qualitative Research in IS: Issues and Trends* Idea Group Publishing, Hershey, PA, 2001.

321.   Trauth, E.M. "Achieving the Research Goal with Qualitative Methods: Lessons Learned Along the Way," in: *Information Systems and Qualitative Research,* A.S. Lee, J. Liebenau and J.I. DeGross (eds.), Chapman & Hall, London, 1997, pp. 225-245.

322.   Trompenaars, F., and Hampden-Turner, C. *Riding the Waves of Culture: Understanding Diversity in Global Business* Mc-Graw Hill, 1988, p. 274.

323.   Tsai, W., and Ghoshal, S. "Social Capital and Value Creation: The Role of Intrafirm Networks," *Academy of Management Review* (41:4) 1998, pp 464-476.

324.   Turner, J.H. *The Structure of Sociological Theory*, (5th ed.) Wadsworth Publishing Company, Belmont, CA, 1990.

325.   Uzzi, B. "Social Structure and Competition in Interfirm Networks: The Paradox of Embededdness," *Administrative Science Quarterly* (42:1), Mar 1997, pp 35-67.

326.   Uzzi, B. "Embededdness in the Making of Financial Capital: How Social Relations and Networks Benefit Firms Seeking Financing," *American Sociological Review* (64: August) 1999, pp 481-505.

327.   Vandeven, A.H., and Koenig, R. "A Theory on Pair-Wise Inter-Organizational Relations," 1975.

328.   Vaze, S. "The Politics (and Economics) of Outsourcing," Express Computer, 2005.

329.   Vandeven, A.H., Delbecq, A.L., and Koenig, R. "Determinants of Coordination Modes within Organizations," *American Sociological Review* (41:2) 1976, pp 322-338.

330.   Vernon, M. "If You Focus Solely on Cost When Outsourcing - Your Deal May Be for the High Jump," TPI, Houston, TX.

331.   Violino, B., and Caldwell, B. "Analyzing the Integrators," *Informationweek* (709), November 6 1998, pp 45-113.

332.   von Hippel, E. "'Sticky Information' and the Locus of Problem Solving: Implications for Innovation," *Management Science*, 1994, p. 429.

333.   Walsham, G. "Interpretive Case Studies in Is Research: Nature and Method," *European Journal of Information Systems* (4) 1995, pp 74-81.

334.   Walsham, G., and Waema, T. "Information Systems Strategy and Implementation: A Case Study of a Building Society," *ACM Transactions on Information Systems* (12:2) 1994, pp 150-173.

335.   Weiss, R.S. *Learning from Strangers* The Free Press, New York, 1995.

336.   Wetzels, M., Ruyter, K., and Birgelen, M. "Marketing Service Relationships: The Role of Commitment," *Journal of Business and Industrial Marketing* (13:4/5) 1998, pp 406-423.

337.   Whang, S.J. "Contracting for Software-Development," *Management Science* (38:3), MAR 1992, pp 307-324.

338.   Willcocks, L., Fitzgerald, G., and Feeny, D. "Outsourcing IT: The Strategic Implications," *Long Range Planning* (28:5) 1995, pp 59-70.

339.   Willcocks, L.P., and Kern, T. "IT Outsourcing as Strategic Partnering: The Case of the UK Inland Revenue," *European Journal of Information Systems* (7:1), MAR 1998, pp 29-45.

340.   Willcocks, L.P., and Lacity, M.C. "Information Systems Outsourcing in Theory and Practice," *Journal of Information Technology* (10:4), Dec 1995, pp 203-207.

341.   Willcocks, L.P., Lacity, M.C., and Kern, T. "Risk Mitigation in IT Outsourcing Strategy Revisited: Longitudinal Case Research at Lisa," *Journal of Strategic Information Systems* (8:3), SEP 1999, pp 285-314.

342.   Woolcock, M. "Social Capital and Economic Development," *Theory and Society* (27) 1998, pp 151-208.

343.   Wright, P.M., and Snell, S.A. "Social Capital and Strategic HRM: It's Who You Know," *Human Resource Planning*) 2000, pp 62-65.

344.   Wu, W.-Y., Chiang, C.-Y., Wu, Y.-J., and Tu, H.-J. "The Influencing Factors of Commitment and Business Integration on Supply Chain Management," *Industrial Management & Data Systems* (104:4) 2004, pp 322-333.

345.   Yin, R.K. *Case Study Research: Design and Methods*, California, Thousand Oaks, 2003, p. 171.

346.   Zaheer, A., McEvily, B., and Perrone, V. "Does Trust Matter? Exploring the Effects of Interpersonal and Interorganizational Trust on Performance," *Organization Science* (9:2) 1998, pp 141-159.

347.   Zaheer, A., and Venkataraman, N. "Relational Governance as an Interorganizational

Strategy," *Strategic Management Journal* (16:5) 1995, pp 373-392.

348.   Zatolyuk, S., and Allgood, B. "Evaluating a Country for Offshore Outsourcing: Software Developers in the Ukraine," in: *Information Systems Management*, Auerbach Publications Inc., 2004, pp. 28-33.

www.ingramcontent.com/pod-product-compliance
Lightning Source LLC
LaVergne TN
LVHW022301060326
832902LV00020B/3213